W9-CRA-567

Europe Reconsidered

Europe Reconsidered

Perceptions of the West in
Ninteenth-Century Bengal

Tapan Raychaudhuri

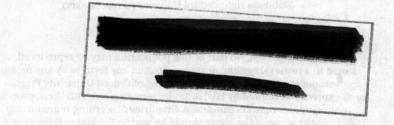

OXFORD

UNIVERSITY PRESS

OXFORD
UNIVERSITY PRESS

YMCA Library Building, Jai Singh Road, New Delhi 110 001

Oxford University Press is a department of the University of Oxford. It furthers the
University's objective of excellence in research, scholarship, and education
by publishing worldwide in

Oxford   New York

Auckland   Bangkok   Buenos Aires   Cape Town   Chennai
Dar es Salaam   Delhi   Hong Kong   Istanbul   Karachi   Kolkata
Kuala Lumpur   Madrid   Melbourne   Mexico City   Mumbai   Nairobi
São Paulo   Shanghai   Taipei   Tokyo   Toronto

Oxford is a registered trademark of Oxford University Press
in the UK and in certain other countries

Published in India
By Oxford University Press, New Delhi

© Oxford University Press, 2002

The moral rights of the author have been asserted
Database right Oxford University Press (maker)

First published 2002

ISBN 019 566 1095

Typeset in Bodoni
By Le Studio Graphique.
Printed by Roopak Printers, Delhi 110 032
Published by Manzar Khan, Oxford University Press
YMCA Library Building, Jai Singh Road, New Delhi 110 001

To

the memory of my teacher
Professor Susobhan Chandra Sarkar

Contents

Preface to the Second Edition

On Matters Relevant and Not So Relevant

This edition of *Europe Reconsidered* does not aspire to present a substantially altered text. Its main claim to be considered a 'new' edition consists in the present exercise to spell out its implications with reference to a number of themes implicit in the text which bear upon the ongoing discussions regarding several themes: the cultural nexus between the dominant West and the colonial middle classes; the nature of that social group and its achievements (considered by some of their intellectual and social descendants to be both minimal and vastly inflated in the relevant literature); and, finally, the relationship between the individuals and the trends of thought discussed in this volume with the phenomenon of Hindu 'revival' past and present, especially the very different perceptions of Hindutva. As none of the many reviews of the book, both favourable and dismissive, picked up the points which, to my understanding, were central to my arguments, it seems worthwhile to spell them out in a new introductory statement. Evidently, I had failed to communicate with sufficient clarity my major conclusions and hence further explanations are necessary.

For the same reason, I have appended the text of a lecture delivered in memory of my teacher, the late Professor Susobhan Sarkar, which has a direct bearing on the subject matter of this book. Professor Sarkar introduced me to historical studies and shaped my thinking on the subject. And it was his writings that first kindled my interest in the nineteenth-century 'enlightenment' in India, still described by some as a Renaissance. This edition is dedicated to his memory as an insignificant payment of my *gururina*, debt to one's mentor, which is beyond my ability to repay in full.

The memorial lecture is printed here as it was presented, without notes, for I do not feel scholarly annotation would add anything to what I had to say.

By now there is a substantial body of literature which argues (a) that central to the colonial enterprise in India as elsewhere was the agenda projecting the superiority of western civilization and (b) that the middle-class collaborators of the regime, especially their ultimate exemplar, the Bengali babu, accepted this paradigm *in toto* and without any question. These perceptions are integral to the wider discussion of Orientalism which sees Europe's scholarly quest for knowledge of Asian civilizations as an accessory to the consolidation of imperial controls; the knowledge sought by the western Orientalists and the scholar-administrator alike was 'power-knowledge', to use a widely popular if somewhat infelicitous expression. The end product of that quest is an essentialist paradigm, the East, one of the several 'Others' of a fundamentally different and necessarily superior West. The basic formulations of this radical critique have been questioned and I do not intend to contribute further to that debate, except to point out that it has a relevance to the subject matter of this volume. What follows, however, is directly concerned with the cultural agenda of colonialism and its supposed impact on the collaborating classes. To anticipate my argument, it is time one questioned the near-consensus view regarding the colonial intelligentsia's unquestioning acceptance of western superiority and the corresponding inferiority of the colonized; again, this volume offers some clinching evidence to the contrary.

Much has been written about the diversified content of the Orientalist enterprise. I should like to emphasize only one well-known fact which has been generally ignored in the relevant debate. In the Orientalist controversy in the nineteenth century, it was the Anglicists who rubbished Asia's cultural heritage and the Orientalists who defended it. True, William Jones aspired to be a new Justin, salvaging the true law of the Hindus from the alleged Brahminical monopoly and thereby help consolidate the hold of *pax Britannica*. But the same person sought in Persian and Sanskrit literature a possible source of inspiration for a new cultural Renaissance in Europe: the model he had in mind was the impact of classical learning and Graeco-Roman art on Renaissance Europe. This latter aspiration certainly has little affinity with any quest for 'power-knowledge' and neither project suggests a clear sense of western superiority. The young Max Mueller's romantic dreams, inspired by pictures of the Benares *ghats* on the cover of a school exercise book in Paris, may suggest a fascination with the exotic, one of Europe's

'Others' if you like, but surely no sense of cultural superiority. The latter is even less evident in his adult perception of the Upanishads as his source of consolation in life, and, he hoped, also in death. Arguably, the sense of otherness is not pronounced in the writings of the great Orientalists; there is a deep feeling of identification with their subject of study, a profound intellectual and aesthetic pleasure which counterbalances any sense of separation.

Another component of the current radical discourse on Orientalism and the cultural nexus under colonialism is centred on the derivative nature of the modern Indian perception of Indian and, more generally, Asian civilization. The derivation is allegedly from Orientalist scholarship. Hence, the perceptions consist in essentialist paradigms, the East and the West, their irreconcilable 'mutual otherness', and the quintessential inferiority of one in relation to the other. As this particular component of the discourse is directly relevant to the subject matter of this volume—how Indian intellectuals perceived Europe, especially in comparison with their own heritage—some assessment of its validity is necessary.

True, the Indian discovery of the region's heritage owed much to the Orientalist enterprise. Much, but not all. Rammohan acquired his Vedic learning from pundits in Benares, not British scholars, and his knowledge of Islam, which influenced him profoundly, from the *maulanas* in a Patna *madrassa*. Till well into the mid-nineteenth century, the educated Bengalis had access to Persian learning. Their delight in Hafiz and Rumi were not of western derivation in any sense. As Rabindranath Tagore explained about his father, Devendranath, the mystic owed his intellectual perception of the Divine to the Upanishadic texts, first edited by Rammohan, but his deep devotionalism to Hafiz. Rajnarayan Basu also underlined his belief that the element of *rasa*, aesthetic-emotional joy, in their religiosity was of Islamic derivation. Orientalist scholarship had nothing to do with it.

The three thinkers discussed in this volume derived their knowledge of their Indian heritage from a variety of sources. Western Orientalist scholarship was only one and not the most important among these. For the most part they emphasized the elements in the received tradition which were marginal to the concerns of Orientalism. Bhudev read into the Puranic tradition meanings totally unrelated to any scholarship of western derivation. The notion that the fifty-two *pithasthanas*, sanctified by parts of the goddess Sati's body, symbolized the unity of Indian civilization was an entirely original interpretation of an ancient myth. This projection of unity is, of course, informed with the modern ideas of nationalism, but the scriptural knowledge underlying the paradigm is entirely indigenous. And, Hinduism to Bhudev meant above all the Tantric tradition and the Brahminical rituals prescribed in the *smritis*, both central to his family's religious culture. His formal initiation into Tantric practice was by his mother, who had no access to western learning in any form. His prescriptive essays on ritual duties, *Achar Prabandha*, owed nothing to Orientalist scholarship. Bankim's initial introduction to the Hindu scriptures and the civilization of ancient India may well have been through Orientalist writings, but in his effort to gain a direct knowledge of that heritage he chose the pundits of Bhatpara as his mentors. His projection of the Mother Goddess as the motherland and a heavily armed Vishnu as the object of adoration were nationalist in inspiration; these had little if anything to do with Orientalism or, for that matter, with the inherited tradition. His interpretation of the Mahabharata and the Gita had obvious traces of contemporary western philosophy but was equally distant from both Orientalist perceptions and the received wisdom. Vivekananda's induction into the mystical tradition was through the discipleship of a man who knew nothing of the West. In fact, the nearly illiterate guru derived his knowledge from a purely oral tradition and as a disciple of 'adepts' untouched by any extra-Indian knowledge.

What is true of the three protagonists can be shown to be largely true of the other major exponents of the nineteenth-century enlightenment in Bengal. Their knowledge of the Indian tradition had important sources other than Orientalist scholarship and the use they made of it emphasized concerns very different from those of the Orientalist agenda. Knowledge of the Puranas and of rituals as prescribed in the *smritis* was very much a part of the Hindu's life experience. The former was integral to the cultural tradition embodied in the vernacular literature as well as folk memory. Neither the rural Bengali nor the urban babu learnt his Ramayana and Mahabharata stories or the Puranic myths at the feet of any sahib. And the great Orientalist scholars of the West did not dispense Indian nationalism in their writings; the results of Orientalist scholarship were put to a totally unintended and unexpected use. That use, arguably, had as much to do with the colonial experience as with the spread of nationalist ideology, a major element in the intellectual and political history of the nineteenth century. It affected Europe's emerging nations as well as the western dependencies and the threatened nation states of Asia. Even the study of Indian history and culture by Indian scholars, who certainly used methods learnt from European masters, expressed nationalist concerns—in its emphasis on the discovery of pan-Indian polities, the autonomy and excellence of artistic traditions, and the tolerance and superior refinement embedded in the 'Hindu view of life'. In short, Orientalism was but one element in modern Bengal's self-discovery. And that discovery was a part of the proto-nationalist agenda and was in no way a component of the colonial project.

Current literature establishes beyond reasonable doubt the existence of a colonial agenda to convince the subject population, especially the collaborating classes, that the rulers represented a superior civilization. One component of this project was to underline the inherent inferiority of Indian culture—its failure to emerge from a cretinous childhood into adult rationality in terms of social evolution, and the pervasive decadence manifest in contemporary Indian life. Incidentally, the negative perceptions were no part of Orientalist paradigms. They were central to the world-view on which the 'progressive' modernizing projects of the Utilitarians were based. James Mill's description of Indians as inferior to the nobler animals was not a racist statement; it articulated his 'scientific' beliefs. So did Macaulay's notorious declaration rubbishing the entire body of Oriental learning as inferior to a single shelf of books in the European languages.

The new-found confidence and uncomplicated belief in cultural superiority almost certainly had causal links with imperial domination. They emerged at a time when the empire felt secure and triumphant. But the fact that the Utilitarians had an equal contempt for the 'irrational' elements of the received tradition in the West, deficiencies which would be rectified in due course by reason, science, and progress, suggests that more than a quest for power and domination was involved in their project. It is difficult to dismiss Macaulay's hopes for England's 'proudest day' when Indians, their consciousness restructured by western education, would achieve self-rule, as mere rhetoric. He was not addressing an already disgruntled class of collaborators but his own sceptical countrymen. The faith in science and reason, and the consequent rejection of the 'irrational' both in the dependencies and at home, was the hallmark of the new bourgeois ideology. It often coincided with the ideology of empire and the purpose of domination. Again, often but not always. The first English decision maker to question the exclusion of white British subjects from the jurisdiction of Indian magistrates was Macaulay; such privilege went against his notion of rational justice.

The comments made in the last paragraph are not intended to deny the colonial project for cultural domination. They only underline the complexity of that project, its internal tensions and wider context. That complexity, interacting with the multiple and often mutually conflicting strands in the colonial experience, especially its intellectual dimension, produced results which cannot be summed up in any uncomplicated conclusion such as the unquestioning acceptance of western superiority by the collaborating classes, easy victims of colonial propaganda. The essays in this volume discuss perceptions which do not at any point accept the unquestioning superiority of western civilization. Bankimchandra, the thinker who comes closest to a belief in such superiority in one phase of his intellectual development, focused on very specific elements and particular periods of Europe's history. He saw post-Renaissance Europe as the high watermark of human civilization with which neither India nor Europe's earlier past had anything to compare. But he was no uncritical admirer. Mankind, in his eyes, had still a very long way to go. His awareness of India's backwardness did not blind him to modern Europe's many inadequacies, especially its horrendous record of colonialism and violent conflict for the acquisition of territories; he equated the right to conquest with the right to steal and compared the great powers fighting for colonies to pariah dogs squabbling over a piece of bone. Vivekananda greatly admired the quality of *rajas*, manly this-worldly virtues, of western civilization which Indians should emulate. But he was one of the pioneers of the belief in cultural relativism—'they are all right and so are we'. India had much to learn but could offer in exchange her immense wealth of spiritual knowledge. Bhudev's rejection of western values was total and genuine: the core value of individualism was to him an apotheosis of selfishness; Europe's past was an object lesson in what mankind should avoid.

The element of cultural self-assertion is certainly there in the writings of these three thinkers. But it is well to remember that their appreciation of their Indian inheritance is almost as selective as their assessments of the West. They are not unthinking chauvinists out to rubbish the civilization of the ruling race at any cost. Their assessments of the West are products of deep and careful study; its spirit is not xenophobic. The end product of this careful study is not any unquestioning acceptance of western superiority. If the colonial agenda was to project such superiority, it had obviously failed in the case of these very influential thinkers of the nineteenth century.

One could argue that all three belonged to a certain phase in the intellectual history of Bengal, the age of 'Hindu revival'. And if they were, as is claimed, protagonists of that revival, then they would expectedly focus on the negative features of western civilization. But unqualified admiration for the West, the civilization of England in particular, was not the characteristic feature of Indian perceptions in the nineteenth century. I have illustrated this point at some length in my essay 'Europe in India's Xenology: The Nineteenth-century Record', published in *Past and Present* (November 1992) and reprinted in my *Perceptions, Emotions, Sensibilities: Essays on India's Colonial and Post-colonial Experiences* (Oxford University Press, Delhi, 1999). All assessments of the West did recognize the advantages which they had over other civilizations, past and present, especially in science, technology, economic growth, and military-political domination over less fortunate races. Enquiries into the reasons for such advantages highlighted the positive features of European society and their comparative absence in the East in general, and in India in particular. But nowhere do we come across a concession of superiority across the board. Historical Christianity as encountered in Europe was one stumbling block. In no way could one see it as more rational than the religious beliefs and practices in India. Even its most ardent non-Christian admirer in Bengal, Keshab, was disappointed by the shallowness of Christian devotion and piety and had even less patience with its dogma. Rammohan found the Anglican acceptance of the 39 Articles hypocritical. And Christian intolerance, especially the ignorant missionary propaganda against Hinduism, provoked not merely resentment but a measure of real contempt. The individualistic values as also the growing consumerism of the West were off-putting to many. And no Indian observer saw any virtue in Europe's colonial wars and territorial acquisitions, especially the sad record of massive genocide. The criticisms focused on such matters were unrelated to any urge to cultural self-assertion or the psychological need to rubbish the alien ruler. The colonial project to convince the subject population of their cultural superiority was not a grand success.

Yet, there were elements in the cultural consciousness of the Bengali middle class, especially of people not engaged in serious intellectual assessment, which suggest a concession of superiority with few qualifications. The insignificance of Indians in general, Bengalis in particular, on the world stage is a recurrent theme in nineteenth-century writings. On the one hand, there is a recognition of great nations dominating the world and, on the other, there is a perception of Bengalis as a poor, weak, and worthless people, without any honour in this world and deserving no honour. The vague belief in a great past accentuated the sense of unworthiness: if the past was great, the fall from grace was all the more shameful. The emphasis on Hindu glory, on a worthy inheritance which was still a part of middle-class life, was partly inspired by this pervasive sense of worthlessness.

Yet, it would be incorrect to trace its source to the success of any colonial propaganda. The inferiority of Bengalis was not a theme in the academic curricula. Macaulay's rolling phrases rubbishing the hapless Bengalis or the steady stream of racist abuse in the Anglo-Indian press was unlikely to have been accepted as literally true by the colonial middle class. Their sense of low worth derived from a growing sense of hopelessness rooted in the colonial experience—their meagre material prospects, their low status in the colonial hierarchy, and their total exclusion from any access to political or administrative power. Worthlessness was literally a fact of life. It tortured generations of Bengali intellectuals, from Akshay Datta to Nirad Chaudhuri. The failure to alter the situation or the absence of any viable agenda for the attainment of a more honourable future generated a pattern of self-hatred evident in the writings of most Bengali thinkers and creative writers. Bankim's lampoons on the babu have to be read along with his private letters in which he describes himself as a mere servant of the British. Rabindranath castigated his people for the absence of a burning resentment against the daily insults which were their fate. Nirad Chaudhuri's hatred of his own social class has to be read in the context of the many humiliations he suffered till quite late in life. Arguably, the Bengali radical intellectual's contempt for the babu is in the same tradition—a tradition of self-hatred objectified as social criticism of one's social class. The critic somehow conjures a false self-perception which leaves the self untouched by the stigma of babuhood. There are rare exceptions such as Bankim talking of the curse of his life, service under the British which he was not strong enough to reject or, in more recent times, the author of *Babu-brittanta*. Samar Sen was not fooled by his own radical stance.

The superiority of the West as a part of the popular common sense was the logical other side of this self-perception of worthlessness. The superiority was evident in their domination, the military and political might on which that domination rested, their affluence, and their high achievements in the fields of knowledge as well as the creative arts. The drunken box-wallah or the not very educated missionary might not be the best representative of the civilization which claimed Shakespeare and Newton among its protagonists, but they too did belong to the same race and, in terms of dominant nineteenth-century beliefs concerning race, the fact gave them a claim to shared superiority. Besides, they had power and wealth. How could the poor Bengali clerk and schoolteacher not see the totality of their English civilization as superior to their own? The continual rubbishing of things Indian, the paeans of self-praise by the English in India, and the colonial project of preaching western superiority probably did not convince many. But the life experience under colonial rule did what conscious propaganda failed to achieve. The serious efforts to assess the relative worth of Europe's civilization were meant to counter the mindless acceptance of one's hopeless inferiority.

The social and political chasm which separated the two races in the colonial context buttressed the sense of mutual otherness. The intellectual perceptions of the period confirmed it partly on the basis of serious cogitation, partly through an unthinking acceptance of western paradigms: the East and the West. Orientalism did contribute to this simplistic perception. And some of the basic formulations of India's proto-nationalist thought were derived from the same source. The belief in 'unity in diversity', is a proneness towards political unification manifest in the region's history from the beginning of time, as also an alleged other-worldliness being the dominant concern of its culture were all of western Orientalist derivation. Some of these notions were mobilized in the service of nationalist consciousness; others fed into the agenda of cultural self-assertion. But to recognize these facts of the country's cultural history does not imply the acceptance of the thesis that the colonial agenda for brainwashing the collaborator was an unqualified success. This volume tries to show among other things that it was not.

This book is structured around one central argument. It questions the adequacy of paradigms such as westernization and modernization and suggests instead an alternative concept, that of a catalytic or chemical reaction generating phenomena which do not represent the synthesis of two cultures or any simple importation of artifacts from one culture into another. The encounter generated unpredictable responses, often complicated by the colonial experience. The cultural encounter with the West is an analytically distinct phenomenon from the colonial encounter though the two overlapped and influenced each other. One reviewer of my recently published volume of essays stated that I treated all cultural development in nineteenth-century India as a product of the encounter with the West. Nowhere have I stated or implied any such thing. On the contrary, it is my view that the encounter with the West resulted in often unexpected developments which acquired a measure of autonomy.

There are two other mutually related themes I wish to touch upon before I conclude. The first is the question of 'Hindu revival' in the late nineteenth century. My contention is simply that the vast majority of the Bengali population, both the élite and the masses, never swerved from their commitment to popular Hinduism, both its socioritual practices and its underlying system of beliefs. Western education and the reform movements, especially the emphasis on rational thought (of which more later), generated doubts about some of the sastric prescriptions, especially those such as *sati* and the enforced celibacy of widows. Deviation in practice from the prescribed conduct was rare. *Sati*, which was never the practice of the majority, was prohibited by law. And widow remarriage, which secured legal approval, never gained wide acceptance in Hindu society. The Brahmo movement was in decline partly because of its internal squabbles, and partly because many of its ideas had been taken on board by the educated bhadralok who did not join its ranks. On the other hand, the continuous denigration of Hindu practices and beliefs by westerners as well as the Brahmos, accessible to many through the growing print culture, resulted in a backlash. The mammoth meeting to protest against the Age of Consent Bill can be interpreted not as a symptom of Hindu revival but as an attempt to ward off an attack on the very heart of Hindu patriarchy. Only changed social and economic circumstances and very slow cultural change would render any significant rise in the age of marriage for women acceptable to the majority of the bhadralok. Comparable changes even in industrialized countries have taken ages. These issues are discussed at some length in the lecture appended to this volume.

The articulation of Hindu ideology, its more conservative strand hostile to changes in inherited social practices, is not a late nineteenth-century phenomenon. The tension between the reformers and the orthodox goes back to the days of Rammohan and Radhakanta. Rammohan did not have an easy victory at any point, and the famous 'silent majority' evidently did not deviate from orthodox practice. The vigorous defence of the received tradition acquired a new cutting edge in the late nineteenth century, thanks partly to the burgeoning national consciousness of the time. But the defence of Hinduism took many forms. It would be an error and a serious misrepresentation of facts to lump them together. Bankim and Sasadhar Tarkachudamani were not ideological bedfellows. And I have argued at length why identifying Vivekananda as the ultimate protagonist of Hindu revival and dragging his mystic guru into the unlikely scene of Hindu chauvinism are probably the height of absurdity. It is my contention that in the context of the emerging nationalism the hard core of Vivekananda's message, empowering the masses and preaching universal tolerance as well as his utter contempt for much in popular Hinduism, got overlooked. And it is probably true that the frustrated and humiliated clerks of Calcutta found a vicarious source of pride in the Swami's success abroad or the advent of a great Hindu saint on their doorstep, one whom even a great reforming babu like Keshab admired, and about whom even the sahibs wrote. To conclude for such reasons and on the basis of a few stray statements that Vivekananda and his guru represented the high point of Hindu revival seems rather unauthorized.

Historical studies, to make an obvious point, are not produced in a political or cultural vacuum. Much of the historical literature on India produced since the Second World War was part of an ideologically inspired debate on colonialism and the nature of the successor states, even though the fact is not overtly stated. A new ideological debate now occupies the political centre stage in India—on the Hindu identity, Hindutva, and its claim to a position of privilege in the structure of the country's polity. I have failed to discover so far the precise connotation of Hindutva as envisaged in the current discourse of the Sangh Parivar except that it excludes people who believe in faiths of extra-Indian origin, those to whom India may be the fatherland but certainly not the holy land. The Vishwa Hindu Parishad has laid amazing claims to Vivekananda as their 'intellectual' ancestor. Several possible meanings of the Hindu identity were projected by the thinkers whose ideas are discussed in this volume. I would like to point out that attacks on missionaries, destruction of mosques, and dictating what college girls should wear, and similar other elevated concerns were no part of Hindutva as they saw it. Vivekananda in fact advised Hindus who had the welfare of their country in mind to throw all temples and other impedimenta of popular but very expensive Hindu worship into the Ganges and concentrate instead on the service of God incarnate as the dispossessed—the dispossessed of all communities.

all temples and other impedimenta of popular but very expensive Hindu
worship into the Ganges and concentrate instead on the service of God
incarnate as the dispossessed—the dispossessed of all communities.

Preface to the
First Edition

This volume, though self-contained, is part of a more wide-ranging study on the history of changing perceptions and attitudes in nineteenth-century Bengal. A fact not sufficiently emphasized in the literature on the East-West encounter in modern times is that the Bengali intelligentsia was the first Asian social group of any size whose mental world was transformed through its interactions with the West. In 1817, Bengal's social leaders took the initiative to establish the first institution of western higher education in Asia. By then, through trade and colonial government, Bengalis had had more than six decades of close contact with a European nation. The change in their mental world has a relevance to wider themes. It is part of a process described very unsatisfactorily by the two expressions, 'modernization' and 'westernization'. Without entering into a discussion of the inadequacy of these two terms, one can note that élite groups throughout Asia experienced a revolution in their world-view and expectations from life which crucially influenced much that has happened over the last hundred years or so. Basic changes in the political, economic and sociocultural world of Asia were mediated by this transformation. Arguably, neither Indian nationalism nor Japanese industrialization nor Chinese communism could have emerged in its absence. Fundamental discontinuity in perception and outlook was confined to a minority of the population. Its impact was not so restricted. To give one example, the principles underlying the Indian Constitution represent the values of a minority. Their formal acceptance by a nation through representative institutions introduced potentialities of vast changes affecting hundreds of millions. The nineteenth-century Bengali experience is thus a part of a global phenomenon. Chronologically, it is perhaps the earliest manifestation of the revolution in the mental world of Asia's élite groups.

The specific context of colonial rule and absorption into the international economic order were important factors in the transformation, but the basic determinant of the change, arguably again, was the close contact between two entirely different cultures of which one was perceived to be dominant. The changes occurred, not through any simple transmission of 'influences' manifest in the straightforward adoption of cultural artifacts like specific elements in western life-habits or belief systems (though such adoptions were not absent), but through processes which went much deeper. The contact was a catalyst. It induced mutations in the inherited ways of thinking and conduct, both individual and social, and initiated unprecedented departures from established patterns of responses even in the most intimate areas of life. For instance, at one level, western education was simply an equipment which helped one earn one's living under the colonial regime. At another level, it destabilized established norms and mores of intra-family relationship. The belief in one's inalienable duties to a large kinship group, especially one's parents and one's own siblings and their progeny and the prescribed distance between parents and children and husband and wife— the two props of Bengali family life—were shaken to their foundation. Nirad Chaudhuri has argued convincingly[*] that the perception of man-woman relationship was transformed through exposure to western romantic literature. Like all discontinuities in such areas of life, the changes were not uniformly distributed over the relevant social space. Large joint families with nearly hundred members survived until very recently. Norms of deference and distance within the family circle also remain strong in many sections of the urban and rural middle class. But the new patterns of response and behaviour, through confined to a small minority, created waves and echoes which reached even remote corners. For instance, militant nationalism, the most powerful and unintended product of the East-West contact, might be the centre point in the lives of only a few young men and women, but its resonances can be noted even in rural ballads. The constitutional politician of a later age also used to his advantage the emotive associations of past martyrdom. The changes in the mental world of the élite are thus not an isolated historical phenomenon, but a crucial determinant of far-reaching developments. The Bengali experience is of particular interest in the Indian

* See his *Bangali jibane ramani* (Women in Bengali Life), Calcutta.

context, for it mediated at least some of the new ideas and influences which shaped modern Indian life. This is true not only at the level of 'proto-nationalist' consciousness and the growth of liberal-humanist values, but because the Bengali officials, clerks, lawyers, teachers and doctors were the first groups of western-educated Indians who went out to almost every part of the subcontinent to earn their livelihood.

The new perceptions and attitudes of the western-educated Bengalis derived of course from the historical forces at work, e.g. the working of the colonial government which altered the material bases of their life, shifting attitudes towards the fact of political dependence, growing familiarity with an alien culture which attracted and repelled often at the same time and new movements which consciously sought to alter social practices and inherited systems of belief. But whether the change was induced by self-conscious effort or impersonal influences, one notes an all-pervasive concern, almost obsessive, in their social and intellectual life—an anxiety to assess European culture in the widest sense of the term as something to be emulated or rejected. Whether it is a question of religious belief or one of ideal domestic conduct, the western example is a continual referent. Sometimes it appears as an impossibly superior ideal of a high civilization which an inferior subject race can never hope to match. Sometimes in a mode of self-assertion European ways are described as unworthwhile, not to be compared with the living heritage of the great Hindu civilization. Sometimes, a cautious and careful assessment is recommended as a basis for adopting selectively what might be acceptable in the Indian context. The inevitable resentment against alien rule, aggravated by Anglo-Indian *hauteur*, introduced an element of xenophobia in these judgements. The end products of this persistent preoccupation were a series of stereotypes, often mutually contradictory, which influenced social attitudes and informed political consciousness.

The stereotypes coexisted and interacted with a high intellectual tradition of serious evaluation. The latter can be traced back to the earliest beginnings of modern Indian thought to Raja Rammohan Roy and his contemporaries. This tradition too was inspired by a serious social purpose rather than mere intellectual curiosity. The object was to determine what India could adopt from the West and, as important, what elements in western life must be rejected at all cost. Needless to say, these exercises were not straightforward academic analyses. The author's ideological preference determined his prescription *a priori* and consequently the details of his evaluation. The attempt at objectivity, often supported by profound scholarship and great intellectual skill was, however, seldom absent.

Nationalist consciousness acquired a measure of clarity and was expressed in specific programmes in the latter half of the nineteenth century. One component of this developing awareness was a great pride in the Indian past, especially the high traditions of Hinduism. Cultural self-assertion centring on this new-found pride in the Hindu past at times assumed bizarre forms. Hindu 'revivalism' in late nineteenth-century Bengal was an extreme example of the psychological need felt by a colonial élite to assert its superiority in relation to the ruling race.

The term 'revivalism' in the context of nineteenth-century Bengal is applicable, strictly speaking, to a movement led by a small group of self-consciously 'traditionalist' intellectuals. This point is argued at some length in the text of the present volume. The movement, despite its great popularity, was short-lived. The major figures in the cultural life of the period distanced themselves from its antics, though some, like Bhudev Mukhopadhyay, had a cautious regard for some of its leaders. But pride in the Hindu past and strong nationalist sentiments informed by that pride were powerful influences at the time. One can think of hardly any Bengali Hindu leader, writer or publicist of the period untouched by this preoccupation with Hindu glory.

The three persons whose perceptions of Europe are discussed in this volume were all profoundly influenced by these two interacting trends of the time. They also contributed to the further development of a nationalist ideology. All three were concerned, *inter alia*, with the clarification and projection of a Hindu view of life, though I would not use the term 'revivalist' in relation to any one of them.

My choice of these three thinkers is based on several reasons. First, their statements on the West have a quality of fulness, depth and sophistication, based on very considerable scholarship and intellectual power, hardly matched in any other nineteenth-century Asian writing I have come across. This assessment, of course, may be entirely mistaken because my reading is confined to secondary material and translations. But even if the comparison is erroneous, the quality of the writings discussed in this volume is not in doubt. The other Bengali writer I would have liked to discuss is Rabindranath Tagore who continued to develop his ideas on Europe well into the 1930s. Since the scope of the present study is confined to the nineteenth century, I decided reluctantly to leave out his assessment of the West. A second reason for my choice is the influence of these three men on the cultural and political life of the region. Bhudev, as the great exponent of traditional virtues, Bankim, the most famous novelist and thinker of his time, and Vivekananda, the 'patriot-prophet' whose impassioned preaching influenced generations of idealistic youth, are among the most respected culture heroes of late nineteenth-century Bengal. What they wrote mattered. Their perceptions of Europe became part of the region's cultural heritage and even influenced popular stereotypes. There is the third reason for my choice. In a way, all three came from very similar backgrounds. Upper-caste Hindus, they were products of the new middle class and western education. In so far as they saw Europe through books, their reading covered more or less the same ground. There were basic similarities in their ideological outlook. The questions they asked were determined by the same historical circumstances—the contact between two very different cultures and the responses, both negative and positive, to the civilization of the politically dominant nation. Inevitably, their questions are very similar, if not identical. The answers are not. These talented men, very close to one another in their social origins and historical experience, assessed the civilization of Europe each in his own distinctive way.

One purpose of this book is simply to present their ideas as representative samples of the nineteenth-century Indian perceptions of the West at their most complex and well-informed level. Compared to the substantial literature on western views of Asia and even on the perceptions of the West in China, Japan, Southeast Asia and the Arab world, very little has been written so far on Indian perceptions of the West. I hope this book will go some way towards filling an obvious lacuna.

My second object is to focus attention on the diversity of experiences and personalities which explain the diversity in their assessments. Contact between different cultures and the experience of colonial rule may effect different individuals and groups very differently indeed. To make an obvious point, neither cultures nor historical situations are monoliths. Within the apparently narrow range of upper-caste Bengali Hindu culture, there are possibilities of very substantial variations. There is a world of difference between the life experience of an orthodox Brahmin, punctilious in his observance of ritual requirements and that of a high-living professional person, devoted to the Mother Goddess, but no less devoted to Mughal cuisine. The colonial experience itself subsumes a variety of possibilities.

The middle-ranking bureaucrat constantly at odds with his European bosses is likely to take a view of the British personality which would be very different from the perceptions of a famous *sanyasi*, revered by western scholars and heiresses alike. Besides, even colonial rule subsumed a pattern of modernity, however stunted, and hence contributed to a proliferation of personality types. Few individuals could be more different, one from another, than Bhudev, Bankim, and Vivekananda. Finally, while their lives overlapped chronologically, these were fast-moving times and in a sense the three belonged to three different generations, though Bankim was younger to Bhudev only by twelve years. When the Queen-in-Parliament assumed responsibility for the governance of India, Bhudev was a mature man and Bankim a precocious youth of nineteen. Interestingly, the former considered the Company's rule in many ways superior to its successor. Bankim's nationalism and gut reactions to British rule were influenced *inter alia* by the Indigo Rebellion and the Anglo-Indian* agitation against the Ilbert Bill. But he, like his senior contemporary, could still maintain some faith in at least the objectively beneficial role of the British presence. The attitude of total rejection, the increasingly dominant response to colonial rule, is already there in Vivekananda. His American audiences discovered that the one topic which could disturb his equanimity was the British rule in India.

Each of the three main chapters in this book has two parts. The first part explores the specificities of background and life-experience, which help explain the thinker's point of view in his assessment of Europe. I have, however, avoided any reductionist effort to trace particular ideas to clearly located sources in the life-stories. In presenting their ideas, I have been guided by the nature of the source material. Bhudev, in his *Samajik prabandha*, offered a closely argued critique of western civilization. It seemed worthwhile to follow his sequence of ideas as developed in this major work and supplement the statements from material in his other writings. Bankim's observations are scattered over a wide range of literary products—fiction, *belles lettres*, and didactic works. A thematic treatment was obviously suitable in his case and also in dealing with the writings of Vivekananda, even though the nature of the material is different. Vivekananda did write one book specifically comparing the East and the West besides a fascinating travelogue, but some of his most significant perceptions are to be found in dialogues recorded by his admirers and in personal letters. This book has not been

---

* The term is used in this book in the old sense of the English in India.

written exclusively for readers with a specialized knowledge of modern Indian history or of Bengal, because its subject matter may be of some interest to people whose primary concern is with other areas of study. Therefore, I have filled in the relevant background information which the specialist reader may find trivial. I have not, however, provided references for information well-known to students of the subject. Hence the introductory chapter contains very few footnotes.

In referring to the authors discussed in this book, I have used generally the first name following the Bengali convention. Where there are thousands of Mukherjis, Chatterjis, and Dattas, this practice makes obvious sense. I have also taken the liberty of using only the first part of the name, i.e. Bankim and Naren or Narendra rather than Bankimchandra and Narendranath. This usage implies an abbreviation permissible in the language. In transliterating Bengali words, I have followed no fixed principle but sought a compromise between the scholarly convention of transliterating Bengali words as if these were Sanskrit ones and a system of transliteration which seeks to convey the actual pronunciation. Hence *Samajik prabandha* and not *Samajika pravandha*. Diacritical marks have not been used. Sometimes, I have had to use different editions of an author's work for his various writings, because the relevant volumes in one standard edition were not readily accessible. However, the accuracy of all the editions used has been carefully checked.

The research for this work was funded by generous grants from the British Academy and the Economic and Social Research Council. It is not possible to list the various individuals and institutions without whose help this book could not have been written. I should, however, like to express my deep sense of gratitude to Professor Ashin Dasgupta, Director, National Library, Calcutta, and Swami Lokeswarananda and Miss Abhaya Dasgupta of the Ramakrishna Mission Institute of Culture. Professor Dasgupta has dealt very patiently with my requests with exceptional kindness over the years. Swami Lokeswarananda has helped valuable advice and Miss Dasgupta placed at my disposal all relevant material on Vivekananda, much of which is not easily available elsewhere. I am especially grateful to Professor Manoranjan Mohanty for helping me in various stages of this work. My colleagues, Dr Ann Waswo and Dr Mark Elvin, helped me with bibliographical information on Japanese and Chinese perceptions of Europe which proved useful in working out my approach to the subject matter of the present volume. I resisted the initial temptation to compare the Indian perception with their Sino-Japanese and other Asian counterparts. Such comparisons, based inevitably on secondary literature or, at most, translations of primary material, can lead to disastrous mistakes. My thanks are also due to Mr Partha Ganguly who did a splendid job in producing a very accurate typescript in record time.

The subject matter of this book was first presented as the Sakharam Ganes Deuskar lectures at the Centre for the Study of Social Sciences, Calcutta. The lectures have been published separately as a pamphlet. That pamphlet is in no sense a summary of this volume.

I find it necessary to add a curious word of explanation. While delivering lectures on the subject matter of this volume in different countries, I encountered a startling response, at times from highly educated people. I was called upon to defend the opinions of my authors as if these were my own. One Calcutta newspaper quoted one of Bankim's more abrasive comments on Bengalis and did the honour of attributing it to me. An angry member of the audience in the Antipodes harangued me on the unfairness of Vivekananda's criticisms of Christianity. A good friend who kindly read parts of the manuscript keeps referring to his 'piratical forebears', following Bhudev's description of European exuberance in the Middle Ages. In the light of such experiences, I feel I should dissociate myself entirely from all opinions cited in this book on the Europeans and Indians alike. I hold no brief for my authors. Besides, they have been dead for nearly a hundred years!

Abbreviations

(See Bibliography for publication details)

AP	Bhudev Mukhopadhyay, *Achar pravandha*
Basu	Pramathanath Basu, *Swami Vivekananda*
Bch	Mukundadev Mukhopadhyay, *Bhudev charit*
BD., SV	Bhupendranath Datta, *Swami Vivekananda*
Bj	Mahendranath Datta, *Swami Vivekanander balyajibani*
BP	Bhudev Mukhopadhyay, *Bibidha pravandha*
BPr	S Samajpati, ed., *Bankim prasanga*
BPra	Bankimchandra Chattopadhyay, *Bibidha pravandha* Centenary Edition
BR, EW	J C Bagal, ed. *Bankim rachanavali, English Works*
Burke	Marie Louise Burke, *Swami Vivekananda in the West— New Discoveries*
BY	Bengali Year
CW(B)	*The Complete Works of Swami Vivekananda* (Bengali)
CW(E)	*The Complete Works of Swami Vivekananda* (English)
Dhar	S N Dhar, *A Comprehensive Biography of Swami Vivekananda*
Ghat	Mahendranath Datta, *Srimad Vivekananda Swamir jibaner ghatanabali*
Life	*The Life of Swami Vivekananda* by his Eastern and Western Disciples
Londone	Mahendranath Datta, *Londone Swami Vivekananda*
POP	Swami Vivekananda, *Prachya o paschatya*

PP	Bhudev Mukhopadhyay, *Parivarik pravandha*
RKA	Mahendranath Datta, *Sri sri Ramakrishner anudhyan*
RKK	Sri Ma (i.e. Mahendranath Gupta), *Sri sri Ramakrishna—kathamrita*
RLP	Swami Saradananda, *Sri sri Ramakrishnalila prasanga*
SP	Bhudev Mukhopadhyay, *Samajik pravandha*
SSS	Saratchandra Chakravarti, *Swami-sishya samvad*
VB	Swami Vivekananda, *Vartaman Bharat*
VIN	Sankariprasad Basu and Sailendranath Ghosh, *Vivekananda in Indian Newspapers*
VSB	Sankariprasad Basu, *Vivekananda o samakalin Bharat*

chapter 1

The Background

The title of this book, *Europe Reconsidered*, has reference to evaluations which preceded in time the writings discussed here. It also implies that the earlier assessments projected a somewhat more positive image compared to the views held by Bhudev, Bankim, and Vivekananda. In fact, some of their contemporaries, like the poet, Michael Madhusudan Datta, the Brahmo leader, Keshabchandra Sen—the Indian best known in England at that time—and his close associate, Protap Mazoomdar, among others, retained an almost unqualified admiration for many facets of European culture. It would be incorrect to suggest that all earlier assessments were exclusively favourable. The statements which constitute the subject matter of the present study, however, do differ from earlier as well as some of the contemporary Indian opinion on Europe in several ways. First, objective or not, these statements mostly consist in reasoned arguments based on a large volume of data derived from reading and observation. We have here a body of considered opinion, rather than casual or fragmentary comments. It reflects a measure of intellectual self-confidence in relation to Europe. That confidence was founded on the social experience of several decades of contact. Knowledge of western civilization was no longer the prerogative of a few individuals but, at some level or other, very much a part of contemporary 'élite'* culture in Bengal. Second, these considered judgements question the explicit or implicit assumptions of western superiority as expressed, for instance, in the opinion of the Indian Anglicists or the reformer Vidyasagar, dismissing Indian philosophy and much of Sanskritic culture as useless. 'Useful knowledge' in this view could come only from Europe. While such assumptions had

---

* This imprecise term, albeit somewhat misleading, has been used here to denote the western educated intelligentsia as a short-hand description.

always been questioned, the reasons for rejecting these unequivocally are clearly spelt out in the second half of the century—in such writings as are discussed in this book. Finally, though the three thinkers had very different things to say about Europe, the questions they ask and the answers they provide reflect the ambience of strong nationalist concerns.

An increasing clarity of nationalist consciousness informs all their writings. There was a continuous tension between the evolution of this new consciousness and the growing familiarity with European culture. As the new middle class of colonial Bengal emerged from their role of mere compradors and assumed a variety of roles as bureaucratic, professional, and tenure-holding collaborators, they also became avid students of western knowledge, especially the humanities and the social sciences. The early products of the new schools and colleges[1] had an almost unqualified admiration for the unfamiliar learning now accessible to them and, presumably, for the civilization which produced it.

The embryonic national consciousness in the 1920s and 1930s manifest concerns for the improvement of 'society' and a burgeoning pride in the inherited culture, coexisted easily with a total acceptance of colonial rule. Criticism of arbitrary or unjust action was already there. Derozio and his students also showed an occasional romantic concern for the motherland's state of bondage. Such signs of disquiet were however no more than very minor deviations from the dominant attitude of enthusiastic loyalty.

The admiration for the alien rulers and their civilization was, however, subject to certain social and psychological constraints. The alien authority's reforming legislations which interfered with matters of ritual practice, like the abolition of *sati*, were not universally popular. The implied condemnation of the established social order—the ascription of barbarism—was resented. Defensive postures were a natural outcome of such resentment. Further, the acceptance of liberal-humanist values and the consequent rejection of irrational codes of social and ritual conduct had very limited impact on practice for a long time. Conformity rather than deviation from the prescribed codes was almost certainly the rule so far as the majority of the western-educated intelligentsia was concerned. The consequent need to justify the much criticized practices reinforced defensive attitudes. The Christian missionaries' criticism of everything Hindu—often crude and ill-informed,[2]— provoked anti-Christian sentiments, at times a thinly veiled surrogate for anti-European feelings. The negative dimension of nationalism—its xenophobic content—began to emerge almost as early as the proud sense of a new identity and commitment to social change. Conversion of high-caste Hindus to Christianity was a prospect which few could accept with equanimity.[3] The often frantic efforts to set the neglected house of Hinduism in order were inspired by fears of proselytization under the protective aegis of the British rule.

Modally, the emerging nationalist consciousness adopted the heritage of Hindu culture as the focus of its identity and gloried in the Hindu past. Yet well into the 1870s, it also rejoiced that India was part of a glorious, world-wide empire and nurtured hopes of a steady progress under Britain's providential guidance. The contradiction between pride in the Hindu identity and faith in a regime seen to be identified with the most vicious critics of the cherished culture was apparently not obvious in the early phases of nationalism. Besides, not all patriots were uncritical admirers of Hinduism. The sceptical products of the new enlightenment, reformers, both Brahmo and Hindu, and, by the seventies, the positivist disciples of Comte rejected many features of the established socioreligious system. Yet a devout Brahmo like Rajnarayan Basu could avow publicly the superiority of Hinduism over all other religions.[4] Even the secular agnostic trend in Bengali middle-class culture, traceable back to the early days of the Hindu College— if not to the even older tradition of *Navyanyaya*[5]—was subsumed by the ill-defined sense of national identity built around the Hindu heritage and its social body.

A selective veneration for elements in the Hindu tradition was thus the cultural bedrock of the nationalist awareness. It coexisted, but not very easily, with at least an equal veneration, also selective, for the civilization of the master race. We do not have the data to decide what proportion of the new intelligentsia thought of western culture as something wonderful and believed, overtly or otherwise, that it represented heights India could never hope to attain. The evidence, however, suggests that such attitudes were fairly pervasive. The fact of dominance was evidence enough of superior might. That might was seen to be based on formidable material and intellectual achievements. The excitement over the literature, history, and philosophy of Europe as well as the less familiar scientific knowledge was deep and abiding, even though any intimate knowledge of western learning was really confined to the few with access to higher education. Macaulay's theory that education would filter down from the privileged few to much larger social groups did not quite work. But the knowledge acquired by the few provided the basis for admiration by many. In a culture which had always admired scholarship, the pundits of the new learning were objects of awe. And as to the new knowledge itself and its source, the civilization of Europe, an acceptance of their superiority informed cultural stereotypes widely in vogue.

Theoretical analysis of colonial cultures and Third World nationalism tends to explain such admiration in terms of political domination and the dependent character of the colonial intelligentsia—their failure to aspire after hegemony or attempt basic transformation of the society within a political framework that forges a consensus involving all classes of the population. In short, the acknowledged limitations of nationalism in Europe's Afro-Asian colonies, especially in its earlier phases, are emphasized in this context. Alternative or complementary theories identify colonial nationalism itself as a notion imported from nineteenth-century Europe, a rather unwholesome product of a sense of inadequacy in comparison with the pace-makers of modern civilization.[6] The implied positive image of European nationalism—the conscious or unconscious inclination to ignore its many unacceptable faces—is surely questionable. The autonomous and 'positive' cultural content of Afro-Asian nationalisms—their efforts to devise new goals and criteria for man's progress—is also no part of such theories. Yet their hard core of partial truth should not be denied, so long as one remembers that it encapsulates a purely negative, and hence distorting, assessment.

A weak and dependent intelligentsia necessarily admires its masters. The admiration for their civilization is, however, not exclusively a result of dependence. Such responses are very much a part of the history of cultural encounters. Equality or inequality in terms of power is not the sole determinant of their content. The evolving values of the parties concerned and the specific historical situation determine what people nurtured in one civilization admire in another. It is significant that the very first generation of western-educated Bengalis felt attracted to the ideals of national liberation and post-enlightenment rationalism, which were by no means the only components of the nineteenth-century European tradition. Mazzini and Garibaldi, but not Bismarck, were the admired heroes. The rational-sceptical tradition won many converts, not Roman Catholicism despite its evident affinities with the symbolic ritualism of the Hindu religion. Negatively, one dominant drive of European nationalism—colonial expansion and aggressive wars—was universally detested in nineteenth-century Bengal. This unqualified rejection coexisted paradoxically with a genuine sense of wonder about the British empire as a marvellous feat, albeit the product of many ruthless wars of aggression.

Then there are areas of response hardly touched by relationships of power. The fact that Bankim preferred Shakespeare to Kalidasa has causal links with the education he received and the tastes formed thereby. The sense of inadequacy in relation to the ruling race does not come into the picture here. The same is true of his and Vivekananda's negative aesthetic judgements concerning Indian sculpture and their preference for the art of the Greeks. Thus strongly positive responses to specific elements in an alien culture are not necessarily linked to dominance, though the latter may reinforce it. Dominance provokes revulsion and hostility as well. Theoreticians well aware of this phenomenon often interpret it as a manifestation of ambivalence. A different explanation noted above is perhaps more convincing. The particular components of the cultures concerned at the time of encounter and circumstances of the encounter determine what one admires and emulates as well as what one detests and rejects. In the colonial context, a hopeless aspiration towards power and the sense of inadequacy it generates are transmitted to areas of encounter where they have no obvious relevance. Bankim's statements avowing British superiority and Bengali worthlessness in every sphere are prime examples of this generalized sense of inadequacy. But the evaluation of the dominant culture is seldom a seamless web. It stretches across a spectrum, however limited in range. The precise point that an individual occupies along that spectrum is determined by his/her relationship to the inherited tradition and the specific experience of encounter with the alien civilization. One object of this book is to explore and explain the possibilities of the consequent variation in Indian perceptions of Europe. Colonialism does tend to define the contact between cultures in terms of power relationships and thus limit and distort its potentialities. Nevertheless, the transmission of ideas, especially when the latter act as a powerful catalyst, often works as an autonomous force. All responses to the West in colonial India were not within the two polar limits of slavish admiration and xenophobic rejection. There is an extensive area of rational and scholarly assessment untouched by hang-ups of one sort or another.

In any given situation, individual responses are shaped by the impact of relatively rigid structures as well as the more elusive influence of an amorphous and shifting milieu. The colonial structure impinged on the lives of the intelligentsia in a way that was more or less uniform. Exclusion from positions of real authority, a limited range of opportunities, racial discrimination built into the legal system, and an economic nexus seen to be unfavourable to Indian interests were all parts of their shared experience. A measure of criticism and resentment was the inevitable response to these structurally determined negative experiences. Even there, however, some individuals had better luck than others. Besides, a phlegmatic personality and a highly strung man reacted very differently to the same set of shared misfortunes.

The scope for variation was much greater when it came to the influence of milieu. The colonial experience itself was not rigidly structured all along the line, but contained the possibility of a variable milieu. The Indian official working for the regime might have to work with friendly or unfriendly European colleagues. The work experience might offer job satisfaction or fail to do so. The encounter between different cultures under the aegis of colonial rule subsumed a much wider range of possibilities. Such encounters might have points of institutional focus—like schools, colleges, associations, etc.—but these were seldom structured in the same way as political or administrative authority. The young educated Bengali encountered Europe mainly through books. The dominant trends in the intellectual life of the period created a general interest in certain areas of western thought. They did not determine what an individual should read or accept. The cultural milieu thus offered a range of choice. A novelist and a *sanyasi* would respond to very different elements in that milieu though the structural compulsions of the colonial experience might focus attention on the same set of questions. Such reasons explain why the three thinkers discussed in this volume followed very different lines of analysis and reached substantially different conclusions in their assessments of the West, even though they belonged to the same small subset of the intelligentsia—champions of the Hindu way of life in one form or another. Vivekananda offered spontaneous worship in a Catholic church. Both Bhudev and Bankim found the Christian conception of the Deity a monstrous construct.

The milieu created by the encounter between two very different cultures, interacting with the colonial structure, helps explain some of the major developments in the concerns of the Bengali intelligentsia. So long as a relatively small middle class—bureaucrats, men in the professions and rentier proprietors of landed estates—were contented beneficiaries of British rule, happy with the modest quantum of new economic opportunities, their embryonic national consciousness subsumed very little criticism of the colonial regime. The element of xenophobia in their world-view was a direct reaction to the Christian missionary onslaught on their cherished beliefs and practices. The criticism by foreigners resulted in attention being focused on one's Hindu identity and the need to defend it against all assailants, native or foreign. The Dharma Sabha established by notables like Raja Radhakanta Deb expressed institutionally this new anxiety. Defensive postures thus became an important component of emerging social and political consciousness even at a very early stage. By the 1830s, it had crystallized around the resistance to the proposal to abolish *sati* and a new educational policy shifting the emphasis of state support from oriental to western education. The 1830s also saw the first conversion of educated young Bengalis to Christianity and Reverend Duff's vigorous campaign for proselytization.

Defensive attitudes were, however, not the only, or even the central, concern of the burgeoning nationalism which emphasized the Hindu identity. Its components included an informed delight in past glory, necessarily idealized, but often based on the results of serious research by European and Indian scholars. The *Tattvavodhini Patrika*, established in 1843 and edited by the rationalist Akshay Datta, explored *inter alia* the ancient traditions in a sober and respectful mood. In the 1850s, the movement for the legalization of widow remarriage and prohibition of polygamy, no doubt inspired by the new liberal values, invoked the authority of the Smriti texts. Even earlier, Rammohan's pioneering efforts at reform had also sought *sastric* sanction and his syncretic monotheism interpreted one particular Hindu religious tradition in the spirit of a new commentary. The English title of his bilingual journal was the *Brahmanical Magazine*. The young radicals who denounced Hinduism in *Gyananwesan* and the *Enquirer* in the 1830s were the only real exceptions to this pattern of concern with the Hindu heritage but they had very limited influence and were soon marginalized. The self-conscious nationalism of the 1860s and 1870s—expressed pointedly in Nabagopal Mitra's *National Paper* and National Society—owed much to *The Hindu Mela* (Hindu Fair) he first started in 1876 'to promote the national feeling ... among the Hindus'. The literature of the period is replete with patriotic passion, but the referent in most cases is the medieval Hindu chiefs' resistance to Turkish rulers—an obvious surrogate for the unlikely revolt against a more contemporary alien regime. The tradition of serious investigation, inspired by Western Orientology, developed further in the

1870s and produced *inter alia* the superb antiquarian research of Rajendralal Mitra.

The sense of inadequacy one inevitably finds in a subject people did inform many areas of Indian life. A lack of cultural self-confidence, the continual need for assurance, preferably from reputable European quarters, was very much a part of the preoccupation with the Hindu heritage. Max Mueller's scholarly theories concerning the common origin of all Indo-Aryan races based on his linguistic studies were received with incredible enthusiasm. The belief that the white masters were not very distant cousins of their brown Aryan subjects provided a much needed salve to the wounded ego of the dependent élite. A spate of 'Aryanism' was unleashed. The word 'Aryan' began to feature in likely as well unlikely places—from titles of periodicals to the names of street corner shops. Even the serious writers of the period were not unaffected by the particular plague. The Tagores—Rabindranath and Dwijendranath—might poke fun at the new Aryanism, but they were almost certainly in a minority and it is doubtful if their irony was appreciated by many.

Tributes from the West were especially welcome because uninhibited and offensive criticism of Hindu ways had not ceased by any means. The controversy between Reverend Hastie and Bankim, discussed in this volume, shows how far even a highly educated European could go in his use of abusive language while describing Hindus and Hinduism. If such vicious criticism was hurtful, it was even more so when it came from one's own countrymen. The resentment against Brahmos—expressed *inter alia* in a scurrilous and highly popular novel, Jogindrachandra Basu's *Model bhagini* (The Ideal Sister)*—was partly provoked by their overt contempt for traditional practices. Parodies of westernized Bengalis—whose lifestyle implied an unfavourable comment on 'unreformed' Hinduism—recur continually in the popular literature of the period. The criticism of 'native' ways by Europeans and their Indian imitators induced a quest for the deficiencies in western culture. To an orthodox Hindu conditioned by the habits of his own society, much in western life—from beef-eating and sanitary habits to the relative freedom in man-woman relationship—was genuinely repellent. A movement, described somewhat inaccurately as Hindu revivalism, arose on

---

* Among Brahmos, it was customary to refer to the women members of their 'society' as '*bhagini*', i.e. sister.

the twin foundations of wounded self-esteem and an aversion to the ways of the ruling race.

The said description is inaccurate for two very different reasons. First, all writers and publicists who evoked the Hindu past as an ideal to live by or defended the inherited beliefs and customs have been described at times as revivalists. The three thinkers discussed in this volume are often included in the same category. I have argued in the relevant chapters the reasons why such inclusion is fallacious. To put it briefly, Bhudev did not seek any 'revival' of lost ways. He simply pointed out the need to preserve the inherited practices for otherwise there was a danger of losing all sense of cultural identity. Bankim interpreted, in an explicitly patriotic mood, certain elements in the old traditions as a viable basis for national regeneration. I have argued that the ideal he projected had more to do with nationalist purpose and certain schools of European thought than with the ancient *dharma* or Lord Krishna as depicted in the great epic. Vivekananda, who preached Vedanta in the West, was concerned almost exclusively with national regeneration at home, especially the uplift of the masses—not a preoccupation one usually associates with the Hindu past. His guru did revive an ancient tradition— that of syncretism, avowing faith in the fundamental truth of all religions, not in Hindu orthodoxy.

The second reason why the term 'revivalism' is misleading is that it is difficult to revive something which is far from dead. The hold of traditional Hindu practice on the lives of all but a few among the Bengali Hindu intelligentsia was still very strong in the second half of the nineteenth century. It is well to remember in this context that Hindu orthodoxy demands conformity in practice rather than in belief. The urban Bengali might have departed from the punctilious observance of ritual purity, though even this statement would not apply to their womenfolk. But very few other than the Brahmos had discarded the life cycle and daily rituals or, more crucially, the practice of child marriage. *Bhakti* to the deities one worshipped was still very much the hard core of religiosity. Brahmos were few in number. The Christian proselytizers had little joy of the Bengali intelligentsia. Vidyasagar's heroic efforts for the legalization of widow remarriage produced one more law on the statute book, still virtually ignored by the Bengali caste Hindus. The curious movement pioneered by men like Sasadhar Tarkachudamani and Krishnaprasanna Sen with its doctrine of Hinduism *uber alles* should perhaps be described by some suitable epithet other than revivalism. 'Aggressive chauvinism' is perhaps the appropriate term. The three writers here were, in any case, no part of that movement. But there was tension between the more sober evocations of the Hindu heritage and the bizarre projections of Pandit Sasadhar. The latter sought to justify every Hindu practice—ranging from child marriage and *sati* to popular beliefs in the occult implications of untimely sneezing or the clicking sound produced by house lizards. The pandit discovered the core of all advanced scientific knowledge in the ancient Sanskrit texts. Their hidden meaning deciphered by the new seers had eluded everyone else until then. They dismissed the civilization of Europe as an inferior culture; its progenitors were but brutish savages when the great Aryan sages propagated the Vedas revealed by the Infinite. Pseudo-scientific arguments were marshalled to establish this thesis. Such pathetic attempts to bolster up Hindu self-esteem had immense appeal. Sasadhar and Krishnaprasanna could fill any hall to overflowing in the metropolis and district towns.[7] The bruised ego of the less sophisticated middle-class Hindus floated happily on the hot air of the new gospel.

Euphoria turned into ecstasy when three renowned white persons, Mrs Besant, Colonel Olcott and Madame Blavatsky arrived to declare India's great spiritual superiority. Hinduism, people were told, was the ultimate fountainhead of ineffable wisdom and the western world must sit at India's feet to seek salvation. Even people of great learning and intellectual calibre found this sight of famous westerners kneeling before India's spiritual authority quite irresistible. If Indian nationalism had an element of anxious quest for something to counterbalance a sense of inadequacy, the Theosophical movement's success is its most telling example. Even the acerbic and cynical Krishna Menon in his youth was an activist in the cause of this cult, which claimed access to esoteric knowledge communicated by great souls resident in Tibet and visible, occasionally, only to Madame Blavatsky. The relationship of Bhudev, Bankim, and Vivekananda to Hindu 'revivalism' is clarified by the fact that all three found Theosophy disreputable. The Swami actually courted considerable unpopularity by his unequivocal condemnation of theosophy and the theosophists. Yet, the almost hysterical excitement in India over his *succès d'éstime* in the West had obvious links with the same sense of inadequacy which explains the appeal of theosophy, Max Mueller's theories on race, and Pandit Sasadhar's ludicrous claims. In Madras and Calcutta, excited young men insisted on drawing Swamiji's carriage when he first returned form the West—a response which suggests something other than legitimate pride at a fellow countryman's success abroad. One notices an element of social neurosis in the late nineteenth-century preoccupation with Hindu glory among a large section of the Bengali intelligentsia. In that blind alley of Indian nationalism, many Bengalis—Positivists or Utilitarians in their youth—abjured agnosticism and the westernized lifestyle to rejoice in Hindu rituals and the unrestrained emotionalism of guru cults. A well-known socialite, who in his youth had achieved notoriety through his seduction of and later marriage with a widowed maharani, acquired in his middle age the pigtail prescribed by orthodoxy to go with his well-tailored suits.[8]

The power of this movement should not be underestimated. One of its important organs, *Bangabasi*, had 50,000 subscribers, a record number in those days. Its editor, Jogindranath Basu, and his friend, Indranath Bandyopadhya, a highly talented satirist, reduced Brahmoism to an object of ridicule through their often scurrilous writings. No writer of the period could ignore the phenomenon. Its bizarre and often extremely tasteless manifestations soon had a sobering effect on the enthusiasts. All major thinkers and publicists distanced themselves from it. Yet, some of them, Bhudev and Bankim included, had tenuous and short-lived links with Sasadhar. Vivekananda had no patience with the pandit's inanities, but his infinitely tolerant guru expressed an interest in the latter's preaching. The pandit and the sage, however, failed to establish any rapport, though Ramakrishna's standard biography projects a somewhat inaccurate picture of cordiality. Rabindranath ridiculed the false glorification of the Hindu past, but his portrayal of individuals caught up in the throes of Hindu chauvinism in two of his best-known novels—*Chaturanga* and *Gora*—is remarkable for its quality of empathy. The anxious and neurotic effort at cultural self-assertion was a major trait of the milieu in late nineteenth-century Bengal. One inevitably notes its resonances in the more sober attempts to evaluate European civilization.

Potentially, one of the most dangerous features of this aggressively Hindu orientation was a new tendency to rubbish the rule of Muslim dynasties. The quest for a nonexistent patriotic tradition inevitably fastened on the Rajput and Maratha resistance to the Muslim dynasts. A characteristically middle-class desire to play safe and avoid giving offence to the British partly explains this preoccupation; acts of resistance to the British were not a safe subject. However, to be fair, Bengali journalism in the 1970s showed no excessive anxiety about the consequences of criticism.[9] As Bhudev pointed out, the Bengali intelligentsia had been successfully brainwashed by the

British writers on Indo-Muslim history. The continual use of a pejorative—
jaban (*yavana*) with reference to Muslims—expressed this new xenophobia.
Of our three writers, Bankim while evoking the Hindu identity in his
passionately nationalist writings, hardly ever missed the chance of a dig at
the Muslims. Bhudev and Vivekananda had very positive attitudes towards
Islam and the Indo-Muslim past. But even they occasionally referred to
'Muslim tyranny'. Nearly all evaluations of the British presence were coloured
by this negative attitude towards Islam's role in Indian life.

I have written at some length about the Hindu component of nationalism
in nineteenth-century Bengal, because to a large extent the perceptions
discussed in this volume were profoundly influenced by it. All the three
writers whose ideas constitute our subject matter contributed to the definition
of a nationalist goal as well as a positive Hindu identity. One even helped
foster anti-Muslim sentiments. Yet, by the 1860s and 1870s, nationalism
developed other concerns which transcended the limits of a particular religious
tradition. As early as 1861, Rajnarayan Basu established a Society for the
Promotion of National Feeling among the educated natives of Bengal,[10] which
sought to encourage a return to Indian life-habits in preference to the
denationalizing imitation of European manners. The Society did not emphasize
the ways of any particular community. Later in life, despite his declaration
of faith in the superiority of Hinduism over all other religions, for which he
was hailed as the saviour of the ancient religion, his famous pamphlet,
Briddha Hindur asha (The Hopes of an Old Hindu), emphasized the need
for cooperation with 'our Muslim brethren'.[11] An awareness that the Indian
nation had to comprehend ethnic groups other than the Hindus had been
the basis of political organization as far back as 1851 when the British
Indian Association was founded. A union of all religious and ethnic groups
in India on the basis of a common political programme was its stated purpose.
A branch in Madras and contact with the leaders of public opinion in all
parts of India were the programmatic expressions of this ideal. In 1876,
Surendranath Banerjea established the Indian Association as 'the centre of
an all-India movement' to realize the vision of 'a united India'. 'The
unification of the Indian races and peoples upon the basis of common political
interests and aspirations' and 'the promotion of friendly feeling between
Hindus and Muhammadans' were two of its declared objects. Surendranath
launched the first all-India agitation—against the regulation which would
further handicap the Indians competing for entry into the ICS—under the
Association's auspices. It was a symbolic gesture for very few Indians could

ever hope for admission into the heaven-born service. Surendranath's hope that it would awaken 'a spirit of unity and solidarity among the people of India' was not misplaced. His speeches in the major Indian cities attracted thousands and the campaign acquired the features of a triumphal march.[12]

The National Conference which met in Calcutta in 1883 and the Indian National Congress established two years later were expressions of the same political impulse towards a unity transcending parochial barriers.

There was a tension between the emphasis on Hindu identity and this pan-Indian ideology—most evident in the writings of Bhudev and Rajnarayan. It is by no means certain that the way they resolved the conflict in their statements, e.g. that a united Hindu community would work closely with their Muslim brothers, had a clear counterpart in popular consciousness. The uneven development of the Bengali Hindu and Muslim middle classes and the distance which most Urdu-speaking Muslims of Bengal maintained from the nationalist organizations ensured the failure of nationalism in Bengal to absorb the Muslim intelligentsia. The anti-Muslim rhetoric of the patriotic Bengali Hindu writers and the stage-plays provoked before long an inevitable retort—in the works of the poet Kaikobad and the later writings of the erstwhile tolerant Mir Musharraf Hossain. The nationalist backdrop to the perceptions of Europe discussed in this volume was tarnished dangerously by incipient communal hatred.

Europe as perceived by our three writers reflected and influenced the changing content of nationalist consciousness in Bengal and, up to a point, in other parts of India. The ideal of liberty—in every sphere of life—was first absorbed by Young Bengal from the teachings of their famous mentor, Derozio. The dream of independence appears as the theme in the first English poem, written in 1830 by an Indian—one of Derozio's students. The Derozians had limited influence on the basically slow-moving society of middle-class Hindus. But the same is not true of their contribution to political consciousness. The journals published by the students of the Hindu College between 1828 and 1843 were influenced by the ideals of the French Revolution and projected a radical ideology anticipating the popular political concerns of a later period. The following extract from an article in the *Hindu Pioneer* of 1838 was fairly typical: 'The Muhammadans patronized merit wherever it was to be found; the English, like the primitive Hindus, have one caste of men to govern the general body. The violent means by which foreign supremacy has been established and the entire alienation of the people of the soil from any share in the government, nay, even from all offices of trust and power, are circumstances which no commercial, no political benefits can authorise or justify.'[13] Another Derozian, Dakshinaranjan Mukherji (1814–78), declared his faith in the doctrine of equality in his essays and public lectures in the 1840s. A few years later, in 1854, Akshaykumar Datta, the editor of *Tattvavodhini Patrika*, a major influence on the intellectual development of an entire generation, described political dependence as worse than hell.[14] The ideal of national independence became very much a part of intellectual discourse in the 1860s. Jogendranath Vidyabhushan serialized his biographies of Mazzini, Garibaldi, and Wallace in the monthly *Aryadarsan*. Surendranath's speeches projected Mazzini's life as the ideal Indian youth should live by. In the 1870s two other highly influential monthlies, Bankim's *Bangadarsan* and the Tagores' *Bharati* explored with earnest sobriety various issues of national interest. The *Sanjibani*, established in 1883, had for its motto 'Liberty, Equality and Fraternity'.

Indian nationalist consciousness, especially its Bengali variant, was no simple mirror image of European aspirations for political liberty. Its concerns had a certain autonomy, partly due to local circumstances peculiar to the region. There were distinct 'schools of thought' and, even within these, individuals spoke in very different voices. Attempts to classify such individuals under headings such as 'conservative' or 'liberal' have tended to ignore these complexities. Furthermore, the Indian predicament raised serious doubts about the political and economic doctrines in vogue in Europe and at times the intellectuals came up with distinctly original ideas.

One question at issue in permanently settled Bengal was the conflict of interest between the landholders and the tenants, mostly peasants. Several of the political organizations, including the British Indian Association, were keenly concerned to protect the zamindars' interests. Harish Mukherji, the editor of the *Hindu Patriot* who championed the peasants' cause during the 'Indigo Rebellion', considered the zamindars an 'estate', a countervailing power in society whose rights deserved respect. Others opposed the levy of an education cess on the zamindars to provide for mass education. 'National' Nabagopal objected to mass education because it might create a distaste for agriculture among peasants and was hence not to be encouraged at the cost of higher education. He had the interest of the intelligentsia rather than that of the zamindars in mind, though there was a substantial overlap between the two. But other intellectuals whose social origins were very similar to his were strongly in favour of mass education funded by taxes on zamindars. The ideological and programmatic responses to the horrific conditions of the peasantry were not determined simply by class origins. Raja Rammohan had been deeply concerned with the ryots' fate but unwilling to subvert the zamindars' interests. Rasik Krishna Mallik, a leading Derozian, condemned the Permanent Settlement for its 'utter neglect' of the rights of the humbler classes as early as 1833. In 1864, Kishorichand Mitra, anticipating Bankim, invoked Buckle's theory to explain the degradation of the Indian peasants. The highly influential *Tattvavodhini Patrika* with which Debendranath Tagore, himself a big zamindar, was closely associated consistently championed the ryots' rights. The Hindu chauvinist Chandranath Basu pleaded for mass education as a means towards redressing the peasants' grievances.

The differing views on the rights of the peasants had their counterparts in the area of purely political questions. For instance, both Bhudev and Nabagopal were opposed to the idea of political democracy and the editor of *Sadharani*, following Bankim, considered society rather than the state the appropriate arena for efforts at national regeneration. The emphasis on *dharma* as the necessary and sufficient basis for political as well as social and personal conduct, central to the arguments of both Bhudev and Bankim, is echoed by other writers as well—most notably the Positivist Jogendrachandra Ghosh. This emphasis derives partly from an introspective quest for an Indian political ideal and partly from a sense of futility about any political agenda under colonial rule. It also expresses an aversion for the egalitarian values implicit in political democracy and the outlandish practice of agitiations.[15]

A distinctive product of Indian nationalism was its analysis of the economic problem, especially, the problem of poverty. While the classic statement of economic nationalism is Naoroji's *Poverty and un-British Rule in India*, many of his ideas were anticipated by Bholanath Chandra in his articles on commerce and manufacture published in *Mukherji's Magazine*, 1873–4, where the idea of *swadeshi* was first broached. The theory of drainage of resources from India as well as the notion that the colonial impact had destroyed Indian manufactures also appear as parts of a nationalist statement in these essays. Chandranath Basu, among others, questioned the validity of the *laissez-faire* theories and pleaded for an interventionist policy for India's industrialization. Interestingly, he saw a moral and cultural purpose in industrialization—the achievement of a 'position of dignity in ... the great commonwealth of nations'. An expected by-product of that achievement would be a friendship with England on the 'basis of mutual esteem'.[16] The theory of *laissez-faire*, unlike the issue of democracy, did not become a subject of debate in Bengal. But, as discussed later in this book, Bhudev and Bankim had almost diametrically opposed perceptions on questions such as the drainage of resources and the ruin of handicrafts.

The more basic tension in nationalism in Bengal centred round the question of loyalty to the British rule. As a dependent and basically contented élite, for a long time the Bengali intelligentsia had genuine enthusiasm for the regime. It provided an acceptable livelihood and opportunities for some upward mobility. It was also seen—not quite accurately—as the channel through which western knowledge and enlightenment had come to India. The British faith in the beneficence of their rule appears to have been fully shared by middle-class Bengalis. The Derozian Dakshinaranjan Mukherji, despite his belief that alien rule was evil, was at pains to declare that 'he was no enemy of the British rule in India'.[17] Ramgopal Ghose, considered to be the 'king' of the western-educated intelligentsia,[18] who refused to accept employment under the British, similarly desired 'the perpetuity of the British sway'.[19] There is some scope for doubt as to the absolute sincerity of such sentiments of loyalty. In view of the manifold resentments provoked by the colonial experience in the very same people, the avowed loyalty suggests at best an ambivalent attitude—an appreciation of Britain's 'objective role' in India modified by a perception of injustice in the government's policies and executive action. The declarations may also reflect the characteristic caution of a colonial middle class, even though the defiant note in the criticisms of the Raj grew sharp by the 1860s. But there is nothing false about the British Indian Association's unqualified faith in the British Parliament, shared by many individuals. The distrust of agitational politics—explicit in Bhudev and Bankim—had other exponents as well. The conservative satirist, Indranath Bandyopadhyay, summed up his assessment of patriotic aspirations in his famous 'epic', *Bharat-uddhar kavya* (The Lay of India's Liberation); 'No matter, let India become free and we will fill our pockets as we will.'[20]

The enthusiasm for the British rule was, however, on the wane. Between 1854 and 1882, the total number who obtained Arts degrees of the Calcutta University was 11,589. The figure does not include the dropouts and failures. The number of school students increased from 91,145 in 1870–1 to 139,198 in 1881–2. The number of colleges increased from 7 in 1855 to 46 by 1902. Of the latter, 26 were outside Calcutta. The number of schools stood at 1,783 already by 1870 and the number of secondary schools increased from 132 in 1870 to 535 in 1901–2.[21] As early as 1874, the title of an article in *Mukherjee's Magazine* read: 'Where shall the Baboo go?' People with some English education far outnumbered the jobs available and the increasingly politicized Bengalis were not popular as employees. An official advertisement for the post of a clerk in the North West Provinces stated simply, 'Bengali Baboos ... need not apply'.[22] A confidential letter from Sir Ashley Eden to his successor in office as Lieutenant-Governor refers to this new pervasive sentiment against the Bengalis in the bureaucracy.[23] The Anglo-Bengali honeymoon, such as it was, had definitely come to an end.

Even the early enthusiasts for the colonial regime had been acutely aware of its unacceptable face. Rammohan himself had been insulted by a British official for his failure to show due deference to a member to the master race. The biographies of many notable Bengalis, including the three whose ideas are the subject matter of this book, contain accounts of similar experiences. Self-respecting Indian officials often found the racial attitude of their British superiors quite intolerable.[24] Particular features of the administration were severely criticized even in the 1830s. A correspondent in the *Samachar chandrika* described the petty police and revenue officials as worse than thieves in their dealings with the poor.[25] Rasik Krishna Mullick felt that the very 'source of justice' was corrupted and that the poor had no chance against 'men of wealth and influence,'[26]—a sentiment later echoed by Bankim in his long essay on the Bengal peasants. The tendency to trace the misfortunes of the rural poor to the British arbitrariness and exploitation also go back to this period.[27] Akshay Datta stated categorically in his *Bharatvarshiya upasak sampraday*[28] that under the British, the people had suffered a general degeneration in every area of their moral and material life.

The Anglo-Indian agitation triggered off by the bills introduced in 1849, intended to bring non-official European under the jurisdiction of the Mofussil Courts, further alienated middle-class Bengali opinion. The Anglo-Indians fought viciously against the 'Black Acts' in defence of the status quo under which they were subject only to the jurisdiction of the Supreme Court. The attempt to bring them under the criminal jurisdiction of Indian officials had to be abandoned. A second and a third attempt to establish equality in the eyes of law, in the 1856–7 and 1883 respectively, met with a similar fate.

The campaigns against these bills, especially the so-called 'Ilbert Bill' of 1883, were marked by racist invectives of exceptional violence. Such language had already become familiar through the columns of some Anglo-Indian papers. On one notorious occasion, the *Englishman* had advised Europeans to first kick and only then speak to the Bengalis. Such invectives had a long history. Dwarkanath Tagore, his biographer informs us, became a part proprietor of the *Bengal Hurkaru* in order to counteract 'the savage and unscrupulous attacks of the John Bull upon the natives.'[29] The intelligentsia perceived another dimension of John Bull's arbitrary ways when the *Hindu Patriot* took up the cause of the indigo ryots and in a famous trial the Reverend Long was sentenced to imprisonment for publishing the *Mirror of Indigo*, a translation of Dinabandhu Mitra's *Nildarpan*. The Arms Act and the Vernacular Press Act (1878) during Lytton's highly unpopular viceroyalty, followed by the contempt of court case against the *Bengalee* leading to Surendranath's imprisonment (1883), helped sharpen the militant edge of nationalist consciousness.

Nevertheless, the protestations of loyalty persisted. These were certainly genuine when expressed in relation to the Empress of India. But one finds a new tone of racial bitterness in the nationalist propaganda from the 1860s onwards, and in some instances earlier. 'They have taken all which the natives possessed', the loyalist Dwarkanath stated in 1836.[30] Some three decades later, in 1864, the vernacular monthly *Sikshadarpan o sambadsar* edited by Bhudev coined the phrase *jativairita*,[31] or racial animosity. That negative feelings was identified as an unavoidable concomitant of alien rule. Bankim's essay on *Jativaira* welcomed it[32] as an evil yet necessary sentiment, essential for the progress of a backward people. The necessary sentiment was much in evidence in the Bengali press. It gave the Vernacular Press Act its *raison d'être*. The *Amrita Bazar Patrika* emphasized the racial divide as a basic social and political reality: 'We are we' and 'they are they'. A leader in the issue of 31 December 1868 was in the nature of a manifesto. 'The Bengalis are determined to oppose the tyranny of Englishmen', it declared, adding that 'thousands of Bengalis were now willing to lay down their lives' in the cause.[33] The statement was somewhat premature, but the patriotic press and literature of the period did their best to foster a spirit of self-sacrifice in the national cause. In *Surendra-Binodini Natak*, a play in somewhat poor taste, a tyrannical district magistrate is lynched by a group of prisoners. After several performances the theatre manager and leading actor were arrested and prosecuted in August 1877 on charges of obscenity, but acquitted by two liberal English judges.[34] The ideal of violent rebellion to achieve independence was expressed more directly by the Maharashtrian Brahmin, Basudev Balwant Phadke in 1879–80. The *Amrita Bazar Patrika* published an admiring account of his life and activities. Some believe that Bankim's famous novel, *Anandamath*, was inspired *inter alia* by Phadke's rebellion.[35] A militant and defiant mood was certainly one face of Bengali nationalism by the 1870s. Bankim and Vivekananda shared this outlook and were major influences on the development of revolutionary politics. This was probably an unintended consequence of their programmes for national regeneration. It is difficult to be certain that the result was entirely unintended.

Nationalism provides but one context, however important, for the complex responses which conditioned the Bengali perceptions of Europe. As the intelligentsia's encounter with the West was mainly through the written word, what they read and what appealed to them most in European thought marked out another boundary of their perceptions. The curricula and contemporary tastes in England communicated through the European teachers and their pupils partly explain the literary preferences of the Bengali intellectuals and creative writers. And, of course, there was an element of individual choice. Shakespeare and Byron appear to have been universal favourites, but Bhudev admired Goethe, barely mentioned in one statement concerning Bankim. The latter's extreme admiration for Walter Scott, dismissive attitude towards Jane Austen, quotations from Campbell and Southey in introducing the various chapters of his novels, distaste for Zola, and deafening silence about Dickens suggest a pattern of curious preference contradicted by the sensitivity of his critical writings. Vivekananda, who admired Shelley and could quote page after page from *The Pickwick Papers*, is on record expressing his greater pleasure in a shoddy play by Girish Ghosh than in anything written by Shakespeare. Encounter between mutually alien cultures obviously produces unexpected responses. The extant theoretical literature on culture contact offers no explanation of these specificities.

Other areas of selective interest in Europe's intellectual traditions had more easily identifiable links with the historical experience of the nineteenth-century Bengalis. The intellectual core of that experience was an awareness of the West's success in the conquest of nature. The European dominance was ultimately traced to this basic victory. There was also an acceptance of liberal humanist values and a tendency to identify man's future progress with the restructuring of the social and political order in terms of these values. A world so restructured would, among other things, exclude political dependence. The latter, we have seen, was perceived quite early as a fall from grace because it implied a humiliating state of subordination to aliens who monopolized all levers of authority. It also meant a lowly status in the comity of nations. The humiliation was matter of daily experience. It informed and sharpened the awareness that a dependent people was without any honour and that men and women in other parts of the world were willing to sacrifice all to achieve the honourable state of independence. The tension generated by the twofold perception that national independence was desirable and that it was absent—similar to the characteristic impulse towards industrialization identified in Professor Gerschenkron's seminal essay, 'Economic Backwardness in Historical Perspective'—derived from something more than a desire to keep up with the western pace setters of civilization. It implied a redefinition of social goals in terms of newly perceived possibilities. The fact that these possibilities were first realized in the West does not justify the ascription of derivativeness to Third World nationalisms. Otherwise the transmission of any idea from one culture to another, including religious ideology, can be described as imperfect adaptation of something not fully understood. The western model of national sovereignty founded in popular will was a catalyst. It induced exploration of historical experiences leading to the emergence of independent nations. The roots of Europe's aggression against other peoples was an inescapable theme in that enquiry. Social thought seeking to iron out the multiple imperfections of politically independent societies and projecting new norms of human conduct were also attractive to the Bengali intelligentsia. This was so because new goals required the foundation of systematic thought as guidelines for positive action.

The emphasis in all this was on reasoned thinking rather than emotive responses to given ideals. Post-enlightenment rationalism was at the heart of the intellectual tradition encountered by the Bengali intelligentsia. It disturbed their faith in the received tradition. Even efforts to restore that faith had to be in terms of rational thought, not unquestioning acceptance. Reason was the foundation of scientific enquiry. Exploration of matters pertaining to human society and even the norms of personal life were within the latter's purview. 'Pure rationalism is our teacher', wrote Akshay Kumar Datta in his very influential adaptation of George Coombe's treatise on man's relationship with external nature.[36] The Society for the Acquisition of General

Knowledge established in 1838 sought to cultivate 'useful knowledge' in terms of rational enquiry. Its predecessor, the Derozians' Academic Association (established 1828) explored themes like free will and the arguments for and against the existence of God as expounded by Hume, Reid, Dugald Stewart, etc. The first number of the journal *The Parthenon* (February 1830) described itself as the organ of people who were 'Hindu by birth, yet European by education'.[37] One such Hindu, Tarachand Chakrabarti, invoked Bentham's deontological maxim—'What it is a man's duty to do, cannot but be also his interest'—in his plea for the introduction of moral education.[38] Raja Rammohan, his guru, was a great admirer of Bentham's ideas. From the very beginning of the Utilitarian impact, however, Bengali intellectuals questioned its individualistic assumptions. The organismic view of society was the theoretical basis of such criticism,[39] but its roots probably lay deep in the Hindu social experience, with its emphasis on the values of the 'joint family'. Akshay Datta, in emphasizing altruism as a necessary corrective to the love of self-interest, cited the authority of the Upanishads. One may note here in passing that neither he nor Rammohan and his contemporaries derived their acquaintance with the Sanskritic tradition from western Orientology. An unbroken indigenous tradition of Sanskritic scholarship was an autonomous source of knowledge of the past so far as the Bengali intelligentsia was concerned. Among the Utilitarian philosophers, Mill, more than Bentham, attracted the Bengali intelligentsia. But at times, his liberal values had a greater appeal than his specifically Utilitarian ideas. A paper read before the Bethune Society, for instance, drew attention to Mill's rejection of the idea that 'national character' reflected inherent natural differences. Liberal values were not always acquired from philosophical studies. Dwarkanath Vidyabhushan, the editor of *Somprakas*, got his liberal ideas from the study of European history. Others too studied with interest the French and English constitution, as well as the history of Europe in search of programmes for national regeneration and also a basis for the better governance of India. By the 1870s, the conservative adherents of the ideal of stability and progress had discovered Comte's Positivism, first introduced in Bengal in 1857.[40] Jogendrachandra Ghosh, a frequent contributor to Bankim's *Bangadarsan*, was its high priest in Bengal. Its social ideology which glorified the priestly class had an appeal for men like Bhudev and Bankim who rejected its agnostic religion of humanity. I have discussed in the relevant chapters the range of authors and subjects studied by our three thinkers. While all three were exceptionally voracious readers, the range of their interest in European thought was in no way atypical.

Despite the individuality of their outlook, their perceptions of Europe have a certain representative quality. They were but three among many who commented extensively on western civilization. Hardly any issue of a major periodical of the period failed to include some statements on the theme. None of these exercises in assessment was concerned exclusively or primarily with a scientific study of an alien culture. They all had one basic referent in common: comparison with Indian or what, accepting the familiar western stereotype, was often labelled as 'Oriental' culture and an analysis of what one should or should not learn from Europe. Implicitly, the Bengali intellectuals examined afresh the two components of their own cultural identity—the indigenous and the acquired elements. The inspiration was derived from the emerging outlook on alien rule and the psychological need to do something about the state of apparently helpless dependence which hurt one's ego as much as one's prospects. To repeat, the dominant context was a clear articulation of nationalism, the often declared feeling that nationhood was necessary and possible no matter what lay in the region's political past. In many parts of the world from Russia to Japan latecomers to the field of self-conscious nationhood and material progress based on modern industries felt a similar concern to evaluate themselves in relation to the dominant civilization of western Europe. The debates which derived from this concern and the issues thrown up were strikingly similar in Russia, China, Japan, and India.

Theoretical studies of the dependent élites' response to the dominant culture mentioned earlier in this chapter surely go some way towards explaining the Bengali intelligentsia's interest in and qualified admiration for European civilization. A weak and dependent intelligentsia looked up to the master race which was perceived as the source of the imported elements in their ideology and the models they sought to emulate. Eventually nationalism in the colonies psychologically rejected alien rule. The superiority of the ruling race was inevitably questioned. Till then, admiration for the dominant culture was the most natural response.

As noted earlier, strongly positive responses to specific elements in an alien culture are not necessarily linked to domination, though these may be reinforced by the experience of dependence. The latter can, of course, generate revulsion and hostility as well. Theoreticians, well aware of such rejection, often see it as a manifestation of ambivalence. But one fact not explained by the relevant theoretical literature is the abiding attachment in one culture to a whole range of cultural artifacts of another civilization both in and outside the context of domination. The adoption of Persian language and literature by the Central Asian Turks, of Indian cultural motifs in Southeast Asia, or of Hellenic culture by the Romans were not linked to political–economic domination. Besides, whatever the context, the patterns of admiration and adoption were selective everywhere and varied widely within the same society from group to group and, in fact, from individual to individual. The Bengali intelligentsia's very selective excitement over European civilization which has survived decolonization was rooted very probably in specific cultural traits of the Hindu castes with literary traditions, but we do not know enough to suggest any definite causal connection. The popular pastime of comparing Sanskrit poetry with its English counterpart offers one tantalizing hint towards an explanation. A familiar but probably valid cliché suggests that the different sub-continental cultures responded very differently to the western presence. If this is true, the differences in the chronology and content of the colonial experience in different parts of India or the undeniable limitations of the colonial intelligentsia would not explain it all. The finer points of difference can be explained historically up to a point, but 'history' in this context may well mean the experience in time of particular groups or even individuals.

If the Bengali excitement over Europe's civilization was selective at the first close encounter, it becomes far more so by the latter half of the nineteenth century. One notes also a much wider range of variations in assessment. Strong nationalist sentiments and the new mode of cultural self-assertion accentuated the critical note in all evaluations of Europe. The critics did not speak in the same voice, but they were all in the business of reconsidering earlier judgements—at times their own.

Notes and References

1. Some of these schools were established in the first decade of the century in response to very considerable public demand. See George Smith, *The Life of Alexander Duff*, I, 96, quoted in R.C. Majumdar, 'Education', in N.K. Sinha, ed., *The History of Bengal* (1757–1905), Calcutta, 1968, 434. By 1819, there were four colleges in Bengal, including the Bishop's College which admitted a few non-Christians. The popularity of English is indicated *inter alia* by the fact that by 1835 the School Book Society sold two books in English for each book in Bengali. Majumdar, *loc. cit.*, 436.

2. The missionary perception was summed up in a classic phrase—'The monster of Hinduism, the enemy of both God and man'. See G. Gogerly, *The Pioneers: A Narrative of Facts Connected with the Early Christian Missions in Bengal*, London, n.d., 5. Also see Weitbrecht, *Missionary Sketches in North India*, London, 1858; K.A. Ballhatchet, 'Some Aspects of Historical Writings on India by Protestant Christian Missionaries during the Nineteenth and Twentieth Centuries', in C.H. Philips, ed., *Historians of India, Pakistan and Ceylon*, 344 ff. and M.A. Sherring, *The History of Protestant Missions in India*, London, 1884, 96.

3. See Sibnath Sastri, *Ramtanu Lahiri o tatkalin bangasamaj* (Ramtanu Lahiri and Bengali Society in His Times), Calcutta, 1903, 112f.

4. Rajnarayan Basu, *Atmajivani* (Autobiography), Calcutta, BY 1315 (1908), 86f.

5. The school of logic developed in Bengal, especially at Nabadwip.

6. For a critique of the relevant theories of nationalism, see Partha Chatterjee, *Nationalist Thought and the Colonial World: A Derivative Discourse?* Delhi, 1986, chap. 1.

7. Bipin Chandra Pal, *Memories of My Life and Times*, I, 2nd edn., Calcutta, 1957, 347–9. The classic statement of Tarkachudamani's ideology was in his *Dharmabyaksha* (A Commentary on Dharma), Calcutta, 1884.

8. Rajnarayan Basu, *Atmajivani*, 116–17.

9. 'The Bengalis are determined to oppose the tyranny of Englishmen at every step', the *Amrita Bazar Patrika* commented on 31 December 1868. See R.C. Majumdar, *The National Movement* (1833–1905), in N.K. Sinha, ed., *op. cit.*, 206.

10. *Op. cit.*, 83. The correct date, it has been suggested, was a few years later.

11. Rajnarayan Basu, *Briddha Hindur asha*, Calcutta, 1887.

12. See Surendranath Banerjea, *A Nation in Making Being the Reminiscences of Fifty Years of Public Life*, Oxford University Press, London, New York, etc., 1925, chap. 5.

13. Quoted in Bimanbehari Majumdar, *History of Political Thought from Rammohan to Dayananda* (1821–84), vol. I, *Bengal*, Calcutta, 1934, 91. His Chapter on 'The Philosophical Radicals', 78–156, contains *inter alia* a detailed discussion of early radical thought in Bengal.

14. Quoted in Bimanbehari Majumdar, *History of Political Thought from Rammohan to Dayananda*, (1821–84), vol. I, *Bengal*, Calcutta, 1934, 153.

15. For a detailed discussion of the different 'schools' of political thought in Bengal in the nineteenth century as well as the individual authors mentioned here, see Bimanbehari Majumdar, *op. cit.*, Chapters 2–5 and the sources cited there.

16. Ibid., 276–9; Bipin Chandra, *The Rise and Growth of Economic Nationalism in India*, New Delhi, 1966, 125f., 153–4, 229f.

17. Dakshinaranjan Mukherji, 'The Present State of the East India Company's Criminal Judicature, and Police under the Bengal Presidency', *The Bengal Harukaru*, 18 February 1843.

18. Rajnarayan Basu, *Atmajivani*, 30.

19. *The Bengal Harukaru*, 24 April 1843.

20. Ramdas Sharma [Indranath's pen-name adopted in this particular work], *Bharat-uddhar Kavya*, Calcutta, 1877.

21. Indian Education Commission, 1882, *Report*, 269; R.C. Majumdar, 'Education', N.K. Sinha, *op. cit.*, 446–50.

22. Bimanbehari Majumdar, *op. cit.*, 323–4, fn.

23. See chap. 2.

24. Bimanbehari Majumdar, *op. cit.*, 105–6, fn. 118.

25. Quoted in *Samachar darpan*, 5 June 1830.

26. His article in *Gyananneshan*, quoted in the *India Gazette*, 12 April 1833.

27. D. Mukherji, *loc. cit.*

28. Akshay Kumar Datta, *Bharat-varshiya upasak sampraday* (Indian theistic sects), Calcutta, II, Introduction.

29. Kishorichand Mitra, *Memoirs of Dwarkanath Tagore*, rev. and enl. edn., Calcutta, 1870, 39.

30. Quoted in Bimanbehari Majumdar, *op. cit.*, 183.

31. See R.C. Majumdar, *loc. cit.*, 206, in N.K. Sinha, *op. cit.*

32. Quoted in ibid., 206.

33. Brajendranath Bandyopadhyay, *Bangiya natyasalar itihas* (A History of the Bengali Stage), Calcutta, BY 1340 (AD 1933), 201-2.

34. See chap. 3.

35. Quoted in Bimanbehari Majumdar, *op. cit.*, 127.

36. *The India Gazette*, 17 February 1830.

37. *The Bengal Spectator*, September 1842, 88.

38. See for instance, Akshay Kumar Datta, *Dharmaniti*, (Principles of Right Conduct), Calcutta, chap. 5.

39. Bimanbehari Majumdar, *op. cit.*, 245.

40. G.H. Forbes, *Positivism in Bengal: A Case Study in the Transmission and Assimilation of Ideology*, Calcutta, 1975.

chapter 2

Bhudev Mukhopadhyay
(1827*–1894)

I

The responses of the traditional Brahmin scholars to the West have not been recorded. Arguably, Bhudev Mukhopadhyay's assessments of European civilization are in some ways a fair indicator of their likely reactions. By birth, upbringing, and inclination, Bhudev felt most at home in the social world of the orthodox Bengali Brahmin. He accepted its values both emotionally and intellectually. His self-perception largely excluded any awareness of the fact that his aspirations and preferences had been modified by his western education and career in the colonial bureaucracy. In fact, his experiences at Hindu College and his aversion to the ways of the westernized Indians—including their initiatives in social reform—were major reasons why he decided to write at length about Europe. His purpose was to protect his society from servile imitation and inform it with self-confidence based on sober appraisals of western life in relation to traditional Indian values. His concerns were, of course, also causally linked to a new articulation of nationalist identity and, marginally, to its more frantic expression, the bizarre glorifications of Hinduism. In this, he expressed as well as influenced the trends in social change in post-1857 Bengal. And necessarily, in writing of Europe, he drew upon his two sources

---

* The date of Bhudev's birth, as given in his biography written by his son, is 12 February 1825 (*Bhudev charit* I, 20). The correct date, 22 February 1827, was however established on the basis of his horoscope discovered among his papers. (See Brajendranath Bandyopadhyay, *Sahitya-sadhak charitmala—Bhudev Mukhopadhyay*, 6).

of knowledge—his extensive reading and the numerous personal contacts with Europeans since childhood, the latter somewhat distorted by the frustrations and humiliations of the kind of jobs which he had under the British.

'You are my progenitor and my teacher. I have not learnt even one per cent from books or anyone else of what I learnt from you.'[1] This statement, part of Bhudev's dedication of a book to his dead father, is an important key to our understanding of his attitudes and perceptions. Its literal truth is questionable. His considerable scholarship, despite his Sanskritic studies, owed more to Europe than to India and his father Viswanath, a formidable scholar in Sanskrit, was unacquainted with western learning. Yet Bhudev protested elsewhere what he owed everything to his father and nothing to western learning.[2] These assertions are valid in so far as the publicist's fundamental values are concerned. His deep regard for the particular variant of Brahminical culture his father represented was central to his world-view and shaped all his perceptions.

What one knows of this key figure in Bhudev's life comes from his own writings and the biography written by his third son. The portrait, necessarily idealized, is not unconvincing. What is more important, it surely represents Bhudev's perception of the man's personality, the ideal he tried to live by. By this account, Viswanath Mukhopadhyay was an impressive specimen of the old culture. Learned, upright, and uncompromisingly faithful to his norms, he accepted poverty because he would not record views critical of his society, as required by a European association for which he temporarily worked.[3] His principled behaviour went beyond the limits of worldly matters; as a believer in the doctrine of action without attachment (*nishkama karma*), he refused to pray for worldly benefits, despite his faith in the efficacy of prayers, even when his only son was seriously ill. For he would not call upon the Deity to perform the lowly task of curing disease ordinarily left to doctors.[4]

Bhudev's induction into the system of Brahminical values was by way of his deep attachment for this very remarkable father. In his brief treatise on education, he noted with regret the lack of affection between fathers and sons which, in his view, was a characteristic failing of Indian society.[5] He himself suffered no such deprivation. To the believing Hindu of his days, parents were living gods. For him, these objects of adoration were also the objects of intense affection. His mother died when he was sixteen and thereafter all his emotions were centred on his father.[6]

The latter carefully nurtured in his son a genuine devotion to traditional ways and a sense of reverence for Hindu culture. He went about this task with considerable finesse. Bhudev went to Hindu College at the age of twelve. Open defiance of Hindu social conventions in matters of food and drink was then considered almost *de rigeur* by the avant-garde students of the college.[7] To be reckoned a civilized person, one had to eat beef and consume alcohol. Viswanath simply expressed his apprehension that his son would also take to prohibited food and Bhudev took a vow never to eat or drink anything he could not consume in his father's presence. He did stick to his promise.[8] His contemporaries at college remembered with awe the severity of his Brahminical self-discipline.[9] A more serious crisis developed when the son, under missionary influence, declared his lack of faith in idolatry and refused to do his part in the daily ritual worship at home. His father agreed that worship without belief would be a sacrilege, adding with conviction that his son's views would certainly change in due course. In the days which followed, he developed a dialogue with his son about the symbolic meaning of image worship and then introduced him to the study of the Gita and Sanskrit poetry. Day after day, he would request Bhudev to explain what he had learnt at college and then place before him parallel ideas and passages from Sanskrit. Bhudev's incipient faith in Christianity had already suffered through his introduction to Hume, Tom Paine, and Gibbon. Viswanath's subtle indoctrination restored his belief in the ancestral religion. The process was completed through his initiation into the Tantric cult followed by his family.[10]

The strength of his commitment to Indian ways—which explains his genuine rejection of much in western civilization—derived in large measure from his happy experience of family life. His belief that the Bengali Hindu joint family—which he described as the most natural institution in an agrarian society[11]—was a profoundly satisfying arrangement embodying very worthwhile values, had for him pragmatic validity. In his treatise on family life, he drew upon the happy memory of his grandfather, a noted Sanskrit scholar like his father, to project the abstract ideal of the grandfather as *pater familias*, a positive influence on the grandchildren in particular as playmate and teacher whose affection was uncluttered by parental anxieties or lack of objectivity.[12] Child marriage seemed natural and acceptable because over three generations he had seen it blossom into abiding love. His grandfather and father, both widowers in early middle age, spent the rest of their lives in the firm and happy expectation that they would join their wives after death.[13] His own child bride grew up into an ideal and much loved companion. The poignant dedication in *Paribarik Prabandha* (Essay on Family) is witness to his heartbreak at her death. For three generations, the idea of remarriage had been repugnant to the men in his family. No wonder he resented the reformists' efforts to legalize widow remarriage.[14] His mother, whose regal exterior dazzled his iconoclastic friend, Michael Madhusudan Dutt, was the mistress of a joint family. Under her guidance, the characteristic tensions of such families were apparently avoided, though the household included her husband's brothers who did not earn their living. For his initiation into the Tantric cult, Bhudev chose his mother as the guru.[15] In short, despite the brief flutter in his *vita religiosa*, his integration with the values of his family, based on intense emotional attachments, was unaffected by the characteristic schizophrenia of his times.

Family loyalty meant total acceptance of the severe discipline imposed on the growing child in an orthodox Brahmin milieu—a regime of strict ritual observances and absolutely correct conduct, as prescribed in the Smritis, in matters of food, drink, and virtually every detail of daily life. In his maturity, Bhudev traced all that he cherished in his own personality and ideals to the traditions of his family. He took an immense pride in his Brahmin identity. The shift from the life of a poor teacher to a deputy magistrate's comfortable existence was for him a degradation in terms of values. He evidently believed that the Brahminical values marked the highest point in human development. In his *Achar Prabandha* (Essay on Correct Conduct), he recommends the meticulous observance of *sastric* injunctions in every detail, even when they appeared to be superstitions. He considered most of these injunctions actually beneficent, even if the fact was not always obvious, for he had implicit faith in the wisdom of the Aryan seers; western science and scientific reasoning were not necessarily more advanced in every way. Besides, if one accepted the totality of a tradition, one did not quibble over particular details. Ritually prescribed conduct was like the codes of decent behaviour in civilized society—not necessarily rational. One accepted them without question. Traditions prescribed for the good of an entire society were based on an intuitive assessment of modal needs. It had to be accepted as such in its entirety. A society grew strong by such acceptance. Hindus, deprived of all but their distinct identity, could not afford to discard the inherited way of life. 'What else is left to us?' Bhudev quipped, when asked about his strict adherence to orthodox ways. He gloried in it, for he had imbibed its values through severe discipline. More importantly, he had loved it deeply in the persons of his grandfather, parents, and wife. By comparison, everything else seemed unsatisfactory. In his study of Europe and contact with Europeans, he failed to discover anything which could compensate for the loss of ideals by which his forebears had lived. He saw these as still a vital, if threatened, component of Indian life.

The threats to the cherished values were all around him, but they had one common source—western civilization, or rather its manifestation in India, especially in the lives of westernized Indians. The Brahminical ideal his father had inculcated emphasized one particular tradition out of the wide choice offered by Hinduism—*nivrittimarga*, the path of renunciation implying abstinence and freedom from worldly desires. Nineteenth-century consumerism, especially the westernized Indians' imitation of the European lifestyle, was hence repugnant. He was disgusted by the ways of his westernized fellow-students at Hindu College. For a Brahmin youth brought up in the orthodox tradition of ritual cleanliness, the sight of twice-born Hindus consuming beef *kabab* from Muslim shops washed down with whisky, was of course nauseating. A curious advertisement quoted by another classmate, Rajnarayan Basu,—'Yorkshire ham in canvas for Pooja'—shows how bizarre the results of thoughtless deviation from established mores could be. To appreciate the enormity, a westerner only needs to substitute 'Pooja' with some Jewish festival. Bhudev's aversion to the lifestyle of his peer group was not simply the Pavlovian reaction of a culture-bound Brahmin. Their imitation of the ruling race was an affront to his sense of dignity and self-respect. It hurt most when the person he admired more than any other contemporary. Madhusudan Dutt,—a much-loved friend whose genius he was among the first to recognize—exhibited this tendency in its extremest from. He referred repeatedly to 'Madhu's despicable inclination to imitate' '*Madhur hin anukaran pravritti*'. When Madhusudan gave up his ancestral faith and became a Christian, allegedly in the hope that this would facilitate his visit to England, Bhudev saw in this act the tragic result of alienation from one's culture. The poet's stormy life and multiple misfortunes confirmed this assessment. If all this could happen to the most outstanding talent of the epoch, Indian society had to be protected from the deluge of uncritically accepted western influence.

Bhudev's ideological distance from his peer group in college went beyond matters of external conduct and attitude to orthodoxy. Nearly everyone around him was either a sceptic or indifferent to questions of religon.[16] By contrast, he had acquired a profound religiosity, especially since his formal initiation into the Tantric worship.[17] Thus, early in youth, he came to regard western influence as a threat, a root cause of alienation from the ancestral tradition he had accepted *in toto.*

His misgivings about the western impact were widely shared. In fact, such doubts were as much a part of the nineteenth-century Bengali culture as the impact itself. Their roots can be traced back to developments in the first half of the century—the Derozians' open defiance and conversion of a few upper-caste young men to Christianity, the missionaries' ill-informed criticism of Hinduism, Raja Rammohan's attack on idolatry, the prohibition of *sati* resented by many as an alien interference in matters of faith and ritual, and the Orientalist controversy. The perceived threats had not disappeared entirely. Some of the controversial questions at issue earlier were still very much alive, especially in Bhudev's youth. He was eighteen when a protégé of the Tagore family and his wife became Christians. Even the usually tolerant and rational Akshaykumar Datta was infuriated by this incident and described Christianity as a 'poison' in Indian life. A school for Hindu boys, meant to counteract the possible attractions of Christianity, was established. The saintly Devendranath was among the chief organizers of the agitation and the Brahmo periodical, *Tattvabodhini Patrika*, became, for a while, a mouthpiece of anti-Christian sentiments.[18] The *Patrika* itself and its sponsor, the Tattvabodhini Sabha were established a little earlier, with the object *inter alia* of resisting a more insidious tendency—the acceptance by the western-educated youth of Macaulay's contemptuous opinion regarding classical Indian culture.[19] D.L. Richardson's students at Hindu College (of whom Bhudev was one) were not only enthused by his lectures on Shakespeare; they were also convinced of the superiority of English literature and the worthlessness of the Indian literary tradition.[20]

The unhappy consequences of western education are a recurrent theme in Bengali writings of this period, including those discussed in the present volume. Bhudev's contemporary, the Brahmo social leader Rajnarayan Basu presented in his widely popular pamphlet, *Sekal ar ekal* (Then and Now) what was probably a general view on the subject. 'Now our heaven is England': this caustic comment sums up his central argument. The educated Bengali had lost all sense of pride in his culture. Everything European was imitated, regardless of its suitability to Indian conditions. Western clothes, highly unsuitable in the Indian climate, symbolized the alienation of the new élite. They spoke a bastardized Bengali, liberally studded with English words.[21]

All lectures were delivered in English and even letters to friends and relations written in the same language. Rajnarayan quipped that 'the affluent would, if possible, have the *luchi** at their banquets fried by white men' to assert and augment their status. Those who went to England returned as imitation Englishmen. The author's own son-in-law was a sad example of such denationalization.[22] Imitation of the West meant an addiction to western luxuries, but without the industries to produce them at home. The material and moral dependence on the British was total; even intimate issues of social reform were taken to the Privy Council for adjudication with no sense of shame. The end products of this westernizing tendency were physically degenerate specimens, often given to heavy drinking, a habit first adopted as the token of civilized conduct.[23]

Cultural servility in any form went against the emerging nationalist ethos. There were good reasons why the politically conscious Bengalis had become extremely sensitive. Enhanced awareness of self-respect as a nation was a contributing factor. More important, as Indian criticism of colonial rule became increasingly sharp, the diehard elements of the Anglo-Indian community achieved new heights in the art of abuse. In February 1884, the Anglo-Indians launched a campaign against the proposed 'Ilbert Bill' intended to place European offenders on the same judicial footing as their Indian counterparts. One particular speech—by J.H.A. Branson—delivered at the first meeting of the campaign probably surpassed all previous displays of racism. Norris, a judge of the Calcutta High Court, participated actively in the agitation. He had offended Hindu sensibility through a gratuitous insult and when Surendranath Banerjea criticized him, he was cited for contempt of court and sentenced to a month's imprisonment.[24] Such episodes made a deep impact. The persistent abuse of Hinduism produced a counter-reaction—an eagerness to believe that everything Hindu was sublime and essentially superior to all that the West had to offer.[25] The reaction in support of traditional ways met little effective resistance from one likely direction— the Brahmo movement, for it had lost much of its credibility through internal strifes. It had acquired an image of smug arrogance and, occasionally, the conduct of some members violated social norms.[26]

Some of the most pointedly self-conscious expressions of this new trend appeared in two periodicals, *Aryadarsan* and *Sadharani*, both first published

---

* The Bengali version of *puri* (deep-fried puffs made of wholemeal) now popularized in the West by Indo-Pakistani restaurants. *Luchi* is made from white flour.

in 1873. The big boost came two years later. In 1875, Colonel Olcott and
Madame Blavatsky founded the Theosophical Society, a curious amalgam of
Victorian occultism and a belief in Mahatmas allegedly resident in Tibet. As
noted earlier, what mattered was that the founders traced their mysterious
beliefs to unidentified Hindu sources and proclaimed the excellence of
Hinduism. When Colonel Olcott came to Calcutta in 1889, his reception
was ecstatic. The movement became a real power in the land when Mrs
Besant joined it in 1889. She was among the first to declare the superiority
of the Aryan (Hindu) civilization to all else,[27] especially western materialism.
She called upon her contemporary brown Aryans to forsake materialism
and revive their great spiritualist tradition. She praised the laws of Manu
and the system of caste. The effect was electric. The educated Indians had
come to expect nothing but denigration of their culture from Europeans.
The sustained tradition of sober assessment and sympathy spoke in less
strident voices and hence passed largely unnoticed. Now men and women,
famous in the West, had declared Hinduism to be superior to western
civilization itself. To the wounded ego of the colonial élite, who more than
half-shared their rulers' contempt for themselves,* the message was
irresistible. Some of the most enlightened members of the Bengali élite were
attracted to theosophy. They included Swarnakumari Devi, Rabindranath
Tagore's sister, the civilian Asutosh Chaudhuri and Yeats's friend, Mohini
Chatterji. Among the movement's famous recruits outside Bengal in the
twentieth century was Krishna Menon. Even Nehru in his adolescence is
said to have felt attracted to this flattering new cult.[28]

The Hindu self-image had received a moral boost from another important
western source—the writings of Professor Max Mueller. His linguistic studies
stressed the common origins of Indo-European languages and the Aryan
races. These theories, translated into popular idiom, were taken to mean
that the master race and the subject population were descended from the
same Aryan ancestors. The result was a spate of Aryanism. Books, journals,
societies rejoiced in the Aryan identity. The Tagores—Dwijendranath and
Rabindranath—made fun of it and Kipling advised Christians against hustling
'Aryans brown', but those who were caught up in this pathetic euphoria
took little notice.

* The word *hin*, 'despicable', occurs with unfailing regularity as an adjective for
  Bengalis in contemporary Bengali writings and even Macaulay could not have
  improved upon Bankim's accounts of his own social class.

Aryanism and the Hindu reaction found some powerful protagonists though their influence proved to be short-lived. The most effective among them were Sasadhar Tarkachuḍamani and Krishnaprasanna Sen. Chandranath Bose was a milder exponent of the same tendency. Its literary lions included Indranath Bandyopadhyay and Jogindranath Basu. The central message of the movement was clear and simple: Hindu superiority and the unacceptability of western civilization. Indian Hindus were the most superior Aryans, no, even the only true Aryans. Everything in popular Hindu practice was based on higher reasoning and could be explained in a scientific way. All the discoveries of western science and technology had been anticipated by the ancient Aryans. Those who, like Bankim, sought to assess Hinduism in the light of western logic were deluded as were the protagonists of religious synthesis, the basic unity of all faiths.[29] Social reform, especially the Brahmo-style liberation of women, was the high road to immorality and decadence.[30] Since 'only India could produce human beings complete in every sense'[31], the road to salvation lay in the revival of Aryan glory.[32] The conclusions were often based on ill-understood applications of modern physical theories; electromagnetism was especially popular. Sanskrit texts were freely distorted to yield the desired meaning. Truly vulgar puns were used to demonstrate the worthlessness of Christianity. These appeals to a colonial élite's inferiority complex were very successful for a while. Educated young men, in large numbers, affected a demonstrative reversion to the ways of their forefathers—with fasts, pigtails, well-displayed sacred threads, and other stigmata of Hindu orthodoxy. The name 'Aryan' appeared in every possible and impossible context—in the titles of books as much as in the names of drug stores. This reactive Hinduism became a powerful influence on Indian nationalism as well. Rajnarayan Basu, a Brahmo to the end of his days, lectured on the 'Superiority of Hinduism' and expressed the hope that an association would be established under the name 'The Great Hindu Association' exclusively for Hindus, though its representatives in the National Congress would 'work jointly with our Muslim brothers'.[33] All the three thinkers discussed in this volume had at least some sympathetic contact with this reactive movement, even though briefly and rather tangentially.

Bhudev's rationalist approach had little in common with the shrill pronouncements of Tarkachudamani and Krishnaprasanna Sen. Yet, he was not without some sympathy towards their objectives. One scholar has suggested that the Bharat Dharma Maha Mandali (the Great Religious

Association of India) was established by Bhudev and others in consultation
with Sasadhar.[34] There is no reference to the fact in Bhudev's standard
biography by his son, which does not even mention that he was a co-founder
of the Mandali, But he did write to his second son very approvingly after he
had met the propagandist: 'Sasadhar Tarkachudamani is a really good man.
He is very popular and a good Sanskrit scholar, yet the title of
Mahamahopadhyay has not been conferred on him'.[35] The biographer also
mentions another champion of Hindu reaction, Chandranath Basu, as 'a
great admirer of my father'.[36]

Such evidence of mutual admiration does not, however, imply any identity
of views. The Mandali, which did in fact reflect some of Sasadhar's ideas,
set out to salvage Hinduism from its fallen state. Bhudev comments on the
basis of his extensive travels in India: 'Whoever else may say it, I shall never
say that Hinduism is in a fallen state. In truth, if the Himalayan mountains
were to fall, you could not bolster them up with reeds. If Hinduism is in a
fallen state, neither Sasadhar Tarkachudamani nor Raja Pyarimohan nor
Bhudev Mukhopadhyay will be able to salvage it.'[37] A major reason for the
publication of the *Education Gazette* on Bhudev's suggestion was that he
considered *Bhaskar*, a mouthpiece of Hindu reaction, too fanatical, though
the question at issue then was political rather than religious or social. He
described both the uncritical acceptance of whatever is new and the refusal
to change anything at all as forms of superstition.[38] Besides, he had little
sympathy with the crazes of neo-Hinduism. Particularly off-putting was
theosophy, lapped up by Hindus less confident than himself. He described
it as 'adulterated Hinduism'.[39] His position with regard to the relative
excellence of Hinduism—a central theme in all his assessments of Europe—
was quite close to that of Rajnarayan Basu. Commenting on his friend's
highly popular lecture, 'The Superiority of Hinduism', Bhudev wrote under
a pseudonym in the *Education Gazette*: 'I am a fanatical admirer of
Rajnarayan Basu.'[40] Despite his lengthy encomium on the lecture,[41] in his
Essays on Society he struck a more critical note because he found
Rajnarayan's criteria too western for his taste: 'In what way has the author
proved the superiority of Hinduism? He has only shown that it is similar to
the Englishman's religion. In the author's mind, the English are the measure
of all things.'[42]

Bhudev's own reasons for his faith in the superiority of Hinduism are
stated eloquently in the more favourable review of Rajnarayan Basu's lecture:
'Who would not be gratified by paeans of praise for a religious system which

is inspired by far-seeing and profound thought, was created by great seers pure of heart, has saved the children of the Aryans from the contamination of sins for thousands of years, preserved in every Hindu throughout this vast land of India some sense of national unity by acting as steps towards firm social cohesion, introduced the happy and pure family system of the Hindus, achieved in effect the knowledge of God, the ultimate end of all spiritual quest and rendered the Hindus more selfless, godfearing and convinced of a life hereafter, than any other people?'[43] He considered the Hindu social system truly marvellous in the innate strength of its organization and nobility of spirit.[44] The code of conduct prescribed for the Brahmins was worthy of imitation by everyone else.[45] He invoked Comte's category of a society in which the priests as guardians of spiritual and moral wisdom were predominant as an apt description of the Hindu social order. On this basis, he claimed that it was more guided by spiritual concerns than any other society.[46] All the virtues of Christianity and the socioreligious codes of the English people were to be found in Hinduism. Besides, the latter had merits not to be found in Christianity˜ or European life—purity, non-attachment, the realization that the universe represents a unity.[47] Hindus felt no need for conversion to any other faith because they could find everything they needed in their own.[48] He professed amiable sentiments towards the Brahmos because they had resisted the Christian onslaught.[49] Besides, the founder of the movement, Raja Rammohan, having read deeply into all religions, proclaimed the supremacy of the Upanishads. In the West, Schopenhauer had acknowledged the same.[50] For Bhudev, the faith in the superiority of Hinduism, almost absorbed with mother's milk and seriously disturbed only once, was not an affectation. He only projected it in terms of what he considered universally acceptable ethical and metaphysical criteria. He was meticulous in the observance of the Brahminical code—in death as in life. His dying body was carried to the waters of the holy river at his instruction: he ended his life there strictly according to the rules prescribed in the Smritis[51] and in full control of the situation as befitted a very proud Brahmin.

Bhudev's objections to the contemporary efforts at reform derived from this deep faith, which he explained and validated in terms of rational arguments. His orthodoxy was not blind and had nothing in common with the vulgarities of the Hindu reaction. He had some knowledge of the natural sciences˜and hence did not marshal pseudo-scientific arguments to uphold Hindu institutions and popular practices. His defence of the established order was along essentially different lines. The joint family, he argued, affirmed one of the highest Hindu values—the importance of subordinating one's interest to that of others. Moreover, it was the natural product of an agrarian society based on joint ownership of land. The English, with their individualistic preferences, might denigrate joint ownership, but there was no reason why Indians should accept their value judgements. Child marriage, neither universal nor in way essential in Hinduism, was an integral part of India's agrarian society. It was unlikely to die out. The system was unsuitable for those preparing for a career in the modern professions or the idealistic young who, one hoped, would go abroad to learn industrial or agricultural technology for the benefit of their country, but it was stupid to reject it for one and all simply because the English condemned it.[52] He saw much merit in the caste system beyond the usual argument that it had contributed powerfully to survival in the face of almost impossible odds. The very pride of the twice-born was a guarantee against a total loss of self-respect, a likely result of political subjection. In Burma, he had seen members of the élite group literally wash and worship the feet of a British official. This could not happen in India so long as the caste system retained any vitality. Even the lowliest in India would not stoop so low.[53] Hindus had been accused of narrow parochialism, a failing to be condemned in all circumstances. Bhudev, however, saw one redeeming feature in Hindu parochialism: the vast territories of the Hindu homeland were an epitome of the world and tradition prescribed pilgrimages across its length and breadth. Hence even parochialism in India was not to be equated with a total narrowness of outlook. The restrictions on sea voyage probably had historical origins—the destruction of Indian merchant fleets by Arab pirates. The nineteenth-century practice of ostracizing those who had gone abroad, less strong in Maharashtra than in Bengal, owed much to the arrogance of those ostracized. If the 'England-returned' were a little more respectful to their own society, as was the case in Maharashtra, very probably the problem would disappear.[54] Besides, it was well to remember that travel abroad was no proven antidote for narrow parochialism. The attitudes of the English in India should disabuse one's mind of such notions.[55]

Bhudev saw in the reformist efforts a slavish acceptance of British view on Indian society. He hence considered them degrading for no progress was possible without an independence of spirit. In his view, Vidyasagar's agitation in favour of widow remarriage was the one blot on the great man's otherwise many-splendoured career. Still, there was an extenuating circumstance: the scholar's inspiration was the *Parasara-smriti*, a legitimate text in the *sastric* tradition, and not European ideas as the western-educated believed at the time. Bhudev justified this thesis on the basis of Vidyasagar's later opposition to the Age of Consent Bill, also under the authority of the same Smriti text.[56]

'When one protects one's country from the advent of foreigners while living under the authority of one's own countrymen, we say that the independence of the country has been saved. Similarly, the only way to preserve the independence of one's mind is by rejecting as unsuitable for oneself the prescriptions of alien ideas, on the basis of sound reasoning, and under the authority of inherited traditions.'[57] This, for Bhudev, was the essence of a healthy social life. Over the centuries, Hindu society had shown itself flexible and adaptive. The tradition was not averse to change within the laws of its own being as manifest in the *sastras*. Change, hence, could only be gradual and was unacceptable if it rejected tradition. The vaunted freedom of the western-educated was the false name of their slavery to English ideas. The latter too were acceptable, but only where they helped one retain one's true freedom, that is, within the tradition. Freedom, thus defined, was the essential basis of all progress.[58] The continuous adaptation to changed circumstances had always been achieved through *sastric* injunctions. The Brahmin scholar defined and redefined the *sastras* continually to meet new needs. Strategies for progress must not ignore this well-tried instrument. 'Those who instruct are strong through the excellence of self-discipline and scholarship; therefore try to maintain the community of Brahmins at a high level of discipline and scholarship. All desired results will flow from this and Hindu society acquire immense strength thereby.'[59] His allegiance to Hindu society was almost a self-conscious act of transference. 'One's society is like one's father', he wrote, and the profound affection he had felt for the one was effortlessly extended to the other. The Brahminical tradition, implicitly reinterpreted in terms of the new criteria of rationality, was Bhudev's chosen touchstone to test the quality of all cultural phenomena. It necessarily informed his probing enquiry into the civilization of Europe.

Bhudev's love for the ways of his own society was in effect an expression of his very deep love for his country. Perhaps it would be more accurate to say that his two loves were twin facets of an intense and pervasive emotion. If his society evoked for him the image of his father, the personification of Brahminical virtues, the country as the motherland was identified with the mother, the deity 'who always provided her children with nourishment and water to drink'.[60] The body of Siva's dead spouse, Sati, cut into pieces by Vishnu's disc, was scattered all over the subcontinent, creating fifty-two places of pilgrimage sacred to all Hindus. Bhudev read into this myth a new meaning: 'When I was a student of Hindu College, a European teacher told [us] that patriotism was unknown to the Hindus, for no Indian language had any word to express the idea. I believed his word and was deeply distressed by the thought. I knew then ... the mythical account of ... Sati's death, but that knowledge did not help me refute the teacher's statement or console myself. Now I know that to the descendants of the Aryans the entire motherland with its fifty-two places of pilgrimage is in truth the person of the Deity.'[61]

This discovery of nationalist sentiment in a Puranic myth was no doubt contrived, but there was nothing false in the author's own patriotic commitment. It informs all his writings. The didactic and sociological essays offer blueprints for national regeneration under the aegis of tradition. *Anguriya-vinimay* (Exchange of Rings), the first historical novel in the language anticipating Bankim, projects Sivaji as the ideal Hindu hero; its real theme is the rise of national consciousness inspired by the ideal of non-attachment, *nishkama karma*. The romantic plot dwells on the love between a Hindu prince and a Muslim princess. His *Swapnalabdha Bharater itihas* (A History of India Revealed in a Dream) assumes a contrafactual—Maratha victory at the Third Battle of Panipat—and proceeds to project a utopia, a prosperous India under a wise Hindu emperor, its ideology combining quintessentially Hindu virtues with western science and technology, *dharma* with the rights of the people. *Pushpanjali* (An Offering of Flowers) and *Svayamvarabhas parva* (The Chapter on Betrothal by Choice), parts of an incomplete fable, *Unavimsa puran* (The Nineteenth Purana), modelled on the Puranas, describe allegorically the glories of Mother India, conceived as a goddess, Adhibharati[62], and her sufferings under alien rule. Asked about his future ambitions when he was still a student at Hindu College, he had answered somewhat priggishly: 'To work for my country'.[63] The theme keeps recurring in his diary: 'What can I do for the permanent benefit of my countrymen?'[64] The *Vishwanath Fund*, named after his father, and financed from his life's savings, expressed the same aspiration in a concrete form.[65]

The immediate object of the Fund—to support Sanskrit scholars— underlined Bhudev's perception of what the nation needed. Western education had produced false perceptions—the belief that the *sastras* destroyed independence of spirit.[66] In truth, however, their object was to control man's animal nature and its inclination towards self-indulgence. Man also shared with the inanimate world the quality of inertia. The *sastric* regime offered protection against this inherent tendency.[67] The British had achieved their ascendancy not through their excesses or unwholesome habits but 'their will-power, skills and mutual sympathy, the results of observing codes appropriate for their country and their faith .... Therefore the people of this country can acquire qualities even superior to those of the English if they stick to the *sastric* prescriptions.'[68] The statement defines the scope of Bhudev's enquiry into the European experience for object lessons relevant to India.

That query was also determined by the perceptions of barriers to national integration in India. One major failing he noticed was simply the incapacity to organize effectively in the pursuit of self-interest. He did not consider such social skills morally very worthy, but these were essential prerequisites of nationhood. Once in his conversation with an Englishman he had used the word 'we' with reference to Indians. The English acquaintance retorted angrily, 'If you were capable of saying 'we', then we would not have been here.' Bhudev implicitly accepted the criticism.[69] India's lack of unity was manifest *inter alia* in mutual jealousies, a tendency to feel unhappy at the petty successes of one's countrymen vouchsafed by colonial rule. To him, this was a new development. One of its manifestations was a failure to honour the country's great men. Indian achievements under conditions of alien rule were considerable, just as the mastery of the English language was quite a feat. But there was a tendency to take such achievements for granted—until and unless they were recognized by the masters.[70] Above all, there was the basic psychological problem of subjection: '... Subject races can of course defeat the person or race in power, if they offer united resistance, but power inspires such a sense of awe that no one dares look [at the ruler] without fear, let alone attack him.'[71]

The antidote for weakness and disunity was, of course, national unity. Bhudev's conception of the Indian nationhood was comprehensive. In this he was well in advance of other contemporary thinkers and the political organizations of the period. His experience as a teacher at the Calcutta Madrassa had given him an abiding respect for Muslims and their culture. He developed close social relations with them—but strictly within the restrictions on commensality imposed by the *sastras*.[72] He did use the implicitly pejorative expression, *jaban*, at least twice in his references to Muslims.[73] I have not been able to find any other instance of its use in Bhudev's works.

In his numerous statements on Muslims, he always uses the neutral and more respectful expression, 'Mussalman'. Incidentally, the expression which Muslims found objectionable was used even by contemporary Brahmo leaders such as Rajnarayan Basu[74] and Sibnath Sastri[75], but his assessment of Islamic culture as well as the role of Muslims in Indian history was strongly positive. In his imaginary history of India, he ascribed the following statement to a Maratha leader: 'This motherland of ours has always been burnt by the fire of internal strife; that fire will be put out today .... Even though India is truly the motherland of the Hindus alone, even though it is only the Hindus who were born from her womb, still the Muslims are no longer alien to her for long has she held them to her heart and nourished them. Therefore, the Muslims too are her foster children. If a child is born of the mother's womb and another child is breastfed [and brought up] by her, are not the two siblings? Certainly, according to every scripture. Hence, the Hindus and Muslims who live in India have become brothers. This relationship is destroyed if there are quarrels.'[76] In his allegorical piece, *Pushpanjali*, the Muslim contribution to Indian history is thus described: 'They are brave, heroic and determined. They again united the continent under one ruler; nearly removed the linguistic differences, beautified the land with palaces, roads, etc. and tried to achieve unity by reiterating the grand message that all men are equal. But they were a people with a strong worldly spirit, given to luxury and the pursuit of pleasure. Through their advent the qualities of *sattva* (spirituality) and *rajas* (this-worldly manliness) merely coexisted—the two were not united. Only a few among them have seats of honour in the temple of the goddess [Adhibharati].'[77] He was probably the first Bengali Hindu writer to state unequivocally that he considered the reigns of the Muslim dynasties superior to British rule. He shared with several of his well-known contemporaries the belief that as a religion Islam was superior to Christinaty.[78] Arguably, such sentiments were closely linked to anti-colonial attitudes. Bhudev was certainly the first, if not the only, important nineteenth-century Hindu writer who questioned the then current version of Indo-Muslim history and described it as a mischievous fabrication by British historians, which had influenced western-educated Hindus.[79] He rejected Marshman's statement that the Muslim rulers of Bengal had seized the land of Hindu zamindars as a grotesque exaggeration. He argued that the Turks could not have spread out into northeastern India so quickly but for the acquiescence and active support of Hindu zamindars.[80] His attitude even towards the separatist trend in Muslim politics was full of empathy. When the Bengal Muslims stayed away from the Congress in 1886 under the leadership of Ameer Ali and Abdul Latif, he commented that it would be wrong to attribute motives of personal advantage to these leaders. 'They are not so mean-spirited. They expect that the Muslims generally will benefit from this.' He mildly criticized this attitude as unpragmatic, for Muslims should learn from the experience of the Hindus how fickle was the patronage of alien rulers.[81] He did not ascribe any policy of divide and rule to the British Indian Government, but did accuse some officials of inciting inter-communal tension. 'But such efforts will fail', he remarked with confidence.[82] This particular component of his nationalism—the concern for Hindu-Muslim amity and deep regard for Muslims—influenced not only his assessment of British rule in India but his understanding of Europe's historical evolution as well.

By the 1880s the need for Hindu-Muslims unity was a familiar feature of nationalist propaganda. It was in his practical concern and aggressive championship of the underprivileged that Bhudev was truly ahead of his times. While he accepted the traditional Hindu hierarchy of birth, he objected to the new hierarchy based on one's job and income.[83] He had clear reservations about the caste system itself; he described the political history of India as a record of two-fold penitence.[84] Hindus were guilty of practising untouchability, of treating human beings as worse than animals.[85] As an inspector of schools, he pushed hard in favour of a policy of compulsory primary education[86] and was especially concerned to provide education to tribal groups such as the Santals.[87] In his *History of Bengal*[88] he described at length the miseries of the Bengal ryots, especially the depredations of the indigo planters. He resented the allegation that the peasants were spendthrift and lacked foresight. In 1879, he had plans to write an essay refuting this allegation.[89] He identified the persistent indifference of the caste Hindus towards the education and welfare of the untouchables as a major failing of Indian society. He believed that God had sent the Muslims, the most egalitarian of all peoples, to India to teach Hindus the lesson of equality between man and man.[90] Similarly the British conquest was also divine dispensation; for Indians divided against themselves on the basis of race and language would now learn patriotism from the British whose love for their country transcended even their moral sense.[91] This anxious concern for national integration, both vertical and horizontal, prompted his analysis of nationalism in Europe. His comments on class relations in European society, inspired by more universalist sympathies, were analogous to his views on the state of the underprivileged in India.

Indian nationalists and nationalism, especially in the early phase, are often described as ambivalent in their attitudes to western civilization and British rule. Such a description would be inappropriate in the case of Bhudev. He defined very precisely his position *vis-à-vis* his own culture as well as the impact of Europe. It is summed up in the quotation from the *Manusmriti* he chose as the motto of his *Essay on Society*: 'The learned with his eyes of wisdom looks upon the entire world as equal, but in view of the proven authority of the received tradition, he sticks to his own faith.' Despite this ideological clarity, there are elements, not of ambivalence, but contradiction in his ideas and conduct. Some of these derive from the general conditions of colonial rule and his personal position as a bureaucrat. Others are traceable to more subtle influences, the internalization of western, in fact Victorian, habits and values. In a fundamental sense, he too was a westernized oriental gentleman, despite his scrupulous observance of Brahminical codes; but he was not overtly conscious of this dimension of his personality.

His elaborate arguments in favour of sticking to traditional ways in matters domestic and social boil down to two basic propositions. First, there are on uniform principles as to what is good and what is evil irrespective of differences in culture, levels of development, and historical circumstance. 'Therefore it is necessary that the institutions meant to achieve the ends of (different) societies should also be different.'[92] India's moral and social norms were very different from those of Europe. Therefore in matters pertaining to family or society, one could not learn anything from the West.[93] Second, he was convinced that the norms of Indian society, emphasizing a selfless concern for others, especially as enshrined in the traditional family system, were superior to those of Europe. He quotes his wife approvingly on the question of the alleged need to 'enlighten' Hindu society: 'We have kept all doors and windows open. Where is the darkness? There is not much light outside, but only a great deal of heat and dust.'[94]

The prescription for India's social development, based on this commitment to traditional Hindu values had negative as well as positive components. He disapproved of the school books written by Vidyasagar because they projected as models only western men and women.[95] He considered it essential that Indians should draw inspiration from their own past and own traditions. He wanted the mother tongue to be the medium of all instruction[96] for 'only the improvement of our mother tongue can lead to such beneficent results of nationhood as independence of thought and spirit'.[97] He advised Indians to speak and write to one another exclusively in their own language.[98] His gut reactions to the western influence, however, were not simply in terms of the need for self-respect as a nation. These are summed up in a bitter statement quoted by his son: 'I am teaching my sons English because the way things are, they may suffer poverty unless they learn English. But I do realise that [thereby] I am throwing them into hellfire [literally 'drowning them in hell'].' He took good care to ensure that the sons did not develop any taste for luxury and self-indulgence which, to his understanding, usually went with an English education. If one was careful about such things, then 'English education could not lead [children] altogether astray, and much of its evil impact was mitigated'.[99]

Yet in his own life, he went against many of his own prescriptions. He considered allopathy superior to ayurveda.[100] In his moments of relaxation, he recited European, not Sanskrit or Bengali, poetry. Goethe was a special favourite.[101] He kept a diary from his forty-ninth year. This intimate document was written in English. So were his letters to his sons—a characteristic feature of Indian Victorianism.[102] His Brahmin disciplinarianism had a hard Victorian patina. A typical example is his advice that school children should be encouraged to maintain a record of self-analysis.[103] The inspiration for this was surely Samuel Smiles and not his beloved Smriti texts. The *obiter* that there is nothing to learn from the West in matters of morality appears to have been quietly forgotten here. In the context of his firm commitment to Brahminism, his membership of the Freemason Lodge, Anchovy and Hope, seems even more bizarre.*[104] The contradiction went deeper. There is evidence to prove that he deeply resented the fact of British rule.[105] Yet he preached that there should be neither any agitation[106] nor any resentment against the alien rulers, for such actions and attitudes were no part of the Indian tradition.[107] There is an element of not entirely worthy cautiousness in the attitude of this middle-ranking Bengali official. As editor of the *Education Gazette* he advised his friend, Hemchandra Bandyopadhyay, to excise some words from his *Bharat Sangit* (Song of India): 'The line—'we are dazzled by

---

* Bhudev's one brief comment on freemasonry makes curious reading: 'The Tantras are one type of freemasonry. Many important European gentlemen are freemasons. Are they bad people? Has the world not benefited greatly from freemasonry? Who can tell whether the benefits continue to flow or not.'[112]

the sight of a few white guardsmen'—refers to the British government divinely appointed to unite India; this is not proper. If one is to write anything that refers to the present, the voice of moderation is preferable.'[108] Patriotism in his view was best invoked in a historical context. This had the advantage *inter alia* of not breaking the law or exciting sedition 'in this land of peace-loving and self-restrained Hindus'.[109] Where his own emotions on such matters got the better of him, it was expressed in veiled language—allegorical tales.[110] The veil, however, was thin and the allegory quite transparent. One wonders how the bosses never caught on. Some did consider his *Essays on Society* seditious in intent.[111] In truth, his self-conscious professions of the need for loyalty failed to repress his deep resentment against British rule. The contradiction between his two levels of perception informed all his assessments of the British presence in India and therefore his understanding of western civilization itself.

Undoubtedly, he was too disciplined an intellectual to base his analytical statements primarily on his personal experience. His ideology and considerable study of western civilization were the main sources on which he based his assessment of Europe. Yet, as anthropologists now recognize, even their scientific investigation of other cultures is influenced by the manner in which the investigator is received by the community concerned. Bhudev's comments on the West were by no means purely scientific in intent. They were ideologically inspired and deliberate exercises in social and cultural propaganda aimed at his countrymen. His personal contact with Europeans— a type of experience he shared with many other members of the colonial élite—hence had an obvious relevance to his insight into western attitudes and the nature of alien rule.

Bhudev's contacts with Europeans, nearly all Britishers, were of the usual type—usual, that is, for men of his social background. He got to know them as teachers and senior colleagues ('bosses' might be a more correct description for most of his British acquaintances in the latter category). Besides, there were his French neighbours at Chandernagore, the inevitable encounters on train journeys, and the occasional brush with aggressive missionaries, equally inevitable in those days. These encounters, pleasant and unpleasant, are a recurrent theme in his biography and provided illustrative material for many of his statements on the European character.

If it were possible to measure such things, it would be probably correct to say that most of Bhudev's contacts with Europeans were friendly and

pleasant. His obstinate resolve to give up Sanskritic studies in favour of an
'English education' was due to the kindness he had received from an English
teacher at Sanskrit College. He contrasted it with the rather unprincipled
behaviour of his Sanskrit teacher who got young Bhudev thrashed by his
father for no good reason.[113] This memory of kindly concern was reinforced
through his contact with a missionary lady, Mrs Wilson, who helped him
with his English education after he left Sanskrit College.[114] As a student at
Hindu College he met David Hare and was among a group of students who
once 'raided' his house demanding prizes for their excellent performance in
tests set by the philanthropist.[115] The relations between European teachers
and Indian students at Hindu College in his days were close and friendly.
He benefited fully from this fact, especially because he was a bright and
promising student.[116] Mr Halford, an otherwise kindly teacher, had kicked a
student who had pushed him beyond the limits of his patience, and this was
the one occasion when the students went on 'strike'. It was Bhudev who
induced his classmates to spare the old man the humiliation of an apology.[117]
He used to call on the Reverend Long and even came into close contact
with the aggressively proselytizing missionary, the Reverend Duff. He
developed a deep respect for that remarkable man. Duff, in his turn, never
tried to convert Bhudev. His later prescription for Anglo-Bengali relationship
was based on this experience; Indians could learn much from educated
Europeans provided they did not try to show off their western education
and the Europeans gave up their vanity and proneness to sarcasm.[118]

For aspiring Bengalis at this time, European patronage was a *sine qua
non* for success and, in fact, even entry into careers. His senior British
colleagues often became his admirers and then his patrons. He got his first
break, as a teacher at the Calcutta Madrassa, with the help of F.J. Mouat
who was on the managing committee of the Hindu College. As headmaster
of Howrah School, he met Hodgson Pratt, the civilian inspector of schools,
After an initial misunderstanding, the two became very close friends, Pratt's
obituary note on Bhudev in the *Indian Magazine* is an enlightening
commentary on Anglo-Indian relationships and the nature of Bhudev's
intimacy with the civilian: 'He seemed incapable of saying a word more
than he felt, or of resorting to flattery or obsequiousness to his English
visitor and official superior. He could not be ignorant, however, that if he
pleased that visitor, it might not improbably be an advantage to him for his
whole life.'

'When, in after years, I heard Englishmen talk glibly about "native untrustworthiness and duplicity" I used to tell them of Bhoodev Mookerjee, who could not tell a lie or fawn, or, indeed, act otherwise than with the utmost uprightness ... . Yet all this time he was a typical Hindoo, in his wonderful dignity and his almost feminine gentleness, with entire absence of self-consciousness and absolute reliableness. I am certain that these qualities were not peculiar to him, but that they belong to his race. It was this acquaintance with Bhudev Mookerjee that made me, ever afterwards, long to see the existence of close personal relations, deep and hearty friendships, between the men of the West and the men of the East, alike in India and England.'[119] There is a curious and unexplained episode in the history of this friendship. Pratt, on his return to England, wrote to Bhudev. The latter never received any reply to the many letters he wrote to his friend over a period of at least ten years. Pratt, in his obituary note, mentioned 'more than forty years of silence on both sides'. Presumably, Bhudev's letters never reached him[120] and the Brahmin was deeply distressed by Pratt's silence. His *Essay on Society* contains a very bitter comment on friendship with Englishmen.[121] One wonders if the above facts had anything to do with this highly negative assessment.

Friendly relations with his immediate English superiors[*], if not close personal friendship, was Bhudev's usual experience in his official career. The relationship was never exclusively official. The Pratts were frequent visitors to his home. He effectively sought the intervention of Mrs Woodrow, the boss's wife, on a matter involving his career.[122] Inspector Lodge defended him vigorously against the false complaints of a missionary.[123] With Medlicott, who was transferred to the inspector's job from the Geological Survey, he developed what was probably the closest friendship of his life.[124] In his *Miscellaneous Essays* he refers to him as '*nikat atmiya*' (literally, a close relation).

The term *atmiya* or 'someone very close to oneself', a derivative of *atma* (self), is normally applied to blood relations. Bhudev used it here to indicate a very high degree of intimacy. Yet, curiously, the fact that Medlicott was a European is not forgotten. The full phrase runs: '*amar ati atmiya kono europiya*' ('a European who was very close to me'). Had the friend been an Indian, this unselfconscious reference to his ethnic identity surely would

---

[*] Mostly inspectors of schools. As headmaster of government schools and later, as assistant or additional inspector, Bhudev was under their authority.

not have been there. In the closing decades of imperial rule, a rigid protocol kept all but the seniormost Indian officials at a great distance, social as well as official, from those at the top of the bureaucratic pyramid. The rebellion of 1857 is often believed to be the climacteric in Indo-British social relationships. This view is probably incorrect. Indian officials in the provincial services as well as other members of the indigenous élite continued to have, at times, very close social contact with the highest levels of British officialdom, including the governors, at least until the turn of the century. Bhudev came into contact with the Lieutenant Governor of Bengal, Sir Ashley Eden, in connection with official business, while he was still an assistant inspector of schools. His predecessor, Sir Richard Temple, had invited the Bengali writers to a steamer party in 1875.[125] As a literary gentleman, Sir Ashley in fact went further and developed a personal friendship with the celebrated editor, Krishnadas Pal. A similar friendship developed between him and Bhudev while the latter was still a fairly junior person in the official hiearchy.[126] So close was this friendship that when Bhudev, now a Class I inspector of schools, visited Rangoon in 1873, he was the guest of Sir Ashley who had assumed charge as chief commissioner.[127] He reached even greater heights in his official contacts: on 24 March 1886, the Viceroy himself invited Bhudev 'to have a little conversation'.[128]

Bhudev observed rigidly the Brahminical restrictions on commensality in all his contacts with Europeans. In declining invitations to take food in any European home, he explained his reasons according to his assessment of his would-be host's personality. He did not invoke the Hindu scriptures so dear to him, for he was extremely sensitive about slighting comments on them.[129] In his *Miscellaneous Essays*, he wrote at some length on the subject: 'Once a European with whom I was on friendly terms invited me to dine with him. I declined with apologies. He said, 'I shall not insist, if you want to decline, but you must tell me frankly your reason.' I said, 'Dining with you would be an act in violation of our social code. Could there be a stronger reason [for declining your invitation]? Besides, consider, what else are we left with? We have lost our political freedom, our religion is under your attack, our vernacular literatures have not yet reached a level one can be proud of. What else have we got to give us a sense of pride or help maintain our individuality [as a people]? You may call it superstition or a social code, the system of caste and codes of ritual conduct are all that we have now. These I cannot abandon.'[130] His friend Medlicott expressed his respect for such 'superstitions'; to him the only alternatives to conformity were either total wisdom or moral bankruptcy.[131]

Clearly, Bhudev's orthodoxy in these matters had strong nationalist overtones, and with good reason. For some, interdining with Europeans might be an unselfconsciously rational act. For many more, it implied weak-minded indiscipline, deviation from a code which had not been discarded in other respects, but was violated in this particular case out of embarrassment or unwillingness to upset the masters. Many again positively hankered after opportunities to hobnob with Europeans and would forego all ritual scruples in their single-minded pursuit of this objective which could help open doors to a more successful career and higher status. The Anglo-Indian image of the educated Bengali was that of a person who simply hankered for an invitation to an Englishman's table. None of them was expected to be an exception to this rule. Atkinson, the then Director of Public Instruction, said this in so many words to Medlicott, who in turn asked him to try Bhudev. Atkinson contrived a morning interview for Bhudev with the Lieutenant Governor, Beadon, who duly asked the Brahmin to join him at breakfast. The latter declined on the ground that in his youth he had promised his father never to violate the ritual code in such matters: 'If I now eat [with you] in violation of [our] social practice, I shall fall very low in my own eyes for the rest of my life.'[132] His contempt for those who violated the code is on record in an anecdote he cities in his *Miscellaneous Essays*. On his declining an invitation to dinner, a senior English official commented: 'Those we would like to dine with, decline our invitation. Those who come to dinner, are people we would rather not have at our table.' Bhudev quipped, 'If I accepted your invitation, would I not join the ranks of those you prefer not to dine with?'[133]

Once a condescending district magistrate offered to shake hands with Bhudev to say goodbye, adding 'I do not usually shake hands with natives'. Bhudev declined.[134] The explanation he offered is in the nature of an ideological manifesto: 'The modes of courtesy differ from society to society. When I called on you, you did not stretch your hand for a handshake, and I saluted you in the oriental manner (which too is a *namaskar* with one hand in the spirit of obeisance to the Deity manifest in all beings). I found this satisfactory; so you should not worry about it. Our holy scriptures acknowledge God in all beings; to them nothing in this universe is an object of contempt. However, the low-born and *mlechchhas* (impure foreigners) have been designated as 'untouchable' owing to the impurity of their habits or some other reason. My father would ... touch the heads of sick lowborn children ... and bless them with deep affection and without any sense of disgust and then take a [purifactory] bath. If I shake hands with my European friends and so express my friendly feelings, afterwards I change my clothes, wash my hands and also touch water from the Ganges, if convenient. I do not do so out of contempt but only to abide by our codes. Therefore, you will appreciate I am gratified if any European does not shake hands with me. This is not due to any reluctance to shake hands out of national pride. A Hindu is reluctant to touch another person's body even to express his affection. Since on this occasion there was no handshake and we have developed a mutual regard, why don't we forget about it today?' Was this spiel simply a note on Brahminical ways to avoid misunderstanding or a poker-faced expression of 'national pride', meant to put a smug little ass in his place?[135]

All his British friends and colleagues appear to have accepted Bhudev on his own terms. As a guest in the house of Eden or Medlicott,[136] he would set up his tent in their compound and have his food cooked by his own servants. Medlicott stopped eating beef for a month in anticipation of Bhudev's visit.[137] Effectively, the restrictions were one-way. He assured Medlicott that the latter had not defiled the Brahmin's homestead by eating there, for 'a guest was an object of veneration to a Hindu'.[138]

Bhudev's extensive analysis of the European character is identifiably based on his personal knowledge of individual Britishers. Even when he fell back on his favoured historical perspective, often his intention was to try and explain scientifically what he had observed himself. The friendly contact with highly educated and sensitive Europeans partly explains the positive stereotypes projected in his writings. His praise, however, was seldom unqualified. He wrote of different types of British officials and also of unworthwhile traits in the European personality which counterbalanced the good in them. One is left with the feeling that he sought to derive from his very mixed experience of encounters with Europeans an abstract model of the western persona with its many faces, acceptable and unacceptable, in terms of his values.

Both in and out of office, he had his share of humiliating experiences, which was an ever-recurring theme in the life-stories of the colonial élite. This unfortunate feature of alien rule has a long history in Bengal. Raja

Rammohan was insulted by a British official for his failure to show due respect. Vidyasagar resigned from his well-paid job because he felt he could not continue to hold it consistently with his self-respect. Surendranath was dismissed on charges of corruption, presumably flimsy, in view of the knighthood later conferred on him. Bankim was in serious trouble over his patriotic novel, *Anandamath*; he was also once manhandled by an army officer, an incident over which he went to court. Bhudev's biographer mentions several unpleasant encounters—once with a missionary whose street-corner lecture on Hinduism contained bizarre misinterpretations of the Ramayana[139], another time with a bully who jumped on to a boat hired by Bhudev and wanted to be taken to his destination first.[140] On a third occasion, he was requested amicably to quit a railway compartment for the convenience of the European passengers.[141] On the first two occasions, he got the better of his opponents, on the third he complied out of regard for the ladies present.

The confrontations in course of his official career were by no means such mild pinpricks. The experience of humiliations began early. As a young applicant for a job, at the door of important European gentlemen, he received the usual treatment from the sahib's *chaprasis* and dogs.[142] Later, when asked by Pratt the reason for his avoiding social contact with Europeans, he said he did call on some like Duff, Long, and Mouatt who were kind to him: 'They do not keep me waiting outside for a long time and their *chaprasis* do not treat me with contempt or brush past me.'[143] At the Madrassa, a European colonel who used to inspect the school bullied and shouted at him for refusing to provide damaging information about the headmaster. Bhudev stood his ground, but was deeply shaken by the experience.[144] While he was the Headmaster of Hugli Normal School and already a much respected figure in the Bengali literary world, the Director of Public Instruction, Atkinson (later very friendly to Bhudev), called for an explanation for his absence from duty during the director's visit of inspection. In the colonial context this implied questioning the great man's integrity, putting him at once on the same level as a petty clerk. The reason for his absence, incidentally, was the death of his uncle and Bhudev had applied for leave.[145] Things got much worse when Campbell became the Lieutenant-Governor. Allegedly, the new Lieutenant-Governor was prejudiced against him because he had published some articles criticizing the former's ideas on educational policy. His first encounter with Campbell was marked by sharp exchanges and the meeting ended with a snub: 'I see, Babu,* you understand matters of politics. I shall be glad to talk with you on matters of politics.' Soon afterwards he was asked to explain his conduct on a number of petty issues, including his failure to be present during the Lieutenant-Governor's visit. Such attendance, while not 'specially ordered', was considered 'natural and proper'.[146] The strong support of his superiors checked further persecution. But he seriously considered resignation at one point.[147]

His unfavourable impressions of British officials and Anglo-Indians generally were derived not merely from his experiences of personal humiliation. The blunt pronouncements on racial issues and even blunter expressions of racial attitudes made him aware of the empire's unacceptable face and the fact that educated Europeans could be less than civilized in their behaviour. He noted in his diary in 1890 Grant Duff's comments on Indians—that they were ugly, black, and totally lacking in national feelings. The same entry contains another quotation from the same dignitary— recommending relative immunity from punishment for English offenders in India to ensure that the Indians for ever lived in awe of Englishmen.[148] He also noted the confident declaration of the Duke of Argyle, Secretary of State for India, that the central purpose of British policy was to keep India in bondage for ever. This popular view was reiterated many times by others.[149] In commenting on Campbell in the *Education Gazette*, he underlined the lieutenant-governor's opinion of Indians, that they would never achieve any progress and the country should be colonized by South Europeans—the Spaniards, Italians, etc.[150] He was further aware of the growing anti-Bengali feeling among the younger civilians. His son found among his papers a letter from Eden dated 27 April 1873, seeking to intercede with Campbell on Bhudev's behalf. Evidently, it was never sent to the addressee. The letter contains a curious comment: 'Bhoodeb has a fault and that is that he is a Bengalee. This among the present race of civilians is an unforgivable offence I fear ...'[151] He wrote at length on the Anglo-Indian agitation against

* The word had already acquired a negative connotation, especially if not used as a suffix to the first name. It became a respectful or contemptuous form of address according to the social context. Babu used after one's name was the formal way of addressing a gentleman. A servant addressing his master as 'Babu' was the accepted style indicating respect. But 'Babu' was also the word for a clerk and an Englishman addressing a respectable Bengali simply as 'Babu' would not be interpreted as a positive gesture.

Bethune's Black Act*[152] in his *History of Bengal* and noted with equanimity
the hostility of the *Englishman* and the *Pioneer* towards the Indian National
Congress. His advice to his country men was to ignore such expected
opposition.[153] Several notings in his diary express his growing distrust of the
British bureaucracy, or at least of an important section of it. In December
1879, he noted: 'If Lord Lytton is not stopped, the native civil service
examination will be mere pretence. He would like to eliminate competition
from this examination.'[154] An entry earlier the same year reads: 'A curious
belief is gaining ground among the English that there is no real saving in
employing Indian officials in place of Europeans.'[155]

The comments on individual officials in his diary are often very critical.
The Subdivisional Officer of Madhepura in Bihar is described as a 'great
friend' of the oppressive indigo planters.[156] 'I heard of one reason ... why
the English are so infatuated with Patna', he wrote on 4 January 1877.
'The rich in this city very frequently dine (and wine) the Europeans.'[157]
He had a fair amount of personal knowledge of racial attitudes—of the way
the English treated their Indian servants[158], and their feelings about inter-
racial marriage. A Muslim friend of his youngest son had married a
European lady. 'He used to say that every Englishman felt that he had
outraged a close relation of theirs.'[159]

If his pride in his Brahmin identity was one basic fact of Bhudev's life,
the other was his aspiration as an official in the colonial bureaucracy. The
tension between these two sides to his personality was very considerable,
especially so because he was very sensitive and rather shy.[260] The proud
Brahmin was bent on making a success of his career in service[161] and
starting as a teacher in the Calcutta Madrassa (after a brief spell in non-
government schools), he went about as high as any Indian could hope to
go in his days—ending his career as a Class I inspector of schools, an office
held by members of the civil service from time to time. In cash terms the
transition was from Rs 50 to Rs 1500 per month, the latter a very
considerable income in those days. The progress was not easy. There was
strong resistance to his promotion to higher office at each step, in addition
to the not infrequent conflicts with his superiors. Perhaps even more painful
for him was the attitude of his friendly British patrons. He refers more than
once to his deep sense of chagrin at the assessment of his worth implicit in

---

* The object of the Act was to bring Europeans in the *muffassil* under the jurisdiction of
local courts.

the casual comments of these well-meaning persons. In 1862, when he was the headmaster of a government teacher-training school, he sought the help of his superior, Woodrow, inspector of schools, to secure a promotion. As headmaster, he already occupied a post normally reserved for Europeans. Woodrow's response to his request was therefore natural: 'What further promotion do you expect? You have gone as far as is possible.'[162] Referring to this episode, Bhudev wrote in his *Essay on Family*: 'When he [i.e. Bhudev] heard these cruel words from his superior who was English by race, his heart was inflamed,—but he remembered his new born son and his burning anger was quenched.'[163] In short, he had a family to support and could not afford the luxury of anger. On this occasion, as on others, he did get what he wanted through clever arguments and a certain measure of manipulation. The psychological cost of the efforts is not difficult to imagine. A second episode underlines profound ego-frustration self-consciously traced to the fact of alien rule. When he was promoted to the rank of inspector, Class IV in 1876, another 'first' for an Indian, the director of public instruction commented, 'Would you have gone as far in promotion and salary under the Hindus or Muslims?' Bhudev replied, 'Even under the great Muslim empire Hindus rose to the offices of royal minister and commander-in-chief. And under the Hindus? Do you really believe that in those days I would not have been appointed prime-minister in some kingdom?'[164] Bhudev's sons were brought up to believe that for the scions of a scholarly Brahmin family, any service was a form of degradation; the study and transmission of the inherited knowledge were the only appropriate functions. Only circumstances forced one to work for the 'King'[165], an alien king at that.[166] The conflict inherent in his system of values in a colonial situation and the rather inadequate efforts at rationalization became explicit in an encounter between Bhudev and a rather boorish zamindar. Asked to identify himself, the former simply replied, 'A Brahmin', demanding to be treated with the honour due to one. When the zamindar enquired mockingly how a Brahmin could serve a *mlechchha* king, the answer cited scriptural authority: 'one does not ask what caste the king belongs to.'[167] The demands of correct ritual conduct were no doubt satisfied. All conflicts were not resolved so easily. It was painful to work under alien masters, often 'totally ignorant' of things Indian,[168] who could be discourteous to a Brahmin. Especially distasteful were the ways of the young civilians who had no knowledge of the respect due to age in Indian society. An agonized entry in this aged Brahmin's diary[169] reads: 'Oh, how the youngsters lord it over the country.'

When his *Essay on Society* was published, Sir Charles Eliot commented[170] on the 'extensive reading', unique in India in his opinion, on which the work was based. His vivid analysis of European society and civilization necessarily owed more to such extensive reading than to actual observation, for he had never been to Europe. His authorities are often cited in the texts of his essays[171], which show a wide-ranging knowledge of European history, contemporary philosophy, political theory, and sociology. The *Essay on Society* bears the imprint of contemporary social scientific methods even though its conclusions, with their emphasis on 'Hindu' values, are of course very distinctive. His other writings bear witness to his knowledge of European literature.

His contemporary, Rajnarayan Basu, has left an account of the required reading in the seniormost class of Hindu College. There was a heavy emphasis on English literature, especially Bacon, Shakespeare, Milton, and Pope. The syllabus also included Young's *Night Thoughts* and Gray's *Poems.* Next in importance was history. The required reading, which ran into 36 volumes for the one-year course, included Hume's *History of England*, Mitford's *History of Greece*, Fergusson's *Roman Republic*, Gibbon, Elphinstone's *India* and Russell's *Modern Europe.* In addition, there was an extensive syllabus on mathematics, including optics and astronomy, besides moral philosophy, not based on any prescribed texts.[172] Bhudev's introduction to European civilization was thus based on a wide-ranging curriculum.

In addition, already in his early youth he had read into continental literatures in English translations.[173] He was attracted for a while to Christianity and studied with great interest not only the Bible but books intended to establish the 'truth of the Christian faith'. A classmate, Chandicharan Sinha, who later became Christian, joined him in these studies.[174] As noted earlier, his incipient faith in Christianity was shaken by his introduction to Hume's *Essays* ('This volume has knocked off the teeth of Christianity', a fellow student informed him), Tom Paine, Gibbon, and Voltaire's *Muhammad.*[175]

Later, he had plans to write several books on western civilization and he read widely into western writings, partly with this end in view. Only one of these projects, the volume on society, was completed. It includes material bearing on another project, a volume on Hindu and English manners. He never wrote his projected book on 'Nature', but did produce a school textbook on the natural sciences and another on geometry. The other textbooks he wrote include histories of England, Greece, and Rome, all based on standard authorities in the English language.[176] The volume on the history of art and architecture was never started. Stray comments in the *Essay on Society* suggest that he had read into the subject. He wrote to his second son, Govinda, in 1888 that he 'had thought out a number of essays to be entitled 'Philosophical Essays', which would summarize critically the philosophical ideas of Europe and ancient India'. We find him reading Plato in 1878.[177] The comment in his Diary reads: 'Accumulated human experience develops into science. Is virtue true because it pleases the gods, or does it please because it is true?'[178] Another entry, two months later, comments on Lecky's *History of Rationalism in Europe*: 'A fine book! The author observes correctly that rationalism, however congenial to social progress, does not help nurture heroic individuals. The current objections to the German philosophy of Goethe and Fichte support democracy.'[179] In another letter addressed to his youngest son and written the same year, he noted with satisfaction that Professor Huxley's article in the February issue of *The Nineteenth Century* agreed with some of the basic propositions of his own *Essay on Society*; but he rejected Huxley's thesis that 'nature was unmoral'. 'The truth is that European writers are not used to conceding that the root of morality is in nature itself: they say that it is either revealed preternaturally or socially evolved.' The same letter contains critical comments on contemporary writers on government who considered the primary functions of the state the only appropriate field for bureaucratic intervention.[180] Another letter contains a lengthy discussion on the experimental and institutional schools of philosophy—Hume, Mill, Kant, and Hegel.[181] The western thinkers whose ideas he found most acceptable in political economy and philosophy respectively were Malthus and Comte. He saw an affinity between Comte's concept of altruism and the Vedantic doctrine of surrendering 'self' (*atma*) to 'all' (*sarva*).[182] He was also expectedly sympathetic to Schopenhauer's words in praise of the Upanishads.[183] Unlike most of his contemporaries, he rejected utilitarianism, having read deeply into Spencer and Mill.[184] Despite his objections to revolutionary violence, he was an admirer of Mazzini's religious and ethical ideas: 'God is, but he is not the Christian God, arbitrary dispenser of good and evil', 'Life is not a search after happiness, it is a mission'. Presumably he caught in such *obiters* echoes of his own views,[185] and the doctrine of *nishkama karma*. Like other Victorian Bengalis, he too was a great reader of 'improving' biographies of self-made men. Smiles'

Industrial Biography, Davenport's *Lives of Individuals who Raised Themselves*, Brewster's *Martyrs of Science*, biographies of Stephenson. Watt, and Joshua Wedgwood, were some of the works he recommended to a colleague.[186]

Bhudev wrote on Europe in his numerous books as a self-consciously just observer and a man of considerable erudition. His object, however, was propaganda. He was convinced that the truth was on his side. The 'truth', of course, was ideological in content, but he tried to establish it on the basis of rational arguments in the belief that norms could be graded on grounds of reason. The exercise had its expected share of rationalizations and emotional overtones. He was not quite conscious of these. 'Legitimate nationalism' and an emphasis on the Hindu identity, sharpened by his personal experiences, coloured his vision of the West.

'Ever since western civilization penetrated this land, we began to lose our religion, our sense of nationality, our freedom, our Brahminical spirit, and in fact even our identity [literally, 'I-ness']. The superficially attractive manners, customs, dress, ornaments, religion, ethics and style of action characteristic of western countries have dazzled our eyes. We all resolved to imitate the West in such matters and were determined to give up everything that was our own. If this current had flowed unabated a little longer we would have certainly lost our identity by now. But fortunately for us, that terrible current has now slowed down. This was achieved through the efforts of a few great men. I consider the revered Bhudev, now deceased, the greatest among them. He alone toiled hard to protect our religion and national identity, through his teachings as well as his personal example. Hence it is that we rejoice in calling him not Bhudev Babu, but simply Bhudev, a god on earth.' If one overlooks the hagiographic flourish, this assessment by a contemporary writer[187], echoed in dozens of obituary notes[188], identifies probably correctly Bhudev's place in the social history of nineteenth-century Bengal.

II

The central purpose of all his writings was to clarify and affirm the Indian identity, especially its hard Brahminical Hindu core, in which all Indians—to his understanding—had their share, Muslims very much included. This

identity was threatened by the indiscriminate imitation of the West. The
West, in general, the British impact, in particular, hence had to be assessed
carefully, western norms and mores analysed and compared to Indian ones
to decide what was suitable for the country's needs. His best-known work,
Samajik prabandha [Essay on Society][189], is addressed directly to this task.
The same theme recurs in different contexts in his other essays, his allegorical
tales, and even the straightforward historical writings.

Since his first concern was to alter judiciously the nature of the western
impact on the western-educated Bengalis, that impact itself was naturally
the starting point of his enquiry. His findings were almost totally negative.
The roots of the problem lay deep—in the non-Aryan element in the Bengali
personality which produced a proneness to imitate and love of pleasure.[190]
These negative features of the Bengali character—especially imitativeness—
had flourished most under western influence. The results were soul-destroying.
The most tragic consequences were to be seen in the life of his most talented
contemporary, Madhusudan. The latter, on his return from England, called
on Bhudev in western clothes, but asked for a *dhoti* and wanted to eat,
Bengali-style, squatting on a low flat seat. 'I do not know what he was
thinking of at the time', Bhudev writes, '... Perhaps he remembered my
mother. But at that moment I could not bring myself to talk of her in his
presence. For this was not the same Madhu any longer. The Madhu we
knew was a jewel among men, shining with genius, pure, natural, aspiring
to achieve great fame, but this Madhu was perverted through alien contact,
and blemished by an excess of imitativeness, the prototype of Nimai Datta*
to the poet.'[191]

Since the English were at the apex of India's social pyramid, they were
naturally the objects of imitation especially among the educated Bengalis.
'The latter's ways of walking and speaking, jokes, accent, gestures, manners,
in fact everything about them smells English a little.' An old-fashioned Indian,
Hindu or Muslim, however important he might be, had a certain gentle way
about him. By contrast, 'you can hear the loud footsteps of the English-
educated on the staircase. Their shoes will crunch noisily, there will be a
loud bang at the door, great guffaws of laughter will go up at the moment of

---

* Nimai Datta was the anti-hero of a highly popular Bengali farce, Dinabandhu Mitra's
  Sadhabar ekadasi. A drunken and degenerate western-educated Bengali, the
  character was generally believed to have been modelled on Michael Madhusudan
  Datta, though the playwright strongly refuted the suggestion.

encounter and chairs pulled with a mighty screech. Even the ladies indoors realize, 'Yes, indeed, we have some visitor'. Hindus learn from the English their arrogant ways and give up the gentleness characteristic of their race.'[192] If this important degeneration of outward manners was one result of imitating the English, the rot within traceable to the same cause went much further. The old-fashioned Indian worried if he failed to look after his elders. His modern counterpart's main anxiety was about his own comfort. Fortunately, there were still many old-fashioned people among the English-educated. The point at issue was however not in doubt: 'The growth of English [education] and the imitation of the English were aggravating egotistic propensities.'[193]

The results of imitation were both pathetic and laughable, for it was easier to imitate vices than virtues. The English in India earned fat salaries and lived in great style. Their imitators aped them, no matter what they earned. The latter's single servant had to do for the *Koi Hais*' umpteen retainers. The English put in a lot of physical effort to maintain their luxurious life-style. They took good care of their horses and carriages, as well as their clothes and furniture. The babu loved luxury, but not the effort which went with it. He did not have the Englishman's resources, nor did he husband carefully what little he had. Thus the imitation of English ways only led to disarray and eventually bankruptcy. If imitation included a little problem with drinks, the ruin came quick and very effectively.[194] Of course 'only people without a trace of self-respect would try to become Europeans all the way'.[195]

The degeneration implicit in such loss of self-respect could be observed in every sphere of life. It was manifest in an attitude of extreme psychological dependence. The educated Bengali had ceased to care about the opinion of his own society. What mattered was the criticism or praise of the English.[196] They repeated parrot-like whatever they heard from the English. Since the latter were always full of praise for everything pertaining to themselves, their Bengali disciples had come to believe in the ethical superiority of Europeans and in the cliché that the English were improving Indian morals. Hindus, according to Bhudev, had nothing to learn from Europe in the field of ethics.[197] The degenerate imitators had picked up phrases like 'moral courage' and believed that it was courageous of them to defy the scriptures. But since Hindu society had no power to coerce, it was not an object of fear. The English, with their monopoly of power, were. 'Therefore insulting one's own society ... was no evidence of courage. Nor

Bhudev Mukhopadhyay

61

was it courageous to imitate the English. It was only a way of flattering the powerful. The English-educated, unfamiliar with the scripturally prescribed codes of conduct, had lost all humility and attitude of respect. Hence, even their good qualities were not obvious to the society at large.'[198] The ruling race was their new object of worship and, with the encouragement of a class of self-important and flamboyant officials, the ritual obeisance took the form of lavish entertainment, way beyond the means of most Indian.[199] 'The Hindus are also losing their contented attitude and becoming slaves of greed through their association with the English.'[200] Selfishness had been apotheosized in the British Indian law itself; it denied the mother the right to claim maintenance from her successful son.[201] 'No other race ever developed as great a concern for the welfare of others as the Hindus, no other race can match the English in their intensity of selfishness. I say again, if through the mutual contact of these two societies the English and not the Hindu character underwent a change, that would have been for the best.'[202]

Bhudev saw no indication of such a welcome development, only a pervasive degeneration among educated Indians. They joined their objects of adoration to rejoice in the glories of nineteenth-century 'progress', but had no sense of what was happening to them.[203] Their slavishness was deep-seated because their sense of reverence for the English had become truly an article of faith. It was possible for them to sneer at the suggestion that the business of a meeting be conducted in Bengali, for in their view such a course would 'push the country backwards by two millennia'. An 'educated' munsiff called on all his English colleagues when posted to a new place. The local raja was ignored on the ground that no native had any effective power any longer. Even the high-minded and patriotic Rajnarayan sought to justify Hinduism in terms of English values.[204] Evidently, this class of people had become deraciné, forgotten their innate sense of courtesy, and lost even basic human values.[205]

Even the gains were more apparent than real. The much-vaunted western education was tinsel rather than gold. From childhood people acquired all their education through the medium of an ill-understood and difficult foreign language. An alien tongue was always unsatisfactory as a medium of instruction, for it was necessarily full of words denoting unfamiliar objects and, even more, unfamiliar ideas. Hence, the western-educated were brought up to learn things without full comprehension and acquired the habit of not-so-clever guessing. They were thus trained to miss out on the scientific spirit, the true glory of western knowledge. The European teachers in the Indian colleges were seldom very proficient in the sciences and, in the absence of laboratory experiments, science education was reduced to a farce. The world outside hardly helped make up for this deficiency because there were very few factory industries. Hence scientific education in India boiled down to a destruction of the scientific spirit—a half-comprehending acceptance of the words of European authors and teachers, basically no different from memorizing Sanskrit or Arabic grammar. The only change was the replacement of traditional *sastric* authority by that of modern European scientists. This was an improvement, only so far as the West had achieved a greater understanding of external nature. Their Indian disciples, however, had to accept the fact on faith. The uncritical spirit implicit in this entire process of education became manifest in the unashamed adoption of new western superstitions—the sale of *planchettes* by the thousand, the faith in Tibetan Mahatmas embodied in *lingams*. 'They have given up native witchcraft and adopted witchcraft western-style, abjured belief in native ghosts and adopted English ghosts in their stead, abandoned native incarnations and are about to accept a western *avatara*.'[206] An even more serious consequence of western education was the alienation of the élite from the masses. Having invested a lot of effort in learning English and western education, the new élite naturally held dear what they had acquired, no matter what its intrinsic worth.[207] The infatuation with English created a barrier of language between the two sections of society. In practical matters, the chasm was widened by the universal adoption of English in the offices and courts of law. The British officials found this convenient and were impervious to the harassment caused to the poor and the unlettered. The English-educated reacted in the same spirit, for they were infatuated with their own sense of superiority to the masses, which derived from their English education.[208]

Bhudev noted two redeeming features in this otherwise dismal scene. First, there was a growing awareness of the indignity implicit in senseless imitation: 'Now the desire to speak English, wear hats and trousers, dine at table and the like are somewhat in decline.' The new university graduates were less prone towards such things than the students of the Hindu College in an earlier epoch. The tendency to imitate the western lifestyle was somewhat stronger among those who had been to Europe, as was the new fashion of going out with one's wife. Bhudev hoped that as the numbers of those who had been to Europe increased, these tendencies would also disappear.[209] The second reason for hope, to his understanding, derived from the salutary features of the caste system. It ensured that in the eyes of a Hindu, a section of his own countrymen, i.e. the Brahmins, and not any foreigner, would occupy the highest place of honour. The degradation of the western-educated hence could not go beyond a point: 'If an Indian entirely loses his sense of identity, he feels insulted if the Englishman does not shake hands with him: if he has no self-respect, he is pleased to dine with him; if he is totally infatuated, he feels honoured if the English use his first name while speaking or writing to him; if he has totally forsaken all his ancestral virtues, then he feels gratified by imitating the manners and customs of the English; if an Indian reaches the limits of degeneration through his English education, he considers the religion, social codes and morals of the English superior to those of his own people and aspires ceaselessly to be the equal of the English. But in no circumstances will he seek his ultimate fulfilment in handing over his sister and daughter as mistresses to an Englishman or offer flower and sandal paste in worship at the latter's feet.' Bhudev concluded from his visit to Burma under alien rule that it was only the caste system which saved Indians from such total degradation.[210] He built his hopes on these two slender foundations, and the innate strength of the Indian tradition. To repeat, his critique of western culture in all its manifestations was meant to reinforce what he saw as weak but hopeful beginnings in the life of the colonial élite—the first signs of resistance to a degrading loss of identity.

Of course, the most relevant manifestation of western life was the British imperial presence, his attitude towards it, noted above in the context of his life experience, was not ambivalent but marked by genuine contradiction. In his introduction to *Essay on Society*, he speaks of 'the postal system, railway, printing, newspapers, telegraph and other means of spreading knowledge which are gifts of the British government and the unprecedented state of peace and happiness' established by the same agency.[211] In his allegorical *Pushpanjali* (Offering of Flowers), British rule in India is thus described: 'They did not merely unify the country under one rule, but proceeded to bind it up with [chains of] iron. They made no willing attempts to unify the people. But what they did in pursuit of self-interest, helped in the process of unification. They are totally selfish, but farsighted; they are drunk with arrogance, but not given to pursuit of pleasure; possessed of immeasurable strength, both external and internal, but without any concern for the welfare of others; devoted to pursuit of knowledge, but without any concern for salvation. They are in bondage to baser instincts [*tamoguna*]. They go, as they come [but do not stay]. In the temple of the great goddess [i.e. India] not one of them has a seat of honour.'[212] The other allegory, *Swayamvarabhas parva*, is even more critical of British rule. The land of India is conceived there as a goddess, Adhibharati [literally, the sovereign goddess of India], whose husband, Aryaswami (i.e. the Aryan Hindu ruler), was killed by Yavanik, i.e. the Muslim conquerors. The goddess, after her long period of enslavement to Yavanik, was pestered for her hand by three giants, Saint George, Saint Denis and Saint Nicholas, i.e. England, France, and Russia respectively. Saint George gradually usurped Yavanik's power and falsely claimed that he was the legitimate husband of Adhibharati. The goddess scornfully rejected the claim and asserted that George was no more than a dishonest *diwan* (officer in charge of revenue and civil affairs)—a reference to the Company's *diwani*, who had misused his authority. A lengthy indictment of British rule is then followed by an unequivocal statement from Adhibharati to George: '... Do not bother to give us your unsolicited help. Why don't you go away? My children have no need to become so feeble, 'civilized' and 'educated'. Let them remain unlettered, eat the coarse rice they husk from their paddy, wear clothes made of homespun yarn, and use native slippers. Even then we do not need your jean stockings and boots. Our unrefined ways are preferable [to your ways] a hundred thousand times. We have had enough of your luxurious lifestyle. I have no further desire for your 'benign rule'.'[213] All his attempts to assess the pros and cons of British rule point towards this conclusion, but nowhere else has he been so uncompromisingly explicit.

The Nineteenth Purana is however a fictional statement with strong emotional overtones. Originally entrusted to a student, the text was so extensively altered by Bhudev that the two parts of this incomplete work which appeared in print—*Pushpanjali* and *Swayamvarabhas parva*—were really his writings.[214] These chapters are polemical and didactic in approach and in no sense analytical. His essays aim at a more balanced view of British rule and are free from the impassioned flights of fancy one finds in the allegorical tales. The basic judgements are however not significantly different.

Interestingly, his assessment starts with a rejection of the view he found very much in vogue in Europe, that alien rule was necessarily evil: 'But the history of India does not suggest that the present alien occupation of the country is in every way such a poisonous evil.' Expectedly, the familiar facts—unification and tranquility, national integration, freedom from

invasion—were cited as the main evidence in defence of this position.[215] The
contemporary Indians, he pointed out, did desire a continuation of British
rule in view of these benefits.[216] They took pride in the fact that the heroic
English were now their rulers. The fact that they were foreigners generated
no hatred. Despite his many reservations, discussed below, he did consider
the British empire a fantastic achievement. 'Never before had so few
inhabitants of a country so small acquired such a vast empire so far away.'[217]
The Roman empire at its height covered only a twentieth part of the world's
land surface, the Russian a seventh, while the British already occupied
nearly a sixth, Besides, the other two empires were based on agriculture
and, basically, had a single centre of authority. The British empire, based
on trade, was multicentred, which made the task of governance far more
difficult. Hence, the occupation of India was not the only or even the prime
achievement of this marvellously powerful race, but merely an episode in a
monumental saga.[218]

Bhudev did not draw up any simple balance sheet of British rule listing
points for and against. He systematically explored the characteristic features
of the regime and their historic implications. While he was impressed by
the size and complexity of the empire, he noted that if India were not a
part of it, Britain could not have achieved her position of pre-eminence.
She would then be no more important than Portugal.[219] A very unusual
statement follows; this crucial part of the empire was acquired without any
considerable use of Britain's military might. The establishment of Britain's
hegemony was simply the culmination of a strong trend in Indian history
going back to prehistoric times—the effort at unification. The Indian empire
was thus the end result of objective tendencies manifest as willing and
even enthusiastic acquiescence of the Indian people.[220] This formulation
appears in a different and much more aggressive guise in *The Nineteenth
Purana*: 'My children', says Adhibharati to St George, 'sought your help
to escape from the oppressions of Yavanik ... My sons did not realize that
if given an inch, you would claim all.'[221] The Indian acquiescence is
underlined, but paramountcy becomes less than the fulfilment of the country's
destiny in the formulation.

Bhudev saw the East India Company's commercial role in the early
days of British rule as a positive factor in some ways. The traders' cautious
concern for profit imparted a quality of balance and discretion to British
policy. This was absent, for instance, in the Iberian colonies; the Portuguese
and the Spaniards, representing royal authority, behaved with a certain

measure of arrogance which caused conflicts. By contrast, the English acted with circumspection, taking care to reconcile the defeated. Annexation was gradual and unobtrusive. They openly avowed a policy of non-interference in local religion. Not so the French or the Portuguese. The British based their legal system on the laws of the Hindus and Muslims and, under the Company, showed due respect for Indian customs. 'One can therefore unhesitatingly declare that the English have guided India to her destined path, treated their subjects with great discretion and delicacy and achieved in India what no one else could have done. Thus have they earned the gratitude, respect and devotion of Indians.'[222]

His critique of British rule underlines an important distinction between the Company and the post-Company era. He noted some positive tendencies in the earlier epoch which petered out later on. In an evident reference to the Utilitarian phase[223], he wrote: 'So long as India was under the East India Company, the English used to say, 'We are here to prepare the people of India for self-government' ... The statement was entirely false, but it had one great merit. It expressed beautifully [the belief] that the governance of India must be informed by a very high ideal.' It emphasized an altruistic norm: England's gain from the Indian empire was irrelevant; the object of government was the unification, integration, prosperity, and political development of India. Only a prosperous India would be of benefit to England. Such noble sentiments later gave place to crass expressions of .racial arrogance.[224]

The reality of the Company's rule was, however, seen to be very different from the high ideals. The British in India, exempted from the jurisdiction of the Company's *diwani* courts, enjoyed special status in the eyes of the law. No Bengali then considered it possible that they would be treated in the same way as the English by the Company's government. The police were worse than the outlaws. Landed estates declined in value in the 1830s and the wealth generated by commerce was spent largely in litigation and conspicuous comsumption.[225] Besides, there were the multiple forms of obvious and not so obvious exploitation.[226] Against these negative facts, one noted a growing concern for just and equitable government, especially since Bentinck's benevolent regime and the Act of 1833 which threw open middle-ranking jobs to Indians. 'In fine, the people of this country, having lived long under despotic alien rulers, are now under the power of the relatively more law-abiding English. Can one doubt that they are happier and more independent than before?'[227] When some Muslim king accepted the authority of the courts, the fact was celebrated in popular myths. But the British government accepted the judgement of the courts at every step.[228]

The ways of the English in India, when their attitude was that of traders, were consistent with the familiar principles of Hindu scriptures in matters such as the treatment of defeated princes and non-interference in local religion.[229] There was however a fundamental difference between their outlook as rulers and the one familiar to a longstanding Indian tradition, especially after the decline of the Company's commercial activities. The separation of legislative, judicial, and executive functions ran counter to the Hindu principle wherein the law was vested in the ancient Dharmasastras and interpreted by learned Brahmins. The king's duty was restricted to the preservation of the existing order under scriptural authority. The European political tradition was concerned with an internal balance of power among the king, the nobility, and the common people. This was necessarily absent in India, where the king and his subjects were both expected to act according to the universally accepted *dharmaniti*, virtuous conduct, as prescribed in the scriptures. The English in India did not act consistently in accordance with this code, though their practical farsightedness did introduce an element of righteousness in their administration.[230] This fundamental difference had little to do with the alienness of British rule. Communities, social classes, and political parties in England struggled constantly to reduce one another's power. 'On the one hand, the Indians are unfamiliar with the European principle that people must try to curb royal power; on the other, the British rulers know that they have every right to an unrestricted expansion of their authority unless they are restrained by the subjects.' This contradiction produced a deep-seated conflict. Similarly, the feudal traditions of Norman England predicating the conqueror's 'unqualified right of ownership to all land', delegated to the feudal lords, were transferred to India. The tenurial systems expressed this notion of the state's right to ownership. Whatever the legal position, so long as the ryot was subject to claims to be determined arbitrarily by the ruler, they 'do not see that they have any right' of ownership. In the Hindu tradition, the king was the servant of the people, the one-sixth of the produce paid as revenue was his wage. The English claimed revenue as the proprietor of the land by the right of conquest. Additional taxes could hence be imposed to pay for the cost of other services. The stamp duty payable in the courts of law was an unjust imposition in Indian eyes, a demand for payment for a service which was part of the king's duty.[231]

Bhudev summed up as follows the manifest benefits of British rule: 'In India, the Englishman has fearsome power. His administration is highly disciplined. There is hardly any trace of impudence, inequity or favouritism in his style of action; or the little there is, is carefully camouflaged. Under British rule, there are no foreign invasions of India, no internal wars, no menace of thieves and outlaws. The entire land is at peace. Under British rule, the external commerce is on the increase and inland trade flourishes. The administration of law is just, the press free, knowledge of practical affairs increasing and, through the expansion of education approved by the Europeans, the natives are having their eyes opened to certain things. In short, British rule is a phenomenon without precedent [in India].'[232]

The historic character of this 'unprecedented' phenomenon was best appreciated if one compared it to other empires. The closest parallel was the Roman empire. Like the Romans, the British governed the dependency through officials of their own race, responsible ultimately to their Parliament, the equivalent of the Roman Senate. Both opened schools to teach their own language, but the British paid some attention to local languages as well. The Romans collected taxes to be sent home. What the British took from India was not described as tax. The Romans admitted local deities into their pantheon. The monotheistic British made no overt attempts to undermine Indian religions. Roman law was introduced in the conquered provinces. The legal system of India was modelled on British law.

The sharpest contrast was with the Muslim and Iberian empires where every attempt was made to extirpate local religions. Java under the Dutch offered a different type of contrast; the army there was racially integrated without much discrimination against the subject people. The Javanese were also appointed to some high offices. But while the Government of India had a monopoly only of opium, the Dutch monopolized all the export crops cultivated on the basis of compulsory labour. The Russians had pacified Central Asia, but introduced a regime of extreme exploitation. They had no confidence in the local people and as in western Turkistan so in the new territories, there was very little understanding between the ruler and the ruled. The French sought to wipe out the national identity of Algeria and their other colonies. They offered to confer the rights of Frenchmen on the local people—but only on those who accepted the French legal system *in toto*. This would imply the forsaking of Muslim personal law. The English introduced their own legal system in most colonies, but nowhere had they talked of conferring the rights enjoyed by British citizens.[233]

Even the avowed purpose of British rule changed after the Company era. The Duke of Argyle was the first Secretary of State to declare that its prime object was the permanent subjection of India. Hence followed the conclusion that the careful preservation of British ascendancy in all matters was the best way to benefit Indians. The principle was meant to cover even the privileged status of British offenders.[234]

To repeat, the fact that the British were aliens were in itself not a point against their rule in Bhudev's opinion. Yet he traced some of the major deficiencies of the imperial system to that fact, or rather to attitudes and outlook which derived from one particular alien culture. He referred to Lord Dufferin's statement that the Indian's love for British rule was inspired more by reason than by sentiment. While accepting this judgement, he rejected Dufferin's explanation, viz. differences in language and religion, Indian reluctance to introduce their wives and families to outsiders, etc. These things were no different under the Muslim dynasties, yet the Hindus came much closer to the Muslims than they ever would to the English. There was very little understanding between them even when the highly westernized Bengalis introduced their families to foreigners. The roots of the trouble lay elsewhere. In tune with their own tradition, the English expected to push governmental authority as far as public resistance would allow. The idea of such resistance was alien to Indians. They were only mortified by the rulers' excesses. 'For over a century, the Englishman [in India] has been powerful beyond compare ... His self-confidence and pride are now limitless. He can no longer see his own faults ... He now ascribes everything that is undesirable to other people's ignorance, immorality, incapacity, etc. 'The Indians do not care for me and this may be because of some fault in me'—is not a thought that can enter the Englishman's mind. 'The fact that they do not care for me is indeed due to their own failing': he is firmly convinced that this is so'.[235]

Imperfect sympathy with peoples of other races and cultures was not simply the product of imperial arrogance. It had its roots in the social and political culture of Britain. 'In truth, the Englishman sincerely loves only his own country and considers the rest of the world altogether inferior.'[236] On the other hand, their success in colonizing was unparalleled. It was hence evident that the 'English had no hatred of foreign lands, only of foreigners'. They were perfectly happy if the chosen colony could be transformed to resemble England. They had destroyed the aboriginal populations in their settlements and introduced the English language and law everywhere. Settlers from other countries in such places lost their distinctive identity. The English on the other hand never merged themselves into another culture. They resisted racial admixture, especially with the non-European races. In this they had some affinity with other Teutonic peoples. The Spanish, the Portuguese, the Italians and, up to a point, the French, were rather different. The mingling of races in South America was witness to Iberian attitudes in such matters. Even in French Canada, where the aboriginal peoples were largely destroyed, in parts of the country some 10 per cent of the population was of mixed descent. Bhudev cited the experience of Britain's North American colonies to underline the contrast. His other examples were the fate of the South African Blacks, the Maori and the Australian aborigines. 'Feebler races begin to wither at the very smell of Europeans', he quoted an unnamed author and added, 'The English, beyond doubt, smell stronger than all other Europeans.'

Yet in his view they were the least cruel among European nations. Bhudev compared their record with that of the Spanish in Mexico, Peru, and the West Indies, the Portuguese in Brazil and India, and the French in Canada, Algiers, and Amman. Nowhere had the English been guilty of such cruelty.* Yet it was under them that the aboriginals were most thoroughly exterminated. 'Among other European nations', Bhudev concludes, 'the contempt implicit in their racist attitudes [literally hatred of foreigners] has some mitigating features—there is some concession of humanity to other races. The Spanish, French or other Latin Christians appear to tell people of other races, 'Why should you not be like us? Accept our religion and dress and eat the way we do. Then you will be like us.' This is not the Englishman's attitude. He thinks, 'You are not English. If you want to copy my religion, my codes, manners, language, dress, etc. go ahead and do so. But you can never be my equal, for it is I who am English; you are not'.'[238]

Bhudev saw a remote affinity between such sentiments and the Hindu caste system; a person born into one caste could not move into another. The

---

* Here Bhudev contradicts his own statement concerning the suppression of the Mutiny. He describes the conduct of the English as quite unforgivable.[237] 'The children of the goddess [i.e. the rebels of 1857] were infantile and ignorant. That they persecuted George's officials and their families can be ascribed only to their stupidity. They deserve no dreadful dispraise ... But George's clubmen ... carried out a dreadful massacre, for this one must blame George who considers himself wise. In hundreds of villages all the children of the goddess were killed ... such was George's civilized revenge on his enemies.'

restrictions on social contact among different castes did not however imply mutual hatred. In fact the acceptance of the system provided a basis for consensus and coexistence. The English, more racist than others, did not accept caste and hence were punctilious in maintaining social distance in their anxiety to uphold racial ascendancy.

The vast population of India and their firm commitment to inherited traditions and local languages meant that the country could never be satisfactorily anglicized. The English could not therefore feel any attachment for India. Yet as a dependency, it was a source of profit and power and thus valuable to England. The English recognized that their rule, to be permanent, had to be just. Hence their declared policy of India's welfare. Even a lip service to this ideal helped, for it mitigated the ill-effects of their basic lack of sympathy. Their racism was also restrained by their intelligence, knowledge, and self-discipline, even though it was not altogether absent from their actual policies.[239] Modally, they were unconcerned about the righteousness or otherwise of their public action. They also lacked any understanding of what others might find beneficial. Yet up to a point, they introduced measures from which they themselves had benefited in the belief that these must be good for everyone. They also recognized merit and modified their action accordingly. 'The Englishman is selfish and incapable of sympathy, but he is heroic by nature. He honours ability.'[240]

Despite the ascription of arbitrariness to the Muslim dynasts, Bhudev considered their role superior to that of the British in the final analysis. The Muslims too had united India, established a common language for administration[241], and left behind a splendid heritage in architecture. Above all they had preached the equality of all men and thus contributed to integration. Unlike the British, sunk in *tamas*, i.e. the baser qualities in men, they had a surfeit of *rajas*, worldly vigour, but were lacking in *sattva*, man's transcendental attributes. Thus at least a few Muslims had seats of honour in the temple of Mother India. The British, as already noted, had none.[242] A less complimentary view of the Muslims is taken in *The Nineteenth Purana*, where Yavanik, the symbolic personification of Muslim rule, is described as an 'evil-doer' and plunderer.[243] This negative assessment was, however, counterbalanced by statements appreciative of Muslim rule. It was less exploitative than the British; to wit, Murshid Quli maintained an army of six thousand; under Harding, the number exceeded a quarter of a million.[244] More crucially, the Muslim invaders and converts alike had accepted India as their home and were hence 'foster-brothers' to Hindus.[245] They had also kept the highest offices open to Hindus. Not so the British.[246]

His criticism of British rule was based on a more fundamental value judgement, traceable to his Brahminical ideals. It is best stated in his own words: 'Peace-loving Hindu society has bowed before the Englishman whose [highest] goal is [worldly] happiness. People initiated into the path of renunciation have accepted as their ideal men given to the pursuit of worldly desires. People with high ideals have come under the authority of those with low ones.'[247] This conclusion was derived from his wide-ranging analysis of European culture.

Bhudev's works are replete with detailed criticisms of the British Indian administration. Some of the issues taken up come from an expected territory— the classic formulations of India's economic nationalism: heavy taxation, drainage of resources, destruction of handicraft manufactures, British monopoly of business enterprise, hypocritical policies in matters of Indian recruitment to the higher services and their promotion, and the theme of general decline in standards of living despite some growth in output. The case is argued with considerable intellectual energy. The data cited are impressive in depth and range. Yet what Bhudev has to say on these questions is not significantly different from the analyses one finds in Naoroji, Bholanath Chandra, R.C. Dutt *et al.*[248]

Bhudev's primary emphasis was however on ethical issues. His severest criticisms of British rule were hence based on moral arguments. It had emasculated the people of India by refusing them the use of weapons and access to high ranks in the army. The result was total dependence on Britain in the vital matter of defence and consequent enervation.[249] Exploitative policies were to be condemned not merely because they caused misery: '... if the state's policy is such that people do not enjoy the fruits of their labour, they become naturally averse to all effort.' He cited as evidence the fact that in the temporarily settled areas of India, large parts of the arable land were left uncultivated at the approach of each new settlement.[250] Powers of coercion were earlier vested in society to a large extent. Now it was a state monopoly. The state punished only crime. Society took cognizance of vice and sin as well. Its aim was the maintenance of a moral order and a minimum level of welfare for all. Even the offender was not merely a person to be punished. Judicial authority had passed from the rural councils to the zamindars or the courts of law under the British. The latter were often administered by foreigners who had no knowledge of India. The impersonal and expensive justice had led to increased litigation and financial ruin for many. Besides, the legal system was out of tune with social values.[251]

The decline in norms which went with colonial regimes had affected the ruler as much as the ruled. Bengalis had discovered that the English loved a good feast, and hence resources which could be devoted to the welfare of society were now wasted on grand receptions to officials. The first four lieutenant-governors of Bengal were unostentatious in their ways. But Campbell demanded fireworks and grand illumination for his official visits. There was no looking back ever since. The lieutenant-governors become devoted diners and winers. Their underlings, down to the level of petty officers, 'began to go around feasting at the expense of the natives'.[252] While there were a few worthy people in their ranks, Bhudev saw mainly four types among the British officials in India: (1) oppressors, (2) those who favoured people of their own race, (3) superficial observers and (4) persons full of contempt for India. At the other end of the spectrum, there were the men of good will who truly loved India. Bhudev records one incredible scene: a sober Englishman literally dancing with joy when the first Indian mill was established.[253]

That short-sighted and malicious officials could pervert official policy was proved by the practice of *divide et impera*, learnt from the history of imperial Rome as taught in English schools. Divide and rule was not official policy, but the less enlightened official sought to found on it the permanence of Britain's Indian empire. Hence, the persistent vilification of Muslim rule in India and the practice of tempting Muslims with a show of favour.[254]

He was in no doubt as to the immorality of Britain's expansionist policies based in India. He refers in his *History of Bengal* to the Afghan War during Lord Auckland's Governor-Generalship, as follows: 'That war was launched at the will of the British Cabinet of Ministers; hence Lord Auckland cannot be blamed totally for that action.'[255] His comment on the Opium War was even more explicit. 'Nobody can tell what the future holds; but this Chinese War remains a good example of the fact that virtue does not always triumph. In fact victory often lies with the unrighteous.'[256] Europe's ascendancy, he argued at length,[257] was a grand illustration of this unhappy *obiter*.

With all his reservations, Bhudev welcomed the fact that Britain, rather than any other power, ruled over India. He did so because 'in politics, all other nations looked upon them as the ideal'. They never loosened their hold until faced with indubitable evidence of political ability and quit whenever this stage was reached. Association with the English was thus the best possible training in politics.[258]

Bhudev saw no reason for shame in the fact of conquest. All uncivilized peoples loved war and hence excelled at it.[259] 'The ignorant Spartans defeated the learned Athenians, the barbarians of Macedon conquered Greece ... uncivilized barbarian tribes destroyed the Roman empire ...' The *Pax Britannica* in India was a testimony not so much to English might as to the Hindu love of peace. The English did not quite understand this because forbearance or love of peace was no part of the European tradition.[260] Mutual envy and reckless pursuit of worldly goals drove the Europeans to endless conflict within their own societies and to aggressive expansion all over the world.[261]

Bhudev does fall back on stereotypes in his analysis from time to time. The emphasis however is on the identification of long-term tendencies in a given culture. He traces their origins to a dynamic interaction among the values of a society, its systems of belief, and historical trends.

In the *Essay on Society*, the critique of European civilization begins with an assessment of Christian beliefs. It was argued that a shared faith implied a homogeneity in cultural outlook and hence the Christian nations of Europe had many attributes in common. Christianity rejected predetermination or the doctrine of *karma*, the belief that man's fate in lives to come is decided by the results of his actions. It recognized Divine will alone as the root cause of the universe and all that pertained to it. The Christians were monotheists who believed that the universe had a finite beginning in time. This was very different from the non-dualistic concept of Brahman.[262] Christian dogma based on the sayings of Christ affirmed the notion of eternal damnation or eternal heaven at God's will. Virtue and sin were clearly denoted and knowledge thereof not seen to be dependent, as in Hindu belief, on spiritual discipline. For a Christian, heaven or hell might be the just dessert for the life one has lived, but salvation depended on Divine grace. Moreover, it was one's faith and sectarian faith at that, rather than one's actions that drew upon one's head Divine wrath or grace and thus determined one's fate in eternity. The literature, history, and philosophy of Europe were permeated by this belief and thence it had passed into the European psyche as an ever-present current of thought.[263]

The notion that everything in the universe ultimately depended on the Divine will might have subtle and profound meaning for the wise and the virtuous. Bhudev saw it as a dangerous doctrine for the less enlightened. For them, it inspired at best the smug belief that the knowledge of spiritual truth required no patient quest; that right and wrong were clearly demarcated, given 'facts', not something one hoped at best to glimpse through a lifelong search.[264] On the other hand, the absence of any belief in the inevitable consequences of one's actions in future lives had been morally disastrous for the common people in Europe. There was nothing to check their proneness to act as they pleased. 'No other society on earth has produced such malevolent, turbulent, reckless and selfish people.' They had no notion of peace or contentment. Sadistic violence was their normal mode of conduct. European societies were like so many battlefields, arenas for internecine conflict among different groups and communities. Nations and national solidarity emerged more out of such conflicts and mutual pressures than any sense of affinity or spontaneous mergers. Each nation was engaged in perpetual conflict with its neighbours. Internecine conflicts had to be suppressed out of necessity under such conditions; solidarity was essential for military discipline. These perceived needs provided the basis for such ethical principles as obedience to one's leader, loyalty to one's side, etc.[265] But since violence had become a way of life, there was no moral restraint on limitless oppression of other, especially non-European, peoples.[266] The very demeanour of the common people in Europe seemed to betray their descent from the barbarian tribes who destroyed the Roman empire.[267]

The barbarian origins were important; in England, for instance, the laws and customs of the barbarous Anglo-Saxons later developed into the civilized codes of modern Britain.[268] The dominant traits of modern European culture were thus determined by long-term historical forces. In this context, the fact that the barbarian conquerors adopted Roman law and the religion of the vanquished was emphasized. Christianity, as already noted, could act as no check on their violent and criminal propensities, because it denied that a man's future was determined inexorably by his present actions. The native wickedness of these uncivilized races could thus flourish. Roman law, glorifying wealth and individual rights to property, aggravated their natural proneness towards the pursuit of pleasure and self-interest, without any moral constraint. Their religion prescribed the conversion of all mankind to Christianity, but they rushed around the world in the quest of wealth rather than converts. 'The piracy of the ancestors is now camouflaged by devotion to commerce. Yet, a native wickedness and hankering for gross pleasures remain the essential features of the European character.'

Both Christianity and Islam derived from the Jewish faith and all three denied predetermination—the binding consequences of one's actions. The absence of this belief removed a major restraining influence. Islam however did not adopt Roman law or the Roman addiction to bodily pleasures, intermingled with superstitious beliefs, for it emerged when the empire was in ruins. Nor did the Muslims accept the agnosticism of decadent Greek and Latin scholars. Their wars of conquest were inspired by religious zeal, manifest in the actual practice of equality prescribed in their faith, and not by any love of plunder. The egalitarian principle, also preached but never practised by Christians, explained Islam's spectacular success.[269]

To repeat, Bhudev's enquiry into the civilization of Europe had only one ostensible purpose: to find out what India should learn from Europe. Its real object was to stem the tide of western influence. Early in his analysis, he contrasts English and Hindu society, as the former represented Europe in India and was most likely to be imitated. His conclusion emerges from this exercise, like a proved theorem in geometry: 'By nature, Hindu society is marked by love of peace and contentment; by nature English society is marked by skill and efficiency in the pursuit of worldly happiness. Hindu society is mainly agricultural, the English mainly industrial and commercial. Hindu society is based on joint ownership of property and recognized the right to joint ownership, the English recognize primogeniture and are strongly in favour of individual rights. Child marriage is in vogue among the Hindus; marriage between adults is the usual practice in England. The Hindu prefers social control over internal matters, in matters of government the English are anxious to maintain the supremacy of state power. In India these two mutually contrasted societies have come into conflict. The English are work-oriented, skilful, vain and greedy, the Hindus are industrious, gentle and contented. All that the Hindus can learn from the English is their efficiency in matters practical and nothing else.' Bhudev concluded, 'In truth it is better that they do not learn anything else.'[270]

This unqualified value judgement is then supported by a detailed enquiry into western attitudes. The list begins with selfishness, especially strong among the English who, in Bhudev's opinion, were inherently selfish. He recognized however, a quality of innocence, born of narcissistic egotism. Totally absorbed in the pursuit of self-interest, they sincerely believed that there was never any contradiction between their selfish goals and the demands of morality: 'Whatever is to their interest, they find consistent with their sense of what is right at all times.' The very depth of their selfishness deprived them of the quality of sympathy. The Englishman 'fails to understand how his happiness cannot be the source of universal bliss'. 'A childlike infatuation [with self-interest] shrouds the English mind.' Apparently, anyone who had come into contact with them was aware of this trait in their personality. '... So long as the English receive any benefit or help, they are very fond of you. As soon as they think that there was nothing more to be gained, they fail to recall the benefits received.' One wonders if this bitter statement had anything to do with the letters which Hodgson Pratt never received and hence never answered.[271] The evidence Bhudev cited to illustrate this self-regarding incapacity to see the other person's point of view was however drawn from history. When the Greeks of the Ionian island wanted union with independent Greece, the English genuinely wondered why the islanders should seek to forsake the joys of British rule. Similarly, despite their prolonged conflict with Afghanistan, they were evidently convinced that the Afghans loved them dearly. The Burmese too had been waiting eagerly to be conquered. When King Thibaw lost his throne, their joy knew no bounds. Those among the Burmese who were less than jubilant were of course rebels and bandits. Such simple faith might appear to be hypocritical to others, but in truth it was rooted in a blind infatuation with self-interest. In this, the English were unique. The French, for instance, had conquered Algeria and the Russians Turkmenistan, without claiming that the conquered races were eagerly waiting for such blissful subjection and were gratified by the act of conquest. Evidently he had not heard of *la mission civilisatrice*.

A tail piece rounded off this particular assessment. A man carrying a pigeon when asked what he wanted to do with it replied, 'I shall keep it as a pet.' The questioner commented with compassion, 'Why should you kill this God's creature? Give it to me. Let me roast and eat it.' The English 'may roast and eat [a living being]. That is not killing. When another man tries to keep a pet, that is.'[272]

Bhudev concedes another redeeming feature in this pervasive selfishness—an identification of self-interest with the interest of the nation. 'To a large extent, the English do not differentiate between their personal and national interest.' They were 'always intent on the pursuit of national interest, vociferous in the praise of their countrymen, and furious at any

criticism of their people.'[273] It was this patriotism and not the selfishness
which explained their success. The latter quality might lead to their decline.[274]

As a reaction to this excess of selfishness, there was a new trend in
society concerned with the welfare of others. It might bear some fruit in the
future, but Bhudev disapproved of the new philanthropic-bureaucratic
doctrines because they rejected tradition and professed libertarian views
likely to undermine society.[275]

The idea of progress was the second most important attribute of the
western outlook. It assumed progress to be the law of nature—manifest in
the evolution of species culminating in the emergence of the *homo sapiens.*
The same principle was seen to be evident in the development of human
society; and the civilization of modern Europe was the final product. In
Bhudev's view, this self-perception of superiority—most acute among the
English who considered their own ways alone worthwhile[276]—was no
different from that of older societies which described alien cultures with a
variety of pejoratives like 'barbarians', *mlechchhas*, etc. It was necessary to
examine the notion only because it was all pervasive in western social
theories.[277] Bhudev recognized that Social Darwinism was interpreted in a
variety of ways. While one school assumed a purpose in evolution, viz.
progress towards greater happiness, which was identified as progress, others
denied the notion of purpose, but nevertheless perceived in evolution a
trend towards greater well-being. Still others saw evolution as nothing more
than survival through adaptation and change. While this last view was more
acceptable than others, it still failed to take note of the threefold attribute of
all natural phenomena—origin, existence, and destruction—identified in
Indian philosophy.[278] Besides, there was no evidence of unilinear progress
in history. Modern Europe was by no means an all-round improvement on
ancient Egypt, Persia, Greece or Rome. Her children were not physically
stronger than the armour-bearing soldiers of past ages, or, for that matter,
the sturdy Indian sepoy. If Greek sculpture was any indicator, the past
excelled the present in grace and beauty of form. As for human intelligence,
one could only judge it by its products—technological development, social
organization, literary output, etc. Bhudev considered the literary-intellectual
products to be man's highest achievement. By this criterion, the past excelled
because the ancient classics were still the ideals the modern writers aspired
to emulate. Modern Europe had not produced men comparable to Plato,
Aristotle, Archimedes, or the Antonines, partly because the new system of

education was narrow in scope and not concerned, as in the past, with all aspects of the human personality. The one positive development of modern times in this sphere, the limited spread of education among the masses, had not induced any improvement in their nature or ethical conduct.[279] The notion of unilinear progress went against the basic diversity of human society. 'Man's code of conduct, behaviour, religion and government will differ from country to country. Only those without any discrimination or sense of reality seek to mould everyone into a uniform shape. All human beings can never be alike. Nor is it desirable that they should be so ...'[280]

Political economic theory projected the notion of social progress and identified division of labour as a root cause. No doubt such divisions, which went with the technological revolution and the growth of world-wide commerce, increased the output of consumer goods and contributed indirectly to the development of civilization by increasing the leisure of the affluent classes. But working people, Bhudev argued, had benefited nothing from labour-saving technology. In fact, they had lost such leisure as they had and become like machines, divested of their basic humanity. The new technology reduced the demand for labour and thus pushed down wages. The wealth it generated went to the capitalist. Increasing disparity of wealth fostered deep discontent and thus was a threat to the social order. Besides, the limitations of the domestic market and the competition with other countries induced a desperate quest for markets abroad and colonies and thence to the evils that followed inevitably from colonization.[281]

Bhudev's faith in the inherently superior wisdom of Indian society was brought to bear on this discussion. He questioned the view that the transition from mutually exclusive hereditary occupations—the economic basis of the caste system—to unchecked mobility was necessarily a sign of progress. He saw in the trade union movement an analogue of caste solidarity and noted its role as a check on the unrestrained rapacity of employers.[282] Here was one more evidence of the inadequacy of 'progress' in modern times and the fact that at least some Indian institutions could be usefully adopted in the West.

While progress was in no way a law of nature, it could be a legitimate and practicable goal of human societies. This was so because man was unique among the natural species in their awareness of self which produced a will to achieve. It was possible to break away from the cyclical course of natural phenomena through its exercise. Man could self-consciously define and achieve given goals. Bhudev's example of such potentiality in a way sums up his assessment of contemporary western civilization: 'If the Europeans decide to achieve only the beneficial results of division of labour and mechanization to the exclusion of their unwholesome consequences, they can give up their desire to sell their manufactures all over the world by force and deceit and produce only what is needed for their own use and for honest trade. In that case, people in other parts of the world do not suffer and their own workers are spared after a few hours of work [per day].'[283] Besides, he added elsewhere, 'human will was only one factor in shaping man's destiny'. Predestination—or accidents of birth, in more pragmatic terms—and social circumstances were its other determinants.[284]

Bhudev described the principle underlying human progress in terms of ideals deliberately defined and pursued. As ideals in a given time period are compared and contrasted, new ideals emerge and their achievement shifts the goal farther and farther through a continuous process of refinement. But changing values may imply a different pattern of shifts. What is acceptable at one time may cease to be so in another.[285] Bhudev noted in western perceptions a total absence of cultural relativism. Europe graded cultures as 'civilized', 'semi-civilized', 'barbarian', 'stagnant' or 'progressive' on the basis of criteria such as the development of scepticism or social equality or even more crudely, the level of material progress. Technological development, increased output of cheap manufactured goods, increase in wealth or lip service to the principle of equality were not indicative of progress. He suggested, instead, an idealistic basis for the assessment of human cultures— the refinement of ideals and the intensity of effort for their realization. Ideals could be judged in terms of their content of love and sympathy for other beings, the ultimate basis of virtuous conduct.[286] In terms of his two-fold criteria, a society might move forward or backward or stand still.

Bhudev found the ideals of Christian Europe very inadequate by this standard. First, the Christian ideal was embodied in the lives of Jesus and Mary and as such incomplete because they offered no model which men and women involved in a worldly existence could emulate. Christ's saintly life was terminated in youth. His celibate career could offer no guidance to a householder nor did he strive to achieve any public good. Thus Christian Europe had no practical ideal to live by in their everyday life. Besides, it was even doubtful if Europeans had ever accepted seriously the lives of Jesus and Mary as something they could imitate. In the absence of ideals, the instinctive drives like greed* dominated their lives. Christ's words—'It is easier for a camel to pass through the eye of a needle than for a rich man to enter the gates of heaven'—had had the most unfortunate consequences.[287] There was no objective truth in this saying inspired by simple-hearted other-worldliness. But it induced, on the one hand, the monastic rejection of worldly life, and, on the other, limitless greed among those who lived by it.[288] Yet, by virtue of their great enterprise, the Europeans had achieved a quality of dynamism and vitality in their civilization. Besides, though lacking in high ideals of human life, they were concerned with high standards in things material and a formidable capacity to produce such things. The externals of European life could hence mislead one about the real state of their civilization. A close look at their manners and morals however revealed its imperfect and decadent state; their inadequate ideals implied a flawed culture and their indifference even to these was an indicator of decline.[289] By contrast, the Hindus with their ideals of perfection embodied in Rama and Sita represented a higher civilization as did Islam, blessed with the example of the Prophet's life. Only, the Hindu civilization was stagnant, because there was no longer any effort to live up to the high ideals.[290]

But Bhudev rejected without qualification the view—projected by the British and echoed by educated Indians—that the former had improved Indian morals.[291] English ethics had nothing new to offer and lacked much that was contained in Indian notions of morality. European ethics, he pointed out, were derived from Greece, Rome, the ancient Germans, Judaism, and Christianity. The Greeks extolled freedom, patriotism and courage. They also had a highly developed aesthetic sensibility—a sense of physical as well as mental beauty. The Romans, on the other hand, were a fierce people, their animal instincts modified only by their law-abiding conduct. The ancient Germans, habitually given to brigandage, were even more turbulent than the Romans, but civilized in their treatment of women and the practice of monogamy. Their way of life entailed a penchant for group solidarity. The Jews were intolerant of other faiths and entirely worldly in outlook. Of all the sources of European morals, Christianity alone projected a faith in the life hereafter and the terrifying results of sin. It also preached the virtues of peacefulness, humility, and charity. Such merits, however, were counterbalanced by a simple dichotomous view of the world which damned

* Bhudev used the word *ripu*, i.e. 'enemy' in this context. The six 'enemies' in the Hindu tradition are lust, anger, greed, infatuation, pride, and envy.

a large part of humankind—all who were not Christians. Christians, especially Catholics, had no compunction in oppressing or destroying people thus condemned. The Spanish and the Portuguese had tyrannized over non-European races in the belief that they were the devotees of Satan. Second, the Christian doctrine of grace denied that man must inevitably suffer the consequences of his actions. Punishment or reward depended on the Divine will. This attribution of arbitrariness to God had removed all restraint on man's conduct, especially among the Protestants.

Derived from these diverse sources, the English ethical norms emphasized freedom, patriotism, courage, aesthetic sensibility, respect for law, monogamy, group solidarity, and an inclination to act as one liked. There was conflict in values—between the intolerance of other faiths and races as well as worldliness derived from the Jews and the Christian love of peace, humility, charity, and fear of sin. Such conflict was likely to reduce the intensity of both the virtues and vices in question. Similarly, the arrogance characteristic of ancient Germans counterbalanced Christian humility and the two attributes were unevenly distributed, depending on the circumstances of individual lives. The validity of this assessment, Bhudev concluded, should be apparent to those familiar with the way in which the English actually lived and not merely with what they wrote in their books.

The Hindu norms contained all the positive values of European ethics plus such ideals as surrender to the Divine will and, through Vedanta, a sense of identity with the entire universe. The Hindu ideals of purity, freedom from desire, and dedication of the self to the service of others were also, in his view, absent from the European tradition. He referred to the impure lives of the Greeks and the Romans, the unmentionable practices of even the truly great among them (a reference, presumably, to homosexuality). He also criticized the Christian belief in the separation of body and soul, and the implicit notion that the sins of the body did not pollute the soul. Thus, in matters of morality, the only thing Hindus need learn from the English was their skill in achieving solidarity. Those who thought that a sense of beauty had also to be learnt from the ruling race had not seen the great southern temples.

A basic deficiency of European morality lay in the inadequacies of social control. In contrast to the traditional Indian system, society as distinct from the state had no power to punish in Europe. The state punished only crime, not sin or vice. In two phases of European history, this unwholesome dichotomy had been rejected—through the appointment of Censors in Rome and in England under Cromwell. Puritan England, to Bhudev's understanding, marked the true beginning of Britain's glory because Cromwell refused to distinguish between crime and sin and punished both with an even hand. The English then made no distinction between their public and private lives. 'The current view that one's public function was a legitimate object of scrutiny, but nobody had the right to enquire into what one did at home was then unheard of. At that point in time the English stood forth resplendent in their defiant courage and great strength.'[292]

The Christian view that it was for God to punish sin and for the state to punish crime had been questioned by Auguste Comte. Besides, the upper classes in Europe did accept an authority other than that of God and the state. Codes of civilized conduct were with them an important determinant of behaviour,[293]—the decisive hallmark of a 'gentleman'. The civilized ways of the privileged in Europe had, in Bhudev's perception, another layer of meaning. He spoke of a universal tendency in human society—the contradiction between man's bodily functions as an animal and his higher consciousness—which induced a feeling of distress. Hindus had tried to solve this apparent contradiction through their perception of non-duality— the inseparability of consciousness and ultimate reality from the mundane acts of eating, sleeping, or procreation. The awareness was enshrined in daily ritual. Europeans who drew a clear line between their worldly and spiritual dimensions of life abhorred the idea of religiosity in every action. But they too felt the need to spread a cover of decency over man's animal functions. Eating had ceased to be a purely physical act to satisfy one's hunger and formed the basis of a graceful social ritual—with polite conversation, music, dance, etc. This concern for decency did not however extend to all their activities. The habit of imbibing strong drinks, for instance, induced shameless behaviour.[294]

The Hindu tradition recognized multiple sources of authority to guide their lives—the Dharmasastras, the king, traditional practice, and the words of wise and good men. The generality of European people recognized only the authority of the state. The state however had power to deal only with the cruder deviations from morality and in the absence of any other check, the lower orders in Europe indulged their animal instincts without restraint.[295] For Bhudev, the fact was evident in their coarse humour and unabashed use of obscene language.[296] There was a further reason for such unrestrained conduct. Europe received her religion, Christianity, from an alien race, the

Jews, and necessarily rejected the latter's codes of ritual conduct. Thereby
a common and potential source of restraint on their conduct was removed
'and it is for this reason that the lower classes in Europe have remained
bestial in their ways.'[297]

The encounter between India and Europe had produced one very positive
consequence. The missionary criticism of the Hindu religion had induced
an emphasis on the dualistic devotional strand in the Indian tradition. On
the other hand, some German philosophers recognized the identity of their
views with India's non-dualistic philosophy, directly or indirectly. Bhudev
cited Hegel and Schopenhauer as instances of the new trend, especially the
latter's view that the new interest in the Indian tradition might induce a
second Renaissance in Europe. The English too were beginning to give up
their narrow interpretation of Christianity and coming closer to the universal
tolerance of Hindu thought. In other words, the crass materialism of
nineteenth-century Europe was seen to be a passing phase. Here indeed
was the prospect of true progress in terms of Bhudev's categories.[298]

Of all European philosophers, the one Bhudev found most acceptable
was Auguste Comte. This was a preference he shared with many of his
fellow intellectuals in Bengal. In his case, the preference was no doubt
especially traceable to the role ascribed by Comte to the priestly class—
whom Bhudev identified with the Brahmins in the Indian context—teachers
and rulers in future societies. He commented at some length on Comte's
predictions for the future of mankind. He accepted the possibility that religious
differences would disappear in the future, but thought it more likely that
pantheism of the Advaita variety rather than humanism with its worship of
man would be the future religion of mankind.[299] He was less convinced of
the prospect of an end to wars and racial differences for he considered the
causes of these phenomena to be rooted in the nature of man and society.[300]
Nor did he see much sign of any end to the efforts to establish large empires.
In his perception, the contemporary trend in Europe was towards the
formation of empires which would include entire ethnic groups—the Germans
under Prussia, the Slavs under Russia and so on. The trend, helped by the
mutual sympathies within an ethnic group, could be frustrated by clashes of
self-interest. The Slavonic peoples of the Balkans might fight against Turkey
but were no less suspicious of Russia. The Anglo-Saxon colonies of England
were not inclined to sacrifice in the cause of the mother country. Local
autonomy rather than imperial unification might well be the future pattern,
but the roots of imperialism—inequality—were unlikely to be eradicated.[301]

Bhudev foresaw for the British empire an indefinitely long future. For the factors which explained the decline of empires in the past were not yet present in this case. The characteristic love of ease produced by great wealth which marked the beginning of decline was not a feature of British life because the ruling classes—whether as students at Oxbridge or colonial officials—were devoted to manly sports and vigorous physical activity. A second cause of decline, centrifugal tendencies engendered by excessive expansion, had failed to undermine the empire. Witness its vigorous survival after the loss of the American colonies. The third likely cause—defeat at the hands of a stronger nation—was also improbable, because Germany would be no match until she absorbed Holland and Denmark. Russia, similarly, would first need to bring Turkey and Afghanistan under control. Besides, France would act as a check on the growth of Germany and Germany and Austria on that of Russia. Again, though England's exports to Europe had suffered a decline, in many countries including India these were on the increase. There was hence no sign of any decline in England's imperial fortunes in the foreseeable future.[302] One wonders if Bhudev, who had a firm faith in the immutable cycle of origin-existence-destruction as valid for all phenomena, really considered the British empire an exception to a universal law. Was it his caution as an official sharpened, perhaps, by the experience of others like Bankim, who had to pay for their outspoken views on the empire, a factor in the judgement? There is no evidence to justify a clear answer to this query.

In one of his eassys[303] Bhudev states clearly his faith in the progress of mankind based on Hindu ideals. He scoffed at the English-educated babus who had derived from Utilitarianism and the German theory of culture a faith in happiness as man's ultimate goal. Such people failed to appreciate the inherent superiority of societies wherein the individual's primary concern was peace and contentment.[304] Following Comte he affirmed the excellence of cultures in which the priestly class was dominant. Hence the greatness of Brahminical culture. '... If truth be more powerful than untruth, unselfishness superior to selfishness and the pure way of knowledge better than the impure path of emotionally coloured judgements, then certainly Hindu society will achieve its central purpose, i.e., absorb all other Indian cultures and spread to Europe and the entire world the light of true knowledge and virtue. The way of knowledge has been cleared by Bacon, Descartes, Kant and others. The splendour of Hindu scriptures will exceed theirs and just as the Hindus have given China, Japan and the rest of Asia the light of faith, they will bring to Europe an even purer, brighter light of ineffable charm.'[305] This dream of a spiritual conquest with Europe as disciple, shared by others, inspired much of Vivekananda's action. More than the self-assertion of cultural nationalism, such aspirations probably express the need to overcompensate for the fact of subjection and the deprivations, both material and psychological, which went with it. In Bhudev's case, his genuine belief in the superiority of Brahminical values meant a necessary equation between progress and its supremacy.

In his check list of western attitudes, the emphasis on equality comes third—after selfishness and faith in progress. He traced its roots to Christianity. He identified in this context two types of religions—the ones like Hinduism and Buddhism which he described as 'naturalistic' and the others like Judaism, Christianity and Islam which were 'emotive'. The former, based on the analysis of the phenomenal world, emphasized causality—the inevitable cycle of action and its consequences. It conceived the Divinity as bereft of human attributes, eternal, and all pervasive. Knowledge was its preferred way to salvation. The emotive religions, by contrast, arose from introspection into human concerns and ascribed the emotions of charity, compassion, and anger to God. Prayer and Divine grace and punishment were central to these faiths. So was human will as a determinant of man's destiny. The naturalistic religions, by contrast, saw an inexorable causal link between man's action and its results. Neither Divine grace nor man's will could alter the iron law. The hard path of naturalistic faiths was of course the superior way in Bhudev's perception. The need for examples of sanctity in this life on earth, which generated the doctrine of incarnations and prophets, while understandable, implied a deviation from truth. In these terms, the movements in Hinduism away from non-duality and the path of ritually prescribed conduct into devotionalism indicated decline, a sign of growing weakness.

The doctrine of equality was, however, the one apparently superior attribute of the religions based on human emotions. It derived from the observed fact of similarity, but by negating the equally observable fact of difference, it generated an emotion without any pragmatic foundation but nevertheless crucial. Equality was not a fact of nature—'even one grain of sand was not equal to another'—and by attributing man's emotional preference for equality to God, this doctrine confused one's understanding of the universe and rendered, as it were, divine action itself justiciable.

Despite this basic weakness, the protagonists claimed for it a number of beneficial results—a check on man's injustice to man, a concern for the welfare of common man, and a universal impetus to human hope and aspiration. Such claims, Bhudev conceded, were valid up to a point and egalitarian ideas appealed to the suffering masses precisely for this reason. So great was the appeal that these were invoked even in the least likely circumstances—by the English in India, for instance. Bhudev listed the multiple limitations of this false doctrine—how it diminished charity and contentment and aggravated envy, hatred, and spurious ambition. He saw an inherent contradiction between the instinctive drive to excel and the professions of equality. The end result was often no more than a hypocritical pretence of equality alongside an anxious concern to maintain a hierarchical order. The Americans, for instance, who referred to their servants as 'home help' set even greater store by wealth than the English. In fact wealth was the only criterion of status in America. Birth or even education was of little concern. Thus in practice, equality was seldom anything more than a cliché. Even the much-vaunted abolition of slavery was motivated by self-interest because the new technology rendered free labour cheaper than slaves. Inequality was a fact of life derived from nature itself. The 'naturalistic' religions, by which Bhudev really meant Hinduism, recognized it and because of their deep faith in natural or inborn excellence prescribed a hierarchy of birth manifest in the caste system. The system had *inter alia* one great merit: it pushed wealth down to a low rung on the scale of values. Learning, excellence in practical action, seniority, high birth, and wealth were, in his view, the five acceptable criteria of social hierarchy, in that order. In fact, every society accepted these though the order of precedence might vary. Europe had accepted the least worthy of these—money—as the most important. Such a system of values might inspire enterprise, but it was also the source of much that was evil—greed, envy, deceit, and a restlessness of spirit.

If Christianity was one source of the doctrine of equality, the other was the French Revolution,[306] which paradoxically was also seen to be the root cause of the new emphasis on money. To Bhudev, the French Revolution was the beginning of the third, i.e. the modern, age in European history. In his account, the fall of the Roman empire marked the beginning of the second age which ended with the French Revolution. The doctrines of liberty, equality, and fraternity had since been accepted as axiomatic truths. The factors which generated this ideology induced through the Revolution some short- and long-term changes both in France and elsewhere—decline in clerical power, representative government, expropriation of feudal landed property, equality in the eyes of law, expansion of state activities for public welfare, etc. In short, 'the great lesson of the French Revolution was that social effort should have as its steadfast object the welfare of the people.'[307]

'The great lesson' was however flawed, for it was the product, not of any induction into ethical conduct, but of a violent revolution with its 'polluted doctrine of equality'. The emphasis on equality was spurious; it simply expressed the aspirations of the commercial classes for wealth and power through trade and industry. In one of his essays[308] Bhudev discussed the evolution of state and government in terms of the progressive curtailment of royal power by countervailing sources of authority—priests and aristocrats. In the USA and some parts of Europe, state power had passed into the hands of men who had grown wealthy through trade and industry. 'But even in Europe', he concluded, 'the mass of the people have no power till now.' The Revolution so inspired, merely replaced inequality of birth with inequality of wealth. 'There was no end to inequality—only a slight change in its direction.'[309] In fact, the technological revolution which took place around the same time increased inequality and the misery of the working people.[310]

An excessive preoccupation with money was, to Bhudev, one of the least acceptable features of western society and a major reason why Hindus must reject their ethical and social norms. The apotheosis of money made the westerner hesitant to accept or give financial help even where close relatives were concerned. In India, not helping a sibling was social anathema. The shockingly different western norms were illustrated from the lifestory of Garfield who paid his elder sister for board and lodging and the latter accepted it, for otherwise the boy would be too embarrassed to stay at his brother-in-law's. The honourable young man also took out a life insurance when he borrowed some money from his elder brother and the creditor gratefully accepted the certificate of insurance as a guarantee of repayment. These actions, Bhudev noted, are mentioned by the biographer as laudable instances of close fraternal ties. But the biography had nothing to say as to how Garfield treated his siblings when he became the President.[311]

There was no rational reason, Bhudev pointed out, why financial help should be considered taboo. Unless one treated money as the measure of all things, other forms of help which were acceptable in the West were often of much greater value to the giver and the recipient alike. The taboo was thus an indicator of the supreme importance attached to money.[312]

Another expression of this apotheosis was the virtual extinction of hospitality in Europe. Significantly, the westernized Indian were beginning to emulate their preceptors. Bhudev traced this meanness of spirit to self-centred individualism, economic competition among nations, and the breathless anxiety that went with the single-minded pursuit of wealth. He feared that if Indians adopted the western ideals, their social mores in matters of hospitality would suffer correspondingly.[313]

Norms of conduct which idealized selfishness helped aggravate the inequalities of wealth. Since neither charity nor the duty to look after one's kith and kin were acceptable values in Europe, the poor in the West were worse off compared to even the most miserable in India. Thirty-eight per cent of the people above the age of sixty-five in England and Wales ended up in the workhouse, he pointed out.[314]

Bhudev saw a direct causal connection between the growing inequality and the ideologies aiming at a more just society, especially socialism which emphasized social ownership of property: 'If the awareness of corporate rights were not lost through an excessive concern for commercial advantage and if they did not consider that awareness a sign of barbarity or backwardness because it did not conform to their values, then there would have been no such eagerness to establish social ownership as we find in Europe today.' This new anxiety, which had not yet borne any fruit, was simply the reverse side of selfishness, the cornerstone of Europe's political, social, and family system. Bhudev saw no potentialities of 'real progress' in the new ideologies, for 'the more comprehensive truth emerged by absorbing all earlier experience', not through their rejection. The new ideologues had little respect for tradition. They often preached libertarian ideas, which declared sensual gratification to be the highest good, considered efforts to restrain the instinctive drives illegitimate and refused to be bound by the dictates of religion. In his Malthusian anxiety, Bhudev included in this list of unacceptable ideas also the view that there was no need to control the increase in population.[315] He went on to discuss various social experiments with marriage and family which had failed disastrously, creating more bondages than they broke. His conclusion is a classic statement of conservative ideology: 'The body social, in fact, is not like the potter's clay images to be shaped at will; born like animal or plant bodies it grows gradually. It is not even possible to operate on it to any great extent'.[316]

Bhudev discussed the nihilist-anarchist ideal of abolition of governmental authority, the logical conclusion of social evolution, and the doctrine of social ownership of all property as integral parts of the same doctrine. The first was unacceptable because the authority of the state emerged from felt needs. Such needs would have disappeared if men, through education and habit, had reached a level of morality where self-control rendered external sanctions irrelevant. Bhudev considered the prospect of such perfectness very dubious, judging by the record to date. He found the example of Europe particularly discouraging. '... the effort to conquer other people's lands is on the increase and becomes more intense with time among the Europeans: there is a sharp edge to their thirst for material pleasures and it keeps getting sharper; these do not indicate any enhancement of moral standards or any prospect thereof.' So long as they did not give up their obsessive concern for acquiring other people's territories by hook or by crook, any ascription of moral improvement to them would be misplaced. 'In truth, it would be logical to conclude that their descendants also would inherit their penchant for marauding ... If thus Europe does not need external control, who does?'[317]

As noted earlier, Bhudev traced the inequality of wealth in European society to defects in social organization and the absence over many generations of any education in unselfishness. Hence, the way to correct the evil was to attend to such failings. He however emphasized the egalitarians' failure to note one irreducible cause of inequality—the inherent differences in ability as well as the capacity for and proneness to effort. Even if every other source of inequality was ironed out, it would inevitably reappear. Hence the egalitarian doctrines were rooted in man's wish for a better world, not in reason.[318]

He also saw a causal relationship between the social organization of Russia and France and the influence of egalitarian doctrines. The dominance of agriculture was a factor is this influence. In his opinion, the system of the joint family, or at least the idea underlying it, was considered acceptable in all predominantly agricultural societies. In fact, any total departure from the system had a crippling effect on these societies through a massive increase in the number of the landless paupers. In Russia, the villagers' corporate right in the land was a protection against such a calamity. The concern to establish social ownership in every sphere—manifest in the growing influence of socialists and nihilists—was to be traced to this tradition of corporate rights, and not to the Tsar's autocracy or tyranny. By contrast, the emergence of socialists and communists in France was traceable to other factors. There the system of inheritance entailed an equal division of paternal property among the sons and hence a steady decline in the size of holdings, leading eventually to landlessness. As France had no industries or colonies comparable to those of England, landlessness created large-scale unemployment. France's egalitarian parties drew their strength from the consequent social unrest.[319]

If Bhudev was critical of what he described as 'polluted egalitarianism', his rejection of Utilitarian doctrines was even more fundamental 'Greatest good of the greatest number' was to him a false philosophy; for it implied that social action which resulted in such benefit was justified, no matter what it cost particular groups or individuals. Political economic thought based on such goals was 'heartless', for it was wrong for a society to ignore the welfare of any of its component parts. The doctrine of free trade which accepted with equanimity the destruction of particular manufactures for the greater good of society as a whole was hence unacceptable. The American policy of protection for a limited period was preferable because it allowed the threatened domestic manufactures a chance to survive and improve.[320]

Bhudev's final comment on the new political philosophies of the West summed up his own vision of social goals. The coercive power of the state would always be necessary, but its harshness could be reduced and it could be used to educate and not merely to punish. Similarly, it was impossible to eliminate inequality, but not to reduce it. 'Therefore, it would be better if the demands of Europe's social revolutionaries were thus modified: 'humble acceptance of scriptural authority' in place of 'liberty', 'righteousness' in place of 'equality' and 'piety, love and compassion' in place of 'fraternity'. Some such demands, at least one for 'humble acceptance of scriptural authority', were echoed in the English Revolution. Its results were not as evil as those which followed from other European revolutions'.[321]

Bhudev's largely negative assessment of western civilization—past, present and future—pointed to only one conclusion: India should learn from Europe nothing but her 'practical skills' and absorb these into her inherited culture in a gradual, organic fashion. Since the British rule was there to stay for a long time, she must try and protect as best as possible her areas of vital interest—the economy, education and, of course, the inherited social system. And she should wait for the leader to emerge. That leader would be a man of great wisdom, an inheritor of India's moral and religious values, and a person with a profound knowledge of both eastern and western learning.

To conclude, Bhudev, strongly conscious of his social and cultural identity as a Brahmin and with a genuine belief in the unrivalled superiority of the Hindu tradition, was almost unaware of his intellectual debt to the West. His closely argued critiques, based on impressive learning, derive primarily from a set of ethical norms. He found these almost absent in the western tradition and was anxious that the European domination might uproot the inherited norms in his own society as well. His passionate patriotism underlined, not so much any desire for political independence in some distant future, but the preservation of the Brahminical social order. That order must change as it had always accepted change, but according to the laws of its own being. The norms and values at the heart of western civilization were seen to be fundamentally alien and hence a dangerous threat. Their advent was the most sinister invasion with which Indian society had ever had to cope. Bhudev's learned writings on Europe were an elaborate exercise in exposing the true nature of the threat.

Notes and References

1. Dedication, *Pushpanjali* (first published in 1876) in *Bhudev rachana sambhar* (with an introduction by Pramanthanath Bisi), Calcutta, BY 1369 (1962). The citations from Bhudev's works refer to this edition of his selected writings, except where otherwise indicated.

2. *Bhudev jivani*, printed and published by Kasinath Bhattacharya, 1st edn., Chinsurah, BY 1318 (1911), 6–7.

3. Mukundadev Mukhopadhya, *Bhudev charit*, 3 vols., Calcutta, BY 1324–34 (1917–27), I, 12–13.

4. Ibid., 25.

5. Bhudev Mukhopadhyay, *Sikshavishayak prastab* (A Scheme on Education), Hugli, BY 1288 (1881), 30; also Bch, III, 187.

6. Bch, I, 110.

7. Ibid., 51.

8. Ibid., 94.

9. Ibid., 54.

10. Ibid., 97–100, 106.

11. *Parivarik pravandha* (Essay on Family) (first published in *Education Gazette*, 1875–76) 11th edn., Chinsurah, 1939, 102–3; *Samajik*

pravandha (Essay on Society) (first published in 1892), serialized in *Education Gazette*, 1887–89, 50f.

12. See chapter on '*Pitamaha*' (Grandfather), PP; Bch, I, 7–8.

13. PP, 1–5; Bch, I, 8, 110, 176; III, 92.

14. PP, Dedication, 102–3, 149. He quoted Comte's view that a person should marry only once with approval. ibid., 149.

15. Bch, I, 106.

16. Rajnarayan Basu, *Atmajivani*, Calcutta, BY 1315 (AD 1908), 47.

17. Bch, I, 148.

18. Sibnath Sastri, *Ramtanu Lahiri o tatkalin bangasamaj* (Ramtanu Lahiri and Bengali Society in His Time), 183–4.

19. Ibid., 178.

20. Ibid., 181.

21. D.L. Roy, *Hashir gan* (Funny Songs); Rajnarayan Basu, *Sekal ar ekal* (Then and Now), rev. and enl. 2nd edn., Calcutta, Saka 1800 (AD 1878), 60–1.

22. Rajnarayan Basu, *Atmajivani*, 191.

23. Rajnarayan Basu, *Sekal ar ekal*, 32–62.

24. S.N. Banerjea, *A Nation in Making*, London, 1925, chap. 8; also Rajnarayan Basu, *Briddha Hindur asha* (Hopes of an Old Hindu), Calcutta, 1887, 2.

25. S. Raychaudhuri, *Unis satake nabyahindu andolaner kayekjan nayak*, Calcutta, (1983), 28–9.

26. Ibid., 23.

27. In her letter of the *Hindu*, 1893.

28. S. Raychaudhuri, *op. cit.*, 61.

29. Ibid., 54.

30. Jogindranath Basu's *Model bhagini* (The Ideal Sister), projected this image of Brahmo immorality and was highly popular.

31. Sasadhar Tarkachudamani, *Dharmabyaksha* (An Exposition of Dharma).

32. Ibid.

33. Rajnarayan Basu's *Briddha Hindur asha*, 2, 20.

34. *Hindu punarabhyutthan*, 20, 21.

35. Bch, II, 390–1.

36. Ibid., 445.

37. Ibid., 338–9.

38. BP, 177.

39. B Pr, ii, 95.

40. Rajnarayan Basu, *Atmajivani*, 88.

41. B Pr, ii, 152.

42. SP, 66.

43. B Pr, ii; *Brahmodharma o tantrasastra* (Brahmoism and the Tantras), 152.

44. Introduction to SP, Published in the *Education Gazette*, quoted in Bch, i, 83.

45. Notes in his Diary for 22 April 1894, quoted in Bch, iii, 449.

46. B Pr, ii; *Samaj-samskar* (Social Reform), 42.

47. B Pr, ii; *Paradharma grahan* (Conversion to other Faiths), 98–9.

48. Ibid., 96.

49. *Brahmodharma o tantrasastra*, ibid., 153.

50. *Samajik paribartan* (Social Change), ibid., 84.

51. Bch, iii, 454.

52. *Paribarik niti* (Family Norms), BP, ii, 100–5.

53. *Banga samaje Ingraj puja* (Worship of Englishmen in Bengali Society), ibid., 109–10.

54. *Hindu samaje kupamandukata* (Narrow-mindedness in Hindu Society), ibid., 105–7.

55. Ibid., 108–9.

56. *Swadhin chinta* (Independence of Thought), ibid., 128–9; also Bch, ii, 174–6.

57. Ibid., 129.

58. Ibid., 126–9.

59. *Samaj samskar*, BP, ii, 142.

60. *Pushpanjali* (An Offering of Flowers): [Some explanations of the Hindu faith in the form of a dialogue between Vyasa and Markendeya in connection with their visit to some centres of pilgrimage], 89.

61. *Adhikarbhed o swadeshanurag* (Differences in Rights and Patriotism), BP, ii, 247–8.

62. Bch, ii, 85.

63. Ibid., i, 85.

64. Diary of 27 February 1881, quoted in Bch, ii, 271.

65. Bch, ii, 268.

66. AP, Dedication and 1.

67. Ibid., 2–3, 5,9.

68. Ibid., 2.

69. *Hindu samaje dharmaniti* (Ethical Norms in Hindu Society), BP, II, 100.

70. *Irsha prabanata* (Tendency Towards Malice), ibid., 114–15.

71. *Pushpanjali*, 415.

72. Bch, I, 143.

73. *Shikshabishayak prastab* (A Proposal on Education) *Swayambarabhash parba* (The chapter on Goddess Adhibharati's marriage by her own choice), 4.

74. Rajnarayan Basu, *Atmajivani*, 42.

75. Sibnath Sastri, *op. cit.*, 2, 37–8.

76. *Swapnalabdha Bharatbarsher itihas* (History of India Revealed in a Dream), 351–2.

77. Ibid., 422.

78. Rajnarayan Basu, *Atmajivani*, 40–1; Swami Vivekananda, *Prachchya o paschatya* (The East and the West), 1902.

79. SP, 13.

80. *Banglar Itihas* (History of Bengal), 254.

81. Letter to third son, 2 January 1887, Bch, III, 123.

82. *Jatibhed* (The Caste System), BP, II, 76.

83. Bch, III, 389–9.

84. Ibid., 189.

85. Ibid.

86. Bch, III, 379.

87. Ibid., 334.

88. Chap. 6.

89. Diary of 31 January 1879, in Bach, II, 186–7.

90. Bch, I, 185.

91. Ibid., 185–6.

92. PP, 136.

93. Ibid., 102.

94. Ibid., 173.

95. Bipinchandra Pal, *Charitkatha*; Bch, I, 178–9.

96. Bch, I, 218.

97. Quoted in Bch, I, 300, from *Shikshadarpan o sambadsar*, monthly ed. by Bhudev.

98. SP, 243.

99. Bch, I, 419.

100. Ibid., III, 58.

101. Ibid., I, 126–7.

102. Ibid., III, 270.

103. *Shikshabishayak prastab*, 22–3.

104. Bch, II, 384.

105. See below.

106. SP., 228.

107. Bch, I, 187.

108. Bch, I, 395.

109. Ibid., 396.

110. See below.

111. Bhudev's diary of 28 August 1892, quoted in Bch, III, 348.

112. See below; BP, II, *Brahmodharma o tantrashastra*, 161.

113. Bch, I, 31–5.

114. Ibid., 38.

115. Ibid., 60–1.

116. Ibid., 72–3.

117. Ibid., 114–15.

118. Ibid., I, 108–9.

119. Ibid., 158–68.

120. Ibid., I, 383–5.

121. SP, 70.

122. Ibid., 230.

123. Ibid., 222.

124. Ibid., 234f.

125. BP, II, *Paradharmagrahan* (Conversion to other people's faith), 96.

126. Rajnarayan Basu, *Atmajivani*, 218.

127. Bch, I, 240f.

128. Ibid., II, 31.

129. Ibid., III, 96.

130. Bp, II, *Hindu samaje khawa dawa* (Hindu Food-Habits and Ritual Restrictions), 92; for similar sentiments, see *Swapnalabdha*, 54.

131. Bch, I, 263.

132. Ibid., 264–6.

133. BP, II, 93.
134. Bch, I, 270–1.
135. Ibid.
136. BP, II, 31, 269.
137. Ibid., 268.
138. Ibid., 267.
139. Bch, I, 103–5.
140. Ibid., 157.
141. Ibid., III, 82.
142. Ibid., I, 117.
143. Ibid., 160.
144. Ibid., 148–9.
145. Ibid., 219–20.
146. Ibid., II, 24–5.
147. Ibid., II, 26–31.
148. Ibid., 2, 118–19; *op. cit.*, III, 311–12.
149. *Op. cit.*, III, 312–10.
150. *Op. cit.*, II, 51.
151. Ibid., 37f.
152. *Banglar itihas* (A History of Bengal), III, 62.
153. Ibid., III, 124.
154. Ibid., II, 197.
155. Ibid., 194.
156. Bhudev's diary of 25 December 1876, in Bch, II, 137.
157. *Loc. cit.*, 140.
158. *Op. cit.*, III, 184.
159. Ibid., 278.
160. Bch, I, 158–9, 339.
161. Ibid., 142.
162. Ibid., 228f.
163. PP. *Nirapatyata* (The Childless State), 124.
164. Bch, I, 317–18.
165. *Raja-seva* (Service to the King).
166. Bch, I, 270.
167. Ibid., 255.
168. B Pr, II; *Paribarik niti*, 108.

169. 9 February 1878, quoted in Bch, II, 157.

170. Proceedings of the Asiatic Society, 1893.

171. Many of the relevant sources are identified in the text and the fns. below.

172. Rajnarayan Basu, *Atmajivani*, 20–1, 25.

173. Bch, I, 127.

174. Ibid., 89.

175. Ibid., 94, 108.

176. B.N. Bandyopadhyay, *op. cit.*, 26–8.

177. Bch, II, 108.

178. Bch, II, 177.

179. Ibid., 181–2.

180. Letter to son Mukunda, 28 March 1888, Bch, III, 217–19.

181. Letter to Mukunda, 19 January 1889, *op. cit.*, 259–60.

182. See below, Bch, III, 218.

183. Letter to Mukunda, 10 September 1887, *op. cit.*, 173.

184. *Op. cit.*, 218. See below.

185. Ibid., 337–8.

186. Ibid., II, 195.

187. Pandit Bireshwar Pandey, *Swargiya Bhudev Mukhopadhyay* (The Late Bhudev Mukhopadhyay) BY 1301 (1894), 177–81.

188. Bch, III, 456–69.

189. Introduction to SP 68.

190. *Banglar itihas*, 153.

191. Letter to Jogendranath Basu, 17 April 1893, published as appendix to his biography of Michael. See Jogendranath Basu, *The Life of Madhusudan Datta*, BY 1300 (1893).

192. SP, 68.

193. BP, II, *Lakshmichhara Dasha* (A State of Wretchedness), 130–1.

194. SP, 132–3.

195. Bch, I, 303.

196. PP, 109.

197. BP, II; *Hindusamaj o dharmaniti* (Hindu Society and Ethical Norms), 97f.

198. AP, 18.

199. BP, II, *Bangasamaje Ingraj Puja* (The Worship of the English in Bengali Society), 109f.

200. SP, 64.
201. PP, 250.
202. SP, 64.
203. SP, 64.
204. Ibid., 64–6.
205. Ibid., 65.
206. Ibid., 110–13.
207. Ibid.
208. Ibid., 191–2.
209. Ibid., 2–3.
210. Ibid., 109–10. See also *Bangasamaje Ingraj puja*, BP, II.
211. Introduction to SP.
212. *Pushpanjali*, 422–3.
213. *Unavingsha Puran* (The Nineteenth Pruana) (*Swayambaravas parba*), 36.
214. Bch, I, 405.
215. SP, 132–3.
216. Ibid., 263.
217. Ibid., 130.
218. Ibid., 131.
219. Ibid., 130.
220. Ibid., 232–3.
221. *Unavingsha Puran*, 22.
222. Ibid., 135.
223. *Banglar itihas*, 3.
224. BP, II, *Bibhinna prakarer Ingraj rajpurushgan* (Different Types of English Officials), 118–19.
225. *Banglar itihas*, 7, 9.
226. See below.
227. *Banglar itihas*, 44.
228. Ibid.
229. SP, 138.
230. Ibid., 137.
231. Ibid., 137–7.
232. Ibid., 139–40.

233. SP, *Ingrajadhikar—Ingrajer rajbhab* (British Rule—the British Attitude as Rulers), 135–43.

234. BP, II, *Bibhinna prakarer Ingraj rajpurushgan*, 119.

235. SP, 142–3.

236. Ibid., 144.

237. Ibid., 147.

238. *Banglar itihas*, 99; also *Unabingsha Puran*, 7.

239. SP, *Ingrajadhikar—Ingrajer baideshikbhab* (British Rule—the British as Aliens), 142–52.

240. Ibid., 63.

241. Ibid., 192.

242. *Pushpanjali*, 422–3.

243. *Op. cit.*, 5–6.

244. *Banglar itihas*, 45.

245. See above.

246. See above.

247. BP, II, *Bangali samaj* (Bengali Society).

248. SP, *Bhabisya bichar—Bharatbarsher katha* (*arthik abastha vishayak*), (A Look into the Future—India's Prospects [Matters Economic]), 203–22; *Banglar itihas*, 26, 4f, 73f; Bch, II, 120–2; *Unabingsha Puran*, 24f, 34, 29f; BP, II, *Bibhinna prakarer Ingraj rajpurushgan*, 121.

249. *Unabingsha Puran*, 30f, 35.

250. SP, 43.

251. BP, II; *Bangasamaje antahsasan*, 61–70; *Hindusamaj o kupamandukata*, 108; *Banglar itihas*, 60–4.

252. *Bangasmaje Ingraj puja*, *op. cit.*, 111–12.

253. *Bibhinna prakarer Ingraj rajpurushgan*, *op. cit.*, 50.

254. SP, 13f.

255. *Banglar itihas*, 23.

256. Ibid., 29.

257. See below.

258. SP, 28.

259. *Inglander itihas* (A History of England), 15.

260. SP, 32–3.

261. Ibid., 36–7.

262. Ibid., 37.

263. AP, 104.

264. SP, 38.

265. SP, 37–8.

266. Ibid.

267. Ibid.

268. *Inglander itihas*, 10.

269. SP, *Krita Khrishtan* (Christian Converts), 16–19, 39–40.

270. Ibid., 63–4.

271. Ibid., 69–70.

272. Ibid., 71.

273. Ibid., 73.

274. Ibid., 68–73.

275. SP, 165.

276. BP, II, *Paribarik niti*, 105.

277. SP, 73–5.

278. Ibid., 167.

279. Ibid., 75–7.

280. *Inglander itihas*, 362.

281. SP, 77, 163; *Inglander itihas*, 369.

282. *Op. cit.*, 199.

283. Ibid., 78.

284. Ibid., 509.

285. Ibid., 79.

286. Ibid., 81–6.

287. Ibid., 82.

288. Ibid., 86–7.

289. SP, 82.

290. Ibid., 83.

291. BP, II, etc.

292. Ibid., *Bangasamaje atmasasan* (Self-Rule in Bengali Society), 65–6.

293. Ibid., 67–8.

294. PP, 254–5.

295. BP, II, 66–7.

296. AP, 453.

297. BP, II, *Dharmabuddhi, bhaktipriti o achar raksha* (Conscience, Love of God and Man and Ritual Duties), 249.

298. SP, 180–1.

299. Ibid., 155–6.
300. Ibid., 156–7.
301. Ibid., 157–8.
302. Ibid., 175–6.
303. BP, II, *Samaj samskar* (Social Reform), 142–3; *Santi o Sukh* (Peace and Happiness), 140.
304. BP, II, 140–1.
305. Ibid., 142–3.
306. SP, 162–3; *Inglander itihas*, 362–3.
307. Ibid., SP.
308. BP, II, *Sasan Pranali* (System of Administration), 19–22.
309. SP, 164.
310. Ibid., 165.
311. PP, 475–6.
312. Ibid., 475.
313. Ibid., 464.
314. SP, 293.
315. Ibid., 164–5.
316. Ibid., 166.
317. Ibid., 168–9.
318. Ibid., 169–70.
319. BP, II, 102–4.
320. SP, 197–8.
321. Ibid., 169–70.

Select Bibliography

Works of Bhudev Mukhopadhyay

Except where otherwise indicated, the texts published in the collected works, *Bhudev-rachanasambar*, Calcutta, 1962 have been used. These titles are marked with asterisks. The year of first publication is mentioned after each work. Publication details given in square brackets refer to the editions used for this book when these are different from the first published edition and the collected works.

Sikshavishayak prastab, 1856 [Hugli, BY 1288 (1881)].

Aitihasik upanyas, sakabda 1779 (1857).

Prakritik vijnan, 1858.

Puravrittisar, 1858.

Kshetratattva, 1862.

Inglander itihas, 1862.

Romer itihas, 1863.

Unavimsa Puran, 1866. This book, first written by a student of Bhudev, was revised by him so extensively that according to his son, Mukundadev, it would be correct to describe it as Bhudev's work. The last chapter is exclusively his writing.

*Pushpanjali, Part I, 1876.

*Parivarik pravandha, 1882 [11th edn., Chinsurah, 1939].

Bhudev-rachanasmbar contains only selections from this work.

*Svapnalavdha bharatvarsher itihas, 1862.

*Samajik pravandha, 1892.

Achar pravandha, 1895 [3rd edn., Chinsurah, BY 1324 (1917)].

Bibidha pravandha, Part I, 1895.

Banglar itihas, Part III, 1904. The first two parts were written by Ramgati Nyayaratna and Iswarchandra Vidyasagar respectively.

Bibidha pravandha, Part II, 1905.

Dinalipi (Diary), December 1876—extensively quoted in Mukundadev Mukhopadhyay's *Bhudevcharit*.

The undermentioned school textbooks are mentioned in Bhudev's autobiographical letter quoted by Mukundadev (III, 132–33), but not in B. Bandyopadhyay's list of his works.

Yantra-vijnan (1859?)

Vijganit (1863?), *Patiganit* (1863?), *Pranivijnan* (1864?)

Banerjea, Surendranath, *A Nation in Making*, London etc., 1925.

Bandyopadhyay, Brajendranath and Sajanikanta, Das, *Bhudev Mukhopadhya in Sahityasadhak charitmala*.

Basu, Jogendranath, *Michael Madhusudan Datter jivancharit*, Calcutta, BY 1300, (1894).

Basu, Rajnarayan, *Rajnarayan Basur vaktrita*, Part I, 3rd rev. edn., Calcutta, sakabda 1793 (1871).

Atmajivani, Calcutta, BY 1315 (1908).

Sekal ar ekal, Rev. and enl. 2nd print, sakabda 1800 (1878).

Virddha Hindur asha, Calcutta, 1886.

Bhudev jivani, printed and published by Kasinath Bhattacharya, 1st edn.,
  Chinsurah, BY 1318 (1911).

Lahiri, Sipra, *Bhudev Mukhopadhyaya o Bangla sahitya.*

Mukhopadhyay, Mukundadev, *Bhudevcharit*, 3 vols., Calcutta. 1917–27.

Pal, Bipinchandra, *Charitrachitra.*

Sastri, Sibnath, *Ramtanu Lahiri o tatkalin bangasamaj*, Calcutta, 1903.

chapter 3

Bankimchandra Chattopadhyay
(1838–1894)

I

Bankimchandra Chattopadhyay, the first important novelist in the Bengali language and best known to a wider world for his patriotic anthem *Bande Mataram*, came from a background almost identical with Bhudev's.[1] Both were born in Kulin families, ritually the purest stratum of Bengali Brahmins, and belonged to the same subcaste, Rarhi. Only a stretch of water separated the village where Bankim was born from Bhudev's home town. Both families had strong traditions of Sanskritic learning. Born twelve years after the famous educationist, Bankim was for some time a student of the same college as his senior contemporary though in his days it had a new name, Presidency College, Calcutta. Both men were functionaries in the colonial bureaucracy and rose as high as was normally possible for an Indian to do those days (the only exceptions were the Indian members of the ICS whose numbers could be counted on the fingers of one hand). Both tried their hands at a wide variety of literary efforts and their didactic writings were inspired by intense patriotism. It was for the most part an apolitical patriotism—generally suspicious of contemporary organized politics—which informed their self-conscious and avowed adherence to the Hindu tradition, as well as their emotive rejection of social reform which questioned age-old practices like the forced celibacy of Hindu widows or which sought the intervention of an alien government in the intimate concerns of Hindu society. Despite this impressive list of similarities, the two were very different persons. This fact of difference is manifest in their views of their own cultures as well as their perceptions of the West.

As noted in the last chapter, Bhudev was a man at peace with himself and with a sociocultural milieu rooted in ancient traditions. His acceptance of the values of the high-caste Bengali joint family was total—a source of strength, equanimity and, possibly, profound happiness. His attachment to these values had evident roots in his deep love for his parents and the wife whom he had married as a child-bride. The received values were not to be questioned and the foreigners' contempt for institutions like child marriage was of no concern, because to Bhudev the life-experiences of those he held dear were proof enough of their validity. Nothing in the whole world was more worthwhile to him than the family system of Bengali Hindus. Expect for a brief adolescent flutter of doubt, induced by the intellectual ambience of Hindu College, his acceptance of Brahminical doctrine and ritual was equally unquestioning. He would not have bothered, in all probability, about their relative excellence compared to other religious traditions had he not lived under alien rule. As a proud and sensitive Indian, constantly told by foreigners as well as his own countrymen that he belonged to an inferior race, he felt the need to assert Indian superiority at least in some areas of life. Bhudev's faith in such superiority was not contrived. If he took the trouble to state it at great length using a style of argument derived from his western learning, the object was to convince his misguided countrymen, not himself. His ambivalence was in relation to whatever he had absorbed from the West and what, to him, was a mediocre official career under a non-Indian ruler. He was anxious to believe that western education and his job were peripheral to his dominant concerns centred on the Hindu way of life. This was a misperception and probably the only source of conflict in his personality. His departures from objectivity and his angle of vision in assessing the West were conditioned by this conflict. But, to repeat, his total commitment to the Hindu tradition acted as a powerful counterweight and gave a quality of equilibrium to his life.

By contrast, conflict was central to Bankim's personality. The didacticism of his later literary efforts represents an attempt, arguably unsuccessful, to resolve it. His biographies trace the roots of Bankim's ideology and creativity to the traditions of his family and the cultural ambience of his childhood environment, traditions, that is, of Sanskritic learning, Vaishnava devotionalism and the high Hindu ideal of *nishkama karma*, the path of non-attachment.[2] We are told of the Vaishnava cycle of ceremonies held round the year centred on the centuries-old family temple of Radhaballabh, Krishna as Radha's beloved. Bankim's ancestor, Gangananda, was a Sanskrit scholar and founder of a *chatushpathi*, a school for higher Sanskritic learning. The writer's maternal grandfather also ran a *chatushpathi* and Bankim inherited his collection of Sanskrit books. His father is also described as *sastrajna*, a person well-versed in the scriptures and as a man who associated with great Sanskrit scholars of the day, especially those from the famous centre of learning, Bhatpara, only a few miles away. Bankim's first introduction to the Mahabharata—the bedrock of tradition from which he sought eventually to carve out a satisfactory philosophy of life—was through his father's friend, Haladhar Tarkachudamani, one of the most celebrated scholars of his time.[3] He began to learn Sanskrit in his childhood from a reputed Sanskritist in his home town, Kanthalpara. Bankim's father, Jadabendra, is described by his youngest son, Purnachandra, as a person who lived by the doctrine of non-attachment, a judgement endorsed by the writer himself in the dedication of his novel *Debi Chaudhurani*, celebrating the same doctrine.[4] In short, the consensus view suggests a pattern of continuity: the writer who affirmed both in his later novels and non-fictional writing the highest Hindu values of non-attachment and harmonious cultivation of all one's faculties for an impersonal goal learnt these at his father's feet, in the environment of a pious Brahmin home steeped in all that was worthwhile in the ancient tradition.[5]

This tradition, powerfully present in Bhudev's family had helped him achieve a measure of tranquillity and integration. His father, a Sanskrit scholar unexposed to any other tradition, had patiently induced his son's return to the ancestral faith. 'Pure as the sacrificial fire', the epithet reserved for Brahmins unsullied by worldliness and impurity, would not be an inappropriate description of the old scholar. Bankim's family background, scholarly consensus notwithstanding, presents no comparable picture of unfractured integration with the Hindu past. Traces of the conflict ever-present in the writer are already there in his family heritage.

The pure flame of the Brahminical ideal which meant uninterrupted dedication to scholarship over many generations and maintenance of ritual purity through connubium only with one's equals in the caste hierarchy, even if that meant poverty, was no part of his family inheritance. Jadav's father, one learns, 'was also learned', but 'not as renowned a scholar' as his father-in-law.[6] The fall from Brahminical grace had in fact started early— with Jadav's great grandfather, Ramjivan, who married the daughter of wealthy Raghudev Ghoshal whose family's caste status was relatively low. The Chattopadhyay family suffered a loss of ritual status through this marriage of evident convenience and became *bhanga*, literally 'broken' Kulins.[7] In

traditional Brahmin society, more than a loss of ritual status is implied in
such fall from grace. It has a secular dimension, an implication of betrayal
of a proud inheritance for material gain. For the deviant's family and
descendants it entails a loss of social confidence. This remark should not be
taken to mean that the most outstanding literary figure of nineteenth-century
Bengal suffered a sense of guilt and uncertainty because his great-great-
grandfather had married beneath him probably out of material considerations.
I have drawn attention to the consequences of his family history simply to
emphasize one possible reason why his acceptance of and integration with
the Hindu tradition was neither as spontaneous nor as total as that of his
older contemporary. The rigidity of that tradition had inflicted a punishment
on his family. Bhudev's joy in the Brahminical past could be unsullied, for
his family harboured no memory of humiliation or loss of status. Bankim's
family with its five deputy magistrates in two generations achieved a status
in the new colonial context higher than the one they enjoyed in traditional
Brahmin society.

   Deviation from the true Brahminical ideal and the conflicts associated
with such departure were very much a part of Jadav's experience. If he did
acquire a sound knowledge of the *sastras*, he must have done so relatively
late in life and as an autodidact. His Sanskritic education was terminated
early in his childhood in favour of Arabic and Persian. The latter was still
the language of administration and hence a necessary acquisition for useful
employments under the Company. His elder brother was already in such
employment in the salt department. The Chattopadhyay family was thus no
longer in purely Brahminical occupations. Links of dependence on the alien
ruler had already been established in the early decades of the nineteenth
century. Jadav's induction into the colonial bureaucracy was hastened by a
further departure from the tranquil life-style of the traditional Brahmin
family. Something of a wastrel in his boyhood, he was rebuked by his father
for some act of transgression—ritual or moral—the precise nature of which
is not recorded. He ran away from home in protest and accidentally met his
elder brother whom he succeeded as a *darogha* or inspector in charge of
salt refineries.[8] For a person without much formal education, he rose high
enough in his service career and was elevated eventually to the post of
deputy collector. But his progress was not smooth. At one point, he along
with some 600 colleagues had to stand trial on charges of corruption. Jadav's
account of his spirited replies at the trial, which allegedly led to his acquittal
and promotion, may well be true.[9] But one wonders what mark this incident

left on the life of a proud Brahmin. Bankim repeatedly referred to his job as a middle-ranking official as the 'curse of his life'.[10] Was his bitterness informed *inter alia* by the knowledge that his father's career in service also had been no unmixed blessing?

Bankim's biography written by his nephew, Sachis, presents an idealized portrait of the relationship between parents and children in the Chattopadhyay home. His younger brother, Purnachandra, writes with similar eloquence of Bankim's filial piety, his discipleship with the father as guru for the true knowledge of dharma.[11] Sachis records one spectacular anecdote in which the writer, before leaving home to take up his appointment, bashfully collected his parents' *padodaka*, i.e. water sanctified by the touch of their feet.[12] Parents are divinities to the believing Hindu and the worshipful act fits in well with the tradition of heightened deference. Bankim, we are told, never sat down in his father's presence, considered it improper for anyone to speak loudly to one's father and believed that a greater deference was due to one's mother than to the Mother Ganges. If there is any truth in such anecdotes then there was a serious conflict between his norms of filial piety and the reality of his attitude towards his parents.

In describing his childhood to one of his young admirers, he said: 'My father spent most of his time away from home. My mother was excessively old-fashioned; so I learnt nothing from her; I never had any moral training. It is a mystery why I did not end up as a burglar.' In this intimate statement, the only moral influence in his life he recognized was that of his second wife.[13] The living ideal of *nishkama karma* attributed to Bankim's father by the writer himself as well as his chief biographer does not quite fit in with the known facts of the old man's extravagance. As the most solvent among his four sons, Bankim had to pay off the very substantial debts which they inherited from the father. That he deeply resented the consequences of his father's thoughtlessness for which he had to pay throughout his working life is evident from one of his letters: 'No one is more unhappy in this world than the person who has to bear the burden of debts ... You see me as an instance of this fact. Ramesh Mitra is a High Court judge, and I am a petty employee in Maldah. The reason for this is nothing but my father's debts.' The bitter statement occurs in a letter written to dissuade his hapless elder brother, Sanjiv, from borrowing money at the father's behest, to fund a stylish wedding for his (Sanjiv's) only son. Despite his strong sense of filial duty, Bankim advised his elder brother to defy his father rather than incur debts he had no means of repaying.[14] The advice, incidentally, went unheeded. The wedding was celebrated with due *éclat*, the teenage bridegroom riding on a hired elephant to the ceremony. Bankim had to pay in due course for this further display of his parent's taste for the high life. Jadav may well have lived by the doctrine of indifference to the results of one's action enjoined in the Gita. Bankim had less chance of following this high ideal, for he had to foot the bill. The tension between father and son came to a head over Jadav's decision to exclude his eldest son and Bankim from shares in the paternal home in favour of their two less affluent brothers. The novelist left his home town for some time partly in protest against the decision which was resented even more bitterly by the eldest, Shyamacharan.[15]

What must have been particularly unsettling about these tensions for a man of Bankim's sensitivity was that his father was deeply attached to his famous son. We do not know how far this affection was reciprocated. Respectful distance, rather than great warmth, appears to have been the true nature of Bankim's feelings for his father. But the fact of great deference and a strong sense of filial duty is not in doubt. He wrote that he finally left the ancestral home only after his father's death, something he 'dared not' do so long as the old man was alive. He kept up the annual worship of Durga in the family home at considerable expense, because his father had established the practice.[16] As already noted, he ascribed to his father his initiation into the doctrine of non-attachment, central to the philosophy of life he painfully worked out for himself. Evidently, both in terms of inherited values and his own emotional responses, his relationship with his father had a certain centrality in his life experience. Yet his own awareness of this relationship was torn by mutually contradictory feelings—deference, a sense of duty, impatience, and resentment. I have argued that Bhudev's unqualified acceptance of the Hindu tradition was in a way an extension of his attachment to his father who lived by that tradition. Bankim's feelings for his father are not characterized by any such unfractured innocence. His acceptance of the paternal faith, as we shall see, had an element of contrivance as did his ascription of *nishkama karma* to the high-living bureaucrat. The spontaneous negative reactions provoked by his father's unreasonable ways had to be controlled and sublimated: the social conditioning in a traditional Indian family as well as the consciously adopted 'neo-Hindu' ideology both enjoined unquestioning filial piety. Idealization of one's father was a natural corollary. But Bankim's emotional tension in relation to his father was never resolved. A comparable tension marked his attitude towards the Hindu past. His attempt to resolve it with the aid of Utilitarian and Positivist philosophies does not appear to have helped him achieve a state of peace. To repeat, unlike Bhudev, he was not the happily devoted son of a truly Brahminical father. His longing for such a blessed state was evident. Nor was he, unlike his senior contemporary, spontaneously content with the legacy of the ancestral faith as he found it. He tried hard, probably in vain, to carve out of it a satisfying philosophy of life, using imported tools. Arguably, these tools meant more to him than the received wisdom. But he appears to have been reluctant to admit this even to himself. The self-assertion which informed the burgeoning nationalism of the Bengali litterati precluded such admission.

Bankim's strong emotional ties with his brothers and other close relations were also marked by mutually contradictory pulls. All available evidence indicates that the relationship between the four brothers was unusually close. They delighted in one another's company. Three of them were close collaborators in literary activity. Their anxious concern for mutual welfare was expressed in practical terms which implied a measure of self-sacrifice, particularly for Bankim.[17] The second brother, Sanjiv, was always short of money and the youngest, Purna, was also hard up until relatively late in life. Bankim supported the two and their families throughout his life and did so quite willingly. Willingly, but not without frequent exasperation, especially with Sanjiv to whom he felt particularly close. The former's recklessness, irresponsibility and extravagance were really enough to try the proverbial patience of a saint. And whatever Bankim's virtues, saintliness or unlimited patience was not among them. The financial burden imposed on him by his father and brothers kept him in relative poverty, a fact he resented deeply.[18] Yet, he was careful to ensure that the two elder brothers did not suffer from neglect or inadequate medical attention in their declining years.[19] He was also anxious that his eldest brother's excessive proneness to anger did not damage his health.[20] At least once in Bankim's life, the tension with his brothers did reach a breaking point. This was when he decided to quit the ancestral home, peeved by his father's will excluding him from a share in the house. Reconciliation was achieved through complicated arrangements worked out by Sanjiv and Purna. Again, several years later, in a very angry letter to Sanjiv he wrote that he had no desire to return to his home town 'where one had to look upon the face of an elder brother like Baro Babu', i.e. Syamacharan.[21] As a perceptive biographer has commented, Bankim's relationship with his brother never reached a point of actual hostility: their mutual affection and concern to maintain the relationship were too deep for that. It was more a case of continual tension with Bankim's patience approaching a breaking point from time to time.[22] He felt he was a victim of unfair and inconsiderate treatment at the hands of people he was very fond of. This too was a 'curse of his life', as was his job in the colonial bureaucracy. He, too, like Bhudev, lived by the norms of Bengali Hindu family life, but his enthusiasm for these could not have been as great as the older man's. His concern that his nephew, Jyotish, whom he had wanted to adopt, should learn the virtues of self-reliance—irrelevant in an extended family set-up—probably expresses a sense of disillusionment with a system which allowed the failures to live off the more successful.[23] The new individualism which questioned the unlimited demands of the family and kinship group on a man's time, energy, and resources was very much a part of Bankim's personality.[24] Since the family system was central to the Hindu tradition, or at least the form in which it had survived till the nineteenth century in Bengal, any doubts about its norms inevitably merged into reservations regarding the inherited culture as a whole. Both intellectually and emotionally, being a good Hindu involved much effort for the sensitive novelist.

Until recently, the love-life of great men has been a tabooed theme in the modern Indian tradition almost as much as parental sex is in most cultures. The development of a creative writer's emotional life, crucial to any understanding of his or her work, hence remains an unknown territory. In Bankim's case, his writings as well as scattered fragments of information provide hints which tantalize but disclose very little. His fictional works are marked by a profound, if highly refined, sensuousness, an evident joy in the physical world. His adolescent poems have strong erotic overtones. His novels are peopled with women of great beauty. His delight in describing feminine beauty reminds one of classical Sanskrit poetry, except that Victorian inhibitions did not permit references to pectoral muscles or the pelvic zone. Married at eleven to a pretty child-bride of five, he had learnt to love early in life. 'No one can love as deeply as a little boy', the author wrote in one of his novels, *Chandrasekhar*, and went on to comment on the curse which haunts childhood love. One wonders if the loss of his child-bride at the age of twenty-one was a traumatic experience he never forgot. The happy endings in his novels are less appealing than the tragic fate of his star-crossed lovers. The latter is certainly a more frequent theme and the context is often the harsh realities of the human condition rather than high romance.

A recent insightful essay on his novels has drawn attention to the element of liminality, a persistent 'taste for transgression'.[25] In his first novel, *Durgeshnandini*, Ayesha's love for the Hindu Jagatsimha challenges the barriers of community and religion; in *Mrinalini*, Pasupati longs for Manoroma whose supposed widowhood renders such love taboo; in *Bishabriksha* (The Poison Tree), Nagendra's attempt to legitimize his extra-marital passion by marrying bigamously the young widow, Kunda, ends in tragedy; Indira, under an assumed personality as a domestic, seduces her husband; Saibalini, a saintly Brahmin's wife, cherishes a life-long passion for her childhood love, Pratap; in *Krishnakanter uil* (Krishnakanta's Will), Gobinda falls for the siren widow, Rohini, and leaves his wife. This recurrent theme of conflict, of transgression of social barriers, in mind if not in body, presented frequently with empathy, but never with moral approval, is central to the world of Bankim's imagination. We do not know if it mirrors some deep tension in his own emotional life. Two curious statements are ascribed to this highly disciplined person whose private life was very much exposed to the public eye. In one, he referred to the evil company he kept in his youth and the effect it had on his morals.[26] In the other, he admitted that there was an autobiographical element in *Bishabriksha*, a tale of extra-marital passion which ended in tragedy. In the same statement, he referred to the 'many mistakes' of his life which could not be divulged and were known only to his wife. It was for this reason, he said, that it was not possible to write his biography. There is no reason to doubt the authenticity of this conversation, reported by one of his young admirers. The points of reference however remain obscure.

The destructive potential of human passion comes up again and again in his novels, even though in his philosophical writings he acknowledged its legitimacy within given limits. Whatever his intellectual conviction, his imaginative perception underlined the threat to stable happiness posed by elemental desire. The tragedies in *Kapalkundala, Bishabriksha, Krishnakanter uil*, and *Sitaram* are all traceable to unrestrained passion. In *Chandrasekhar*, the heroine's 'immoral' love for a man who was not her husband is burnt out of her soul through a spiritual regime of incredible cruelty. In *Anandamath*, Bhabananda atones for his illicit desire with the sacrifice of his life. Even legitimate love is considered inconsistent with higher purposes like service to one's country. The ascetic Madhavacharya frustrates Hemchandra's efforts at union with his beloved Mrinalini for he must be preserved for the holy task of saving the country from the invading

Turks. The *santans* in *Anandamath*, the 'children' dedicated to the service of the motherland, are vowed to celibacy till their object is attained. Krishna's dalliance with the milkmaids must be rejected as unhistorical.[27] The ideal of restraint is summed up by Sri, Raja Sitaram's queen-turned-ascetic: 'The satisfaction of desires for any purpose other than dharma is sin. Satisfaction of desires [for its own sake] is the way of the beast.'[28] This considered judgement in Bankim's last novel has to be read with Pratap's confession of love for another man's wife before his death on the field of battle: 'I do not love her with a sinful heart. My love is the same as my desire to sacrifice my life. Day and night this love courses through my veins, my blood, my bones.' In reply to his question, 'Am I guilty in the eyes of God?', the *sanyasi* Ramananda replied, 'I do not know. Man's knowledge is helpless here, the scriptures fall silent. He who is the Lord of the [eternal] land you are about to enter alone has the answer.'[29] Evidently beyond a point the line which divides transgression and dharma was elusively thin to Bankim. One wonders if the conflict between ethical norms and passions which tortured so many of Bankim's protagonists was any part of his own experience. One object of his doctrine of 'culture' was precisely to resolve such conflict.[30] The clash of cultures which troubled his intellectual life thrived on fertile ground. Conflict at many levels and in many forms was a basic motif of his life experience. It informed his strivings towards a philosophy of life and his views of the two worlds he lived in—the one of inherited Hindu traditions, the legitimate faith of one's forebears, and the other of western civilization. The latter's seductive charms were consciously rejected, though more in name than in substance—in the last phase of his life. Transgression, however tempting, was ultimately not acceptable.

The nature of Bankim's contact with Europeans in India was very probably a major factor in his eventual rejection of western values. The rejection, of course, was never total. Ideas, absorbed over many years, had struck roots too deep to be weeded out entirely. His carefully worked out philosophy of life is replete with their insidious presence. The impulse to reject was, however, strong; for whatever the attractions of Europe perceived through the written word, the experience of encounters with the ruling race was for the most part deeply humiliating for this proud man.

His contemporaries refer repeatedly to his great pride. His critics accused him of vanity.[31] Even his good friend, Akshaychandra Sarkar, wrote that in discussing his character[32] it would be a travesty of truth not to mention his pride. His Brahmin origin, striking good looks, fame as an author and, above all, confidence in his intellectual and creative talent were the sources of this much-discussed pride. The fact that all the four brothers were 'high' officials contributed to a family reputation for snobbery.[33] Bhudev's son and biographer mentions that Bankim was reluctant to have social contact with those below him in the official hierarchy. Nearly everyone who has written about him mentions a quality of reserve, the virtual impossibility of treating him as an equal.[34] He explained that his literary labours on top of his official responsibilities left him no time for idle gossip and perforce he had to discourage superfluous visitors, the great saboteurs of sustained work in Bengali society. He was quite willing to pay the penalty of being dubbed vain.[35] His reputation for vanity cannot however be ascribed simply to such rational calculation. He did not take criticism very well and is known to have snapped at friends who expressed a dislike of his famous song, *Bande Mataram*.[36]

His sensitiveness was aggravated by what has been described as a nervous temperament. He was rather weak in body and physical courage did not come to him naturally. He never learnt horse riding, an almost essential accomplishment for officials of his rank in those days, and also avoided hills and mountains all his life.[37] He appears to have been somewhat acutely conscious of his lack of bodily strength and prescribed for himself an incredible diet—four chickens and eight eggs a day—in the belief that the hard work he imposed on his frail body demanded such nutrition.[38] His repeated acts of great moral courage suggest a pattern of compensation—conscious efforts of will which must have cost him a great deal. The continual experience of humiliation—and, with some exceptions, that was the record of his contact with Englishmen—did take a heavy toll. For Bankim to describe himself as a humble employee and recognize that while the English could do what they liked, the rules of the game were different for the Bengalis, especially the 'petty servants' of the government,[39] the iron must have entered his soul very deep indeed.

A familiar theme runs through most biographies of famous nineteenth-century Bengalis: tales of humiliation at the hands of sundry Englishmen and of courage shown in the face of such white peril. Bankim's experiences both in and out of office were particularly unfortunate. His initiation into the realities of race relations under colonial rule began early. At the age of six, Bankim was admitted to Mr F. Tead's school in Midnapore. He was a welcome visitor to the Tead home and Mrs Tead used to take him and her own children along on her visits to the District Magistrate, Mr Mollet, a

Haileybury-trained civilian and his family. One afternoon, the white children were asked into the house for tea, but not Bankim. He never visited the Mollets again.[40] One of his best-known essays has for its title *Jatibaira*, i.e. racial animosity. An awareness of this negative phenomenon formed part of his earliest experiences. Even before the episode at the Mollets' home, he realized that the English were objects of fear to his countrymen. One winter morning, there was great commotion in the village for a boatful of English soldiers had landed at the river *ghat*, an event which from previous experiences was known to mean trouble. While the streets were quickly emptied, Bankim alone stood by the roadside watching the bogeymen. 'Every Bengali child is scared of the bogeymen, but there are some boys so wicked that they want to see the bogeyman', he later wrote in one of his novels.[41] As a teenager, he had several unpleasant encounters with Englishmen. Once the local district magistrate entered the Chatterji *zenana* by mistake and was told off by Bankim. In 1857, he confronted an officer from the regiment stationed in Chinsurah who had 'playfully' set his dog on Bankim's younger brother, Purna.[42] These trivial episodes acquire significance from the fact that nearly every biographer of Bankim has considered them important enough to record. Two of them were among his nearest relations. These memories evidently became part of the family tradition.

As tales of racial humiliation and courageous resistance, these were absorbed into the archetypal folklore of modern Bengal. There were other similar episodes, e.g. Bankim's forced ejection from a second-class railway compartment by two drunken Englishmen, after which he advised all self-respecting Bengalis to avoid the second class favoured by the less reputable British and the even more infamous incident involving Colonel Duffin who was in charge of the Berhampore Cantonment. The Colonel physically assaulted Bankim because his palanquin passed through a cricket ground where the officer and some European friends were playing. When a criminal charge was brought against Duffin, he apologized in public, regretting that he was unaware of Bankim's identity. Assaulting lesser natives was evidently permissible in his eyes. Bankim is reported to have said that had he been physically stronger, he would have fought back his European tormentors. His nephew, Kailas, while recording the episode, advised Bengalis to take up physical exercise because it was futile to seek redress in a court of law for assaults by Europeans.[43]

A fundamental contradiction of Bankim's life—one he shared with the entire social class he came from—derived from the fact that his livelihood depended on service to and collaboration with alien rulers whose contempt for Indians was a fact of daily experience. 'Petty servants' is the expression he used to describe Bengalis like himself performing functions which were a constant source of humiliation. This bitter epithet would apply to many of his close relations and friends. His father and elder uncle had worked for the Company. All the four brothers and his eldest son-in-law were deputy magistrates. Two of the brothers, including the highly talented Sanjiv, started their careers as clerks. His beloved nephew, Jyotish, was an inspector of police. Among his closest friends, Dinabandhu Mitra was an inspecting postmaster and Kalinath Datta a head clerk.[44] The badge of servitude; despite a pervasive sense of chagrin, was often taken to be a mark of distinction. Bankim's father had been honoured with a title, 'Rai Bahadur', for his services to the Raj. One biographer proudly quotes a contemporary editorial comment: 'In Southern Bengal, when people talk of Rai Bahadur, they mean only Jadav Chattopadhayay.'[45] Bankim, while mentioning the conferment of the same honour on his friend, Dinabandhu, observed: 'I cannot say how far the recipients of this title feel gratified.'[46] Yet, by a curious anomaly, he was careful to mention the honour in its more flamboyant form in the title of his preface to his friend's work.[47] The uncertainty as to where humiliation ended and honour began in the service to the colonial master was never entirely clear to the men of his generation. Even to Bankim, an Indian deputy magistrate might be a lowly person, but a High Court Judge was not.[48] Evidently, servitude ceased to be a matter for shame if one's rank in service was adequately high.

Bankim's career in the bureaucracy, despite continual friction with British superiors, was successful enough. Starting as a deputy magistrate with fifth class salary and status, he was elevated to the second class in the twelfth year of service. It took another fourteen years to reach the coveted first class rank.[49] On retirement, his name duly appeared in the Honours List, though the twin titles of CIE and Rai Bahadur were sources of embarrassment rather than gratification to the ageing champion of nationalist ideology.

Yet it was the humiliations rather than the modest successes that left their mark on Bankim's assessment of the Indian reality under colonial rule. As a highly sensitive young man, he had been hesitant to accept the coveted post of deputy magistrate and changed his mind without any enthusiasm on his father's instructions.[50] If we are to believe his nephew, Kailas, his troubles began from the day he became a member of the bureaucracy because the Eurasian clerks cunningly prevented his access to the relevant files.[51] In the third year of his service, he had to deal with the notorious indigo planter, Morrel, and his henchman, Denis Hely, who led the planter's private army against local landlords as well as peasants reluctant to cultivate indigo for uneconomic returns. The encounter offered a new insight into colonial relationships, for the Lieutenant-Governor, J.P. Grant, had praised Morrel as a model settler, a view endorsed by the English Special Commissioner enquiring into the peasants' complaints. According to one biographer, Hely offered Bankim a huge bribe and threatened his life when it was refused. This wild adventurer probably provided the model for Foster, the villainous Englishman in *Chandrasekhar*. Both Hely and Morrel were eventually brought to justice and Bankim's action commended by the Government.[52] His assessments of British justice, however, reflect his initial experiences in the indigo affair more closely than the official attempts at rectification at a later stage.

The negative experiences of his first years in service established a pattern repeated many times in his career as a bureaucrat. His relationship with his official superiors, the English district magistrates—Buckland, Macaulay, Westmacott and Baker—was a record of almost continual friction. On more than one occasion, he thought that he would have to quit. In several cases, the conflict arose over his tendency to deal leniently with the accused, especially those committed by the police. He knew from experience that the police were oppressive and rarely to be trusted, a belief evidently not shared by the English district magistrates. In one classiç case, an illiterate old woman was sent up for trial for contravening a building regulation—that combustible material should not be used to thatch houses. The order in Bengali had mistakenly used the word *jaliya* (liquid or watery) instead of *jvaliya* (combustible). Either of these highly Sanskritic words would have meant little to the illiterate woman. Bankim dismissed the case, commenting *inter alia* that dry leaves were by no means liquid (*jaliya*). Buckland described this as 'insufferable pedantry'. He commented, 'Bankimchandra's vanity in the knowledge of the Bengali language has misled the judgement.'[53] The British officials who feature in Bankim's gallery of rogues and fools often share a common characteristic—their mistaken belief that they know the local language. Some of these portraits may well have been drawn from life.

There are reasons to believe—and, what is important, Bankim fully shared this belief—that he was the victim of official displeasure at least on two occasions. In one case, his literary perception of the British role in India was the source of trouble. In the other, his refusal to kowtow to a high official led to sustained persecution for some time. In September 1881, Bankim was appointed assistant secretary, a post created specially to encourage able Bengali officials. In less than five months, on 23 January 1882, he was asked to hand over charge at an hour's notice. The post was formally abolished, but in fact renamed and reserved for European officials. The publication of a particular instalment of his novel, *Anandamath*, in *Bangadarshan* is identified as the cause for this decision. Set against a fictionalized account of the Sanyasi rebellion under Warren Hastings, this novel published in *Bangadarshan* in January 1882, described in its second part the decimation of a British contingent led by a lecherous English officer at the hands of the patriotic rebels. Only a few days separate the date of this publication and the unexplained decision to terminate Bankim's appointment to high office. The worst offending passages were excised when the novel was published as a book.[54]

Bankim was convinced that anyone with a dark skin had little hope of fair treatment in any employment under the Raj. The doubtful honour of a title was all that his friend Dinabandhu received in recognition of his services because, Bankim wrote, 'Dinabandhu was a Bengali by birth.' Had he not been a Bengali, he further commented, 'he would have retired as postmaster general or even the director general of postal services. But just as coal cannot be cleaned of its dirty appearance even if washed a hundred times, so can a man never live down the fact of his dark skin even if he has a thousand merits. Just as charity [sic] covers up a thousand faults, so does a dark skin cover up a thousand merits.' The fact that Dinabandhu was eventually paid the salary of a first class official of his rank meant little, because 'with the aid of passing time even quadruped animals become entitled to first class pay. Everywhere in the world does one find asses elevated to the first class.'[55] The same note of bitterness marks several of his comments on the service career of his brother, Sanjiv. The latter lost his job as deputy magistrate owing to some muddle over the results of a test.[56] But he believed that his dismissal was the result of an unfortunate joke which offended an English judge.[57] Bankim does not refer to this episode, but he writes at some length of his brother's harassment at the hands of a District Collector, Burton, 'a despicable Englishman' whose 'only object in life was to seek out chances to humiliate and insult or dismiss educated Bengali officials'.[58] He also believed that his own transfer in 1882 to noisome Jajpur in Orissa was an act of punishment for he had omitted to greet and salute the Divisional Commissioner, Monroe, one afternoon in Calcutta's Eden Garden.[59] His biographer, Sachis, wrote that a proposal to appoint him district magistrate had to be dropped owing to the objection of the Europeans.[60]

Bankim's bleak experience of service under the Raj was relieved from time to time by friendly relations with a few English officials. Even before he entered service, he had received kindness from his European teachers at school and college. Despite the unfortunate episode at the district magistrate's residence, young Bankim's visits to the Tead home did not stop. At Hugli College, seven of his teachers were Europeans. Their comments on his character and attainments were very positive.[61] Later, during the turbulent years of service at Jessore and Khulna, Mr Benbridge, the District Magistrate of Jessore, befriended and supported the beleaguered young official. Bankim's firm handling of the lawless planter was also commended by the government. Again, during his brief posting at Burdwan in 1880–81, he found a friend in the young Joint Magistrate, H.A.D. Phillips. Besides, he did have friends in even higher quarters. The Lieutenant-Governor, Sir Ashley Eden, took a favourable view of his stand in the case which peeved Buckland. It was at his request that Sir Ashley appointed Purna a deputy magistrate. Lieutenant-Governor Sir Charles and Lady Elliot were personal friends despite his relatively humble official standing. His nephew mentions that he presented a manuscript translation of *Bishabriksha* to Lady Elliot at her request.[62] There is some concession of fair play and goodness to British officials in Bankim's satirical sketches—maybe, as a nod of gratitude towards the few who had treated him with due respect.

Bankim seriously considered quitting his job and taking up law as a profession on more than one occasion. He stopped short of taking such a decision for reasons which are not entirely clear. His heavy financial responsibilities may have been one possible factor. The failure to exorcise 'the curse' of his life meant persistent anxieties which must have been deeply humiliating for this very proud man. He advised his nephew, Jyotish, against running into debt for this might displease his European superior: '...Your first duty is to ensure the security of your job. Or else, you will starve.' His 'special advice' (*bisesh upadesh*) to the same nephew when he first got his job was spelt out under seven headings. The third enjoined obedience, humility and the need to avoid controversy. 'These', he stated, 'were essential for keeping one's job and progress in one's career.' The first injunction commended unflinching honesty, but there too the good opinion of one's superiors was underlined as one, though not the only, object of moral rectitude.[63]

The civil servant, anxious not to lose his job and hence not to displease the rulers, was perforce a part of Bankim's personality and one likely source of his self-disgust.[64] He had to work hard to remove the official displeasure over *Anandamath*. The patriotic protagonists' calls to attack the 'English and Muslims' in the serialized version were modified to exclude the English in the first edition. Besides, the latter, uniquely among his novels, had a foreword explaining the morals of the story. 'The English have rescued Bengal from anarchy' was declared to be one of these. The second edition omitted the reference to Captain Thomas's virile interest in Santal girls and added somewhat gratuitously that the eighteenth-century Englishmen were not as pure in their morals as their contemporary descendants. This was not enough. A high official, probably the Lieutenant-Governor himself, asked Bankim to secure a statement from Keshab Sen—a person trusted by the British—certifying the novel's unseditious intent, or else the book would be proscribed and worse might follow. Probably, a letter containing the required statement was published in Keshab's weekly, *Liberal*, or at least sent to the Lieutenant-Governor. Keshab's brother wrote an extensive review for the weekly. Extracts from it were printed in all the later editions of the novel.[65] Bankim told his friends that he would have liked to write a novel about the Rani of Jhansi, to him the noblest woman in history. But in view of the official reaction to *Anandamath*, he dared not.[66] When the Russian orientalist, Minaev, visited Calcutta, he asked if there was any book in Bengali on the recent annexation of Burma. Bankim told him that no one dared express his real opinion.[67] He himself was not free from this lack of courage, characteristic of a dependent élite. When an unsolicited honour—'Rai Bahadur'—was conferred on him, a contemporary periodical commented that one wished he had refused it and went on to add: 'He cannot say such courageous words to the English ruler, for he is but an employee of the Enlgish.'[68] That perhaps was the central tragedy of his life. It inevitably coloured his percep'ions of the world around him.

A major influence on Indo-British relations in the nineteenth century was the uninhibited expression of racial attitudes on the part of the Anglo-Indians. The educated Bengali—the Shakespeare-quoting seditious

Babu—was the chosen object of scorn. The stream of abuse poured forth in the Anglo-Indian press; papers like *The Englishman* were a perpetual irritant, especially because the victims were in no position to reciprocate in kind. The most blatant and ignorant expressions of racism were a recurrent theme in Bankim's satires. He encountered this unacceptable face of colonial rule early in his official career. When the notorious planter, Morrel, attacked a local zamindar with his armed retainers in November 1861, the *Friend of India* commented that the poor fellow 'having applied in vain for the protection of the police, was obliged to protect himself'. The newspaper later observed, 'The planter—denied laws, courts and police—like Englishmen all over the world became a law unto himself.' The aggressor's self-image as a victim was a major motif in Bankim's well-known satirical piece, 'Bransonism'.[69] The Indigo Planters' Association petitioned the Governor General Canning, requesting him to restrain the Lieutenant-Governor, Sir John Peter Grant, 'from pursuing a course which cannot but be ruinous to the indigo-planters in Bengal'. Canning's refusal to comply and Grant's persistent efforts to curb the planters' excesses were welcomed by the Calcutta intelligentsia. Here again was further material for a familiar stereotype of the colonial era, the 'good' and the 'bad' Englishmen. It is not absent from Bankim's writings.

Bankim's 'Bransonism', however, is about the ultimate in 'bad Englishmen', the racists who agitated against the government's attempts to place the European subjects on the same footing as Indians for judicial purposes. Anglo-Indian agitations against these anti-discriminatory legislations described the latter as 'Black Acts'. Bankim was witness to two of these agitations. The first was against the proposal of 1850 to bring the British residents in India accused of crimes within the jurisdiction of Indian courts. In 1857, the year before he graduated, the citizens of Calcutta congratulated the government for framing an Act which proposed 'to render administration of justice uniform for the British subjects of India'.[70] The second was against the Ilbert Bill of 1882, seeking to empower Indian magistrates and lower court judges outside the metropolis to try European subjects. Mr Branson, a barrister, was the hero of this campaign, remarkable for the ferocity of its racist invective. The nature of racial animosity—Bankim's *jatibaira*—was driven home well and truly, so far as the Bengali intelligentsia of his generation was concerned.

Uninhibited racism was no monopoly of boxwallahs and planters. In his literary career, Bankim felt compelled to challenge an immoderate expression of ethnocentricity on the part of a highly-educated Britisher, the Reverend

Hastie, Principal of the General Assembly's Institution, run by the Scottish
General Missionary Board. The occasion was a funerary ceremony at the
Sobha Bazar Raj family residence in Calcutta attended by the leading Hindu
citizens of the metropolis. The Scots missionary was shocked by reports in
the Calcutta *Statesman* describing the grand ceremony; for the family idol
of Krishna as Lord of the milkmaids, Gopinath, was brought into the assembly,
an idolatrous abomination tolerated, to Hastie's horror, by the highly-educated
Bengalis present. Though he had 'of course not a word to say that would
give the slightest pain to the mourners', he expressed his sense of outrage in
a letter to the *Statesman*. In it he described the family idol as 'a gawky
image gilded and adorned to attract the vulgar eye, but,—like old Marley,—
'as dead as a door nail', and, happily on that account, incomparably less
dangerous than the living god would have been ... to the virtue of the 3,500
ladies who partook of the banquet.' 'As a friend of Hindu society', he
decided to launch a sustained campaign against the 'glaring evil of idolatry'.
But in doing so, he promised to carry with him 'all the breadth and tolerance
of Christian charity'.[71] Expectedly, the columns of the *Statesman* were filled
for some weeks with angry protests. The protesters included Bankim, who
first wrote under a pen name and later revealed his identity. The letters
were eventually published by Hastie under a telling title, *English
Enlightenment and Hindoo Idolatry*. This remarkable volume is full of the
familiar missionary responses to the Puranic deities—'horrid' Kali, scandalous
Sivalingam, ridiculous Ganapati and, of course, lecherous Krishna.[72]
Hinduism was found to be pervaded by 'mere animal licentiousness',
'senseless mummeries, loathsome impurities, and bloody barbarous
sacrifices'.[73] The 'debasing idolatry' produced 'a mass of shrinking cowards,
of unscrupulous deceivers, of bestial idlers, of filthy songsters, of degraded
women, and of lustful men'. The only hope of salvation for the degraded
race lay, of course, in embracing Christianity.[74] There were other signs of
hope, for 'the glory of the English name, since the Battle of Plassey, was on
the lip of every Hindu in Bengal', delivered from 'the hateful oppression of
centuries of Mussulman misrule'.[75] References to the 'English sense of
justice', 'the invincibility of the new power', 'our English enlightenment',
'powerful scholars of Europe' and the like abounded.[76] The sense of racial
superiority was finally encapsulated in the title Hastie chose for the volume
of correspondence. Britain's civilizing mission in India and the ignorance of
amateur orientalists are the pet themes of Bankim's satires. Hastie's rolling
phrases would have been a godsend to any satirist.

Bankim's tension in relation to western culture informed even his life habits. Like many of his contemporaries, he too adopted certain features of the European lifestyle. Suresh Samajpati thus describes his drawing room in Calcutta: 'There was a beautifully embroidered carpet on the floor. Oil paintings hung on the wall. There were portraits of Bankim's father and himself. Attractive divans, chairs, etc. were arranged tastefully. A harmonium stood on a table in a corner.[77] In short, very much the home of a westernized Bengali or an Indian civilian rather than that of a man who wrote *Dharmatatva* or eulogized the ascetic virtues of dedicated *santans*.' He portrayed this lifestyle without satire only once—in an unfinished story, *Nishith rakshasir kahini* ['The Tale of a Night Ogress'], in which two brothers are described as dining off roasted mutton with sherry.[78] In one phase of his life, he had adopted the western way of dining—with knives and forks—along with the other paraphernalia of the western lifestyle and looked down upon the indigenous habit of eating with one's fingers as an uncivilized practice. His wife's gibes made him see his folly one day when he was struggling helplessly with some intractable *koi* fish which would not yield their delights to the alien instruments. This was also a time when imitation of the West in everything was on its way out, a trend much welcomed by the author. He once told an aspiring writer: 'What you write naturally is your style [sic]. Do not try to write like others. Then you will fall between two stools, as we do in our efforts to become Europeans'.[79] Yet, with all his emphasis on the Hindu tradition, he did depart from orthodoxy; for he did not give up tabooed food until 1885—when he became a vegetarian—and remained a moderate drinker all his life.[80] His self-conscious return to Hinduism was a matter of philosophical belief, rather than ritually correct conduct emphasized in the tradition. But his definition of identity emphasized self-respect which basically excluded alien modes of behaviour. An 'England-returned' Bengali once wrote 'Mr Bankimchandra' in the address of a letter to the novelist. Bankim's reply made a significant point: 'There is no one by the name of Mr Bankimchandra in this house. It appears you have forgotten this fact.'[81] Evidently, the intrusion of denationalizing alien ways was to be resisted. But the precise point where the line was to be drawn appears to have remained uncertain to him all his life.

The life-experience of the Bengali intelligentsia was however only one determinant of their world-view and the new sensibilities which shaped their perceptions. The intellectual and emotive response to Europe was largely a function of what one read, especially in the case of those who knew the West through books and the very few westerners they actually met. Bankim denounced in unequivocal language the education he received at school and college and described it as 'insufferable'.[82] His examination results however suggest that he had mastered well the prescribed reading which included, at the school-leaving stage, Addison's prose, Pope's satires, Johnson's *Rasselas*, Bacon's *Essays*, Dryden, Southey, Abercrombie's *Moral Feelings*, Keightley's *History of England*, some mathematics, geography, and some unspecified reading in political economy. This he supplemented with extensive readings into history, biography, and literature. The emphasis in these literary studies was on the classical rather than the romantic tradition in English literature and, as one critic points out, Bankim's literary style appears to have benefited from the exposure to disciplined prose.[83] In 1857, he was in the first batch of students who took the newly established Calcutta University's Entrance Examination. The punishing syllabus covered a wide range of subjects—English, Greek, and Latin; Sanskrit, Bengali, and Hindi; history and geography, mathematics and natural philosophy. As one of the first two graduates of the Calcutta University, he sat for an examination the following year for an identical range of subjects, presumably at a somewhat higher level. His preparation for these two examinations was as an autodidact, for he was at the time a student of law in Presidency College and the College did not provide for the relevant instruction. In short, by the age of 20, he had acquired a fair knowledge of European literature, philosophy, and the natural sciences, mostly through his own effort.[84]

He kept adding to this basic knowledge acquired in youth throughout his life, at the rate of a book a day, according to one source of information.[85] In literature, Shakespeare, Byron, Scott, and, judging by the quotations at the beginning of the chapters in his novels, Southey, Thompson, and Campbell were his favourite writers. The historians he referred to most frequently were Macaulay and Buckle, the latter partly for his Positivist inclinations, because Comte was a major influence on Bankim's philosophical writings. He was well read in classical and contemporary European literature. Dante, Goethe, Hugo, and Balzac were the subjects of heated discussion at the literary gatherings in his house. Though his biographers do not mention the fact, there is evidence to show that he read French, for he reviewed J.B.St. Hilaire's *Le Bouddha et sa Religion* for the *Calcutta Review*.[86] His linguistic skills included some Latin and Arabic, the latter acquired because of his interest in astrology, but there is nothing to indicate that he read the Roman writers in the original.[87]

A recurrent theme in his writings is Europe's scientific spirit. In this he shared the intellectual concern of his generation, deeply inspired by Akshay Datta's impassioned regard for Bacon and his treatise on man's relationship with external objects based on George Coombe's work on the same topic, a prescribed text as well as a favourite reading of young Bengalis ever since its publication in the *Tattvabodhini patrika*. It is unlikely that the courses in natural philosophy which he read for his examinations, evidently without any access to laboratories, provided any sound introduction to scientific knowledge, but he did retain a lifelong curiosity which he sought to satisfy in an amateurish way. A microscope, acquired after his student days, and extensive reading into scientific literature indicate this persistent interest. The eleven essays on popular science he published in *Bangadarshan* and his philosophical discourses which touched on scientific themes drew upon the writings of Darwin, Huxley, Tyndall, and Lockeyer among others. While Bankim's writings were profoundly influenced by the motifs, subject matter, and sensibilities of western literature, he, like the other major writers of his generation, appears to have been attracted most by two schools of social philosophy, Utilitarianism and Comte's Positivism and Religion of Humanity. The implications of this preference are discussed below. Here it is worth noting that the world of contemporary western thought he knew best were the works of Hume, Bentham, James Mill, and Auguste Comte. His assessments of the colonial economic nexus, where he discounted the theories of the drainage of wealth and immiserization through the destruction of handicrafts, indicate his conversion to the doctrine of free trade and a thorough knowledge of classical political economy. His short treatise on equality, which he later repudiated as erroneous, contains evidence of his familiarity with the philosophy of the Enlightenment, especially Rousseau, as well as the nineteenth-century socialist writings. One obscure reference to one 'Mausukh saheb' may be actually to Karl Marx, but the point can never be decided for certain owing to the peculiar transliteration or a printing error.

The central object of Bankim's creative effort was to develop the language and literature of Bengal and create among his countrymen a sense of national identity based on what he considered to be the best traditions of Hindu culture. The Bengali contemptuous of his own language and literature and unable to speak his language fluently was a frequent object of his sarcasm.[88] He started writing in Bengali while in his early teens for the popular literary journal, *Sambad prabhakar* edited by the famous poet, Iswar Gupta. Since the provision for formal instruction in Sanskrit was non-existent outside the Sanskrit College, Bankim was tutored in the language and its literature at home by the famous pandits of Bhatpara.[89] Later in life he devoted a great deal of time to Sanskritic studies and inherited his maternal grandfather's splendid collection of books and manuscripts.[90] Yet by his own admission, his command over Sanskrit never equalled his knowledge of English. What is more, he confessed that both in writing and speaking he was more at ease in English than in Bengali.[91] His conversation as reported by friends and acquaintances contained a large proportion of English vocabulary, especially when the subject of discussion was literary or philosophical. He was evidently not free from the characteristic predicament of the western-educated Bengali, the favourite object of his satires. The mental world of men like Bankim was largely shaped by their western education. This catalytic influence was of crucial importance in their perception of western civilization. To make an obvious point, the perceivers were not Indians encountering a totally unfamiliar civilization, but men and women whose intellection and sensibilities had been radically altered by their exposure to specific elements of the alien culture.

Historians of Bengali literature have explored in some depth the western literary influences on Bankim's writings. His, it is pointed out, was the first successful effort to adopt the novel, a western literary form of relatively recent origin, into an Indian language. The affinities between his first novel, *Durgeshnandini*, and Scott's *Ivanhoe* have been commented upon repeatedly. He acknowledged that his story of the blind girl, Rajani, was inspired by Lytton's *Last Days of Pompeii* and Wilkie Collins's *The Woman in White*. Both his romantic historical themes and the later 'social novels' concerned with ordinary men and women of his own days and the problems of the human condition in a specific cultural context have very obvious western resonances as literary products. Our concern here is however not with his conscious or unconscious adoption of western literary forms or stylistic modes but the sensibilities which informed his world of imagination and intellect. There were at least two attempts to write novels in Bengali before Bankim, the famous *Alaler gharer dulal* and the less known *Anguriya-binimay* by Bhudev. Bankim's writings and these earlier literary efforts do not belong to the same world of emotional, aesthetic or intellectual ambience. The differences derive not simply from one man's individual genius but the complex interaction between distinct cultural influences in a particular historical situation resulting in new patterns of sensibilities.

Perhaps the most strikingly new characteristic of Bankim's novels is an intensely romantic mood expressed in a variety of forms and contexts. It is a romanticism unmistakably different from the delight in the miraculous and the wonderful the educated Bengalis had acquired from their exposure to Arabic and Persian tales. In his evocation of the past, as much as in his description of feminine beauty or of nature in her beguiling or awesome aspects, his prose as well as the subject matter almost invariably sought to transcend everyday reality and project a world of heightened consciousness. The first novel has for its background the struggle between the Pathans in Bengal and Akbar's Rajput generals. It is a world peopled with heroic men and women of transcendent beauty, a world of chivalry and tragic love. The second novel centres on the self-abnegating efforts of a Hindu prince to save his country from the Turkish invaders. Even the villainous Pasupati is a more than life-size character, an extraordinary man destroyed by his unscrupulous ambition. *Kapalkundala* is the story of a ravishingly beautiful woman brought up in total innocence by an ascetic in the middle of an uninhabited forest. Even the more didactic novels are stories of exceptional men and women dedicated to impersonal tasks of great moral grandeur. The social novels are about people in the throes of profound passions. His best works are permeated by a sense of tragedy. There too he was inspired by a romantic rather than a realistic perception of the human condition. His tragedies are rarely those of everyday life. They develop around people of exceptional character or outstanding beauty in circumstances which range from the unusual to the supernatural. Credibility is retained by the novelist's great skill as a writer.

His romantic imagination was no doubt inspired by his deep reading into European, particularly English literature. But here too a personal preference interacting with a particular vision of India's historical predicament appears to have been at work. To him, Walter Scott was one of the great literary figures of all times. He bracketed him with Kalidasa and compared him, favourably, with Shakespeare for his insight into human nature. He was also an assiduous reader of Byron's poetry and Shakespeare's plays.

This may help explain the romantic vision of history in his first novel. But already in his second novel, *Mrinalini*, the romance of history is overshadowed by grim tragedy, the conquest of Bengal by the Turks and the sack of Nadiya. The theme of political disaster or oppression of Hindus or the people of Bengal again recurs in his last four novels, in two of which he spelt out his doctrine of the disciplined cultivation of human faculties as the basis for individual and national regeneration. Two of these four novels end in tragedy. The third, *Anandamath*, also is a story of national failure on which an emotionally acceptable explanation is forced artificially, possibly for political reasons. Bankim's sense of history was thus overshadowed by his perception of the national fate, subjection to alien rule over long centuries. Incidentally, he did note in one essay that the British rule was the only truly alien rule in Indian history. In a statement on the Indian poets of the past, he makes a significant comment on the mediaeval poet, Vidyapati, that he was inward-looking, a man with a knowledge of sorrow, because he had known alien rule and national decline. The relevant passage runs: 'The days of Vidyapati were days of sorrow. The faith had been destroyed. Followers of a different faith were now the masters. The life of the nation was at a low ebb and just beginning to revive. The poet's eyes were opened. In that sadness, he sang his sad songs to point his finger at [the all-pervading fact of] sorrow.'[92] It is difficult to resist the conclusion that Bankim saw his own predicament as similar to that of Vidyapati's, for was he not the poet and preacher of a subject-people on the threshold of national revival, according to his own light? His tragic perception of the nation's fate spread out to include his understanding of the human condition. He too draws attention to the all-pervading fact of sorrow for, as he noted in the same essay, poets and writers were but the products of their times.[93]

The known and probable facts of Bankim's personal life suggest that he had more than his fair share of conflict and unhappiness. One constant thorn in his flesh was his means of livelihood, a perpetual reminder of what political subjection meant to a proud people. The emotional affect of a political perception was at the very heart of his tragic vision. His hopes and blueprints for national regeneration were similarly inspired. Despite all his efforts at objectivity, this man could in no way be a detached observer of the civilization represented by the alien rulers.

His views on the purpose of literature subsumed but transcended the more limited objective of national regeneration. The nation would rise to great heights through the achievement of a moral perfection. Such perfection, *chittasuddhi* (purification of one's heart) was one purpose of literature: 'The object of literature is not ethics; but ethics and literature have the same end in view. The secondary purpose of literature is to elevate the human mind—to achieve a purification of the human heart ... The poets are the teachers of mankind, but they do not instruct by expounding the principles

of morality ... They purify the human soul by achieving the highest level of
beauty. This creation of the highest level of beauty is the purpose of
literature.'[94] This humanist ideal of literature gave him a universalist outlook,
a criterion by which to judge all literature. Literary creation was for him a
common heritage of mankind, an undifferentiated universe of experience
transcending parochial limits, despite the limiting influence of culture and
one's time in history. For him all literary creation was based on a fundamental
unity: 'Poetry has two objects—description and refinement ... the beauty
which is absent even in the beautiful, the aesthetic emotion, the experience
of physical beauty, touch or smell which nobody has ever known, the light
which is nowhere there on land or on water. That bright golden light born of
their own souls is what the poets deploy to suffuse the world and make what
is beautiful even more so. They create that ultimate perfection of beauty
which is transcendentally real. Transcendentally real but not unreal. Nothing
in their creation is untrue, unthinkable, opposed to truth or the laws of
nature, but nowhere in nature will you find it represented exactly. This is
what we have described as refinement at the beginning of the essay. The
poetry which lacks this refinement ... we have called descriptive.' His
perception of these universal criteria counterbalanced his nationalist concerns
when it came to any question of aesthetic judgement. And as an artist, he
inevitably assessed much of human civilization as cultural artifacts within
the purview of such evaluation.

　　'The beautiful includes the good', he remarked to a friend in course of
a literary discussion. But for him, the good included moral and aesthetic
criteria which were not entirely in accord with the universalist literary ideal
expounded above. *Adirasa*, the first or primeval *rasa*, the erotic impulse
transformed into an aesthetic experience, was disgustingly ugly (*kadarya*) to
Bankim, very much a product of the Victorian puritanism.'[95] The poet
Bharatchandra who often rose to great heights of sensitive lyricism was
described as a person of low instincts.[96] The older generation of Bengalis
were, in his view, obscene in their tastes, a fault he attributed even to his
literary mentor Iswar Gupta. In fact, so great was his concern with 'decency'
in such matters that he heavily bowdlerized his edition of the latter's poems
even though he admitted that the true flavour of the writer's poetry was lost
in the process.[97]

　　Bankim's literary sensibility could however transcend such narrow
puritanism. He did see his exercise in bowdlerization as an act of literary
vandalism and justified it as follows: 'But in view of the current situation of

the Bengali writers and readers, in no way can I retain an iota of obscenity.' The sentences which follow indicate a very different level of aesthetic awareness: 'I also know that Iswar Gupta's obscenity is not true obscenity. Only what is written to excite base passions or express the writer's disgusting thoughts can be described as truly obscene. That is obscene even if written in pure and decent language. But that which is written with no such end in view, but only to ridicule or reprimand sin, is not obscene even if the expression and taste are opposed to civilized norms.'[98] These civilized norms were evidently those of another society which the western-educated Bengali had accepted as superior. The older generation were given to foul language. 'Fortunately', Bankim noted, 'those social conditions are gradually disappearing.'[99]

The newly acquired anxiety about language permissible in Victorian drawing rooms was compounded in Bankim's case by a concern for morally correct behaviour. In his case moral rectitude appears to have been equated to a large extent with sexual restraint or single-minded monogamy. His 'Poison Tree', *Bishabriksha*, is really man's unrestrained passion visited inevitably by nemesis. This view of morality may contain some existential truth, but arguably his understanding of ethical norms, despite his later projection of a complex philosophy of life, was closer to copybook morals than to the empathic insight of a creative writer into the human condition. Only the copybook in question derived from two very different sources—the conservative code of family life among high-caste Bengalis and the new code of chaste and restrained conduct by which English gentlemen allegedly lived. But for the fact that Kunda in *Bishabriksha* was a widow, Nagendra's love for the hapless girl would have posed no problem socially in a traditional Bengali context. Taking a second wife was a perfectly acceptable action. In two of his later novels Bankim describes polygamous homes without any moral condemnation. Of the two, one, *Debi Chaudhurani*, is in fact an exemplar of the highest ideal, *nishkama karma*, the doctrine of non-attachment. But *Bishabriksha* ends in grim tragedy, quite convincingly in human terms. Yet one is left with a strong feeling that an ethical lesson is written into the text. The results of Nagendra's sin in deviating from virtuous monogamy is visited on all, the innocent Kunda included. If this lesson derives from an alien ideology—the seductress Rohini's gruesome end is another instance of the same precept. Bankim's exaltation of *satitva*, a woman's unflinchingly chaste devotion to her husband, raised a cherished domestic virtue applauded in the Hindu tradition to the level of the highest ideal. In *Chandrasekhar*, the deviant wife, Saibalini, is made to return to the straight and narrow path through a spiritual regime of excruciating cruelty evidently approved by the author. The one exception to the prescriptions of chastity in Bankim's novels offers an interesting insight into the relevant ideology of the time. In *Indira*, the lost wife disguised as a cook, seduces the husband who declares that he would never take back the wife who had presumably been abducted by robbers. While *Indira* is briefly worried by her husband's readiness to take a domestic to bed, she is advised to overlook this minor deviation natural in a man deprived of sex. The author sees nothing to condemn in the husband's lechery or his cruel determination to abandon an innocent wife. The indulgent view of an affair on the side with a domestic is consistent with Victorian morality. Discarding an abducted wife was in accordance with the ideal of women's chastity dear to Hindu orthodoxy. If Bankim absorbed selectively many of the humane values of western and Indian life, he did not necessarily reject all that was inhuman in the two traditions.

His complex personality and the clash of cultures in his mental world preclude any identifiably consistent pattern of responses. If as a conservative Hindu he deplored a married woman's passion for another man and as a Victorian *pater familias* he felt a similar revulsion for a man's extra-marital love, his novels are no simple lessons in uncomplicated morality. First, in accepting the lives of ordinary people as the legitimate theme of literature, he had adopted an aesthetic ideal virtually unknown in India. In dealing with such themes, his primary concern was not any lesson in morality but artistic perfection as he understood it. The task involved a capacity for empathy. Bankim was not lacking in this quality. His 'sinners' are recognizably human and one can easily identify with their predicament. He has his transgressors punished more in quest of a social ethic than in his pursuit of artistic truth. Arguably, the same logic as the one which inspired his bowdlerization of Iswar Gupta was at work here: morality like discretion in the use of language was preferable to artistic excellence 'in view of the current situation'. Even his ideal of *satitva* is not uniformly projected in all his statements on women. His treatise on equality contains an impassioned discussion on the uneven treatment of men and women in Hindu society. It acknowledges the acceptability of widow remarriage even though his emotional preference went the other way. It is by no means clear that his later repudiation of *Samya* covered these passages as well. As a creative writer and a thinking man, he appears to have been constantly at odds with the mildly conservative to right of the centre social values he consciously accepted. At the same time, he never quite lived down his cultural conditioning as a Bengali Hindu. His gut reactions on questions such as the remarriage of widows were hence often out of tune with his rationalist perceptions. The conflicts in his thought and personality were at many levels and had multiple facets.

There is no conflict or ambivalence, however, in Bankim's intense nationalism. It informed the bulk of his creative writing and social effort and was the mainspring of his emotional life. His formidable reserve disappeared whenever he talked of his country. 'His self-control was swept away by [a flood of emotions]—chagrin, shame, joy, grief, anger and pride.'[100] This impassioned nationalism was very much a part of the contemporary political culture.[101] In Bankim's case, it appears to have reached a level of great intensity owing to his sensitive nature and the negative experiences of his career in service.

There are several elements of apparent contradiction in his nationalist ideology and commitment. First, there is the fact of his faith in the beneficence of British rule and plea for loyalty.[102] The true character of this faith is discussed below. It should, however, be noted in the present context that he shared with his contemporaries the entirely rational belief that the British rule was there to stay for a long time to come and independence was predicated on sustained effort at national regeneration over a long period. In the interim, it was necessary to work out a *modus vivendi* which included obedience.[103] The *Anandamath* episode shows how as a government servant he was forced to modify his initial statements into which an 'anti-British', in the sense of anti-colonial, sentiment was quite correctly read. Bankim's pragmatism in trying to retain his job may not be particularly edifying, but it illustrates the predicament of a colonial intelligentsia and suggests that his positive assessment of British rule should not always be taken at its face value. There is plentiful evidence to show that he saw that rule as painful bondage. A friend offered to show him a souvenir he had brought from the battlefield of Plassey. 'What is the point?', he asked. 'One can only shed tears.'[104] He admired the Rani of Jhansi as the greatest woman ever in human history and would have liked to write a novel about her heroic role. The concluding chapter of *Anandamath* refers to a future day when the *santans*' struggle for the liberation of the motherland was resumed—almost certainly a reference to 1857. In reviewing Nabin Sen's epic poem on the Battle of Plassey, he made two telling comments. The first describes the battle as a historical, yet an unhistorical event 'because its true history had not been written yet'.[105] The second commends the poet as follows: 'If crying out aloud and heart-rending words of genuine pain are the stigmata of patriotism, then Nabin Babu is indeed a patriot.'[106] In *Kamalakanter daptar*, he asks a loaded question as to who was a woman, the deposed nawab Wajed Ali, who spent his time in happy dalliance at Calcutta or the Begum of Oudh, who had fought the British and ended up in painful exile?[107] The message which the writer sought to convey is clear and explicit.

Bankim had no patience however with the organized politics of his days, even though he had some contact with Surendranath and the British Indian Association. 'The blind beggar asking for alms' was his caustic description of the politics of petitioning.[108] He was especially contemptuous of the Indian press whose supreme politics, in his view, was abusing the English.[109] His defence of the Vernacular Press Act, which earned him a great deal of opprobrium, may have been inspired by his contempt.[110] It is difficult to resist the conclusion that he put his faith ultimately in a violent revolution or at least the ability to threaten such a revolution. 'Physical (i.e. armed) strength is the best means of self-defence'—this was his considered judgement. George Washington and William of Orange were cited as examples of beneficial leadership. The Indian subjects, he observed, had been defeated in 1857, but it had been no pleasant experience for the British. 'They avoid their cherished path if there is a threat of violence.'[111] The statement evidently had more than descriptive connota-tions.

In three of his novels he deals with the theme of conflict with the British—*Anandamath, Debi Chaudhurani,* and *Chandrasekhar.* Their heroes and heroines and other protagonists, presented in a favourable light, are either engaged in mortal combat with the British, or, like Debi Chaudhurani and Bhabani Pathak, undertake a Robin Hood-style enterprise to redress the sufferings of the poor induced by the conquest. Each of these novels ends in a British victory. In two instances, the concluding passages contain words of praise for the British rule which sound far from convincing in the light of all that precedes. *Chandrasekhar* even omits this exercise and refers to Mir Qasim's defeat as the end of Bengal's independence. Arguably, such exercises were intended to avoid trouble with the authorities. By then at least one producer and playwright had been prosecuted for the crime of projecting anti-British sentiments.[112] Even before the publication of *Anandamath,* the government's attitude to overt criticism was well known.

Bankim's complex and explicit assessments of the British rule have to be read with the less direct expressions of his true feelings.

His blueprint for a programme of national regeneration, its ethico-philosophical emphasis notwithstanding, was evidently concerned about the physical invincibility of the British power in India. In his didactic writings, he speaks of the need for a spiritual discipline based on a cultivation of all the human faculties, including the physical. The purpose is service to one's country and mankind in a spirit of total detachment. The patriotic monks in *Anandamath* are fictional exemplars of this ideal lifestyle.[113] So are Bhavani Thakur, the high-minded brigand, and his disciple, Debi Chaudhurani. The monks worship Vishnu, the protector, not as the lover god Krishna, but as an embodiment of righteous power, resplendent with all his weaponry, ready to punish the evil-doer and restore virtue on earth. That evil is represented by 'the king who does not do his duty', the Muslim *roi-fainéant* of Murshidabad and, quite explicitly, in the serialized version of the novel, the British, the real power behind the nawab's throne. In devising a symbol for this militant nationalism of his imagination, Bankim evoked the image of the motherland, once glorious, now reduced to shameful misery. She is identified with the mother goddess worshipped as Sakti, i.e. power incarnate, and in his famous hymn to the Mother, *Bande Mataram*, the weapons in her ten arms, her infinite strength, and the sharp swords in the hands of her myriad children evoke an image of great power. His cryptic comment on the song, that its meaning would be fully understood only by a future generation, probably indicates a pattern of hopes which put little faith in constitutional politics. After 1905 *Bande Mataram* became the slogan of Indian nationalism and *Anandamath* the Bible of armed revolutionaries. One has the feeling that their creator had almost hoped for such a result.

If militant nationalism provides the context for his assessment of the colonial presence, the precise content of that nationalism was a major determinant of his perceptions of the West. He had an immense pride in the Indian heritage, especially the Hindu past, but recognized that patriotism was no part of that tradition.[114] He also believed in the decline of Indian civilization over time, a departure from the heroic endeavours of earlier ages into an effete enjoyment of the fruits of civilization, which to him explained the Turkish conquest of India.[115] As to contemporary India, he described the Hindus as a people unaware of their great past. A renewed consciousness of that heritage was essential for national regeneration.[116] As a writer and an educated Bengali, he perceived one duty as incumbent on the people of his social class—instructing his countrymen about the nation's past achievements, current problems, and one's duties to the nation.[117] Even his later philosophical writings were unmistakably dedicated to the same task.

There is some obscurity as to the ethnic identity and the social limits of the 'nation' (which he calls *jati*), whose cause he espoused so passionately. Sometimes it was coterminous with India: the unity of all the races of India, he wrote, was essential for the country's progress.[118] The referent is oftener the Hindus. His more immediate concern was surely with the Bengalis and even in the hymn, *Bande Mataram*, the reference to the 'twice seventy million arms' of the Mother's children clearly equates the nation with that segment of the Indian people. Whatever his misgivings about the role of Islam in India's history, in one explicit statement he recognizes the Muslims as an integral part of the Bengali, and hence, by implication, of the Indian people.[119] And despite his later repudiation of his treatise on equality, his writings repeatedly express his passionate concern for the deprived sections of the population. The lack of sympathy between the poor and the rich was in his view the 'chief obstacle' to India's progress.[120] An equitable distribution of wealth would lead to unlimited progress. 'Now some half a dozen Babus', he wrote, 'sit in the hall of the Indian Association and speak softly softly. Instead one would have heard the loud roar of sixty million subjects, formidable like the sound of the thundering ocean.'[121] Never in his writings on the country's problems did he overlook the fate of the poor. His critiques of the colonial regime focused above all on this question.

His attitude to Indian Muslims, a subject of considerable controversy, is relevant to this study because his assessment of British rule was coloured to some extent by his views on the reigns of the Muslim dynasties. Commentators have drawn attention to the complexity of Bankim's attitude on this issue—his various favourable statements about Muslims and his refusal to describe the Indo-Islamic age as a period of foreign rule—to repudiate the allegations of communalism against the author.[122] The complexity and ambivalence are not in doubt. But it is difficult to overlook Bankim's passionate hostility to Muslims, expressed at times in a totally gratuitous way. I shall give only two instances. In *Anandamath*, the victorious *santans* go on a happy spree of burning and looting Muslim villages apparently inhabited by people who had nothing whatever to do with the nawab's alleged oppressions. The second example is perhaps even more telling. In discussing what really happened at Plassey, he writes, 'If you do not believe what I say read the book entitled *Seir Mutaqqherin* written by a shaven-headed cow-killing Muslim.'[123] Bhudev complained that the western-educated Bengalis had been brainwashed by British writers on the Indo-Islamic period of Indian history. Bankim like many of his contemporaries did look upon those centuries as a period of bondage and considered the resistance of the Hindu chieftains to the Delhi emperors as a form of national resistance. Comparisons between the pre-modern administration of the Muslim dynasts and the more orderly government of the colonial rulers was a necessary corollary of such perceptions.

One characteristic attributed to colonial nationalism is its acceptance of the objectification of its own culture as projected by the protagonists of the dominant culture.[124] The 'they' versus 'us' dichotomy perceived as central to Orientalist thought and the implied inferiority of the subject peoples became, in this view, unquestionable axioms in nationalist thought over a long period. Hence the nationalists' psychological need to assert their superiority, or at least equality, in relation to the West. I have argued in the previous chapter that there were exceptions to this pattern of perception and response. Individuals and groups with undiminished faith in the received tradition were the least concerned with its assessment in terms of alien criteria.

Bankim's acceptance of western superiority is, however, a central theme in the discussion which follows. It has been suggested that he sought to compensate for the resulting sense of inferiority by identifying one area where India, in his view, excelled,[125] namely, her spiritual heritage. Such a view, promoted among others by the Theosophists and Vivekananda in their very different ways, did become a part of the intellectual vocabulary in late nineteenth-century India. Such claims, emphasizing moral rather than spiritual superiority, were part of a fairly universal response to the threatened victory of the West, political and cultural, in many parts of the world, from Russia to Japan. Bankim's enquiry into the Indian past in the quest of ethically and intellectually satisfying answers was idiosyncratic and its direction followed no expected path that can be summed up in such simple clichés as spiritual superiority. His intellect, shaped by the dominant rationalist philosophies of the time which it continually questioned, arrived at a synthesis based on selective features of the Indian philosophical and the modern European traditions. The object, as suggested above, was not simply psychological compensation, but the discovery of an ideal and a programme for national regeneration. He stated in so many words that this was the purpose of his philosophical writings.[126] It is true that he claimed for Hindu thought satisfactory answers to questions raised but not solved by the modern western philosophers. The answers however were very much Bankim's own, though at times no more than a modification of the philosophies he had learnt from the western thinkers he admired. Such idiosyncratic mingling of Hindu and modern western thought with one's own innovations and in terms of one's preferred values was very much a part of modern Indian nationalism: Gandhi is a prime example. The claim that the synthesis was inherent in the received wisdom is also a part of the nationalist perception. The invention of tradition, with a thin veneer of credibility for its claims to ancient origin, fortified the emergent faith in a glorious history. That faith compensated for the unhappy present, the fall from grace inherent in political subjection, and was a beacon of hope for the future.

There are two distinct phases in the development of Bankim's patriotic and ideological concerns and a corresponding change in his evaluation of the West. The disjunction between the two phases is sharp and somewhat sudden. Probably caused by some personal experience not recorded by his biographers, this abrupt transition from a passionate scepticism to a theocentric outlook has not been satisfactorily explained. The discontinuity should not however be exaggerated, for many of the intellectual influences which earlier moulded his world-view are evident in the latter phase as well.

Post-Enlightenment rationalism was a dominant strand in the intellectual milieu of nineteenth-century Bengal, but its attractions were not equally strong for all concerned. Bhudev used its tools to validate the inherited values and the traditional way of life. Bankim's contemporary, Keshab Sen, preached a profoundly emotional faith in God and almost as passionate a loyalty to British rule. His disciples who later left the fold, like Sibnath Sastri, combined a non-conformist piety with dreams of Indian independence. In short, uncompromising allegiance to reason was not the only choice open to the Bengali intelligentsia in the latter half of the nineteenth century. One's background and personal predilection often determined the choice.

In Bankim's case the personal preference was spelt out at a surprisingly early age. When he was probably about ten, he caused a scandal in the village by asking a leading Sanskrit scholar which Krishna he had come to worship—the one who once stole the clothes of the milkmaids bathing naked in the river and who had sixteen hundred of these maids as his mates? He had recently read the Bhagavatapurana in translation and evidently not liked what he had read. His question expresses perfectly two dominant traits of his adult life: disregard for received wisdom and a puritanical distaste for overt eroticism.[127] Bankim told Sris Majumdar that he was an atheist earlier in life.[128] The earliest incontrovertible evidence of his conversion to a theistic faith is in *Anandamath*, written in 1880, though a few references in his writings before that date may have similar implications. His first essay on the subject of the Hindu religion—'On the Origin of Hindu Festivals,' published in 1869—is a social scientific discourse offering anthropological explanations. Two years later, he described without hesitation the entire body of Hindu philosophy as 'a great mass of errors'. *Samkhya*, which he admired for its 'merciless logic' in questioning even the existence of God because of lack of evidence, was denounced for its 'tendency to support the Vedas'. The Buddha's glory lay in taking the final step: 'He denied the authority of the Vedas; and with it caste, sacrifice, superstition, priesthood...' The Smritis 'set unbearable restraints on individual freedom of action'. Jayadeva's *Gitagovinda*, venerated by all Vaishnavas, did not have 'a single new truth to teach'. Only the *nyaya* philosophy was 'splendid' because of its inherent rationalism, especially its clear statement of the laws of causation, anticipating Mill. *Samkhya*'s potentiality for wise scepticism was undermined by its subservience to the Vedas. But these two systems were superior to the others because they recognized the Reign of Law which 'must supersede all the theological conceptions'. Even these were vitiated by the deductive method, for the Hindus found observation and experiment beneath their dignity. The deductive method itself was not pushed to its logical conclusion. Principles were assumed on no grounds and 'the most perfect weapons of deductive logic' were not used; 'fanciful inferences' were the preferred substitutes. He saw an obvious causal link between specific dimensions of the Hindu intellectual tradition and national decline. First, the close link between myth and philosophy permitted fanciful superstition to coexist with rigorously rational thought. The philosophical notions were often suggested by the Vedic nature myths and then developed into profoundly introspective speculation on the nature of the moral and material world. Eventually however the philosophical notions were expressed in myths which subverted all rationality. He cited as example the probable origin of the doctrine of the three *gunas* or qualities, *satva, rajas* and *tamas* in the three Vedic deities of light. But the philosophical concept generated a 'fanciful' doctrine, namely the three attributes of the Supreme Being. Incidentally before long Bankim saw in the same doctrine an innate rationality which came close to the scientific theories of his time. In the earlier phase of his intellectual development he regarded the 'mutual affiliation between religion and philosophy' as the most disastrous feature of the Hindu past.

Philosophy moving within the narrow circles of orthodoxy developed into systems of error. Thus vitiated, it would provide intellectual support for superstitions and sectarian errors which would have died a natural death but for the subtle and illusory arguments of philosophy.[129] A far worse consequence of this *damnosa hereditas* was that it 'taught the Hindu to despise the blessings of existence and to look upon inaction as the ideal of human happiness'. Bankim drew upon Buckle's historical explanation of man's sense of sin to develop his thesis. Man's sense of helplessness in the face of nature's overwhelming power had induced the faith in deities who had to be propitiated all the time. Their anger implied some failure on the part of the mortals. The notion of sin thus engendered led to the idea of penance, self-imposed physical suffering by way of propitiation. In India, the climate 'neutralized' human energies and the philosophers came to perceive in nature, not angry deities, but omnipotent causes of all-pervasive suffering. The major systems, each in its distinctive way, sought the solution of this fundamental problem in life-denying regimes. Asceticism, fatalism, apathy in politics, and sensuality in poetry were the necessary results of the Hindu and Buddhist other-worldliness.[130] He referred to Lecky's grim account of mediaeval European asceticism and its consequences in support of his theory.

Buckle and Lecky were the two chief mentors in his historical enquiries. He accepted the former's views regarding the impact of climate on civilization, a belief frequently invoked in the nineteenth century to explain the alleged decay of Indian civilization. As discussed below, Bankim used these notions as a fairly sophisticated tool of analysis. Lecky's ideas on the source of human progress taken with his own belief in the disastrous consequences of the Indian religio-philosophical tradition led to a somewhat different interpretation of India's decline. With his firm faith in buoyant capitalism, Lecky identified the quest for wealth as the root of all human progress. Contentment was hence inevitably the enemy of progress. And since both the Hindus and the Buddhists had idealized indifference to material pleasures, stagnation and decay had been the fate of India. The impoverished masses had cowered before the might of a malevolent nature. The Brahmins, who encouraged their festering superstitions to shore up their own power, became the victims of their own stratagem and came to believe in what they preached. The pervasive apathy and decline in the spirit of independence affected the polity as well; for as he had learnt from Lecky, conflict was the source of strength in political life. In the absence of resistance and competition from the commonality, the functionaries of state power assumed unwonted authority.[131] It is worth noting that Bhudev identified the self-same conflicts as one of the most baneful traditions of European public life which India should carefully avoid.

Bankim's negative assessment of the Indian heritage went much farther than his critique of the philosophical and religious traditions. He traced the misfortunes of the Indian masses, especially the peasantry, back to the earliest origins of civilization in the subcontinent. Here too his analysis was based on Buckle's ideas. Growth of civilization, in this view, was contingent upon a steady increase in knowledge. The latter in its turn depended upon the creation and maintenance of a leisured class, a division of labour between the toiling masses and those pursuing knowledge freed from the burden of physical effort to produce the necessities of life. The surplus needed to sustain the leisured class was produced easily and early in India thanks to her fertile soil. The monopoly of knowledge which the higher castes, especially the Brahmins, secured through this early division of labour helped and encouraged them to impose their authority on the masses on a permanent basis. Inequitable distribution of wealth and knowledge meant a corresponding inequity in the distribution of power in society, enshrined in the Smritis devised to oppress the Sudras. 'Poverty, ignorance, slavery' were hence the fate of the toiling masses. Their apathy, as discussed above, affected the quality of political life and their ignorance encouraged the growth of superstition among the Brahmins themselves. Besides, the climate discouraged effort (here Lecky's exposition of the climatic influences on the growth of civilization was cited) and religion prescribed indifference to the world. The pervasive apathy which generated this philosophy was thus reinforced.[132]

There was more than patriotic intent in this enquiry into India's fall from grace. A passionate hatred of social injustice in every form inspired much of Bankim's writings in the most productive phase of his career. The egalitarian values projected in his treatise on equality *Samya*, are supported by copious references to Rousseau, Louis Blanc, Fourier, Sully, Proudhon, and Mill's views on inheritance. The International and communism are mentioned as the spiritual descendants of Rousseau's ideas, apparently not without some sympathy. To conclude that Bankim was influenced by his readings into egalitarian philosophies would be easy but not necessarily correct. The intensity of his feelings on inequality suggests something other than calm reflection. Inequality of wealth is thus explained in the introductory chapter of *Samya*: 'Jadu does not know how to steal, how to cheat, how to defraud another man of all that he owns; hence Jadu is a plebeian. Ram has accumulated wealth by theft, fraud and deceit; hence Ram is a rich man.' The most impassioned passages in his entire works are those dealing with the condition of the peasantry in Bengal: '... The goddess of agriculture is smiling on the land. Wealth is raining down by her grace ... Everyone prospers through that prosperity—the king, landlords, merchants, moneylenders, everyone. Only there is no prosperity for the peasant ... The bigger animals like the tiger devour smaller animals like goats .... The big man known as the zamindar devours the small man called the peasant.'[133] Bankim defended his stringent criticism of the Bengal zamindars as follows: 'Let that voice which fails to cry out in pain for those suffering pain be choked. Let the pen which fails to write for the benefit of people [living] in misery dry up.'[134] His portrait of the fictional peasant, Paran Mandal—a description of unending harassment by exploiters, big and small, and consequent hopelessness—was true to life, he claimed. He commended his friend Dinabandhu Mitra's *Mirror of Indigo* as 'the Uncle Tom's Cabin of Bengal'. Very probably it was his exposure to the misery of the rural poor as a young deputy magistrate which attracted him to the western egalitarian philosophy. This concern persisted. *Samya*, written in 1873–5, was published as a book in 1879. In 1892, the chapters dealing with the condition of the peasantry were republished. Only the section on equality was suppressed because the author considered it erroneous. He drew upon his reading into the egalitarian writers to explain the origins of inequality—the distinction between natural and socially imposed inequalities—and the reasons why artificial inequality should be rejected.[135] The structure of arguments were evidently built on a foundation of deep emotions.

At least as late as 1879, the year in which *Samya* was published, his feelings about inequality between men and women were as strong as his attitude to other forms of social and economic inequality. He was revolted by the treatment of women in Hindu society and his arguments castigating the mores of his own people were merely buttressed by references to avant-garde western thought on the subject, especially Mill. Denial of higher education to women, their seclusion (keeping them 'caged like wild animals' was his description of the practice), and the virtual absence of rights to property were in his view the most execrable features of the existing social code. The Dharmasastras were castigated for excluding unchaste women from all rights to their husbands' property while they imposed no comparable restriction on lecherous men. 'If this is dharma-sastra (the scriptures on righteous conduct), what then is adharma-sastra (the scriptures on unrighteous conduct)?', he queried.[136] He saw only one purpose in all laws made by men for women—the latter's total enslavement. Bengal, he pointed out, had even a society for the prevention of cruelty to animals, but none for the protection of women who constituted half the population.[137]

If western egalitarian thought mainly reinforced a strong emotional commitment, Bankim's intellectual debt to certain other areas of European philosophy and social sciences went much deeper. His acceptance of classical political economy, intellectually if not emotionally, appears to have been total at one stage. Free trade, he believed, had increased India's wealth by expanding the market for her agricultural produce. If weaving had declined, others had gained through the cheapness of textiles and the market would reallocate the weavers' labour in some suitable way. What looked like drainage of wealth was no more than the legitimate gains of trade.[138] He recommended Mill to those who wanted to know why protectionism was a false doctrine and Buckle for accounts of its disastrous consequences.[139] He explained the distribution of wealth in terms of returns to factors of production. In this, he did not entirely follow the classical economists, a fact to which he drew attention in his preface to *Samya*, and described the entire income of the leisured classes as profit.[140] In the 1892 edition of *Bangadeser krishak*, he admits to certain errors in his political economic arguments but adds that one is no longer very sure as to what was correct and what incorrect in this particular social science.[141]

Despite his many criticisms of Utilitarian philosophy, the influence of Bentham and Mill is writ large on his ideas of social progress.[142] Even his version of the Hindu ideology as stated in his later writings drew heavily on Bentham.[143] To Mill he owed much of his insight into classical political economy and modern logic.[144] But it was Mill's ideas on social justice that he evidently found most attractive. The obituary published in *Bangadarshan*[145] heavily emphasized the British philosopher's ideas on state support for education, deployment of the incremental income from land for public welfare, and equality between men and women. *Samya* refers repeatedly to Mill's egalitarian ideas. As argued above, an affinity of sentiments probably induced Bankim to look for theoretical arguments and practical programmes in Mill's egalitarian writings.

The most profound and sustained western influence on Bankim's thought is traceable to Comte—his Religion of Humanity and Positivist philosophy. A fair number of Bengali intellectuals in the latter half of the nineteenth century felt attracted to Comte's ideas. Several of those who wrote for Bankim's *Bangadarshan* were very much a part of this group as was his close friend, Jogendrachandra Ghosh, the leading exponent of Positivism and the Religion of Humanity in Bengal. There were several distinct reasons for this attraction. The Positivist idea of order and progress had an obvious appeal for the reformers averse to any sudden and total break with the past. The fact that Comte accorded society priority over the individual, a point underlined in Bankim's obituary note on Mill, was of special relevance in this context. The new spirit of nationalist self-assertion subsumed a sense of loyalty to the Hindu society and religion, especially when these were maligned by the foreigners. Besides, the established social system was genuinely unacceptable in its essentials only to a few and even among them only a handful favoured sharp departures either in theory or in practice. Open rebellion against the dominant codes was confined to small coteries and a few exceptional individuals. Defiance of social or political authority was by no means the hallmark of this colonial intelligentsia, for the most part dependent on the alien ruler for their livelihood. Bankim's horrendous account of what the zamindari system had done to the mass of the peasantry concludes with a recommendation of mild reform and an appeal to the better sense of all right-thinking zamindars because the abolition of the Permanent Settlement would result in 'massive disorder' and breach of promise on part of the British.[146] Progress consistent with order was the logical choice in ideology in such a context. Comte provided the best sustained philosophical argument in its favour. His respectful references to Hinduism and to the sacerdotal class, identified with Brahmins in the Indian context, enhanced the appeal of his ideas. The Religion of Humanity was acceptable to those whose secular rationalism rejected all dogma and hence the allegiance to any denominational faith. In the two distinct phases of his intellectual development Bankim drew inspiration from two very different elements in Comte's optimistic programme for the future of mankind. His own hopes for the future evoke unmistakably the idiom of the Religion of Humanity: '... Is there any basis of human happiness other than the quest for the happiness of others? No ... Just as at present people are in a mad rush for money, status, material pleasures and the like, some day mankind will rush with equal abandon in the pursuit of other people's happiness. I shall be dead and my body burnt into ashes, but some day this hope of mine will be realized.'[147] An individual's love for mankind is not necessarily traceable to his reading into a particular school of philosophy, but when an ideological statement based on theoretical perceptions echoes the words of a writer's favourite philosopher, the fact of influence is a fair assumption. In his later didactic writings, Comte's theories on the need for a balanced development of man's faculties were the more obvious influence but the theme of love for all mankind remained a strong leitmotif.[148] When it was a question of choice, his distinct preference for Comte was made explicit in the statement that Mill's criticism of Comte had done an unintended disservice to mankind.

Bankim's pursuit of rationality however left untouched one important area of his thought and feeling. A belief in the supernatural appears to have been a constant features of his mental world. Ascetics with suprahuman powers appear repeatedly in his novels and often have a central role in the resolution of crises. The family tradition concerning his father's preceptor, a miracle-working sadhu who lived in Tibet and who had revived the young Jadab when the latter was apparently dead, may have powerfully influenced the writer's romantic imagination. But a close friend, Kalinath Datta, who wrote of Bankim's strong atheistic leanings, also describes the latter's faith in the miraculous power of *mantras*, apparently based on his own experience. He also believed in astrology until the tragic circumstances of his youngest daughter's death destroyed his faith in the pseudo-science. This element of ambivalence was never entirely absent—not even in the most sceptical phase of his intellectual development.[149]

The year 1882 marks a climacteric in Bankim's literary career. Everything he wrote then on had a strong didactic overtone. His chosen task in this phase was to construct a philosophy of life, a system of discipline which could be the basis of national regeneration. He projected this new ideology as essential Hinduism, the ultimate in man's religious experience. While his major literary output along these lines began in 1882, a positive and respectful interest both in Hinduism and theocentric ideas can be traced in much earlier writings as well. As early as 1872, shortly after he condemned the entire body of Hindu philosophy as 'a mass of errors', he lampooned his contemporaries for their eagerness to destroy Hinduism. His irony was inspired, significantly, by the slavish imitation of western materialism and the apprehension that it would undermine the Hindu joint family, 'the only basis for social cohesion in a culture without any tradition of national unity'.[150] In 1875 he found the Hindu conception of the trinity, which he had rejected as an aberration two years earlier, to be closer to the laws of nature as expounded in Darwin's theory of natural selection than any other conception of the Deity: an Almighty who destroyed the bulk of the life he created was a less rational concept than that of a threefold Divinity presiding separately over creation, preservation, and destruction. He did not suggest that the Hindu seers had anticipated Darwin or that there was any evidence to prove the truth of the Hindu trinitarian concept. He only emphasized the superior wisdom of the *rishis* in intuitively appreciating the true character of the cosmos and conceiving their godhead accordingly. Bankim's attempt to shore up the new faith in a glorious past was subtle. He was evidently anxious to keep within the bounds of rationality. He never lost this concern entirely.[151]

An essential ingredient of his new philosophy of life, one which is definitely not traceable to his western mentors, is *bhakti*, devotion or love of God. It ran directly counter to his profession of atheism in the earlier phase of his life. But here, too, one can identify a distinct element of ambivalence. His precocious query into Krishna's love-life notwithstanding, he was by no means unaffected by the highly charged emotional faith of his Vaishnava background. The Sanskrit hymn to Krishna the avenger (*Hare murare*), which features so prominently in *Anandamath*, was the favourite song of his childhood.[152] The sceptical editor of *Bangadarshan* was also a lover of *kirtan*, Vaishnava devotional songs, and is known to have given away the journal's funds to a singer on one occasion.[153] There are at least three available references to his deeply emotional attachment to the family deity, Radhaballabh, the beloved of Radha, despite his efforts to dismiss the tale of adultery as an allegory not to be found in the historical accounts of Krishna's life. The seed of devotionalism came to fruition in his later life in a highly idiosyncratic context, but it certainly lay deep in his early conditioning. His self-conscious rejection of western values in the later phase was probably reinforced by developments in his emotional life which drew sustenance from his early exposure to a profoundly devotional cult. Reverend Hastie's crude comments on Hindu idolatry may have helped revive all the emotive associations which that form of warship had in the life of his family.[154] His caustic reply to Hastie's critique of Hindu idolatry in 1882, published in the columns of the Calcutta *Statesman* first under a pseudonym and later under the novelist's own signature, contained his first uncompromising avowal of faith in Hinduism. He questioned the ability of any person, however learned, to appreciate the true implications of a faith he did not share. He declared that the Vedas were dead and defended idolatry as homage to the ideal of Divinity conceived in a physical form.[155]

The subsequent development of his ideas on religion is recorded first in a series of letters, written in English and addressed to his Positivist friend, Jogen Ghosh. These letters, dated 1882, were meant for publication but neither completed nor published in his lifetime. The letters were aimed at a pan-Indian audience. As he explained in the first letter, 'anyone who wishes to address all Hindus must of necessity write in English'. His propagandist purpose is suggested by his comment to a friend that his controversy with Hastie had in some measure helped restore the Hindu intelligentsia's faith in their religion.[156] In 1883, he began to publish his *Dharmatattva*[157] in *Navajivan. Krishnacharitra* (The Life of Krishna) began to appear the following year in *Prachar* (Propagation), a new journal established by Bankim that year. The purpose of the new journal was made explicit in its title. Besides these two major works—the revised version of *Krishnacharitra* published in 1892 was his largest book—he published a number of articles in the two journals on related themes. Some of the ideas contained in these writings were anticipated in his patriotic novel, *Anandamath*, and further developed in *Debi Chaudhurani*. His last novel, *Sitaram*, may be taken *inter alia* as an object lesson in a negative sense, a moral tale showing the consequences of man's fall from dharma.

A student of Bankim's intellectual and artistic development would certainly find shifts in ideas and different shades of meaning in the wide range of works he wrote during this highly productive decade of his life. For the purpose of the present volume, I feel justified in treating his world-view as developed in this final phase as a totality for two reasons. First, there is a basic homogeneity in his ideological outlook during this period; the discontinuity with the earlier phase is quite clear even though the revival of his faith in Hinduism can be traced as far back as 1875. Second, the sharp discontinuity in his appraisal of the western civilization coincided with this ideological change. Our concern here is with these two very different frameworks of perception which defined the limits of his vision in the two phases.

'From a very young age a question used to occur in my mind: 'What should I do with this life? What is one supposed to do?' All my life I have sought an answer to this question.' These words, spoken by the guru to his disciple in *Dharmatattva* (chap. 12) have an unmistakably autobiographical

ring. The answer which Bankim reached at the end of his long quest is
stated at length in the writings mentioned in the last paragraph. It reflects a
curious blend of an individual's intense spiritual yearning, a rational enquiry
into what an enlightened individual should do with his life—which is almost
entirely secular in scope and draws at least as much on Mill, Bentham,
Comte and Seeley as on Sandilya and the Gita—and a patriotic commitment
that nearly equates the motherland with the Deity. In his earlier writings
Bankim had expressed his concern that Indians must feel superior to the
West at least in some respect in order to shore up their self-easteem.[158]
Rational assessment, not stupid claims based on ignorance and blind vanity,
had to be the basis of this necessary sense of superiority. Earlier, he had
failed to locate any area where an Indian claim to superiority could be
sustained with acceptable evidence. Around the time when he began to
write on matters religious, an intellectually aberrant form of Hindu chauvinism
became highly popular among the Bengali Hindu middle class. Its
protagonists, notably Sasadhar Tarkachudamani,[159] claimed that all the
discoveries of modern science were known to the ancient Hindus and that
the apparently superstitious practices of popular Hinduism derived from
profound scientific principles. Bankim attended a few of his lectures and
denounced the ignorant stupidity of such assertions. A religion based on
superstitious practices, he declared, was unacceptable to the western-
educated Indian who needed a more elevated faith.[160] He also disapproved
of Swami Dayananda's efforts to revive the archaic religion of the Vedas.
The need of the day, he felt, could be met only by the rediscovery of
Hinduism in its purest form, cleared of the accumulated rubbish of
centuries.[161] He set about this task with the aid of tools derived from such
disciplines as comparative philology, sociology, study of myths, Christian
higher criticism, and the methodology of 'scientific history'. His loyalty to
the principles of scientific enquiry was at times disregarded to prove preferred
conclusions. In his analysis of myths, tales repugnant to his Victorian sensibility
(he could not bring himself to spell out the story of Ahalya's seduction by
Indra because it was too 'disgusting') were either rejected as interpolation
or subjected to a somewhat arbitrary historic interpretation: their literal
interpretation was rejected as 'spurious Hinduism'.[162]

Bankim's critical method was further developed in *Krishnacharitra.* He
tried to establish a chronology of his source material and identify a core of
historical truth in these works. He accepted the historicity of the events
described in the Mahabharata and of its *dramatis personae*, Krishna in

particular. All miraculous events were rejected as spurious interpolations. Data found only in the later texts were similarly discounted. The end product was a portrayal of Krishna presented as a historical personality based primarily on material selected from the Mahabharata. The legend of his dalliance with the milkmaids and Radha was treated as unhistorical accretion of a later date. Earlier he had suggested that these legends mythified the *samkhya* doctrine of *purusha* and *prakriti*: the historical Krishna, accepted as an incarnation, came to be identified with *purusha*. In Bankim's treatment, he is projected as the ultimate in human perfection and hence all such acts described in the Mahabharata as were unacceptable to the author's ethical sensibility were either rejected as spurious or shown to have a higher purpose not obvious to the lay reader of the epic. He accepted Krishna as an incarnation of the Deity. No arguments are offered in defence of this faith except that his western education had reinforced his belief in this regard.[163] This work of monumental scholarship remains a *tour de force* which had hardly any impact on the reading public. His belief that the superiority of Hinduism was manifest above all in the perfection of its ideal, Krishna, was not shared by many. The flaws in his method were evident to his contemporaries.

His natural preference for rational enquiry is however evident in his search for pure Hinduism despite his proneness to bend his evidence in support of *a priori* conclusions. He rejected the notion of divinely ordained religion. Even the Vedas were human in origin. For him, religion derived from man's intuitive understandings of nature. The truth of Hinduism and its superiority were rooted in that very fact.[164] But Hinduism had been equated erroneously with much that had nothing to do with its religious beliefs and practices. Philosophical ideas, social codes, non-Aryan beliefs and practices similar to elements of folk-religion to be found everywhere in the world and numerous aberrations which had disfigured Hinduism over the centuries were all covered by the one omnibus description. He defined religion as beliefs which provide a common basis of conduct and a common faith and thereby 'a bond union between man and man'. Underlying the diverse forms of what could be legitimately described as Hinduism there was such a set of immutable principles, eternal verities, on the basis of which Hinduism had to be 'reformed, regenerated and purified'. The non-essential adjuncts, the form in which these principles were expressed in practice, had become 'effete and even pernicious' and had to be discarded as unnecessary.[165] Yet there was much of value in the older tradition. The

worship of natural forces embodied in Vedic worship was an enriching
discipline because it filled one with a sense of wonder for God's creation,
a moving spiritual experience he found absent from the more austere
monotheistic faiths like Islam or Judaism.[166] Nor did he see any reason for
shame in polytheism, for though he believed in one God, there was as little
evidence in favour of monotheism as of polytheism. Besides there was 'no
evidence in nature that its author was omnipotent'. He went on to explain
polytheism in terms of an evolving system of beliefs, first in an impersonal
soul of Nature and then in a threefold Deity and so on.[167] The seed contained
in the Vedic religion had produced the great tree of Puranic Hinduism.
'Even though infested by many monkeys', that tree was necessarily superior
to the seed from which it had grown.[168] In justifying idolatry, he invoked
the familiar argument that the less enlightened needed the aid of a symbolic
image to conceive the formless Deity.[169] But in one of his essays published in
1874[170] he had attacked the practice as unnecessary and pernicious because
it was contrary to scientific knowledge, independence of spirit, and social
progress though it could have some beneficial results for the fine arts. His
rejection of the Dharmasastras and the popular superstitions was however
total at all times. He identified the former as one major reason for India's
decline. Dharma presented as the mindless observance of ritual purity was
to him 'a monstrous fantasy'.[171]

'... Religion in its broadest and most legitimate sense is culture', Bankim
wrote in his *Letters on Hinduism*[172], almost paraphrasing the words of Seeley
quoted in his *Dharmatattva* (Appendix B), 'The substance of religion is
culture'. Dharma for the Hindu had, however, a wider meaning. It subsumed
religion, morality, virtue, good deeds and, through natural law, even the
sciences.[173] At the same time, dharma was the essential truth underlying all
religions.[174] But 'culture', or the balanced cultivation of all human faculties,
was the best way of attending to the requirements of dharma in all its
manifestations. The authority of Seeley, Comte, and Mathew Arnold are
cited in support of his contention, but the Hindu tradition of culture or
anusilan is declared to be the very best. The ancient practice of the four
asramas is an example of this high tradition. A Religion of Humanity à al
Comte is described as an essential part of dharma. But Comte's own
prescription is found inadequate because it excludes theistic belief.[175] In
one essay, he echoes Mill's emphasis on the individual in describing self-
improvement and the individual's quest for happiness as indistinguishable
from dharma.[176] The Utilitarian ideal—'greatest good of the greatest

number'—is also recognized as a part of dharma, though its claim to be a complete philosophy of life is questioned.[177] Similarly, the love of mankind which he had adopted from Comte's philosophy at an earlier stage in his life was not claimed to be an integral part of Hindu dharma in which allegedly it was subsumed by the love of God.[178] A life devoted to the gratification of the senses or the narrow pursuit of self-interest is condemned as is asceticism in all its forms. *Anusilan* or culture, it was emphasized, implied involvement, not withdrawal from the world.[179] Happiness and salvation were inseparable, the ultimate results of *anusilan*, the balanced cultivation of all one's faculties.[180] The doctrine of culture was supplemented by, or rather subordinated to, the ideal of *nirlepa* or non-involvement, the surrender of the results of all one's actions to God. The worship of a personal God, even though His existence could not be proved, was essential for dharma because the perfection of all faculties, the object of *anusilan*, is realized only in the Deity and dharma was subject to His laws. To conclude, the purpose of human existence was the balanced cultivation of all faculties in a spirit of dedication to the Deity. It did not matter if one believed in a life hereafter or not, even though there was evidence for its existence, but there could be no religion without God.[181] Only the rationalist in Bankim introduced inadvertently an element of contradiction in his argument. In the *Letters on Hinduism*, written around the same time as the *Dharmatattva*, he argued that he cared little if people believed in God for he was not one of those who thought that belief in God 'or in anything else which does not admit of proof, constitutes religion'.[182]

If *bhakti* or love-devotion for the Deity implied or included all the other duties defined as dharma, *bhakti* itself had for its object several distinct entities. Bankim accepted much of Comte's prescription in denoting these entities. Within the family it was due to one's elders as required in a traditional Hindu home. The Hindu ideal of devotion to one's husband had to be supplemented by an ideal of mutuality for the latter principle preached by Comte was based on a higher morality. *Bhakti* was due to one's society, because civilized existence was not possible in the absence of a social structure. By the same logic, one owed it to the king and the teachers of society. Loyalty to the king, not as a person but as the embodiment of social authority, was prescribed as essential for social cohesion and progress. The recent ovation to Lord Ripon was cited as the sort of activity which could foster a healthy spirit of loyalty.

Subordination to one's official superiors was recommended as a social necessity even though the man in authority was inferior to oneself. But at no time must one cringe in fear. In accepting the colonial regime as inevitable, perhaps even necessary, Bankim was evidently prescribing a moral stance which could safeguard a measure of self-respect. As a further qualification to the ideal of loyalty, he emphasized the duty of all subjects to force the evil king to mend his ways. As noted above, *Anandamath* contained a more radical prescription. In an almost total departure from the position taken in his *Samya* and earlier writings, he entered a lengthy fiat in *Dharmatattva* in favour of *bhakti* towards Brahmins. They were credited with having established a society and civilization which were incomparable. They were the perfect examples of action without attachment in the service of mankind. Even their prescription of *bhakti* towards themselves was inspired by an impersonal concern for social cohesion and progress. Those who thought otherwise were no better than half-educated monkeys.[183] If earlier he had seen the caste system as an institution contributing to the subjection of the masses, he now accepted it implicitly as an equitable and wholesome arrangement.[184] Equality between man and woman was similarly rejected as an impossible ideal, for nature had ordained different roles for the two sexes and social institutions based on that difference could not be altered without destroying society itself.[185] No wonder he decided to suppress *Samya* as erroneous.

The *Dharmatattva* concludes on a somewhat unexpected note. If balanced cultivation of all faculties in a spirit of dedication to the Deity and service to mankind are the goals of human existence, patriotism and nationalist sentiments—described above as Bankim's chief inspiration—become irrelevant or peripheral. But the work also prescribes: 'Do not forget that the highest dharma consists in the love of one's country.' The text, written in the form of a dialogue, ends with this advice from the preceptor to his disciple. The theme of service to the motherland is first introduced as 'a duty approved by God' (Chap. 21). Herbert Spencer's argument that self-preservation is essential for the good of mankind is cited next (Chap. 23). A further quotation from the same philosopher follows: 'The life of the social organism must, as an end, rank above the lives of its units.' In a somewhat free paraphrase of the English quotation, the social organism is interpreted as one's country (Chap. 24). The ultimate goal was to work out a balance between the love for one's own country and universal love, eschewing western-style aggression. But defence of the motherland was an essential duty. The ancients had made a mistake by submerging patriotism into the higher love of all created things and the balance had to be redressed. That service to one's motherland was no simple exercise in high-minded philanthropy is made quite clear. The rigorous discipline in preparation for the great goal—Debi Chaudhurani's long training in *nishkama karma* was cited as a prime example—included physical exercise and training in arms. The human body was to become a 'sharpened weapon' ready for use. The concern expressed in the setting up of gymnasiums, first under the inspiration of the Hindu Mela, had been quietly incorporated into Bankim's new interpretation of dharma. The development of the physical faculties was prescribed as an essential component of 'culture'. Even Bankim's newly found devotion to a personal Deity, so central to his new ideology, is not always clearly differentiated from his patriotic fervour. As early as 1874, his Kamalakanta, the writer's *alter ego*, dreams of worshipping mother Bengal as the mother goddess.[186] The ideal flowers into a full-fledged cult in *Anandamath*; the motherland is worshipped as a Deity by the patriotic monks dedicated to her liberation. The perfection of Krishna in *Krishnacharitra* derives in large part from one alleged act of profound wisdom—the unification of India.[187] *Dharmayuddha*, war in a just cause, is declared to be in accordance with morality. Both *Anandamath* and *Debi Chaudhurani*, each in its own way, can be taken as illustrations of this principle. It is not difficult to see why the early revolutionaries in Bengal derived their inspiration from Bankim.

An iconoclastic attitude towards many aspects of Hinduism, rather than any veneration of the received wisdom, was at the heart of Bankim's patriotic outlook until the last phase of his life though there are anticipations of the new attitude in some of his earlier writings. The reasons for this change, as noted above, are not clear. The change however did help provide him with a satisfactory answer to one of his persistent queries. He had at last discovered an area where India was superior to all other civilizations. In *Dharmatattva*, he quotes a passage from Comte which comes close to his own idea of culture and comments that if this was the most satisfactory definition of religion, then Hinduism was the greatest religion of all (Appendix A). One could argue that having discovered in Hinduism what he considered the essence of religion he praised Comte's definition because it could be interpreted to support the notion of Hindu superiority. The Gita, with its exposition of the three paths to the ultimate realization—knowledge, action, and devotion—was cited as the highest embodiment of the doctrine of culture, the balanced development of all human faculties, and hence the ultimate religious scripture vouchsafed to man.[188] The ideal of devotion to a personal Deity and the mode of worship were also perfected only in the Hindu system. To a Hindu, dharma was not simply a question of the life hereafter, but encompassed this world and the next, God and mankind, in effect the entire universe.[189]

The claim here is not simply to a superior religious tradition but to a higher wisdom and refinement of spirit handed down from antiquity. The creators of this tradition, the Brahmins, were to be venerated because they alone had devised a social system which could do without war and conflict.[190] The late nineteenth-century myth of Hindu spirituality was invoked only once in this lengthy discourse. The basis of all Hindu principles was stated to be spiritual and God-oriented.[191] But the high tradition had got lost in the hypocrisy and pomp of external rituals. '... Yet very soon the Hindus, revived through the propagation of pure *bhakti*, will rise to great power like the English under Cromwell or the Arabs in the days of Muhammad.'[192] The secular objective of dharma was never very far from Bankim's mind. In looking upon religion and its reform as the road to patriotic ends he is in tune with the one powerful school of thought of his days. Dayananda, Keshab Sen, and later Vivekananda are all parts of this same tradition. A more conservative stance compared to his earlier egalitarian concerns implies an increasing emphasis on order rather than an unquestioning acceptance of Hindu practices, for he still rejected much of Hindu orthodoxy. In his selective empathy with Comte as well as the Hindu heritage, one detects the influence of his socioeconomic affiliation interacting with a personal development. Of the latter only the results, not the causes, are known to us. His ardent nationalism remained throughout his life the chief referent of his enquiry into Europe's history and civilization. The perceptions were shaped in the earlier phase of his life by values derived selectively from post-Enlightenment European thought—egalitarian philosophies, Utilitarianism and, later, Comte's Positivism. Probably Positivism was the most powerful influence, partly because it suited best the necessarily gradualist outlook and aspirations of his social class. His eventual faith in the superiority of Hinduism was based on the appropriation of his earlier ideals to a large extent. The change implied a conscious departure from the uncompromising and impassioned rationality which once informed his assessment of both Europe and India.

II

Two of the writers whose works are discussed in this volume have each devoted one or more of their books and essays specifically to the assessment of European civilization. Bankim is the one exception. He returned repeatedly to the theme of western thought and culture, but almost invariably in a comparative context. This concern is of course present in the other two as well, but the preoccupation with comparison is almost an obsession with Bankim. Dissatisfaction with the state of contemporary Indian society, especially a sense of a fall from grace entailed by the fact of political subjection—and the loss of self-respect perceived as its consequence—is very much there in Vivekananda, while Bhudev's sense of disquiet centred on the rootless western-educated Indian. Bankim's anxiety went deeper, for in terms of the nineteenth-century European values he accepted, India's inferiority was a self-evident fact. He saw no hope of national regeneration until India justly felt a sense of pride in her past and present, in fact a rationally sustainable sense of superiority over the dominant civilization at least in some respect. In his review of the anonymously published *Three Years in Europe*, we find an anguished statement of this felt need: 'We are particularly curious to learn what is there in Europe which would not be to our liking ... . Why do we want to hear this? I am not sure if I can explain the reason adequately. We Bengalis are considered to be a people of no consequence compared to the great nations like the English. In comparison with the English, there is nothing praiseworthy in us. Nothing about us is commendable. We do not know for sure if this is true. But we are beginning to believe it because we hear it every day. Such a belief does us no good. It reduces our love for our country, our regard for our own people. If we do not see in the Bengalis as compared to other people ... some unique excellence, we will have no love for our country. This is why we always wish to hear if we are superior on any count to the most civilized nations. But nowhere do we hear any such thing. When we do hear such words, it comes from people given to false vanity and nurtured exclusively in their own country as in a cage, not from people of balanced judgement with a concern for truth. We have no faith in these; they are no source of satisfaction ... . We were reminded [by this book] that we have no right to say that the motherland is 'superior to heaven'. The nation which cannot think of its motherland as superior to heaven, is the [most] wretched among the nations of this world. We are that wretched nation and hence our lament.'[193]

As a person 'concerned with the truth', he sought answers to his anxious query from every possible angle. The result was always the same. Until his discovery of Hindu superiority late in life, he is never in any doubt about the superiority of western civilization. 'Never before has the world witnessed such material progress as has been achieved by the civilization of modern Europe', he wrote in *Samya*, 'nor had earlier generations of mankind ever hoped for such progress.'[194]

This general assessment is repeated over and over again in his frequent comparisons of the Bengalis with the English. The difference between the two was as great in his opinion as that between men and women. The English were strong, courageous, and hardy while the Bengalis were weak, timid, and rather fragile.[195] An individual Bengali might be superior to a particular Englishman but the latter's superiority as a people—in power, civilization, and knowledge—was not in doubt.[196] The attribution of inferiority was not confined to the Bengalis. The totality of Indian civilization, past and present, despite its numerous achievements of great excellence, was but an object lesson in the 'study of arrested development and decay' while Europe represented the 'more perfect type of civilization'. The intellectual history of Europe had the same relationship to that of India as did physiology to pathology.[197]

As to the reasons why the two civilizations followed such different paths, his scattered statements, if put together, offer a multi-layered explanation. First, the most potent philosophical systems of India, especially *samkhya*, and the Buddhist system of thought, overwhelmed by a sense of human misery, became obsessively concerned with the cessation of pain, and even of experience and, ultimately, of the experiencing soul. Hence the exaltation of asceticism. Knowledge became a prime instrument for liberation, the withdrawal of consciousness from the snares of the experiential world. 'Knowledge is salvation'—this belief was the pivot of Hindu civilization, while in Europe knowledge became the means to power. Hence the two civilizations reached very different ends even though they followed the same path of knowledge. The quest for power was at the root of Europe's progress. Their worldly aims had given them decisive victory in this world. The Indians' neglect of power was, by contrast, the prime cause of their decline. The other-worldly aims ensured defeat in this world while the prospects of success in the next were at best a matter for debate.[198] Bankim cited Lecky on the dire consequences which followed from the triumph of asceticism in mediaeval Europe.[199] The material backwardness of European civilization during 'the millennium following the disappearance of Roman civilization' was attributed to the doctrine of indifference to worldly pleasures preached by the priestly class. The evil was rooted out with the revival of classical learning in Italy: the influence of Greek literature and philosophy demolished the other-worldly outlook.[200] He saw in this particular causal relationship a reason for hope for all mankind. Historical processes were not irreversible. The decline induced by the other-worldly ideals of the Middle Ages was reversed by the revival of classical learning. The course of European history might have been very different otherwise.[201]

A second reason for Europe's great success was one particular element of strength in her intellectual tradition—the inductive method based on observation and experiment and the inclination to follow the glimpses of truth revealed to the inspired intellect to their legitimate conclusions. Bankim cites as an example the discovery of atmospheric pressure. When the gardeners of Florence found that the column of water in the water pump would rise to a maximum height of 32 feet, Torricelli formulated the hypothesis of atmospheric pressure as an inspired guess. He next reasoned that the same pressure ought to sustain a column of mercury as well. The hypothesis was experimentally verified with a glass tube filled with mercury. '... European energy of thought would not stop here.' Pascal took the barometer to the Puy de Dôme and successfully tested his own conclusion that if the atmosphere supported the column of mercury the higher one ascended the lower would the column sink. 'A Hindu philosopher in Torricelli's place would have contented himself with simply announcing in an aphoristic sutra that the air had weight. No measure of the quantity of its pressure would have been given; no experiment would have been made with mercury; no Hindu Pascal would have ascended the Himalayas with a barometric column in hand.' Bankim cites one more telling example of the difference between the two intellectual traditions. The diurnal rotation of the earth, the apparent fixity of the heavenly bodies, and the annual motion of the sun were all known to the ancient Hindus. The heliocentric theory, the legitimate deduction from the combination of these facts, 'was never positively put forward, never sought to be proved, never accepted and never followed out to the establishment of the further laws of the universe'. By contrast, in Europe the announcement of the Copernican theory led to the discovery of Kepler's laws and eventually the law of gravitation. 'In India Arya Bhatta's remarkable announcement rendered certain that nothing further would come of it.'[202]

The influence of egalitarian ideology which Bankim later rejected suggested a very different explanation for Europe's success. His enquiry into comparative history convinced him that of all possible reasons for the decline or stagnation of a society, inequality, which had no basis in nature, but was man-made, was by far the most potent. While India had been the worst victim of this particular malaise, no society was entirely free from it. But in cultures which had achieved progress, conflict between different elements in society had ironed out its more damaging manifestations. The history of Rome, in his opinion, was a prime example of such a solution without resort to undue violence. The inequality between the patricians and the plebeians—the bane of early Roman history—was partially resolved through social justice. In the imperial era, the distinction between citizens and non-citizens was removed through the marvellous political skill of the ruling class. This is how Rome came to dominate half the civilized world. Other countries had been less fortunate and required surgical operations to remove the cancer of inequality. 'The greatest surgeons in this line of treatment were Danton and Robespierre.' The USA had only recently had a civil war to sort out the problem of slavery.

Following this line of analysis, he traced the decline of classical European civilization primarily to the reimposition of man-made inequality. The very prosperity of imperial Rome generated a taste for luxury and self-indulgence and a consequent decline in manly virtues. Bankim repeats this familiar explanation, but emphasizes the fact of social inequality embodied in the institution of slavery, present in the later days of the empire on a massive scale, as the prime cause of its decline. The despotic power of the emperors and the Praetorian Guards and of the governors in the provinces further aggravated the pervasive inequality. 'Wherever despotism is powerful, inequality is powerful as well.' But with the advent of Christianity the egalitarian principle triumphed once again. The equality of all men in the eyes of God and the brotherhood of man preached by Christ were central to the doctrine of equality. Christianity questioned the power of the rich and helped liberate the slave. By its grace, the Romans mingled with the barbarian races to produce 'valiant, progressive and warlike races', the ancestors of the modern Europeans. Bankim noted that there were other factors as well contributing to Europe's progress, but Christian ethics and Greek literature and philosophy were in his view the most powerful influences. His emphasis on equality made him recognize one unhappy result of Christianity itself—the excessive power of the priestly class, especially in countries like France and Spain.[203] He compared their abuse of power to the Brahminical hold on the Indian people. The Popes with very little territory oppressed the whole of Europe. 'The excesses committed in Europe by Gregory or Innocent, Leo or Adrian exceeded those of Philip II or Louis XIV, Henry VIII or Charles I.'[204] He saw the roots of oppression in every form of social power. There is a curious digression in one of his passages on the abuse of sacerdotal authority. Such excesses, he comments, were no monopoly of the priests or the ruling class. In contemporary England, for instance, the sovereign yielded no effective authority. Real power had passed into the hands of the journalists and they abused it freely. 'Wherever [one encounters] social power, [one encounters] social tyranny.'[205] Both colonial rule and caste society presumably suggested this pessimistic conclusion, an equation of power with its inevitable abuse.

The unfolding of European history in the long period was interpreted in terms of the same key principle. Departures from the ideal of equality in the distribution of power, resources, status, and social opportunity meant decline or stagnation and the balance was corrected by the reassertion of the egalitarian ideal. In modern times the French Revolution was identified as the climacteric event which saved Europe from her decline into inequality. Bankim drew upon Carlyle and Michelet to portray the excesses of the French aristocracy in the eighteenth century—the ruthless exploitation of the lower orders in society, their powerlessness and poverty as contrasted with the extravagance, debauchery, and corruption at the court of Louis XV. His description of eighteenth-century France is marked by passionate polemics: 'The treasury was empty, the king's subjects were in agony through starvation; then how were the expenses of such luxury, fit for Indra's heaven, paid for? By stealing the starving subjects' means of livelihood. The oppressed was oppressed even more, the emaciated sucked dry, the badly burnt reduced to cinders so that the scandalous Mme. du Barry could adorn her hair with jewels. And the rich? They did not pay a farthing into the treasury ... . The rich paid no taxes, nor did the clergy or the official—taxes were paid only by the poor and miserable peasants.' Inequality of this order was 'revolting', the end result of an evil system of government. And just as Christian doctrine helped bring to an end the oppressive and decadent regime of the later Roman emperors, so did Rousseau's ideas carried forward by his disciples undermine the evil system of government in France. *Le Contrat Social* in this view was at the root of all that happened in the French Revolution. The results of the Revolution are described as follows: 'As a result of that French Revolution the king, the royal family, monarchy and its very name were all swept away. Gone were the aristocracy, the older form of Christianity and the clerical orders. Even the [old] names of the months and days of the week were gone, everything washed away in an endless stream of blood. In course of time everything came back, but the *status quo ante* was not restored. France underwent a metamorphosis. A new civilization was born in Europe. What was achieved was of permanent benefit to mankind. A glorious imperishable achievement was thus based on Rousseau's mistaken words—because those words were egalitarian in spirit. The body of that error was half made of truth.'[206]

As noted above, Bankim's enquiry into the stagnation and decline of civilization in India was guided by his readings into Buckle and Lecky. Progress in Europe, the reverse of stagnation, was also explained with reference to the same 'law' plus insights derived from Malthus. If the ease with which a surplus could be produced from the fertile soil of hot countries like India was the reason for the early growth of civilization in these parts, it also explained the subsequent inertia, stagnation, and subjection of the producing classes, which in its turn induced a pervasive degeneration. The European experience was seen to be the exact opposite of this unhappy story. In colder climes, Bankim writes, following Buckle, people needed a diet which produced body heat. Hence the need for meat as a basic component of man's food in those regions. The bulk of such food came from hunting in the early stages of civilization. The effort, courage, strength, and dexterity necessary for this mode of existence became a part of the European life habits. Contentment, so admired in India and mediaeval Europe, was but another name for habitual idleness and lack of enterprise. Of the two necessary conditions for the growth of civilization—desire for knowledge and desire for wealth—the latter is more pervasive and hence ultimately more beneficial for mankind. The continuous quest for new sources of material pleasure was the key to Europe's progress. That which was unnecessary earlier becomes an essential need and its satisfaction leads to the quest for still more things. 'Desire induces effort, and success.' A steady growth in human happiness and welfare has been the end result of such material aspiration. And as man's material aspirations are satisfied, new desires are stimulated—for knowledge, aesthetic satisfaction, and the like, leading to an efflorescence in learning, literature, and the arts.[207]

The Europeans' love of independence is also attributed, by implication, ultimately to the same climatic factors in an essay seeking to explain the reasons for India's long history of political subjection.[208] Bankim rejected the theory that the alleged Indian indifference to political independence was the result of centuries of foreign rule and inherent cowardice. He pointed out that martial ardour was not absent from the Indian scene even under British rule. By contrast there was no record of any concern for political independence at any time in the Indian past. Nature's bounty and a hot climate had produced a culture of effortlessness and an indifference to material prosperity. The human intellect, looking inwards, produced great philosophy and a considerable literature in India, but it necessarily excluded all serious concern for political independence. The latter was never an object of aspiration in the country. The very different tradition in Europe—the willingness to sacrifice life itself in the defence of freedom, Bankim implied, was traceable to a basically different natural environment. The Indian indifference to the ethnic identity of the ruler might be misplaced, but being a national trait induced by the environment was not a matter for shame.

A Malthusian explanation supplemented Buckle's climate-based theories and Lecky's exaltation of materialistic aspirations. Increase in population, rarely accompanied by a corresponding or greater increase in wealth and income, normally impoverished the labouring masses. England and the US, countries which had achieved increases in wealth greater than the increase in their population, were exceptions to the general rule. Another way of redressing the imbalance between population and resources was the migration of the surplus population. Both England and the sparsely populated territories which received her migrants had benefited from such migration. Control of population through delayed marriage was also common in countries where people were used to a comfortable standard of living and the felt need for large quantities of consumer goods had to be met with a great deal of effort. In such societies, unlike in India, people did not marry until they had acquired their means of livelihood. The influence of other factors favouring material progress was enhanced by the reduced rate of the increase in population.[209]

Bankim tagged on this historical-cum-demographic theory explaining Europe's progress to his other explanation emphasizing the centrality of the egalitarian principle. The people of Europe, aroused from the natural state of apathy and jealous in defence of their material interests, began to fight for the removal of social inequalities. The affluent subjects resisted the abuse of royal power. The apprehension of discontent had a restraining influence on the ruling classes. Free and impartial criticism fostered the virtues of citizenship. The results were beneficial to all concerned. 'The

ruling classes were improved by the conflict with the Plebeians in Rome and
with the Commons in England.' 'The end results were [increased] human
happiness, prosperity and progress of civilization.' By contrast, India with
her vast population of impoverished, contented, and docile masses suffered
a steady decline.[210]

Even before his assessment of western civilization acquired a
predominantly negative character, Bankim's scattered comments on the
European past contained a number of critical observations. Some of these
contained an implicit message of hope for the Indians, particularly the
allegedly weak Bengalis—assurances that their historical record was not
something to be ashamed of. He pointed out for instance that the civilization
of modern Europe was of relatively recent origin. Even as late as the fifteenth
century. Europe was more backward than nineteenth-century India. The
Renaissance changed all that and Europe experienced a flood of creativity
in every sphere of life.[211] Bankim too was not unaffected by the excitement
over the contemporary theories on race and, like many of his contemporaries,
took pride in the claim that it was Aryan blood that flowed in Bengali veins.
The statement however occurs in a context which repeats his
acknowledgement of European superiority: 'That blood the [inherent]
strength of which has conferred greatness on the great nations of this earth
flows in the bodies of the Bengalis as well.'[212]

A less favourable view is expressed, expectedly, on European
aggrandizement, in two of the satirical sketches in *Kamalakanter daptar*. In
one, the essence of international law in Europe is stated to be the right of
possession. 'If you aspire after civilization and progress, you must grab what
you can', because this world is for the enjoyment of thieves. 'If the Right of
Conquest [sic] is a right [sic], then is not the Right of theft [sic] a right [sic]
as well?'[213] Kamalakanta's impeccable logic is echoed by a white parrot in a
lengthy dialogue with the opium addict. The bird's identity is made quite
explicit when it informs Kamalakanta that he and his kind spread their
wings and flew across oceans to settle in lands where food was plentiful.
Those who protested were either killed or driven away.[214] Such transparent
parables on the European expansion were a commonplace in nineteenth-
century Bengali writings.

A more fundamental criticism concerned the values which informed
the nineteenth-century European civilization and had seeped through to
Indian life as well. Material prosperity had become the be-all the end-all of

human existence. The quest for money, status, and fame was accepted now in one's very infancy as the ultimate goal. 'Comfort, and his brother, Respectability' were 'the tutelary deities' of English civilization.[215] The three-fold objective exalted by western civilization and its colonial disciples was dominated by one central concern—money. Bankim's Kamalakanta lampooned this insatiable thirst in a language of rare passion: '*Hara hara bom bom!*[216] Worship material prosperity. *Hara hara bom bom!* Pour more money on the heaps of money! Money is devotion, money is salvation, money is worship, money is the only way! Money is *dharma*, money is *artha*, money is *kama*, money is *moksha!*[217] Do not go that way, for the country will be poorer. Go this way and the country will be richer. *Bom bom hara hara!* Increase wealth, increase wealth. Railway and telegraph produces wealth: so worship at that temple. Do what you can to increase wealth. Let wealth rain down from the skies ... [What did you say? The human] heart? What on earth is that, [the human] heart?[218] Is there any such thing as the heart other than money? We have no heart beyond money. Money equals material prosperity. *Hara hara bom bom!* Worship material prosperity. The English with copper-coloured beard are the priests at this ritual; the *mantras* are read from Adam Smith's *purana* and Mill's *tantra*, ... education and enterprise are the offerings at this worship and the human heart is the animal to be sacrificed.'[219]

Bankim regretted that this exclusive and overriding pursuit of material prosperity had become the ideal, not of the masses alone, but of Europe's leading intellectuals and statesmen as well. His doubts as to its implications for mankind in no way ran counter to his unqualified rejection of life-negating ideals of asceticism. He rejected it as a barren quest unlikely to bring mankind ever any nearer to happiness. The way to such happiness lay only through love of mankind—his mentors in this regard were probably Comte and the egalitarian philosophers—and a balanced development of all human faculties. This faith in the doctrine of culture preceded his conversion to a more theocentric ideology.[220] He then rejected the more crass manifestations of nineteenth-century materialism and the unending quest for ever-growing prosperity for an ideal of balanced development of the human faculties, a quest for the refinement of the spirit that scorned material wealth. Men who achieved this ideal were not unknown to history, though their number was necessarily small. Their lives were more instructive for mankind than ethics, scriptures, science, philosophy, and the like. But unfortunately the deeper truths of their lives were hidden in mystery. Only

two such men, in his view, had left any account of their lives, Goethe and
Mill. In terms of his evolving values, this was perhaps Bankim's highest
compliment to western civilization.[221]

His reservations concerning the West had subtler dimensions as well.
He found some of the apparently harmless features of western social mores
debasing, because they subverted the higher values of human life in an
insidious way. High on the list of the cultural traits against which he warned
his countrymen was hypocrisy. He considered the English language itself
insincere despite his great admiration for its literary wealth.[222] In his well-
known satire, *Byaghracharya brihallangul* (Maître Tiger Longtail)—a fairly
obvious parody of the European perceptions of India—the learned tiger's
account of human society is rudely questioned by an iconoclastic young
tiger in the audience. The chairtiger mildly reprimands the heckler: 'Please
be quiet. It is not customary among civilized nations to abuse anyone so
openly. You may however indulge in far worse abuse with due
circumspection.'[223] Bankim's rejection of what he understood to be the
western perception of truthfulness was spelt out in his controversy with the
young Tagore. The former had commented with reference to a particular
episode in the Mahabharata that there are occasions when departure from
satya, truth—the word also means promise or troth in Sanskrit—constitutes
true dharma, Brahmo puritanism was outraged by this comment and Tagore,
among others, publicly criticized Bankim's alleged approval of lies. Bankim
stated in his reply that the source of the confusion was the new tendency
to translate age-old Indian concepts into English which had become a barrier
to independent thought. He referred to the closely related yet two distinct
meanings of *satya* to justify his position. But he went further and made a
distinction between the lie direct, often no more than a superficial verbal
deviation from truth of little significance, and the lie buried in the human
heart under a cover of formal truthfulness—the sin of hypocrisy. To him
both were sins, but he had no hesitation as to which was the worse of the
two. The older generation of Hindus, he admitted, thought little of the lie
direct, but were less given to hypocrisy, 'the English sin.' He was worried
that English education while eradicating the older sin had greatly fostered
the new sin of hypocrisy. The great emphasis on verbal truth might easily
lead to an indifference to the truth that lies close to the human heart.[224]

He recognized that there were points of difference between the two
civilizations which were culturally determined and hence by and large outside
the scope of value judgements. Yet though his own sensibility was largely

moulded by Victorian attitudes, especially on such matters as any overt discussion of erotic themes, he found western views as to what was obscene unacceptable beyond a point. Tastes differed from country to country as they did from person to person. Words tabooed in mixed company in England—thigh or pants for instance—had no obscene connotations in India. Kissing in public, on the other hand, the height of impropriety in India, was a socially acceptable practice in Europe. There were areas however where the perception of obscenity ceased to be simply a matter of attitudes. As examples, he cited a verse in Kalidasa describing the mountains as the earth's breasts which he thought would be considered obscene in Europe because such references to the female anatomy were tabooed. But since the earth was the mother of all living beings, he perceived a quality of innocence and purity in Kalidasa's imagery. Only a dirty mind, he implied, would detect erotic undertones in the verse. In such instances, the European taste which approved *inter alia* of Zola's novels, and not the Indian one, was at fault. This discussion was part of his many admonitions against the uncritical acceptance of European values and social attitudes.[225]

Until he abandoned his egalitarian convictions, Bankim wrote with deep admiration about the greater equality of opportunity in European society. He contrasted the Brahminical monopoly of learning in India with Europe's free access to knowledge. He was convinced that not only the great traditions of science, philosophy and literature but even the technological revolution in Europe would have been impossible had education been confined solely to the upper strata of society.[226] The greater equality of men and women in the West and the relative freedom enjoyed by European women as compared to their Indian counterparts were interpreted as further expressions of the wholesome egalitarian values which counterbalanced unavoidable social inequities. The abuses which went inevitably with the necessary concentration of social and political power in the hands of a few were not absent in Europe any more than its unfailing consequence—inequalities which were socially contrived and had nothing to do with the natural differences in human abilities. Even 'natural inequalities' were no equitable basis for inequality of opportunity. And in Europe too the worst manifestation of social inequity was in man-woman relationships. This was especially evident in the laws of inheritance which excluded women. On this point the Hindu law and even more the Muslim *sharia* were distinctly superior. Some people in India alleged that the freedom of social contact had affected women's morals adversely in the West. This assumption of corruptibility was an insult to womanhood in

Bankim's opinion. He wrote approvingly of the movements in Europe for
equality between men and women in all respects and expressed the hope
that these would achieve at least some measure of success in the foreseeable
future.[227]

He did find the western civilization wanting in many ways in terms of
the liberal and humanitarian values. The two forms of social oppression—by
the majority and by those vested with authority—were by no means absent
there. He cited the problems which Mill had to endure because of his
atheistic beliefs as an instance of extreme intolerance, of social persecution
that should be totally unacceptable in civilized societies. The barbaric survival
of harsh punishments, including the death penalty for minor offences until
very recently, was another extreme manifestation of social inequity.[228]

His regard for some of the sacred cows of western civilization was less
than total. He wrote approvingly of the minute attributed to Mill which
questioned the sagacity of the measure placing India directly under
parliamentary control on the ground that the dependency would become a
pawn in the factional struggles within that body. This apprehension, he
believed, had proved to be true.[229] He was never particularly impressed by
the British parliament in which Gladstone's demagogy was more appreciated
than Mill's intellect.[230] He was equally sceptical about the glories of the
British constitution in general.[231] He considered the jury system introduced
by the British in India an obsolete and positively harmful survival from
mediaeval times. When first introduced, it served the useful function of
protecting the weak and the poor from the influence of powerful men on the
judiciary. It had survived after the conditions had changed owing only to
the innate conservation of the British. It reduced the judicial process to a
farce by entrusting intricate matters of interpreting evidence to the judgement
of often ignorant laymen.[232] And of course his most serious criticisms were
reserved for the phenomenon of nationalism itself, which he urged his
countrymen to adopt as an ideal. Nationalism's most serious limitation was
seen to lie in the fact that a wholesome concern for the welfare of one's own
nation was counterbalanced by a willingness to inflict suffering on other
people in the interest of the same welfare. There could never be any moral
justification for such a world view. The much harsher criticism of western
nationalism in the last phase of his life was clearly anticipated in some of the
earlier writings.[233]

The sharpest discontinuity in his assessment of the West was necessarily
with reference of Europe's religious faith, Christianity. Though he never

lost entirely his earlier belief in the historically liberating role of the Christian faith, his discovery of Hinduism's ultimate superiority, especially in relation to the religious beliefs and practices of Europe, went with a denigration of the religion he once admired. As noted above, his regard for Christianity was based on two interlinked perceptions—Christ's egalitarian message as an embodiment of the noblest truth revealed to mankind and Europe's rise to the highest levels of civilization ever achieved by man partly as a result of her accepting that message. The brotherhood of all men and their equality in the eyes of the Lord—the belief that the poor and the meek were especially blessed—were the doctrines extolled for their innate nobility. Christ's injunction calling upon all men to do unto others as they would have done unto themselves was described as the ultimate, in fact, the only basis of morality. It was also the core of egalitarian doctrines. Its only parallel was the ancient Hindu saying—the wise look upon others as identical with their own selves. The message that Christ's kingdom was not of this world—the vanity of worldly power and happiness—was described with respect, not because of any admiration for asceticism. The contempt for wealth and power was seen to reinforce the egalitarian message which 'destroyed the pride of the rich—the pride of the ruler; even the mutilated beggar could now be exalted above the emperor'. There is not a word in all this about the Christian love of God or surrender to God's will. Christ is described as '*samyavatara*', the principle of equality incarnate as a great human being. Europe prospered because his egalitarian message helped level out inequalities. Decline set in when the concentration of unwonted power in the hands of the clergy meant a new pattern of inequality and Christian asceticism discouraged the healthy pursuit of material improvement.[234] Besides egalitarianism, Christianity also prescribed love for all men, an ideal projected in the writings of Bankim's favourite philosopher, Comte. To this discovery in Christianity of ideologies learned from other sources one can add another—somewhat unexpected—reason for his admiration. Spirituality is not a concern one associates with his early writings. Yet in his highly secular enquiry into the study of Hindu philosophy, there is a curious passage with an unmistakably Christian resonance. In explaining the origins of Hindu asceticism, he wrote: 'When man is unable to rise to the lofty doctrine of Repentance, the only form which penance can assume is physical privation.'[235] The implicit tribute to Christian spirituality is counterbalanced by ascriptions of a lower level of rationality as compared with Hindu thought. The concept of a three-fold divinity, with a destroying Deity functioning in the cosmos separately from the Creator and the Preserver, was described as being more in tune with nature as unravelled by nineteenth-century science than with the Christian notion of an Almighty.[236] Bankim's scorn for ritualistic observances and all infringement of humane values was not confined to Hindu practices. To observe the sabbath, sit in a church with one's eyes closed, and nurture a hatred of all religions other than Christianity were not his idea of virtue.[237]

A refusal to accept without due assessment any ideology or intellectual position, however attractive, informs his understanding of all philosophical traditions, western as well as Indian. A doctrine or regime devised by anyone but himself was never acceptable to him *in toto.* The European philosophers who were his intellectual mentors were all discussed with a degree of critical rigour. In his egalitarian phase, Rousseau is placed on a pedestal as one of the incarnations of the egalitarian principle—with the Buddha and Christ. The reader is however reminded that the French philosopher is of course not to be compared with the two great teachers of mankind, for what he preached was not pure and unalloyed truth. With his magical command over the written word, he offered a curious mixture of beneficial moral truths and mischievous lies and captivated his countrymen. Bankim summarized Rousseau's egalitarian ideas with accuracy—the notion that equality is the law of nature, that even the 'natural' inequalities were the products of civilization, the result of a fall from the gracious state of noble savagery, that land belongs to all men and property in land is based on deceit, that law is an institution to perpetuate that deceit. He noted Rousseau's modification of his earlier ideas in *Le Contrat Social*—the view that the noble savage's natural wisdom was replaced by a sense of justice in civilized man and that under certain conditions property was legitimate. Bankim implied that the theory of a social contract was erroneous, but the egalitarian principle which informed it was founded on truth. In pronouncing that land belonged to everyone, Rousseau had sown a seed of great power. Communism and the International were among its products. The theories which preached the social ownership of property were, in Bankim's opinion, the work of learned and wise men of great insight. The social ownership of the means of production, land and capital he described as the 'real communism' preached by Owen, Louis Blanc, and Cabay, but he noted that Blanc favoured a system of distribution in proportion to one's input of labour rather than an equality of income and the affinity between his ideas and Saint-Simon's. The account of egalitarian theories also refers to Fourier's and Mill's views on inheritance; the latter too are identified as essentially part of egalitarian doctrine. Bankim concludes that all existing laws of inheritance were unjust. Fools might laugh at this idea, but some day the injustice would be rectified throughout the world. Of all western social philosophies he admired, he appears to have accepted without qualification only the egalitarian ideology, though only for a brief period. Even 'natural inequalities' did not justify in his eyes inequality of rights: 'You are well born through no merit of yours; another person is low born through no fault of his. Therefore the low-born person has as much claim to whatever happiness the world has to offer as you have .... Do not forget that he too is your brother, your equal.' He cited with approval Mill's opinion that today's good practices were no more than the correction of past evil and that there was a long way to go. He hoped for the day when wealth, instead of stinking like natural manure when heaped up in one place, would be spread out evenly and fertilize the soil.[238] Bankim never explained why he later rejected egalitarianism as erroneous. It is worth noting however that Bhudev also discussed the same ideas in his *Samajik prabandha*, but as unrealistic doctrines rooted in violence trying to correct one set of evils with another. The younger Bankim had no such hesitations in theory. But in applying the egalitarian principles to his immediate environment, he recommended a cautious policy of reform despite his total rejection of the land system in Bengal as being worse than useless. His eventual rejection of his youthful ideals was perhaps no more than the logical triumph of his concern for orderly progress. Comte, Seeley—and the Gita—were better guides than Rousseau and the socialists in terms of such a preference. Only Bankim's exposure to the miseries of the Bengal peasant had produced in his mind a focus of rebellious ideas. To Bhudev, secure in his faith in the inherited social order, western egalitarian thought was never a siren song.

The influence of Utilitarian and Positivist ideas on Bankim has been discussed briefly above. While their influence can be detected in much of his writings, his assessment of these philosophies are confined to a few scattered statements and a couple of satirical sketches in *Kamalakanter daptar*. His high regard for one of the chief exponents of Utilitarianism is expressed at some length in his obituary note on Mill.[239] 'We have never met him', he wrote, '...yet we feel as if we have lost forever someone very close to us.' In his view, the whole of mankind was indebted to Mill for all times. The brief review of the philosopher's achievements, however, contains very few references to his Utilitarian ideas. The contributions emphasized are

those in the fields of political economy, logic, anti-absolutist theories, and
egalitarian ideology. His disagreement with Comte was described as centering
around one fundamental issue. Mill saw social progress as ultimately
dependent on the freedom of the individual, while Comte regarded the
emphasis on the individual as detrimental to social progress because man's
concern for others would never transcend his innate selfishness and hence
it was essential to restrict the pursuit of self-interest for the good of society.
Mill's other criticisms of Comte—denial of justice to women, the ritualism
and authoritarianism of the new religion, the ludicrous practice of *hygiene
cerebraire*, the rejection of all liberal thought, etc.[240]—were ignored in this
summary statement which did focus on the heart of the controversy. In a
very modest disclaimer, Bankim pleaded his inability to judge between two
such great thinkers but one is left in little doubt as to which way his sympathies
lay. Mill's tract is described as having done some harm even though this was
not the intended result. His presentation of Positivism. it was implied, could
be as misleading as the Christian missionary tracts on the Hindu religion.
Bankim, unlike Bhudev, never described individualism as downright evil
but his spontaneous preferences were in favour of doctrines which emphasized
the interests of the larger social group. Both egalitarianism and Positivism,
at the two ends of the ideological spectrum, hence had an appeal which
individualism never had. He parodied more than once the pursuit of self-
interest as projected in Utilitarian doctrines. The title of one skit in
Kamalakanter daptar equates Utilitarianism with a philosophy of the
stomach.[241] The philosophy itself is not the object of satire in this piece as
much as the alleged application of its principles in the author's country.
However, filling that enormous cavity in the human body known as the
stomach is described as its ultimate ideal. He did see a causal link between
the endless pursuit of material prosperity and this school of thought. When
the human heart is described as the animal offered as sacrifice in the temple
of material prosperity, the person invited to yield the knife is the Utilitarian
philosopher.[242] In one brief passage, Bankim posits a very different criticism
of both Utilitarianism and Positivism, later elaborated in his *Dharmatattva* in
a theocentric context. In an essay analysing the roots of oppression in human
society, traced to individual and social necessity, he suggests that oppression
and excess go invariably with power. The human intellect itself is not free
from this tendency towards aberration. The two philosophies are cited as
instances in point. He considered their effects on human emotions deadening

and believed that mankind would have to fall back on intellect itself for correcting its excesses.[243]

There is one area in Bankim's assessment of European civilization virtually untouched by his ideological or nationalist concerns—his appreciation of western literature. The preoccupation with comparison is still there, but his statements in the field of literary criticism are informed much more by a universalist aesthetic sensibility than by the need for any nationalistic self-assertion. He was convinced that human emotions were the same in all ages and climes; the apparent differences were merely external.[244] The ultimate purpose and achievement of great literature was the same everywhere—refinement of the human spirit and to lead men thereby to a higher level of morality.[245] He used the word '*kavya*', usually translated as 'poetry', to cover all forms of creative writing and suggested a new basis for the classification of all such works because he found both the Sanskritic and western traditions in this regard unsatisfactory. He prescribed a three-fold classification. Words like drama which could be presented visually (*drisya kavya*), narrative or epic poetry (*akhyan kavya* or *mahakavya*)[246], and a residual category, *khandakavya*, covering all other literary forms, including lyrics. The superficial form and the real nature of a literary work could be different. Comus, Manfred, and Faust for instance were narrative poems in a dramatic form, while the 'Bride of Lammermoor' was more a drama than a poem. The object of this classificatory exercise was stated very clearly: 'Where there is no difference in substance, difference in nomenclature is both superfluous and harmful. But when we speak of different objects, it is necessary to use different names.'[247] Confusion in the use of terms might induce wrong judgements in literature and hence the necessity for precise nomenclature. Goethe's '*Faust*', treated as a play, might be unimpressive, but as a narrative poem it was an outstanding work of literature. His exercises in comparison between Sanskrit and western classics transcend clearly all cultural conditioning and show the depth of his literary sensibility. Shakespeare is a frequent referent in these comparisons. Bhavabhuti's *Uttararamacharitam* is criticized for its lack of unity in time—an indirect acceptance of a western literary ideal—but the reader is reminded that Shakespeare himself had deviated from this particular unity in his *Winter's Tale*. The Sanskrit play is also found lacking in action compared to its length. Bankim cites *Macbeth* by way of contrast; the marvellous literary impact of plentiful actions, their speed and convincing sequence. In another essay, Kalidasa's *Sakuntala*, the daughter of a heavenly being brought up in a forest by the ascetic

Kanva, is compared first to Miranda and then to Desdemona.[248] Miranda and Sakuntala, in his view, could have been portrayed by the same pen. Their captivating innocence derives from their having grown up away from all contact with human society. Had the same poet written both the plays, 'he would have known that Sakuntala, aware of social conventions [and hence] shy, would not express her love except through indirect signs. Miranda, not so conditioned, has no knowledge of shyness.' Hence her love finds a clearer expression in words. 'If Sakuntala in her sylvan setting is less complete a character than Miranda on her island, there is artistic justification for the difference.' The latter meets a ship-wrecked youth, her equal in every sense, while the former's personality is overshadowed by her royal lover, lord of the earth and a friend of the divine Indra himself. He is like an amorous elephant at play and she the lotus held playfully in the elephant's trunk. The forest maid rises to the full grandeur of her personality when she is rejected by the king in his court as a scheming strumpet. 'For then she is a wife, a queen, a woman about to enter motherhood', and the poet paints her in colours appropriate for the new Sakuntala. Bankim's gloss on the famous play was inspired by a desire to prove that in this particular context the author of *Sakuntala* was not inferior to that of *The Tempest*. Sakuntala was next compared to Desdemona because they both fell in love with heroic men and were both rejected by the men they loved. 'Yet they were not comparable, because one cannot compare things which belong essentially to different orders. This play of Shakespeare is like the ocean; Kalidasa's play is like the garden in paradise. A garden cannot be compared to the ocean.' One technical reason as to why the two cannot be compared is cited. *Sakuntala* is essentially a narrative poem, while *Othello* is a play par excellence. But this explanation is really peripheral. He found in *Othello* all the depth and terror of the open sea—the towering waves of emotion and fierce winds of anger and jealousy, but also the enchantment of blue waters, murmuring breakers, and sunshine scattering on the spray. It was the one incomparable play. Almost every time he cites a gem from Sanskrit literature, he adds that its parallel can be found only in Shakespeare, 'the immortal poet of universal human nature'.[249] His plays were to him 'the highest poetry'.[250] Elsewhere he speaks of the 'immeasurable' superiority of English literature, but the context suggests a comparison with the literature of modern India, particularly Bengali.[251] He also commented that the European works could hardly be described as books if compared to the works in Sanskrit. 'Compared to the Ramayana or the Mahabharata, a European epic is like a terrier as compared to an elephant, the willow or cyprus as compared to a banyan tree or a mountain stream compared to the Ganges, Godavari or the Indus.' Clearly, he had more than size in mind.[252]

There are many dimensions to Bankim's appreciation of western literature. In one perceptive essay he compares *Paradise Lost* to Kalidasa's *Kumarasambhava*, the epic poem on Siva's marriage to Uma, Himalaya's daughter, and the birth of Kartikeya. The point of comparison lies in the fact that the main protagonists in both the works are superhuman. In fact there are no human characters in Kalidasa's poem. Despite its great literary merit, Milton's masterpiece is described as tiresome reading because it is impossible to empathize or identify with the superhuman protagonists who are not modelled on human prototypes. Even Adam and Eve in their innocence have little about them that is recognizably human. Only Milton's supreme genius as a poet saves the work from utter unreadability. The appeal and excellence of *Kumarasambhava* lie in the convincingly human characterization of the divine *dramatis personae*. Since literature is to be judged by its impact, Kalidasa's poem is declared to be the superior work.[253] Against such literary insights one has to place Bankim's enthusiasm over the lesser poets like Thompson and Southey and, above all, his great admiration for the Waverley novels as works of supreme literary merit.[254] He also dismissed Jane Austen and George Eliot as rather insignificant novelists.[255] One fellow-admirer of Scott he mentions in his writings is Gladstone, but in nineteenth-century Bengal probably the only writer more admired than the said novelist was Shakespeare himself.[256]

Scattered comments in his writings indicate his cultivated pleasure in European literature in languages other than English as well, though he very probably read these works in English translation.[257] Sometimes a moral judgement intrudes on his literary tastes. In two separate discussions on the nature of humour and satire the ethical concerns are explicitly present. In one essay he refers to the coexistence of the divine and bestial elements in the human personality and describes a balanced portrayal of both as the function of literature in its perfect manifestation. Some authors, he continues, deal exclusively with all that is noble in man. Victor Hugo is cited as an example. He introduces in this discussion a theme that is not obviously relevant—that of incongruity, and adds quite convincingly that those concerned with the incongruities in human nature were usually humorists, citing Cervantes as the prime example.[258] He was however less tolerant of the true western satire 'full of hatred, malice, crudity, pessimism and envy'.

European wars and European satires were to him like brothers born of the same maternal womb, with one purpose in common—to inflict misery on mankind.[259] An even more severely puritanical judgement castigates the degradation of European taste in accepting the novels of Zola as serious literature. Purity of taste in literature was not one of the many things one could learn from Europe, he concluded.[260]

His excitement over European literature might have transcended his psychological need for cultural self-assertion, but the patriotic concerns were not absent even here. This was inevitably so, because he considered a literary revival an important lever of national regeneration. He had great faith in the potentialities of imitation in literature, for no literature except that of Greece was 'independent and original in its youth'. Horace, 'the most spontaneous and genuine of all Latin poets', equated originality with the importation of a new poetical form from Greece, imitation of Greek being considered a necessary mark of excellence at the time. The European Renaissance focused its energies on the study and imitation of the classical writers. There was an element of imitation even in Dante. And if 'the little remnant of intelligence in the Latin Church' plus the study of classical antiquity could eventually produce the greatness of the modern Celtic and Teutonic nations, perhaps there was hope for the Bengalis as well. Perhaps they would never really assimilate European ideas and at most acquire 'a superficial varnish of sham intelligence'. At the moment they seemed to lack the fibre for any great achievement—in thought or in action. But the Renaissance began among the supple and pliant Italians. The Bengalis, 'the Italians of Asia', might similarly act as a conduit for western thought to be received thereafter 'by the hardier and more original races of Northern India'.[261]

Despite his continual references to European history as an object lesson for the less fortunate nations of this world, Bankim's admiration for western historical writings was less than total. A memory of past glory, he recognized, was an essential component of a nation's greatness. It spurs on efforts to maintain that greatness and efforts to regain it if lost. Blenheim and Waterloo were achievements inspired by the memories of Crecy and Agincourt. Italy's revival was similarly inspired.[262] But Europeans in their great pride were obsessed with the writing of history. Even if they went shooting birds, a history of the event had to be written. They considered every act of theirs an achievement. 'Even if we yawn, the act should be acknowledged as one of immortal glory in this world and hence duly recorded.'[263] But the history inspired by this great self-esteem was not always very objective. Historians who admitted the limitations of their own nations and acknowledged their enemies' merit out of a concern for truth were indeed rare. Even great scholars who took pride in their regard for truth were guilty of despicable lies.[264] Bankim was especially critical of the work of British writers on Indian history. He regarded Macaulay's *Clive* and historical essays more as fiction than history. The extant accounts of the Battle of Plassey were to him a gross distortion of the truth.[265] Historians like Marshman were oblivious of India's past glory.[266] The vilification of Napoleon in British historical writings was equally untrustworthy.[267] This pervasive scepticism regarding western, especially British, historiography might be partly grounded in valid scholarly criticism, but Bankim's language suggests patriotic anger. Besides, most of these statements occur in a self-consciously nationalistic context as part of a plea for Indians to be aware of their past glory.

The achievements of European civilization recommended to Indians in general and Bengalis in particular as ideals for emulation included the fine arts, especially sculpture. Through in one ecstatic passage in the novel, *Sitaram*, the lost glories of ancient Hindu sculpture are eulogized, Bankim was generally of the opinion that India had no tradition of sculpture and should learn this art from the Europeans. The achievements of western art were incomparable and one's aesthetic sensibilities were deepened if one saw these. In his controversy with Hastie he commented that it would be a good idea to have the images of the deities worshipped by the Hindus made in Italy. He considered the European's taste in matters artistic far more refined than that of the Bengalis. This superiority was evident even in the way a poor Anglo-Indian decorated his home. Bankim had little hope that the Bengalis would ever acquire a taste in the fine arts even remotely comparable to European sensibilities.[268] So deep was his pessimism that he did not even recommend sober imitation in this regard as a likely road to any refinement of taste.

For one area of Europe's intellectual effort his assessment ranged from sardonic rejection to strictly qualified admiration. In his opinion, the English especially had failed to understand anything of India despite their close contact with the country for some hundred and fifty years.[269] His contempt for the less informed European critiques of Indian life and civilization is expressed powerfully in some of the best-known satires in the Bengali language. *Maître Tiger Longtail* is fairly typical of this genre. The learned tiger spends a few days among men in a cage, a device he interpreted as a temple constructed by humans, an inferior species, for the worship of tigers. He then becomes an authority on all things pertaining to man. He believes in a remarkable version of the evolutionary theory—the notion that the inferior species gradually acquire the features of those superior to them. Since humans bear some resemblance to monkeys, the Maître is optimistic that the former will some day achieve monkeyhood and sprout tails. These delicious creatures were physically so weak and easy to catch (evidently like the Bengalis as portrayed in English writings) that they could have been created by the merciful Lord only for the delectation of His favoured species, the tigers. The humans were indeed renowned for their devotion to the nobler animal. The tigers had a deep affection for this hapless species, especially in view of their delicate flesh. Some popular notions regarding the said creatures were evidently false. The houses they lived in were not constructed by them, for the learned tiger had never seen them construct buildings. A footnote confirms the reasonableness of this argument for James Mill had concluded through similar reasoning that Sanskrit was a barbarian dialect and the ancient Indians were an uncivilized people.

Max Mueller's thesis that ancient India had no written language was also cited as an instance of such sound logic.[270] Bankim's imaginary letter from one of the special correspondents who accompanied Edward, Prince of Wales, on his tour of India[271] focuses on Britain's civilizing mission in India. It opens with the casual assertion that the Indians know very little about their own country. They were unaware, for instance, of the well-known fact that Bengal was named after a great Englishman, Benjamin Gall, who had discovered this land. Since most Bengalis were clad in the products of Manchester, evidently it was the British who had rescued them from the shame of nudity, a remarkable achievement for a government barely a century old. The large number of English words in the Bengali language—high court, rail, decree, etc., for instance—proved beyond reasonable doubt that it was an offshoot of English. In any case, Dr Lorinzer and others had proved that the name of their god Krishna was derived from Christ and the Gita was but a translation of the Bible. And of course the so-called Sanskrit language was a forgery by William Jones for purposes of self-aggrandizement, *vide* Dougald Stuart. 'A review of the Ramayana by some European critic'[272] notes with some surprise that the work is nearly as good as inferior European poetry, a considerable achievement for a Hindu poet. The epic's purpose is explained as the glorification of the monkeys. Rama, the son of a polygamous barbarian, went on exile at the behest of his father as one would expect an unenterprising Indian to do. His wife Sita eloped with Ravana because Indian women were generally unchaste and so on and so on. In a more direct description of European racial prejudice, he wrote, 'In the opinion of some seers endowed with copper-coloured beard, just as the Creator collected particles of beauty from all that is beautiful in the three worlds to create [the divinely beautiful damsel] Tilottama so did he collect particles of animal nature to create this unprecedented phenomenon, the modern Bengali character.' These double parodies of Europe's racial vanity and ignorance of India masquerading as learned expertise were only an exaggerated version of Bankim's seriously held opinion on Orientalism and British perceptions of Indian life.

Yet Bankim had a deep respect for what he considered the acceptable face of European Orientology. '... There is no study which does not yield its secrets to the European scholar when he takes it up ... earnestly, divesting himself of his prejudices.' This considered judgement comes from that final stage in his career when he rejected much of what he had admired in the West earlier in life. It refers specially to Vedic polytheism which had been 'thoroughly studied in Europe'.[273] He was also appreciative of the work on the Vedic and Puranic legends which had converted 'unintelligible nonsense' to a subject of accurate scientific study.[274] At a much earlier date, in his essay on the study of Hindu philosophy he had acknowledged the debt owed to European scholars, 'giants of another clime', for their reconstruction of the Indian past. The Indian scholars had merely thrown handfuls of material on the structure raised by the Europeans.[275] Respectful references to Max Mueller abound, though gibes at the German scholar's real or supposed errors are almost as numerous.

One of Kamalakanta's sketches describes an imaginary market where one stall displaying dry coconuts belongs to Sanskrit pandits with long pigtails. The pandits have no instruments to cut open the coconuts and are hence content to eat the fibre. European shopkeepers attack their stall, seize and cut open the fruits with various western implements and feast on the kernel. This western enterprise is explained as 'Asiatick Researches'. Europe's appropriation of Indological learning is mentioned with some concern for the narrator escapes in a hurry, apprehending 'Anatomical researches' on his own person.[276]

The caricature, with its several layers of meaning, is a summary statement of a spectrum of responses to the western assessments of India, scholarly

and otherwise. There is admiration, and some gratitude, that western
instruments had cut through the fibres and the shell of the Indian heritage
which the pandits had reduced to useless nit-picking. The invasion however
demanded very careful handling. First, one had to retain one's critical
independence in learning from western Indology. Even the Homers of the
discipline, in Bankim's view, were inclined to nod quite frequently. He
questioned some of the established notions in this field of study. For instance,
he saw no basis for the theory that the *Rik samhita* was the earliest to be
composed. He also dismissed the quest for sun-worship—in myths which
could be interpreted more satisfactorily otherwise—as heliomania, a disease
from which Max Mueller in particular suffered very badly. He saw no reason
for accepting the western notion that the Vedas were polytheistic when all
commentators from Yaska to Satyabrata Samasrami declared that 'owing to
the greatness of the Deity, the one soul is celebrated as if it were many'. An
element of self-assertion was not absent from these criticisms. The educated
Indian was advised to pay attention to what the Indian scholars had to say
on such matters.[277]

The European scholarship on India was seen to suffer from a number
of handicaps. First, the belief that the western scholarship had achieved a
knowledge of Sanskrit superior to that of the Indian scholars was mistaken.
Language, Bankim pointed out, had deep roots in the entire life and culture
of a people and the native thus had a necessary advantage in interpreting
it over any foreigner, however learned. Second, the Europeans lacked the
necessary sympathy and sense of identity to understand Hindu philosophy
fully.[278] These limitations were compounded by misunderstandings, downright
ignorance and distortions, deliberate or otherwise, traceable to racial
arrogance and prejudice. While Bankim saw no reason for shame in
polytheism, practised by the great civilizations of antiquity, he was convinced
that the Vedas were not polytheistic, but simply theistic. The Europeans
failed to recognize the fact because they were wanting in sympathy and
breadth of vision. Max Mueller, quite unnecessarily, delved deep into Greek
lexicons to invent new words—henotheism and kakenotheism—to describe
the Vedic religion. Herbert Spencer in his *Principles of Sociology* affirmed
that the Hindu 'adored' their objects of daily use—a carpenter his adge, a
scribe his stile, a mason his trowel. Sir Alfred Lyall went a step further to
state that the peasant prayed to his plough. The only parallel to such
misunderstandings was the Indian servant's belief that his English master
while saying grace at table was actually worshipping his food. A quotation

from Max Mueller's Hibbert Lectures underlined the true nature of such misunderstandings: 'What is meant here by adoring?'[279] There was also a great deal of genuine ignorance, especially regarding modern Indian life, even among the great European scholars. Max Mueller, who noted the misperceptions of Spencer, and Lyall himself accused the modern Hindus of worshipping cows and monkeys. Goldstucker described the Reverend K.M. Banerji as a Hindu and Mueller thought that the Kayastha scholar Rajendralal Mitra was a Brahmin. A learned correspondent of the Calcutta *Statesman* first wrote that the cow was the mother of the Hindus and later modified his statement to say that only the Hindu gods were her offsprings. Bankim gently pointed out that this was not so, only the calves were. The educated westerner, while full of negative notions regarding Hinduism, if pressed for an answer as to what Hinduism was could only say that it was the religion of the Hindus and that the latter were people who believed in Hinduism. The Census of 1881 virtually said as much. The average Englishman's knowledge of the educated Indian was restricted to the specimens he saw in the courts of law.[280] In his later years Bankim was convinced that with rare exceptions the European scholars were deeply prejudiced against India and that racial arrogance was a mainspring of their academic judgements. They took great pains to prove that only the Buddhist texts, hostile to Hinduism, contained some truth. The rest of India's literary heritage was either false or borrowed from other cultures. The Ramayana to such men was but an imitation of the *Iliad*, the Gita an adaptation of the Bible, Hindu astronomy borrowed from the Chinese and the Greeks, and their script was learnt from some Semitic race. Such conclusions derived from a method based on a clear principle: anything favourable to Indians found in Indian texts were either false or interpolated. The heroism of the Pandava brothers was but a poet's imagination, but the legend of Draupadi's five husbands was true for it proved that Indians were polyandrous and hence barbarous.

Ferguson concluded on the basis of some nude sculptures that the women in ancient India went about naked while the excellence of the sculptures at Mathura and elsewhere convinced some other scholars that these must be the work of Greek craftsmen. Weber, unable to question the antiquity of Hindu astronomy, concluded that they got their lunar calendar from the Babylonians. He only forgot that the latter had no such calendar. Despite the absence of evidence, Whitney theorized that Weber was probably right, because the Hindus lacked the intellectual ability for such achievements.

These scholars rejected the evidential value of any text which contained fanciful accounts. The Mahabharata was thus worthless as a source of historical information, but the fragments from Megasthenes, rich in incredible tales, constituted high authority. Weber was firmly of the view that the Mahabharata had no existence in the pre-Christian era. The only reason why he was willing to concede its existence in the early Christian centuries was that a European traveller, Chrysostom, heard of its existence from Indian boatsmen around that time. In a rare departure from the language of moderation, Bankim commented that Weber was anxious to prove that the Indian civilization was of recent origin because 'the glory of India was intolerable to this descendant of barbarians who roamed the forests of Germany only the other day.'[281]

He also accused European scholars and the 'half-educated missionaries' of having a double standard in their judgements on India and the West which at times led to distortions, deliberate or otherwise. Those who accused Hindus of polytheism ignored the fact that the belief in many gods and goddesses was not essentially different from or less rational than the Christian belief in angels, saints, and devils. Many popular religious practices and superstitions like the animistic rituals of the tribal peoples and popular fetishes were cited as evidence of the essentially barbaric nature of the Hindu religion. But no one considered similar practices in Europe, a survival from pagan times, as an integral part of the Christian faith or as evidence of Europe's barbarism. At the level of scholarly discourse, ancient legends which were fairly transparent allegories and noted as such in ancient commentaries, like the story of Ahalya's seduction by Indra, were interpreted as examples of a strong propensity towards licentiousness among ancient Hindus. Max Mueller in a highly emotional passage accused Brahmins—he called them 'an unscrupulous priesthood'—of deliberately distorting a passage in the scriptures to justify the monstrous custom of *sati*. It never occurred to the great scholar that the mistake might have arisen from some genuine error in the oral transmission of an unwritten text, that the Brahminical record was not one of blood-thirstiness, and that they were the only legislators in recorded history who had declared the taking of a woman's life as a crime worse than other forms of homicide. Bankim's profound sense of disquiet at the unflattering overtones of western Indology is expressed powerfully in the concluding passage of this discussion: 'As a Brahmin, as an humble member of the caste thus vituperated, as a descendant, however unworthy, of that great priesthood who formed the noblest intellectual aristocracy that the world has ever seen, I may be pardoned if I venture to call on the great German scholar to count up the victims of the Inquisition, add to them the slaughtered thousands of St. Bartholomew's Day and the Sicilian Vespers, and then add again the untold millions who fell in the Crusades; and then lay his hand upon his heart and say, if he cannot recollect instances of priestly unscrupulousness more flagrant than he can lay at the door of the Brahmins of India.' This highly charged passage covers a range of emotional effects which moulded nationalist perceptions of the West. The dominant culture, admired for its manifold excellence and considered superior to the Indian heritage in so many respects, was repeatedly found lacking in an essential moral quality—a capacity for detached self-examination and a minimal fairness in judging the vanquished. Even the noblest western mind was seen to be capable of slinging mud at the cherished traditions of a defeated people. The desire to hit back focused almost always on the poverty of western ethics, past and present.[282]

Bankim's evaluation of British rule is however much more complex. There is no scope for doubt on one point. His gut reaction to the fact of political dependence was entirely hostile and, if there was any recipe for instant independence, almost certainly he would have prescribed it to his fellow countrymen. Arguably, the regimes of long preparation for service to one's country recommended instead in *Dharmatattva* and, indirectly, in *Debi Chaudhurani*, were counsels of despair. The emphasis on acquiring physical fitness in both these works, despite the argument that it was essential for the balanced development of the human spirit, suggests that he probably looked forward to the pattern of confrontation described fictionally in *Anandamath* in some remote future. The duty to defend one's country is quite central to the message of *Dharmatattva*.

His stray comments and satirical sketches draw attention to the many blemishes of the British rule in India. Its benefits are also described at some length and these judgements have to be regarded as the author's considered opinion. A very different type of statement occurs in the stories of conflict with the British—*Anandamath* and *Debi Chaudhurani*. The advent of the British is there described as ordained by God for India's regeneration. Such sentiments are nowhere echoed in the serious essays and one wonders if these are to be taken at their face value or as devices to counterbalance the seditious undertone of the novels in question. Official sensitivity to seditious intent in literary works was well known at the time when Bankim wrote these novels. The later editions of *Anandamath* had to be censored by the author to excise passages which were considered anti-British. Apprehension of official displeasure might have influenced even the first version of the novel and *Debi Chaudhurani* was published after the author had been in trouble over the earlier novel.

Bankim's most considered judgement on the British rule appears in an essay, *Bharatvarsher svadhinata evam paradhinata* (India's Independence and Subjection).[283] It is an exercise in the objective assessment of the alleged benefits of independence. It first makes an important distinction. A country is not invariably dependent whenever the ruler is of an alien race. England under George I and Rome under the emperors of barbarian origin were not dependent countries. On the other hand, the American colonies of Britain ruled by the people of their own race were not independent. A country was dependent when its ruler was alien and located outside its territory. One likely consequence of the situation was racial discrimination in favour of the ruling race. Whatever the other conditions, a country was in effect independent when not subject to such oppression by an alien race. By this logic England under the Normans was not free, nor was India under the early Turkish kings. Under Akbar India was independent in every sense. Alien rule so defined might generate two evils. First, maladministration through the ruler's absenteeism. Second, the interest of the dependency might be sacrificed for that of the metropolis. Both were to be found in India under Britain. If the seat of the British authority were located in India, the administration would have improved. On the other hand, India was not a victim of oppression through the excesses of any autocratic ruler. But Indian interests were sacrificed in favour of Britain's. The Home Charges and the deployment of Indian resources for Britain's Abyssinian War were instances in point. However, when India was independent, the subjects were at times oppressed by unworthy rulers. Besides, while the bias in favour of the ruling race was a source of oppression in British India, ancient India had its equivalent of racial discrimination. The distinction between the Brahmins and the Sudras was not less discriminatory than that between the English and the Indians. Discrimination usually takes two distinct forms—preferential treatment of the ruling race incorporated into the law of the land and favour shown to them in matters involving state patronage, especially appointment to high offices. In India there were separate courts for the Europeans and the natives and while the latter could be judged by Englishmen, the Indians had no jurisdiction over the Europeans. But the same law applied to both. But in ancient India, not only could a Sudra never sit in judgement on a Brahmin but the penalty for homicide was different for the two castes. The high offices in British India might be a monopoly of the British, but the Indians had access at least to the lower rungs. In ancient times, though Sudra kings were not unknown, very probably all offices of the state were in the hands of the Kshatriya and Brahmin castes. The argument that in those days the rulers were at least of one's own race was not very convincing. 'It seems unlikely that oppression by one's own people is somehow rather sweet and that by an alien race is especially bitter.' In short, the bulk of the population was not better off under Indian rulers. But the upper strata of society had suffered under British rule for they were denied opportunities appropriate to their intelligence, education, and status. Besides, the English monopoly of all positions of authority meant a denial of access to the skills essential for running one's own affairs. If dependence thus hindered progress, the rule of a European nation had brought with it the invaluable knowledge of western science and literature. The concluding paragraph of this essay contains a revealing statement: '... Is there no difference then between freedom and subjection? ... We are a subject people and will remain so for a long time to come. There is no point in our debating that question.'

In his quest for the merits of a situation that could not be altered, Bankim's concern was for something more than balanced judgement. It was a quest for some silver lining, a measure of consolation when there was no hope of redress in the foreseeable future. This too is made quite explicit in the opening paragraph of the essay discussed above: 'Even in our worst misfortune one can discern some blessing. He who looks for what is good amid [pervasive] evil is a wise person. In these days of our sorrow there is some consolation in the thought that even misery is not unalloyed misery'. His discovery of the said blessings was seldom unmixed with sarcasm. A well-known passage describing England's good work in India opens with a sardonic comment—that there was a great deal of excitement over the rumoured prosperity of the country. 'Until now our country was on its way to perdition, now we are becoming civilized thanks to the Englishman's skill in the art of government.' It is difficult to accept the flamboyant passage which follows entirely at its face value. The blessings of British rule are duly listed—the technical wonders of railways, steamships, telegraph and modern medicine, the breathtaking grandeur of the new cities, the delights of the western lifestyle, the deliverance from the darkness of superstitions into the light that is modern science and the like. A rhetorical query follows, 'Amidst this surfeit of blessings, I want to ask one question—who is it that benefits from this abundance of good fortune?' The answer to this query leaves one in little doubt that the author's enthusiasm for England's work in India was less than total.[284] Even in his apparently straightforward appreciations of the British connection, there are shades of meaning which imply that the most important gains were those not intended by the rulers. The concluding paragraph of the essay entitled 'India's shame' (*Bharat-kalanka*), the English are described as the great benefactors of India, for 'they teach us new things' hitherto unknown in the country. 'They show us how to walk along ways we have never trod before.' Among these priceless lessons there were two, unfamiliar to the Hindu tradition: love of independence and nation building. Evidently, the priceless lessons derived not from alien rule, but in reaction to it and from the example of sovereign nations, especially the English themselves. The preceding discussion hints at the implicit meaning. It focuses on the pre-British attempts to establish sovereign states in India based on some sense of nationality. The Khalsa under Ranjit Singh's leadership is cited as an instance in point and the writer wonders if a sense of unity was achieved in one province, whether it was entirely impossible that the country as a whole could have achieved nationhood. If he relevant lesson was being learnt at last from the British, obviously it was not dispensed through the process of government.[285]

The most explicit criticisms of the British are to be found in the novels dealing with the early days of the Company's rule. These are precisely the works full of protestations about England's divinely ordained role in India. The worst invectives are counterbalanced by statements to the effect that these were lawless times and no one was really in control. Even the English did not know at the time of the noble task that God wanted them to perform in India. The Lord alone knew and He was holding His cards close to His chest.[286]

Only one result of the British connection was greeted as an almost unqualified blessing—western education. The English language was a storehouse of unlimited treasure and its cultivation could only be beneficial for the nation. It was also the rope with which the bonds of pan-Indian unity were to be tied, for Sanskrit was no longer there to serve that purpose.[287] And the benefit of western education, Bankim believed, would not have come except through European rule.

Arguably, Bankim's psychological rejection of alien rule, his deep-seated resentment against the fact of subjection, was articulated in the three novels set against the background of the Company's rule. *Chandrasekhar*, the earliest of the three, has for its setting Mir Qasim's wars with the English. It contains the following passage: 'The English who lived in Bengal at this time were incapable of doing only two things. They could not control their greed and they could not accept defeat .... They would never concede that a certain act was immoral and that hence one should desist from it. The world has never seen men as tyrannical and powerful as the people who first founded the Britannic empire in India.' 'The English who came to India in those days were affected by an epidemic disease—stealing other people's wealth. The word morality had disappeared from their vocabulary.'[288] In this tale, rich in villains, the arch villain is Lawrence Foster, an English factor who kidnaps the heroine, Saibalini. The event is anticipated in a dream in which Foster appears as a white pig. The avenging hero, Pratap, takes a vow to throw out the English, because there were many Fosters among them and dies fighting for Mir Qasim, 'the last king of Bengal'—so described because the nawabs who succeed him reigned but did not rule. There is no reference in *Chandrasekhar* to Britain's providential role in India. Only the saintly Ramananda Swami speculates that the English will probably capture the entire country some day because they were 'very fortunate, strong and dexterous'.[289] Both *Debi Chaudhurani* and *Anandamath* describe in horrendous detail the sufferings of the people in the early days of the Company's rule. But direct criticisms of the English are avoided by a clever device. In the former novel, the philanthropic and saintly bandit, Bhabani Pathak, justifies his role on the ground that the country had no lawful authority at the time. The Muslim rule had ended. The English who had come only recently neither ruled nor knew how to rule. A description of the atrocities committed by the zamindars follows. The true culprits, Debi Singh and Gangagobinda Singh, are mentioned in the next chapter and the fact that Debi Singh's power derived ultimately from Hastings is mentioned casually in half a sentence.[290] Again, the reader of *Anandamath* is informed that at the time of the great famine the company as the Diwan collected revenue, but had not yet assumed responsibility for law and order, left to the worthless Mir Jafar. It is extremely unlikely that Bankim did not know this statement to be incorrect. His remark that Mir Qasim was the last king to rule Bengal, written at an earlier date, otherwise makes no sense. In any case, the cryptic sentences which follow leave one in little doubt about the author's true sentiments concerning the role of the British at the time: 'Mir Jafar takes opium and sleeps. The English extract money and write despatches. The Bengalis weep and are ruined. The revenue of Bengal belongs to the English. People might die of starvation, but the collection of revenue does not stop.' The choicest invectives in the language are used to describe Mir Jafar—'the worst among sinners, despicable, treacherous, a blot on the human species'.[291] Moral indignation at the practice of betraying one's master to gain a throne, not uncommon in eighteenth-century India, does not explain this outburst. It has to be read with an episode described earlier in this chapter—Bankim's perception of Plassey as a tragedy for the nation and his rejection of the British accounts of the battle as pure fiction.

How is one to explain then the several references in the two novels to the beneficence of British rule at a later date? The time of the famine is described as one of anarchy, when the country did not have the benefit of British justice.[292] Bankim's real evaluation of that system of justice in its heyday is discussed below. *Debi Chaudhurani* ends with a brief eulogy of British rule. Bhabani Thakur's role as a self-appointed dispenser of justice ends because the English assume full authority and the country comes to enjoy good government.[293] Also discussed below are Bankim's thoughts on what this good government meant for the bulk of the population. Finally, there are the passages in *Anandamath* which refer to the British conquest as divine dispensation. Hastings forges an iron chain with which to bind the whole of India and the Lord on His throne says, 'So be it'.[294] Bhabananda informs Captain Thomas that the Muslims, not the English, were their real enemies. And then, there is the concluding chapter in *Anandamath* where the divine purpose behind the monks' rebellion is explained. The British as traders were reluctant to take charge of government. The rebellion forced their hands. Thus alone could the ancient faith of the Hindu be restored to its pristine glory, for their knowledge of external phenomena was weak compared to their spiritual knowledge and they must learn the former from the English. Until the Hindus were again strong, the British rule would endure and the people of the land enjoy peace and prosperity. The English were friends, not enemies. Besides, no one was strong enough to defeat them ultimately.[295] The relevant passages occur in the first serialized version of the novel as well and hence cannot be dismissed as cautious afterthought.

Undoubtedly, Bankim admired certain features of the British rule in India. He was convinced that western education was the best thing that had happened to the country in a long time and was grateful to the British for this 'priceless gift'. As noted above, he considered the British administration of justice despite its limitations an improvement on earlier systems. He appreciated the public works; a throw away comment in *Anandamath* compares the 'wonderful' Mughal roads with those constructed by the British later.[296] Like many of his contemporaries he also thought of the long period when Muslim dynasties ruled over India as a period of oppressive alien rule. He does note the many exceptions to this generalized assessment. Bengal under the 'Pathans' even experienced a Renaissance, according to his judgement. A country is not necessarily under subjection merely because the ruler is alien by race, he commented in this connection.[297] For Bengal, Mughal rule is described as an era of true dependence because the region's resources were drained away and there was nothing to show for it even in the form of monumental constructions.[298] Elsewhere he says that India under Akbar was not under alien rule and praises the monarch for promoting Indians to high office.[299] Yet his over all assessment of this long period of Indian history is decisively negative. The following sentence is fairly typical of his considered judgements on the subject: '... The iron heel of the Musalman tyrant had set its mark on the shoulders of the nation.'[300] His tears over Plassey notwithstanding, he surely thought of the British regime as an improvement on its predecessor. This preference was enhanced by his admiration for some individual personalities, especially Warren Hastings. He explained away the charges of oppression against the pro-consul on the ground that men in high office were often forced into acts of injustice for reasons of state. Only large-hearted men who were also just and generous could achieve something so stupendous as the establishment of an empire. Hastings definitely was one such man.[301] He also attributed to all his British protagonists, the vile Foster included, an indomitable courage and patriotism.[302] And he believed, pragmatically, that there was no foreseeable end to British rule so that one had to live with the unpalatable fact of dependence and make the best of it. The impassioned accounts of suffering under alien rule in the early days of the Company's government have their counterparts in essays and satires on the later period as well. Only the admiration for the rebels is tempered with cautious praise for the later years of the Raj, in which the author only half-believed. In the last scene of *Anandamath*, the rebel leader, Satyananda, agrees to lay down his arms only as an act of surrender to the Divine will, revealed to him by an all-knowing superman. But he does so with tears in his eyes. He would have preferred to die fighting the English. If the author really believed that the British conquest was divinely ordained he must have seen in that ordinance an element of severe punishment.

Bankim's concern for fair and balanced judgement did lead him to
recognize that there were at least two sides to every question. His essay on
the Bengal peasants contains his severest criticism of the Raj. In the same
essay, he presents a reasoned evaluation of the progress achieved under
British rule. Increased security, law and order, and an end to arbitrary
exactions by men in authority had led to the accumulation of wealth and
undisturbed inheritance. The new sense of security had contributed to an
increase in population, leading in its turn to an expansion of the arable.
Agriculture was further stimulated by the demand in the British market and
hence the steady growth in trade implied a corresponding expansion in
agriculture and the nation's wealth.[303] The price rise which many regretted
really meant that money had become cheaper and that income from
agriculture was on the increase. The view that Bengal was impoverished
under British rule was not based on any evidence. The trade with England,
again contrary to popular belief, enriched rather than impoverished India.
The import of textiles lowered the price of cloth. If the weaver lost his
livelihood in the process, it was because of his failure to compete. Protection
was a counsel of disaster—*vide* Mill and Buckle. If the weaver could no
longer earn a livelihood by weaving, agriculture offered an alternative means,
for 'all occupations produced comparable [rates of] return'. The thesis that
agriculture was under pressure through such dislocation was answered with
another classical economic argument. Trade was but exchange. If the import
of textiles reduced the demand for domestically produced cloth, the export
of agricultural products created a corresponding shortage in the domestic
market, creating a demand for additional labour in agriculture. The market,
in other words, allocated resources optimally. If owing to the system of
caste, the weavers did not take to alternative occupations, this would indeed
be a misfortune. But the demand for labour in agriculture would then be
met by other people and the loss of income in textiles compensated by the
augmented income in agriculture and the nation's income would suffer no
decline. The theory of the drainage of wealth was rejected. First, the outflow
of bullion was more than counterbalanced by the inflow. The country was a
net gainer from trade. The foreign investments in India, especially in railways,
proved the point. The outflow of resources through the Home Charges was
insignificant compared to all the gains of trade. The preface to the 1892
edition of the essay qualifies this analysis with an admission of errors. But
since 'no one knew any longer what was correct in political economy', he

did not amend his statements. Only a single footnote describes his comment on the Home Charges as a 'great error'.[304]

There is no admission of error as to the hard core of his statement regarding the condition of the peasantry. And if the acknowledgement of benefits has the cold trappings of the social sciences, the peasants' misery is described in a very different language: 'Hasim Sheikh and Rama Kaibarta are ploughing [their fields] knee-deep in mud, bare-headed and bare-foot in the midday sun, with a blunt plough they had to borrow and a pair of bullocks, mere skin and bones. What benefits have they received? The heat of the ... sun is about to burst their skull, they are half-dead from thirst which they try to quench with handfuls of mud from the field. They are nearly dead from hunger, but there is no time to go home and eat for the field has to be ploughed first. In the evening they will return to eat some coarse red rice with a little salt and chili from a broken piece of stone, their platter, and remain half-starved. Then they will lie down on a torn mat or on the ground in one corner of the stable. Mosquitoes do not sting them. Next morning on their way to the field through knee-deep mud, they may be seized by the landlord or the moneylender and detained for non-payment of debts; so no work will get done. Or else at the time of cultivation the landlord will confiscate the land. What then will happen that year? Starvation— starvation for the entire family. Tell me, you Babu, with spectacles on your nose, what benefit have they received? What good have you done them with your education? And you, Sir Englishman, you who sit on your chair, quill- pen in one hand with plans to reshape God's creation, the other hand engaged in scratching your beetle-black beard—you tell me what good you have done to Hasim Sheikh and Rama Kaibarta? I say, not an iota, not a speck. And if this be the case, I shall not join you all in the grand jubilations over the great good fortune of our country.'[305]

The reason for this state of affairs is then explained. The income from agriculture had probably increased three or fourfold since the Permanent Settlement, but the cultivator had benefited little from the fact. Part of the incremental income was siphoned off as revenue, but the bulk of it went to the zamindar. Whatever the law, the peasant was in effect a tenant-at-will and the increased demand for land was an incentive to evictions. The rental demand had increased three to four times since the first settlement and by ten times in some places. It was farcical to talk of legal redress, for the law was but a farce which only the rich could afford to witness. A graphic account follows of the ruthless extortions by the zamindar and his agents, aided by the police who too were in the zamindar's pay.[306] The story ends with the peasant left landless and totally ruined.[307]

The ultimate responsibility for the situation was traced to the policies of the government. Under the Muslim rulers, the zamindars first emerged as contractors for collecting revenue who were allowed to keep the surplus over and above the stipulated amount. The resulting oppression was augmented when Cornwallis conferred proprietary rights on the contractors. The peasant virtually lost all his rights and the promised regulations for his protection were long in coming. Meanwhile new regulations tightened the stranglehold legalizing 'the banditry' of the zamindars. The remedial measures 1859 onwards helped little. The zamindar's legal right to seize everything belonging to the tenant on default of rent was not affected nor his right to enhance the rent. Such policies were the results of the foreigners' mistakes rather than evil intention. But whatever the reason, 'If the subject population is oppressed, one must blame the ruler'. Moreover, the mighty English who terrorized the whole of Asia and evicted the emperor of Abyssinia from his throne for a paltry offence did nothing to stop the excesses of the petty zamindar. Their law never punished the landlords, their courts always gave victory to the powerful. The British with their much-vaunted expertise in the art of government either could not or did not do anything to redress the intolerable situation.[308]

The law was of no help, for the courts, far from the peasants' home, were the playground of the rich. The poor stood no chance there and actually got ruined if forced into litigation. The inadequate number of courts and judicial officers meant infinite delay. Under the British system such ruinous delays were acceptable, but not any departure from the letter of the law.

If there was a criminal case against the zamindars' men, the jury system ensured that the ignorant and incompetent jurors would allow the benefit of doubt to the accused in the majority of cases.[309] The accused then returned to wreak vengeance on the poor complainant and the hostile witnesses. The English judges were well-intentioned and highly educated, but they were ineffective because they had very little knowledge of local conditions and the local language and were lacking in sympathy. The importation of good laws from England, Bankim commented, was one of the tokens of India's progress. The lawyers, judicial officers, clerks had all prospered under the shadow of the good law now administered in every court. 'No one can dispense [true] justice any longer in ways not sanctioned by the law. The poor and the meek suffer a little as a result, for they have no appreciation of the glorious law, but [merely] seek justice. That error of course is the result of their ignorance.'[310] The Penal Code is described elsewhere as an instrument for the suppression of the law-abiding as well as the wicked and for punishing one man for the guilt of another.[311] Kamalakanta in his opium dream sees the court of justice as an abattoir. The judges are butchers. The bigger cattle manage to escape somehow, but the smaller ones do not have a chance.[312] In another dream, the machinery of justice is conceded omnipotence. No one escapes. The rich are ruined and honest men end up in prison.[313] A third question refers to the need for the provision of credit to the peasants. The peasants' indebtedness to usurious moneylenders was attributed to the British failure to attend to this duty.[314]

The process of government itself was described with an equal degree of cynicism. The author's experience as an administrator as well as documentary evidence were drawn upon to support such assessments. In his view, the administration functioned most of the time as a mindless machine with a great show of deliberation. The majority of the officials were mere cogs in the wheel. An example, perhaps not entirely imaginary, was cited to explain how the system worked. The lieutenant-governor asks for a report on the condition of the embankments. The secretary writes to the Board; his letter neatly copied goes out to the eleven divisional commissioners who dutifully note the date of receipt. Their clerks send out copies of the august missive to the district collectors, the latter to the native deputy magistrates who ask for reports from the sub-inspectors who then send the constable to the village watchman. The latter's statement, that the zamindars were neglecting the embankments, travels back through each rung of the official ladder. The Board of Revenue deliberates on the basis of this enquiry in depth and a resolution based on their deliberations is signed by the lieutenant-governor, whose fame as a great administrator reaches the four corners of the world. Officials who thus played safe, like Sir William Gray for instance, seldom caused any discontent. The other type of officials who used their own judgement and took independent initiative seldom escaped unscathed. Sir George Campbell, the *bête noire* of the Bengali press because of his plans to restrict higher education, was an example of the latter type. The two contrasted personalities exemplified two very different traditions in another sense as well. Sir William lived in fear of the press and cherished the British Indian Association's good opinion. Sir George had faith in the intelligence and judgement of only one person—himself. He had nothing but contempt for

Indians, delighted in saying unpleasant things, and knew very little about the country where he served. Expectedly, such attitudes resulted in serious mistakes besides great unpopularity.[315]

The biography of Muchiram Gur, a fictional account of a scoundrel's progress from the post of a petty clerk to the dizzy height of Rajahood, offers a more lively set of pictures of Anglo-Indian officialdom. Muchiram is semi-literate but rises high through his insight into the true nature of English officials, and his skill in using that invaluable knowledge. First, as a petty clerk he profited from the fact the English district magistrates did not write down themselves the evidence at the trials. What Muchi took down as evidence varied according to the 'fees' paid to him by the parties concerned. He was also entirely useless at his job. The sahib was peevish but kind, otherwise our hero would have been sacked. His successor, charmed by Muchi's act of obeisance, concluded that here was the man most worthy of his trust. As the new boss never did any work, he had no reason to lose his total faith in the scoundrel, who was duly promoted. Muchi next applied for a job in the collectorate. His English being not equal to the task of writing an application, he sought help in the matter. The man who wrote it for him was instructed to avoid correct English, for the sahibs had no fondness for educated Bengalis. The application was also duly sprinkled with honorifics to which the official had no title. Muchi turned up in shoddy Indian clothes, armed further with a testimonial from his English boss. The applicants included holders of university degrees, impeccably dressed in western clothes. Those so dressed were dismissed forthwith for their presumption. The degree-holders were told that quotations from Shakespeare were not required for the job which went, expectedly, to Muchiram. The new boss, Mr Home, asked why Muchi addressed him as 'My Lord'. Well, Muchi had heard that the sahib had aristocratic connections. This ascription caused great pleasure to Home. Though a man of considerable ability, he was after all human. Muchi continued to address Home as 'My Lord' and prospered. Home's successor, Read, a shrewd man, realized that he had inherited as his subordinate a true 'monkey that had just left his arboreal home'. But a Haileybury-trained civilian, paternal in his attitude to Bengalis, he decided to act kindly. The scamp was kicked up to the rank of Deputy Magistrate, for Read saw no harm in adding one more to the vast number of idiots to be found in that service. But the new job brought only the monthly pay as remuneration. Unused to such privation, Muchiram retired, bought a zamindari estate, moved to Calcutta, and began to hobnob with the highest in the land. The lieutenant-governor decided that here was a fit person for nomination to the Council. Now landlord and Member of Council, Muchiram was destined to rise even higher. A famine in the land opened the door to ultimate glory. A just, hardworking, and philanthropic magistrate-collector, Meanwell, ever anxious for the welfare of the queen's subjects, rode into Muchiram's village to enquire into the causes of the famine. An encounter with a group of Muchi's tenants, who were cooking a meal for themselves, convinced him that the philanthropic landlord had opened a free kitchen for the famine-stricken. The misunderstanding occurred because the sahib's knowledge of Bengali did not measure up to his great goodwill, even though he had won a medal for his proficiency in the language. No matter. Muchi at last received the ultimate reward—the titles of Raja and Rai Bahadur. The tale ends with the Hindu equivalent of alleluiah.[316]

The British bureaucrats in the history of Raja Muchiram are not evil tyrants. The worst among them merely shirk work. But with hardly any exception they are susceptible to flattery. Even the best take a cynical view of the Indian bureaucrats. And India is a closed book to them. Under their benign authority they sycophantic and rascally Muchirams flourish and so does corruption in the public services. An even more unfavourable view is presented in the satirical sketch. 'Bransonism'[317], inspired by the Anglo-Indian agitation against the Ilbert Bill. A dark-skinned Indian Christian with an English name claims to be outside the jurisdiction—or 'justication' as he puts it—of an Indian magistrate on grounds of racial superiority. His claims are ignored and the black sahib is fined for stealing some fish. An Anglo-Indian newspaper takes up the cause, describes a native conspiracy led by the influential complainant (who in fact was the local fisherwoman), and screams for justice. The Indian deputy magistrate is summoned by the English superior, admits he had acted wrongly in sentencing an 'Englishman' for it was sheer presumption on the part of an inferior race to try their superiors. The cringing pays and the man is actually promoted. The British superior recommends his promotion on the ground that though the man was sly and sycophantic, he was at least free from the intolerable conceit of the so-called educated classes. This ascription of overt racism probably derived from the fact that the anti-Ilbert Bill agitators did have the sympathy of some British officials. The Anglo-Indians' weakness for sycophancy and their animosity towards educated Bengalis are recurrent themes in the literature of the period.[318] 'Bransonism' reflects a popular perception confirmed by the tone and style of the Anglo-Indian resistance to the Ilbert Bill.

Bankim saw racial animosity, a marked feature of the relationship between the Indians and the English, as not only inevitable but desirable. The Anglo-Indian journals invariably contained unfair criticism of Indians and the compliment was returned with unfailing regularity in the Indian press. The mutual recriminations were part of a long-established tradition, a source of deep distress to well-meaning Englishmen who organized associations and wrote to the press in vain efforts to mitigate the evil. Given the superiority of the English in so many areas of life, racial amity would have been possible if they acted with detachment, goodwill, and restraint and Indians accepted a position of humble subordination. Such a relationship was impossible between the conquerors and the conquered. The latter could neither believe in the dispassionate goodwill of the victors nor feel any loving regard for them. The conquerors would have to be more than human to act with due restraint. 'Subordinate we are but humble we can never be,' Bankim wrote. So long as the Indians had their pride in their ancient civilization they might be humble in their words, but never in their hearts. His earnest hope was for the continuation of this mutual animosity, until the Indians became the equals of the English. Insults and ridicule were better spurs to effort in that direction than friendly encounters, for competition comes easier with one's enemies than with one's friends.[319] But the mutual sentiments of dislike should only inspire positive effort, not malice or ill will. Bankim evidently did not see the psychological impracticability of his prescription.

The essay cited in the last paragraph speaks somewhat hopefully of the British impact on the Bengalis even if the beneficial element in the situation derived from competition inspired by animosity. Most of his statements on the subject, however, highlight the negative dimension of the impact. Here his own assessment of the Bengali culture and personality in a historical context, not confined to the British advent, is of relevance. Despite references to occasional periods of glory and cultural achievements of great value and his doubts concerning the ascription of weakness to Bengalis even in the historical past,[320] some of the contemporary British views on the worthlessness of his people appear to have rubbed off on him. In his opinion, the climate and Turkish rule had induced a degeneration in the Bengali personality and over time it had lost all dignity and manly feelings, though not a certain acuteness of intellect.[321] Even their intellectual position in India in earlier times 'was one of the lowest'.[322] The races of northern India were sturdier and more original than the Bengalis—partly an echo of British views on the martial races of India.[323] The comparisons, of course, underline above all their inferiority in relation to the English. The prologue to the journal, *Bangadarshan*, states unequivocally that there was no hope that the Bengalis would ever be the equals of the English. It might not be a bad idea if they could be transformed into Englishmen, but efforts in that direction were likely to produce only asses in lions' skin.[324]

Comparisons aside, Bankim's opinion of his fellow Bengalis, the English-educated Babus in particular, was remarkably similar to that of their worst critics, the Anglo-Indian press. He saw them as the end product of a long process of degeneration, 'crushed and spiritless'.[325] 'Most Bengalis nowadays are either hypocritical and deceitful or like animals', the disciple in *Dharmatattva* comments and the Guru agrees wholeheartedly.[326] This perception of decline over a long period influenced the assessment of the British impact. If alien rule was the prime factor in destroying the moral fibre of the Bengalis, they had reached their nadir under the British. Cowardly, half-educated, devoid of all self-respect, they slavishly copied the externals of the English lifestyle without taste or any sensitivity.[327] Imitation of a superior race was an acceptable way to progress sanctioned by man's historical experience. The Romans had imitated the Greeks, the progress of modern Europe had been triggered off by their imitation of the ancients, and even the contemporary English imitated the French in matters of food and dress. Perhaps the only hope for the Bengalis lay in the fact that they were imitating the English. But unfortunately, they were prone to copy English vices and less adept in emulating the virtues.[328] Worse still, they were left with no sense of shame in the fact of bondage and the size of their meagre salaries had become the criterion for the measurement of social status. 'The length of its tail determines the rank of a monkey. The prisoner prides himself on the length of the chain that binds his feet.'[329] The Babus' craven spirit is parodied in *Ingraj-stotra* (Hymn to the English): 'Whatever I do is for your pleasure ... I do good to others so that you will call me a philanthropist; I cultivate learning, so that you will call me learned. Therefore, oh Englishman, look upon me with favour, I bow to thee in adoration.'[320] A vitriolic definition sums up Bankim's view of the British impact on the Bengali spirit: 'They indeed are Babus whose tongues have been sanctified by the aliens' spittle.'[331]

The alienation from the masses of the population, the lack of fellow-feeling between the educated and the underprivileged, was identified as the worst consequence of western education. The Babu had nothing but contempt for his mother tongue and the language of his intellectual discourse created a permanent barrier between him and the poor. He rejected Macaulay's filtration theory, the hope that education would filter down from the educated to the rest of the population, in characteristic language: 'Until now the country was on its way to perdition, thanks to the dry-as-dust Brahmin pandits. Now the new avant-garde, having absorbed the water [of western knowledge] will save the land, for by virtue of the perforations in their system even the lowly will be duly humidified.'[332]

In the final phase of his ideological development, Bankim, now self-consciously Hindu and devoutly theistic, speaks in a very different voice. He is at last convinced of India's superiority over Europe on many points and he writes more about his reservations than his admiration for the West. His opinion of his fellow Bengalis has not changed, but the imitation of Europe is no longer prescribed as the road to salvation. His discovery of Hinduism no doubt was highly idiosyncratic, but it at last provided an answer to his nationalistic quest for valid grounds which would justify a claim to equality with Europe.

Expectedly, Hinduism as interpreted by Bankim was the central focus of the claim to superiority. He may have derived his doctrine of culture from western models, but was convinced that it had attained dizzy heights in the Hindu tradition way above the comprehension of the European protagonists like Matthew Arnold.[333] The Hindu ideal of prayer went much deeper than the principles of Christian worship. Ideal men, whom people have adored down the centuries as incarnations, appear in the Hindu tradition with an aura of perfection and a completeness of development not encountered in other cultures. Christ, 'once the ideal to Christians', was indifferent to worldly concerns. Not so the Hindu ideal, Krishna, the Lord incarnate, who was king, philosopher, diplomat, and warrior.[334] Some elements of this version of Hinduism might resemble Comte's ideas, and Spencer's theories in criticism of Comte approximated the Hindu doctrines of non-duality and illusion. Spinoza's philosophy also had Vedantic resonances. But these 'European Hindus' were merely groping towards the cruder aspects of the Indian tradition, for Hinduism alone catered to all the needs of mankind.[335] Much that the Vedic Hindus had intuitively understood was still obscure to the West. European philosophers were still trying to grapple with the concepts expounded as *purusha* and *prakriti* in *samkhya*.[336] The doctrines of devotion and surrender to the will of God did occur in Christianity, but they reached their logical culmination only in Hinduism. The egalitarian doctrines were no monopoly of Christianity or Buddhism. These are stated in the Gita quite explicitly.[337] The exclusive preoccupation with western education had resulted in ignorance of this tradition.[338] All the vaunted literature of Europe had nothing to offer comparable to the high ideals of morality and devotion projected in the Puranic legends.[339] The civilization which the Brahmins had created in the past could still offer a solution to Europe's problems.[340] In one of his novels written in this phase, *Rajani*, a miracle-working *sanyasin* explains that while the ancient Hindus did not know much that the West had discovered, the English had no monopoly of knowledge and there were things unknown to modern man the Indians had mastered in their own way.[341]

As Hinduism was declared to be superior, Europe's religion, Christianity, inevitably came under serious criticism. Some of Bankim's assessment of Christianity even in this phase has the neutral quality of social scientific enquiry. Like the other great religions founded by individual prophets, its governing principles were seen to be explicit, something that could be easily apprehended by the outsider. At the outset such religions, he explained, had little beyond the fundamental principles; the legends, rites, mythologies, superstitions were mostly later accretions.[342] These fundamental principles were the common foundations of Christianity in all its forms and the religion should be assessed with reference to these only. Saint worship, belief in ghosts or the various pagan legends and festivals which were a part of Europe's religious life were not integral to Christianity. The ascription of polytheistic elements to Christianity, seen in the belief in angels, devils, and saints, was also a part of this neutral enquiry.[343]

The same cannot be said of the more critical comments. A partisan spirit, informed by the desire to establish Hindu superiority and his old quest for elements of weakness in European civilization, is quite evident here though the method of rational argument is never abandoned. First, the narrower form of monotheism which excludes an imaginative cognition of the Divine in nature and hence nature worship is identified as a relatively crude expression of the religious spirit. It is seen to be present in Christianity and traced to Judaic influences which are also described as the source of Christian intolerance. Bankim questioned the identification of God with the Jehovah of Judaism for though He was the only object of worship to the Jews, He was no more than an anthropomorphic deity given to human foibles like anger and malice. The Christians, through Saint Paul, received

their conception of God at least in part from the Greeks who had a much
nobler conception of the Divinity.[344] The Christian conception of God however
is castigated in terms very similar to those used by Bhudev. He was an
unjust Deity, condemning innocent souls to eternal perdition for their non-
acceptance of Christianity, even if they were born before the advent of
Christ. Besides, the Deity is pictured as for ever peeping into human souls
to detect sinful thoughts. The language used in condemning such beliefs
almost reminds one of Hastie's remarks on Hinduism: 'That God is unfit for
that holy name. He is the lord of the universe, but no devil in human shape
would ever be such an oppressive unjust tyrant.' Such a religion, he concludes,
can only be described as devilish.[345] A more tolerant perception of Christianity
is however not absent from these discourses. The translation of the Bible
into modern European languages is mentioned in a passing comment as
having freed Europe from superstitious beliefs and opened the way to
progress.[346] Contemporary Christianity was criticized for its departure from
the ideals of love and peace as was Hinduism for its abandonment of *nishkama
karma*. Further, the Christian faith in a life hereafter was seen to have been
undermined by the new faith in science. It was the scientists' superstition
which precluded a satisfactory conclusion to the ongoing debate on the
question.[347]

Western science and the scientific spirit, once considered the surest
foundation for man's progress, was now seen in a very different light. Now
science was a monster stinking of human blood and bedecked with the
weapons of destruction. With one hand it ran the machines producing goods
and with the other it brushed away 'all that was ancient and pure, the
cherished treasures of many millennia'.[348] The Europeans wrongly accused
the Hindus of worshipping inanimate objects. In fact they themselves had
become the worshippers of lifeless things. They had harnessed the forces of
nature but never stopped to think that these were permeated by the Divine
consciousness. Nor did they enquire into God's purpose as revealed in nature.
To play around with natural forces without such knowledge was a mortal
sin. The consequences of such folly had already become obvious the day
dynamite was invented.[349] Science had become a handmaiden to the intense
materialism of nineteenth-century Europe, 'deadliest moral poison'.[350]

The expansionist tendencies of the modern European states and their
mutual aggression were criticized in Bankim's earlier writings as well.
Kamalakanta had equated the right of conquest, honoured in international
law, with the right of theft.[351] In *Dharmatattva*, the conflict among nation

states is seen in a somewhat different light. Europe is not singled out for its record of aggression. The absence of any supra-national authority is identified as the root cause of international conflicts. Just as in the absence of a powerful government the strong try and exploit the weak, so do powerful nations exploit weaker ones because there is no one to stop them. European expansion and mutual aggression were a part of this wider phenomenon. Bankim's sentiments on the subject are made explicit by the language he uses: 'Just as the [pariah] dogs in the marketplace snatch from one another whatever they can, so do the nations, civilized and uncivilized, seize from others what they can at every opportunity.' The examples of conflict and aggression are, however, all taken from Europe's recent history. The purpose of this particular discourse is not any assessment of Europe but simply a plea for national self-defence as an essential duty of man.[352]

Europe's patriotism is, however, also identified as a specific contributory factor in aggression and on that ground condemned as a 'devilish sin'.[353] The causal links between patriotism and aggression and the reasons for the relative narrowness of the former are explored along lines somewhat similar to Bhudev's analysis. Patriotism is recognized as a stage in the gradual expansion of man's capacity for love. In Europe the development of the human spirit stopped at that point. The Europeans love their own people and detest other nations. The roots of this limitation are traced to the Graeco-Roman sources of European civilization in the first place. The religion of classical Europe was no more than the worship of power and beauty in nature and offered no reason why one should love all mankind. The natural excellence of the two ancient races generated their patriotic sentiments which acted as a powerful lever of progress. A third influence derived from the Jewish tradition which too emphasized the love of one's own people. Christianity introduced a nobler ideal, but in effect the Graeco-Roman and Judaic influence had a greater hold on the European mind and hence the Christian love for all men had remained a distant goal. The Europeans paid only lip service to the Christian ideal, but really cared only for their own country. The Christian conception of the Deity as a ruler of the universe, not manifest in the created world itself, also did not help equate love of God with love for all his creation.[354] The end result of all this was an intense patriotism which saw nothing wrong in inflicting injuries on other people in the interest of one's own country.

If European patriotism had ceased to be the ideal which it once was to Bankim, even though *Dharmatattva* preaches patriotism as one of the highest virtues, he does not entirely reject even in this phase the Utilitarian and Positivist philosophies which influenced his earlier thinking. I have argued above that his neo-Hinduism drew heavily on those two philosophies and the doctrine of culture. His direct statements on the subject of Utilitarianism in this phase are actually less critical than the earlier assessments. He sees Utilitarianism as a worship of the good and hence attributes to it the characteristics of religion. But it is an incomplete religion, because it does not include the worship of the Beautiful and the True as well. Apparently, a moral implication is attributed in this statement to the ideal of the greatest good of the greatest number. The lengthy discussion on the subject in *Dharmatattva* accepts the Utilitarian ideal almost in its entirety, but argues that it is not enough and must be subsumed by the doctrine of culture.[355] On Comte, *Dharmatattva* comments that some of his ideas are similar to Hindu doctrines.[356] His definition of religion, that it 'expresses the state of perfect unity which is the distinctive mark of man's existence both as an individual and in society ...' is described as the best available.[357]

Bankim's final verdict was that even the civilization of nineteenth-century Europe, which he once considered the highest level of progress ever attained by man, was but an immature stage in the development of human society.[358] He now had doubts regarding his earlier prescription that the Indians should imitate the English, for the latter suffered from a narrowness of intellect and the knowledge they had to offer was a pain. Even as an insignificant Bengali he presumed to make this statement for 'it was not possible that I should describe a fishpond as the ocean because I happen to be a mere puddle'.[359] The alleged failure of the English to understand anything of India despite a hundred and twenty years of contact was to him the most convincing token of their narrowness of intellect. Yet the patriotic virtues he prescribed were to be practised within the bounds of loyalty to the British. The Arms Act was a mistake, but it should be abolished so that the Queen's loyal subjects could defend her empire. An alien ruler could often be a friend of true liberties and though Europe had lost the virtue of loyalty to the king, Indians could cultivate it for the good of their country because it implied loyalty not to an individual but to the embodied authority of a given society. The representatives of state power were to be treated with due respect. Only sycophancy was to be avoided.[360] The implied evaluation of British rule in India is of course positive. I have argued above that the overt loyalty of these statements may not reflect the writer's true sentiments. When independence was not attainable in the foreseeable future, loyalty was prescribed as a counsel of despair and hostile assessments of the colonial rule camouflaged in historical fictions with multiple layers of meaning.

In one of his early essays Bankim identified himself as a member of the group known as 'Young Bengal'. The term is applied in later writings primarily to the first generation of Hindu College students, especially the pupils of the maverick teacher, Derozio. Those who belonged to the 'Young Bengal' group were well known for their admiration for everything western and their unlimited contempt for the Hindu tradition. In his youth and early middle age, Bankim shared these attitudes and the fact is reflected in his earlier writings. His aesthetic, moral, and nationalist aspirations sought and found satisfactory structures on which to build a body of creative works and a philosophy of life within the rationalist-humanist traditions of modern Europe. Europe was then declared to be incomparably superior to everything India, past and present, had to offer. His education, personality and, perhaps above all, his bureaucratic middle-class background explain this positive assessment. Arguably it reflects the values and sentiments of the dominant element in the Bengali intelligentsia of his days, especially the group which identified itself with the periodical he started, *Bangadarshan.*

Unqualified adulation of the West however was unacceptable to the new nationalism of that time. Resentment against the evident inequities of colonial rule and the Anglo-Indian denigration of everything Indian, especially the Bengalis, was aggravated by a new-found confidence in the Indian heritage. Bankim states quite openly the psychological need to feel equal, if not superior, to Europe at least in some ways. He could not however adopt the way of the ignorant and discover electricity in the Vedas or explain the Brahmin's pig-tail with the aid of schooltext physics. A transformation in his personal ideology, an unexplained conversion to theistic faith which induced a return to the traditional religion, in a way, solved Bankim's dilemma. He had discovered to his satisfaction an area in the indigenous tradition which was superior to the highest values of European life. He looked at Europe in the light of this new ideology in the last phase of his creative life and rejected as tawdry, if not positively harmful, much that he had admired in the West at one time.

Notes and References

1. There is a fairly extensive biographical literature on Bankim's life. I have used mainly the undermentioned works: Sachischandra Chattopadhyay {Bankim's nephew], *Bankim jibani*, Calcutta, 1901, 3rd edn., 1931; Rabindrakumar Dasgupta, 'Bankimchandra' (incomplete), *Kathasahitya* BY 1369–70 (1963); Sureshchandra Samajpati, *Bankim-prasanga* [a collection of reminiscences by the writer's relations and friends], Calcutta, 1922, new edn., 1982; Brajendranath Bandyopadhyay and Sajanikanta Das, *Bankimchandra—* in *Sahitya-sadhak charitmala*, vol. 2, Calcutta BY 1349 (1942), 5th edn., BY 1369 (1962) and S.K. Das, *The Artist in Chains: The Life of Bankimchandra Chatterjee*, New Delhi, 1984.

2. See, for instance, Dasgupta, *loc. cit.*, chap. 2, *Kathasahitya, sraban*, BY 1369, 1436f.; Brajendranath Bandyopadhyay and Sajanikanta Das, *op. cit.*, 7.

3. Brajendranath Bandyopadhyay and Sajanikanta Das, *op. cit.*, 7; Purnachandra Chattopadhyay, '*Bankimchandrar balya-siksha*' (Bankimchandra's Childhood Education), Narayan, BY 1322, reprinted in BP, 23.

4. Purnachandra Chattopadhyay, '*Kamalakanter, "eso eso bandhu eso"*' (The Song—*Come, my Beloved*—in Kamalakanta), *Sahitya*, BY 1320 (1913), reprinted in BP, 32.

5. This view is stated most pointedly by Professor Dasgupta: 'Bankim was the righteous son of a righteous father.' *loc. cit.*, *Kathasahitya*, BY 1369, 1316. Also see Purnachandra Chattopadhyay [Bankim's younger brother], *Bankimchandrer dharma siksha* (Bankimchandra's Education in Dharma), BP, 56–60.

6. S.K. Das, *op. cit.*, 3.

7. Dasgupta, *loc. cit.*, *Kathasahitya, ashad* and *sraban*, BY 1369 (1963), 1317 and 1436; S. Chattopadhyay, *Bankim jibani*, 3rd edn., Calcutta, 1931, 12–17.

8. Dasgupta, *loc. cit.*, 1318.

9. Ibid.

10. H. Sastri, *Bankimchandra* in BP, 120.

11. See P. Chattopadhyay, *Bankimchandrer dharma siksha*, BP, 57. For Bankim's account of his father's *nishkama karma*, see BP, 176.

12. S. Chattopadhyay, BJ, 161–3.

13. H. Sastri, *Bankimchandra*, BP, 119–20.

14. Gopalchandra Ray, *Anya ek Bankimchandra* (Another Bankimchandra), Calcutta, 1979, 35–8. This volume is mainly a collection of his hitherto unpublished letters written to close relatives and friends.

15. Ibid., 2, 7–10, 11–12, 197.

16. Ibid., 9, 17, 30. Also Chandranath Basu in BP, 68.

17. The reminiscences published in BP frequently mention that the brothers spent much of their leisure together. The rules of deference which guide the relationship of the younger with the elder brothers in traditional Hindu families were seldom observed. See H. Sastri *Bankimchandra kanthalparay* (Bankimchandra in Kanthalpara), BP, 93; also his *Bankimchandra* in BP, 100; G. Ray, *op. cit.*, 40, 42, 134, BJ, 131–2 (friendly relations with eldest brother).

18. G. Ray, *op. cit.*, 20–8.

19. Ibid., 44–5, 221.

20. Ibid., 198–9. For another instance of tension between the brother, see 221 where Bankim refers to unkind words written by Syamacharan about the younger brothers.

21. Ibid., 14–15; also 206 for a letter complaining of 'cunning, deceit and ingratitude' on the part of the youngest brother Purna and nephew, Jyotish.

22. Ibid., 24.

23. Ibid.

24. See below for allegations of 'vanity' in the novelist's personality.

25. Sudipta Kaviraj, *The unhappy consciousness: Bankimchandra Chattopadhyay and the Formation of Nationalist Discourse in India*, Oxford University Press, Delhi, 1998, Ch. 1.

26. BP, 120 (Srischandra Majumdar, *Bankimbabur prasanga*).

27. Bankim explained to a friend that the tales of dance and dalliance simply referred to Krishna's effort to teach dharma to women through the fine arts. BP, 125.

28. *Sitaram*, BR, I, 792.

29. *Chandrasekhar*, ibid., 383.

30. See below the discussion on the philosophy of '*anusilan*' (culture or cultivation), an ideal of balanced cultivation of all one's physical and mental faculties.

31. In one scurrilous satire, he was described as Barairam, Mr Vainglory, who considered himself superior to all others in every way. Barairam

had no friends because he considered no one his equal. See G. Ray, *op. cit.*, 151.

32. See his *Bankimchandra o Bangadarshan* (Bankimchandra and *Bangadarshan*) in *Sahitya*, BY 1308 (1901), reprinted in BP, 82.

33. His contemporary, Justice Dwarkanath Mitra, once remarked that the proud steps of the four deputy magistrates could be heard from a fair distance. G. Ray, *op. cit.*, 87.

34. See the reminiscences of Chandicharan Bandyopadhyay, Kalinath Datta, Haraprasad Sastri, and others, BP, 83, 95, 111, 151, 191.

35. G. Ray, *op. cit.*, 88.

36. See Srischandra Majumdar, *Bankimbabur prasanga*, BP, 129; Rabindranath Tagore also mentions in his *Reminiscences* that he found Bankim rather distant in his youth. See Ray, *op. cit.*, 137–8. Haraprasad Sastri, *loc. cit.*, BP, 107.

37. A. Sarkar, *loc. cit.*, BP, 75.

38. For instances of his awareness of physical weakness, see Kailas Mukherji, *Sayings of Bankim* (n.d.), 12; also BP, 28; for his dietary habits, see Srischandra Majumdar, BP, 116.

39. See fn. 14 above. In a letter to his nephew, Jyotish, he wrote, 'The English can do what they like. But know for sure, the words of a Bengali, especially a petty servant like you, carries no weight.' G. Ray, *op. cit.*, 223. Jyotish was an inspector of police (ibid., 53), not a petty job by Indian standards of expectation at the time.

40. This episode is described both by his younger brother, Purnachandra (see BP, 20–1), and nephew, Sachis (see BJ, 23–4).

41. Purnachandra Chattopadhyay, *Bankimchandrer balyakatha* (Bankimchandra's Boyhood), BP, 27–8.

42. See BJ, 102; R. Dasgupta, *op. cit.*, *Kathasahitya*, BY 1369 (1962), 361.

43. BJ, 139; *Amrita Bazar Patrika*, 8 and 15 January 1874, quoted in Bandyopadhyay and Das, *op. cit.*, 92–3; K. Mukherji, *op. cit.*, 11–12.

44. See G. Ray, *op. cit.*, 50, 53, 54, 87; Bankimchandra Chattopadhyay, *Ray Dinabandhu Mitra Bahadurer jibani* (Biography of Rai Dinabandhu Mitra Bahadur), in *Bibidha pravandha*, Centenary Edn., Calcutta, BY 1348 (1941), 74.

45. G. Ray, *op. cit.*, 87.

46. *Ray Dinabandhu Mitra Bahadurer jibani*, 79.

Bankimchandra Chattopadhyay   205

47. Bankim wrote 'Ray Dinabandhu Mitra Bahadur' in lieu of the more humdrum 'Ray Bahadur Dinabandhu Mitra'.

48. See fn. 14 above.

49. Brajendranath Bandyopadhyay and Sajanikanta Das, *op. cit.*, 27–31.

50. BJ, 108.

51. *Sayings of Bankimchandra*, 15–16.

52. BJ, 119f.

53. Ibid., 149–56, 171–2, 183–5, 191; S.K. Das, *op. cit.*, 13.

54. Chittaranjan Bandyopadhyay, *Sri Bankimchandra Chattopadhyay o Anandamath* (Sri Bankimchandra Chattopadhyay and *Anandamath*), Calcutta, 1983, 30–4; also Bandyopadhyay and Das, *op. cit.*, 30, 97.

55. See his sketch of Dinabandhu's life, *op. cit.*, 80.

56. Bankimchandra Chattopadhyay, *Bhumika: sanjibani sudha* (Introduction to the Collected Works of Sanjivchandra Chattopadhyay), B Pra, 152.

57. The judge had proposed that street signs should provide English translations of Bengali names, e.g., 'Daughter-in-law's Lane' for *Boumar gali.* Sanjiv proposed similar translations of the names of all Bengali employees, e.g., 'Blackfooted friend' for Kalipada Mitra. The judge left the meeting in a huff and refused to see Sanjiv when he called on him to apologize. See BP, 98.

58. *Bhumika: sanjibani sudha*, B Pr, 154.

59. BP, 125.

60. BJ, 204.

61. Ibid., 24. Brajendranath Bandyopadhyay and Sajanikanta Das, *op. cit.*, 11–17.

62. BJ, 118–19, 145–6, 195–7 Brajendranath Bandyopadhyay and Sajanikanta Das, *op. cit.*, 95; G. Ray, *op. cit.*, 186.

63. G. Ray, *op. cit.*, 23, 59–60. Also see BP, 139. He particularly resented the fact that young civilians he had trained later appeared as his bosses and sometimes took particular pleasure in humiliating him.

64. He discouraged his friend, Srischandra Majumdar, from collecting information for a biography. 'My life is worthless', he commented (BP, 119). In a letter to Sanjiv, he wrote of his many ailments and added: 'I do not try for their cure; for I have no desire for a long life. The longer one lives, the more one suffers.' See G. Ray, *op. cit.*, 37.

65. C. Bandyopadhyay, *op. cit.*, 32–4, 37–41.

66. BP, 121.
67. C. Bandyopadhyay, *op. cit.*, 35.
68. Nagendranath Gupta, *Upadhi utpat* (Harassment of Titles), *Sahitya, sravan*, BY 1299 (1892), quoted in BJ, 227. That Bankim was ashamed of what had happened is indicated by his anonymous letter to the editor of *Sahitya* denying all prior knowledge of the title.
69. BJ, 119–20.
70. See R.K. Dasgupta, *loc. cit., Kathasahitya*, BY 1369 (1962), 549.
71. Rev. Hastie's letter to *The Statesman*, reprinted in Hastie's *English Enlightenment and Hindoo Idolatry* (Calcutta, 1883). 8–9.
72. Ibid., 12–13.
74. Ibid., 30. 31.
74. Ibid., 32.
75. Ibid., 49, 52–3.
76. Ibid., 53, 54, 68; BJ, 404.
77. BP, 186.
78. See *Bibidha*, Centenary Edition, 301.
79. Kalinath Datta, *Bankimchandra, Pradip*, BY 1305 (1898), in BP, 152–3. He gave away his knives and forks to an English colleague. G. Ray, *op. cit.*, 123, 179.
80. G. Ray, *op. cit.*, 178; S. Majumdar, *Bankimbabur prasanga, pratham prastab* (About Bankim Babu: First Essay), BP, 120.
81. G. Ray, *op. cit.*, 178.
82. BP, 119–20.
83. Dasgupta, *op. cit.*, 1639f.
84. Brajendranath Bandyopadhyay and Sajanikanta Das, *op. cit.*, 14–23.
85. K. Mukherji, *op. cit.*, 14–15.
86. BR, EW, 125F.
87. *Bankim Kahini*, 61–3.
88. Several sketches in *Lokarahasya* deal with this theme, e.g., *Hanumadbabusambad* (The Encounter between Hanuman and the Babu).
89. Brajendranath Bandyopadhyay and Sajanikanta Das, *op. cit.*, 19.
90. See above.
91. See BP, 78, 118; Das, *op. cit.*, 38.
92. *Krishnacharitra, Bibidha, II*, 381.
93. Ibid.

94. B Pr, *Uttaracharit*, 41.

95. BP, 23, 119. His literary judgement was profoundly influenced by this aversion to explicit and, what he considered, obsessive eroticism. He accused Jayadeva, the poet of *Gitagovindam*, of excessive sensuality (*Bibidha*, 386).

96. Ibid., 129, 133.

97. See his introduction to the collection of Iswarchandra Gupta's poems, *Bibidha*, 125.

98. Ibid.

99. Ibid., 125–6.

100. Mohitlal Majumdar, *Bankimbaran*, Calcutta, BY 1356 (1949), 6.

101. See Introduction.

102. *Dharmatattva*, 33, 36.

103. Ibid., 36.

104. BP, 125.

105. In his *Banglar itihas sambandhe kayekti katha* (A Few Words about the History of Bengal), he wrote: 'History says that a few Englishmen and Telenga soldiers won a marvellous victory at Plassey by destroying thousands and thousands of native soldiers. This is pure fiction. There was no real battle at Plassey. What happened was something of a farce'. *Bibidha*, *II*, 322.

106. *Palasir yuddha* (Battle of Plassey), *Bibidha*, 384, 386.

107. *Op. cit.*, 35.

108. *Kamalakanter daptar*, 90; *Rajani*, 411.

109. *Kamalakanter daptar*, 33.

110. Bandyopadhyay and Das, 91–2.

111. *Bahubal o bakyabal* (The Strength of Arms and the Power of Words), B Pr, II, 376–7.

112. See Introduction.

113. Recent research suggests quite convincingly that *Anandamath* was inspired *inter alia* by the armed rebellion of Basudev Balwant Phadke in Maharashtra (1879) and the life-story of Mazzini. Phadke, a Brahmin, aimed at independence, collected funds through brigandage, and imposed on his followers a discipline which had identifiable affinities with the lifestyle of the *santans*. The *sanyasi* rebels of the eighteenth century, supposedly the model which Bankim had in mind, bore no resemblance to the *santans*. See Chittaranjan Bandyopadhyay, *op. cit.*, Also Jiban Mukhopadhyay, *Andandamath o Bharatiya jatiyatabad* (*Anandamath* and Indian Nationalism), 9f.

114. *Bharat-kalanka* (India's Shame), B Pr, i, 138f.

115. *Krishnacharitra, Bibidha*, 380–1.

116. See his review of *Three Years in Europe, Bibidha*, 323: 'The people who cannot think of their motherland as 'superior to heaven' are an unfortunate people.'

117. See *Bangadarshaner patrasuchana* (Introducing the journal, *Bangadarshan*), B Pr, ii, 221f.

118. Ibid., 222.

119. See his review of Mir Musharraf Hussain's *Bishadsindhu* in *Bangadarshan*.

120. *Bangadarshaner patrasuchana*, B Pr, ii, 224.

121. *Bangadesher krishak* (The Bengal Peasantry) B Pr, ii, 280.

122. See S. Das, *op. cit.*, 230–8, for a summary of these arguments.

123. See *Bangalir itihas sambandhe kayekti katha, op. cit.*, 322.

124. See Introduction.

125. See Partha Chatterjee, *loc. cit., Economic and Political Weekly*, 18 January 1986, 120–8.

126. BP, 106, 180.

127. See BP, 25.

128. BP, 119.

129. See *Buddhism and Sankhya Philosophy*, 126, 129, 1321–32; *The Study of Hindu Philosophy*, 144–8; BR, EW; *Samkhyadarshan*, 119–23, 132 in BP.

130. *The Study of Hindu Philosophy*, BR, EW, 143–4.

131. *Bangadesher krishak*, BP, ii, 255, 258–63.

132. Ibid., 254–63.

133. *Bangadesher krishak, op. cit.*, 241.

134. Ibid., 242.

135. *Op. cit.*, 4.

136. *Op. cit.*, 44.

137. Ibid., 46.

138. Ibid., 236–8, 274–5.

139. Ibid., 275.

140. *Samya*, 27.

141. Ibid., 234.

142. Bankim's criticism of Utilitarian ideals are discussed in the second part of this chapter.

143. See below.

144. See the discussion on protection in *Samya*, 275 and *The Study of Hindu Philosophy*, BR, EW, 147–8, for examples of his reliance on Mill in these two fields.

145. *John Stuart Mill, Bibidha*, 338–42.

146. *Bangadesher krishak, op. cit.*, 272.

147. *Kamalakanter daptar, amar man* (Kamalakanta's Notebook–My Mind), 28–9.

148. See R. K. Dasgupta, *loc. cit., Kathasahitya*, BY 1370 (1464–66); S. Das, *op. cit.*, 161f; Geraldine Forbes, *Positivism in Bengal*, Calcutta, 1975; S. Das, *Bangadarsan o Bangalir manan-sadhana* (*Bangadarshan* and the Bengali Intellectual Tradition), 44–5, 133. Professor Yasodhara Bagchi's research emphasizes the pervasive influence of the ideology of order and progress in Bankim's novels as well, notably *Anandamath*.

149. BP, 18, 19, 147–50.

150. *Confessions of a Young Bengal*, BR, EW, 139–40.

151. *Mill, Darwin o Hindudharma*, BP, II, 219f.

152. BP, 24.

153. Ibid., 96.

154. For a discussion of theistic beliefs in Bankim's writings before 1882, see S. Das, *op. cit.*, 143–5.

155. BR, EW, 210, 216.

156. BP, 118.

157. For an English translation of this work, see Manomohan Ghosh, *Essentials of Dharma*, Calcutta, 1979.

158. See below.

159. See Introduction.

160. *Devatattva o Hindudharma* (The Concept of Gods and Hinduism), B Pr, II, 187; also BP, 557, 106, 180.

161. *Letters on Hinduism*, BR, EW, 235.

162. Ibid., 244.

163. *Krishnacharitra*, chap. 1.

164. *Kon pathe jaitechhi?* (Which Way Are We Going?), *Bibidha*, 213.

165. *Letters on Hinduism*, BR, EW, 235–7.

166. Ibid., 264–5.

167. Ibid., 268–9.

168. *Devatattva o Hindudharma, Bibidha*, 204.

169. *Gaurdas babajir bhikshar jhuli* (The Begging Sack of Gaurdas, the Mendicant), B Pr, II, 196.

170. *Bange devpuja, Bibidha*, 360–5.

171. *Dharma evam sahitya* (Dharma and Literature), BP, II, 179–80; *Bahubibaha* (Polygamy), ibid., 284.

172. *Op. cit.*, 264.

173. Ibid., Appendix A; also chap. 6.

174. Ibid., chap. 3.

175. Ibid., chap, I; 'Letters on Hinduism', BR, EW, 264.

176. *Dharma o sahitya, op. cit.*, 181.

177. *Dharmatattva.*

178. Ibid., chap. 21.

179. Ibid., chap. 7.

180. Ibid., chap. 7.

181. *Chittasuddhi* (Purification of the Soul), BP, II, 183–4; *Dharmatattva*, chaps. 7 and 11.

182. *Op. cit.*, 137.

183. *Dharmatattva*, chap. 10.

184. Ibid., Appendix G.

185. Ibid., chap. 23.

186. *Kamalakanta—amar durgotsav* (Kamalakanta—My Durga Puja), *Bangadarshan, Kartik*, BY 1881, reprinted in *Kamalakanter daptar*, chap. 11.

187. *Krishnacharitra, Bibidha*, 378.

188. *Dharmatattva*, chap. 13.

189. Ibid., chap. 5.

190. Ibid., chap. 10.

191. Ibid., chap. 13.

192. Ibid., chap. 18.

193. *Loc. cit., Bibidha*, 322–3.

194. *Op. cit.*, 10.

195. Ibid., 35.

196. *Jativaira* (Racial Animosity), *Bibidha*, 344–5.

197. *The Study of Hindu Philosophy*, BR, EW, 142.

198. Ibid., 146; *Samkhyadarsan*, BP, 118.

199. *The Study of Hindu Philosophy, op. cit.*, 145.

200. *Bangadesher krishak*, 260–1.

201. Ibid., 263–4.

202. *The Study of Hindu Philosophy*, ibid., 146–7.

203. See *Samya*, chap. 1.

204. *Bahubal o bakyabal*, BP, II, 372.

205. Ibid.

206. See *Samya*, chap. 2.

207. *Bangadesher krishak, op. cit.*, 259–60.

208. *Bharat kalanka—bharatvarsha paradhin kena* (India's Shame—Why is India a Subject Nation), BP, I, 133–44.

209. *Samya*, 28–30.

210. Ibid., 32–3.

211. *Banglar itihas sambandhe kayekti katha* (A Few Words about the History of Bengal), BP, II, 325.

212. *Bangalir utpatti* (The Origin of the Bengalis), ibid., 340.

213. *Op. cit.*, 118.

214. Ibid., 129.

215. *The Confessions of a Young Bengal*, BR, EW, 139.

216. An invocation to Lord Siva often used as a battle cry by the Hindu warriors in the past.

217. These are the four objects of human life according to the Hindu tradition. The nearest translation would be righteous conduct, material wealth, bodily pleasures, and salvation.

218. The Bengali word used, *man*, literally means the mind, but the context emphasizes human emotions and hence 'the heart' is perhaps a more appropriate translation than 'the mind'.

219. *Kamalakanter daptar—amar man*, 29–30.

220. See his article, *Manushyatva ki?* (What is Humanity?), Published in BY 1284 (1887), BP, II, 388–91.

221. *Manushyatva ki?, op. cit.*, 391.

222. BP, 109.

223. *Lokrahasya*, 13–14.

224. *Adi Brahmo samaj, Bibidha*, 400–4.

225. See his introduction to the collected poems of Iswar Gupta, *Bibidha*, 127–8.

226. *Samya*, 7.

212

x

x

212 — *Europe Reconsidered*

227. *Samya*, 35, 41, 43, 44; *John Stuart Mill, Bibidha*, 339; *Prachina evam nabina* (Women Ancient and Modern), BP, I, 162–3.

228. *Babhubal o bakyabal*, BP, II, 373; *Prachin Bharatvarshe rajniti* (Politics in Ancient India), ibid., I, 155.

229. *John Stuart Mill, op. cit.*, 341.

230. *Op. cit.*, 42.

231. *Muchiram Gurer jibancharit* (Biography of Muchiram Gur), 5–6.

232. *Sir William Grey o Sir George Campbell, Bibidha*, 358–9.

233. *Bharat kalanka*, ibid., 141–2.

234. *Samya*, 9–10; *The Study of Hindu Philosophy*, BR, EW, 145.

235. *Op. cit.*

236. See above.

237. *Manushyatva ki?, op. cit.*, 388.

238. *Samya*, 14–16; *Bangadesher krishak*, BP, II, 279–80.

239. *Loc. cit.*

240. J.S. Mill, *Auguste Comte and Positivism*, London, 1865, 67–200.

241. *Utility ba udar-darsan* (Utility or the Philosophy of the Stomach), *op. cit.*, 17–21.

242. *Amar man*, ibid., 130.

243. *Bhalobasar atyachar* (The Tyranny of Love), *Bibidha*, 98–9.

244. *Sakuntala, Miranda o Desdemona*, B Pr, I, 84.

245. See above, for a discussion of his literary ideals.

246. The contexts to which he applies this term suggest that he meant it to cover only sustained narrations of an entire story, rather than parts thereof. The Ramayana and The Mahabharata would be included in this category, but not the *Iliad*.

247. *Gitikavya* (Lyric Poetry), BP, I, 46–7.

248. *Loc. cit.*, B Pr, I, 80–6.

249. *The Confessions of a Young Bengal*, BR, EW, 138.

250. Letter to Bhudev Mukhopadhyay, ibid., 184.

251. *A Popular Literature for Bengal*, BR, EW, 97.

252. *Uttaracharit*, BP, 39.

253. *Prakrita evam aprakrita* (The Real and the Non-real), B Pr, I, 49–52.

254. See his introduction to the works of Dinabandhu Mitra, *Bibidha*, 82.

255. *Kamalakanter daptar*, 14–15.

256. *Aryajatir sukshmasilpa* (The Fine Arts of the Aryan Race), BP, I, 59.

257. I have cited above evidence of his knowledge of French. The title of French works are always cited in the original in his essays. It is therefore possible that he did read French literature in the original. The curriculum for the examinations he passed also included Greek and Latin and his transliteration of Greek and Roman names do suggest some familiarity with the classical languages.

258. *Kalpataru* (The review of a satirical Bengali novel, 'The Wish-fulfilling Tree'), *Bibidha*, 365–6.

259. Introduction to the collected poems of Iswarchandra Gupta, ibid., 121.

260. Ibid., 128.

261. *Bengali Literature*, BR, EW, 124.

262. *Bangalir itihas sambandhe kayekti katha*, BP, II, 320.

263. *Banglar itihas* B Pr, II, 309.

264. *Bharat kalanka*, BP, II, 134.

265. *Palasir yuddha, Bibidha*, 384; *Kamalakanter daptar*, 88.

266. *Bharat kalanka*, B Pr, II, 316.

267. *Dharmatattva*, chap. 13.

268. *Aryajatir sukshmasilpa*, B Pr, I, 60–1; Review of *Three Years in Europe, Bibidha*, 324; Introduction to Iswarchandra Gupta's poetical works, ibid., 128.

269. *Dharmatattva*, chap. 9.

270. *Loc. cit., Lokrahasya*, 3–17.

271. *Kono 'Specialer' patra*, ibid., 58–62.

272. *Ramayaner samalochan—kono bilati samalochak pranita* (A critique of *The Ramayana* by an English critic), ibid., 51–3.

273. *Letters on Hinduism*, BR, EW, 263.

274. Ibid., 241.

275. *Loc. cit.*, ibid., 143.

276. *Op. cit.*, 58–9.

277. BR, EW, 153, 159–61.

278. Ibid., 143, 204–6, 209, 211.

279. Ibid., 153, 157–9, 261; B Pr, II, 254, 260–1.

280. EW, 111, 116–19, 156, 228–9.

281. *Krishnacharitra*, chaps. 2, 34.

282. BR, EW, 165–6, 228, 232–40, 262; B Pr, II, 211, 244.

283. B Pr, 145–50.

284. *Bangadesher krishak*, B Pr, II, 234–5.
285. *Loc. cit.*, BP, II, 144.
286. In *Anandamath* for instance we have the following passage: 'The *santans* did not understand at the time that the English had come to save India. How would they know? Even the English who were contemporaries of Captain Thomas did not know this. It was only in the heart of God at that time'. *op cit.*, 636.
287. Ibid., 222.
288. *Op. cit.*, 320, 321.
289. Ibid., 352, 378, 380.
290. *Op. cit.*, 691–2.
291. *Op. cit.*, 604.
292. *Anandamath*, 616.
293. *Op. cit.*, 739.
294. Ibid., 635.
295. Ibid., 661–3.
296. Ibid.
297. *Banglar itihas*, 311–12.
298. Ibid., 313.
299. *Durgeshnandini*, 5.
300. *A Popular Literature for Bengal*, BR, EW, 98.
301. *Chandrasekhar*, 372; *Anandamath*, 635, 655.
302. *Chandrasekhar*, 360, 361, 378; *Anandamath*, 606, 608, etc.
303. The term which Bankim uses, *dhan*, can actually be translated as income in this context.
304. *Loc. cit.*, BP, II, 234, 236, 273–9.
305. Ibid., 235–6.
306. In one of his novels, *Rajani*, the heroine is described as a victim of police corruption, and the relevant episode is presented as fairly typical. *op. cit.*, 410.
307. Ibid., 238–51.
308. Ibid., 264–8.
309. In his essay on politics in ancient India, *Prachin bharater rajniti* (Politics in Ancient India), he quotes Narada's question to Yudhishthira in the Mahabharata enquiring if the king did prevent thieves from getting away with burglaries and adds that the question was equally relevant in a country where the jury system was in vogue. Another of Narada's

questions refers to the king's responsibility to provide irrigation and
ensure that agriculture was not dependent on rainfall.

310. Ibid., 269–72.
311. *Debi Chaudhurani*, 714.
312. *Op. cit.*, 61.
313. Ibid., 80.
314. *Loc. cit.*, BP, i, 158, 159.
315. *Sir William Gray, Sir George Campbell, Bibidha*, 351–61; also *Bangla sasaner kal* (The Machine that Rules Bengal), B Pr, ii, 304–8.
316. *Muchiram Gurer jibancharit.*
317. Branson, a barrister, was the leader of the agitation against the bill which sought to bring the European accused under the jurisdiction of Indian magistrates.
318. 'Bransonism', *Lokrahasya*, 63–7.
319. *Jativaira* (Racial Animosity), *Bibidha*, 344–6.
320. *Banglar kalanka*, BP, ii, 314.
321. 'A popular literature for Bengal', BR, EW, 98–9; *Bidyapati o Jayadeb*, B Pr, 54–5; *Manas bikas* (Flowering of the Human Mind), *Bibidha*, 348.
322. *Bengali Literature*, BR, EW, 103.
323. Ibid., 124.
324. *Loc. cit.*, B Pr, ii, 222.
325. 'A popular literature for Bengal', BR, EW, 99.
326. *Op, cit.*, chap. 20.
327. *The Confessions of a Young Bengal*, BR, EW, 137f; *Adhahpatan sangit* (The Song of Degeneration), *Gadyapadya ba kabitapustak*, 26–32.
328. *Anukaran* (Imitation), B Pr, i, 76–7.
329. *Muchiram Gurer jibancharit*, 9.
330. *Loc. cit., Lokrahasya*, 19–20.
331. *Babu*, ibid., 19–20.
332. *Bangadarshaner patrasuchana*, ibid., 223–5.
333. *Dharmatattva*, chap. 1.
334. Ibid., chap. 4.
335. Ibid., chap. 5.
336. *Hindudharma, Bibidha*, 228; *Krishnacharitra*, ibid., 380.
337. *Dharmatattva*, chap. 17.

338. Ibid., chap. 19.
339. *Letters on Hinduism*, BR, EW, 254.
340. *Dharmatattva*, chap. 10.
341. Ibid., 424.
342. *Letters on Hinduism, op. cit.*, 240.
343. Ibid., 234, 262.
344. Ibid., 265; *Devtattva o Hindudharma, Bibidha*, 251–2.
345. *Dharma o sahitya* (Religion and Literature), BP, II, 180–1.
346. *Devtattva o Hindudharma, Bibidha*, 258.
347. *Dharmatattva*, chap. 7.
348. Ibid.
349. *Devtattva o Hindudharma, Bibidha*, 250.
350. *Letters on Hinduism*, BR, EW, 253.
351. *Kamalakanta*, 118.
352. *Op. cit.*, chap. 8.
353. Ibid., chap. 24.
354. Ibid., chap. 21.
355. *Op. cit.*, chap. 22; *Letters on Hinduism*, BR, EW, 237.
356. Chap. 5.
357. Ibid., Appendix 2.
358. Ibid., Appendix 4.
359. Ibid., chap. 9.
360. Ibid., chap. 8 and 10.

Select Bibliography

Of the various editions of Bankim Chandra's works the three mentioned below have been used.

Bagal, J.C. ed. *Bankim Rachanavali*, 2 Vols., Sahitya Samsad, Calcutta, 1983. *English Works*, Calcutta, 1983.

Bandyopadhyay, Brajendranath and Sajanikanta Das, eds., *Bankim Granthabali*, Bangiya Sahitya Parishad, Calcutta, 1983–42 (Known as the Bankim Centenary Edition).

Bankim Rachanavali, Patra's Publications, Calcutta, 1983.

These include the undermentioned works referred to in this chapter.
Novels

Durgeshnandini, 1865.

Kapalkundala, 1866.

Mrinalini, 1869.

Bishabriksha, 1873.

Indira, 1873.

Chandrasekhar, 1875.

Rajani, 1877.

Krishnakanter uil, 1878.

Anandamath, 1882.

Dedi Chaudhurani, 1884.

Sitaram, 1887.

Other works

Lokrahasya, 1874.

Kamalakanta (1885?), 'Kamalakanter daptar', 1875.

Kabitapustak, 1878.

Samya, 1879.

Muchiram Gurer jibancharit, 1884.

Bibidha Prabandha, vol. I, 1887; vol. II, 1892.

Krishnacharita, 1885.

Dharmatattva, 1888.

Srimadbhagavadgita, 1902 (partly published in Prachar, 1886, 1888).

English Works
Novel

Rajmohan's Wife, first published serially in The Indian Field in 1864, published as a book in 1935.

Essays

'A Popular Literature for Bengal', 1870.

'Bengali Literature', 1871.

'Buddhism and Sankhya Philosophy', 1871.

'The Confessions of a Young Bengal', 1872.

'The Study of Hindu Philosophy', 1873.

'Letters on Hinduism', 1940.

N.B. The Sahitya Samsad edition, J.C. Bagal, ed., has been used for Bankim's English writings; the Patra's Publications edition for his novels, and the Bangiya Sahitya Parishad, Bankim Centenary Edition, B.N. Bandyopadhyay and S. Das, eds., for his other works.

Secondary works

Brajendranath Bandyopadhyay and Sajanikanta Das, *Bankimchandra, Sahitya-Sadhak Charitmala*, vol. 2, Calcutta, 1942, 5th edn., 1962.

Chittaranjan Bandyopadhyay, *Sri Bankimchandra Chattopadhyay o Anandamath*, Calcutta, 1983.

Satyaranjan Das, *Bangadarshan o Bangalir manan-sadhana*.

Sachischandra Chattopadhyay, *Bankim jibani*, Calcutta, 1901; 3rd edn., 1931.

S.K. Das, *The Artist in Chains: The life of Bankimchandra Chatterjee*, New Delhi, 1984.

Rabindrakumar Dasgupta, *Bankimchandra* (incomplete), *Kathasahitya*, 1963.

Bhabatosh Datta, *Chintanayak Bankimchandra*, Calcutta, 1961.

Geraldine Forbes, *Positivism in Bengal*, Calcutta, 1975.

Sudipta Kaviraj, *Bankimchandra Chattopadhyay and the Formation of Nationalist Discourse in India*, OUP, Delhi, 1998.

Mohitlal Majumdar, *Bankim Baran*, Calcutta, 1949, reprint 1964.

Kailash Mukhopadhyay, *Sayings of Bankimchandra* (n.d.)

Arabinda Poddar, *Bankim Manas*, Calcutta, 1951, 2nd edn., 1995.

Gopal Chandra Ray, *Anya ek Bankimchandra*, Calcutta, 1979.

Sureshchandra Samajpati, ed., *Bankim prasanga*, Calcutta, 1922, new edn., 1982.

Subodhchandra Sengupta, *Bankimchandra*, Calcutta, 1945; *Bankimchandra Chatterjee*, Calcutta, 1940.

Rabindranath Tagore, *Reminiscences*, London, 1917.

chapter 4

Swami Vivekananda
(1863–1902)

I

A somewhat obvious yet crucially important aspect of Swami Vivekananda's[*] role and personality has not been sufficiently emphasized in the literature on nineteenth-century Bengal. In India, the ancient tradition of *sanyasa*, or renunciation of the world in quest of spiritual realization, has claimed individuals from all walks of life down the centuries. But though a vivid interest in the Hindu religio-spiritual heritage was very much a part of the Bengali intellectual concerns in the nineteenth century, the expression of this new religiosity was modally within the limits of a colonial middle-class lifestyle. The social origins of the young men led by Vivekananda, who became disciples of the mystic. Ramakrishna Paramahamsa, and who were later duly ordained as *sanyasis*, were in no way different from those of other well-known protagonists of the new enlightenment.[**] Children of bureaucrats, men in the learned professions or zamindars, they were also products of the western education dispensed in Bengal's schools and colleges. It is their decision to abandon the comfortable occupations of their forebears in quest of the ultimate spiritual experience in the older religious tradition that marks them out from their predecessors and contemporaries. The Hindu tradition offers *inter alia* the promise of that ultimate experience if one follows prescribed disciplines under the

---

[*]   Narendranath Datta is known by this name which he adopted as a *sanyasi*.

[**] Latu Maharaj (Swami Adbhutananda), originally a domestic servant from Bihar, was the one exception.

direction of an adept. The Paramahamsa's chosen disciples accepted a life of extreme deprivation with total faith in that ancient promise.

Their aspiration itself marks them out as distinctive. The nineteenth-century religious quest in Bengal was a mixture of piety, this-worldly morality and cultural self-assertion, the last partly provoked by the challenge of Christianity and the European criticism of Hindu ways. With the exception of a few rare individuals, like Debendranath Tagore and, possibly, Keshabchandra Sen, the western-educated Bengalis were not inspired by any yearning to encounter the godhead in their own lifetime. Even the two exceptions mentioned were content to limit their aspirations within the four walls of a middle-class existence. Besides, their *vita religiosa* was not basically alien to the traditions of liberal humanism, including its component of tolerant Christianity. This statement would in no way hold true of Vivekananda and his fellow ascetics. Their reversion to an ancient mode of religiosity was the expression of a spiritual angst which cannot be explained in terms of cultural self-assertion or any concern for socioethical reform. The western-inspired enlightenment had no solution for their predicament nor did they look for it in that direction. Thus we have in Vivekananda an unquestionably patriotic Indian whose primary concern in life was articulated in a context peculiar to the Hindu tradition: it had nothing to do with society or polity. The youthful monk's encounters with the West are overshadowed by his deep conviction, based on his life experience, that in his chosen field of endeavour he had nothing to learn from the dominant culture of the day. Instead, he offered to teach the West and advised his fellow countrymen to learn from those areas of western life where contemporary India was obviously deficient. His perceptions of Europe and America were deeply coloured by his faith in what has been reduced to a clumsy cliché—India's spiritual superiority. Cultural self-assertion was very much a part of his mission both abroad and at home. But his belief in the ultimate excellence of the Hindu spiritual inheritance—the Vedantic concepts as well as the way of Yoga in particular— was not informed by any need to compensate for the sense of inadequacy, the characteristic predicament of Europe's Afro-Asian subjects. Bhudev derived his cultural self-confidence from his happiness in an inherited way of life. Vivekananda found his in following a demanding and esoteric tradition which apparently had answers for his somewhat uncommon queries.

A particularly unnerving question Vivekananda put to the saintly Debendranath, among others, was thus worded: 'Have you seen God?' The affirmative answer came at last from a nearly illiterate man of God whose spirituality was rooted in the Hindu tradition. It is unlikely that in the nineteenth century such a reply could have come from any other source, least of all liberal humanism or scientific rationality.

Yet, the Hindu ascetic in search of God was but one facet of Vivekananda's many-sided personality. His family, Kayasthas* by caste with a long tradition of service under the Muslim rulers, was among the early recruits to the new professions created by colonial rule. An ancestor moved from the home village in Burdwan to the new metropolis even before the Fort William had been constructed and at some point the family took up the profession of law. Vivekananda's great-grandfather, Rammohan Datta, practised law in Calcutta's Supreme Court, probably as a Persian *Vakil* since only Europeans could practise as attorneys in his days. He started his career as superintendent in an English attorney's office.[1] He amassed considerable wealth and appears to have adopted the elegant lifestyle of Calcutta's newly rich, including a taste for such western luxuries as chandeliers and oilpaintings.[2] Other ancestors included Rajiblochan Ghosh, the Company's treasurer at Alipore, according to one account. One of Rajib's grandsons and another relation, Gopal Datta, were associated with such products of the new enlightenment as the newspaper, *Hindu Patriot* (Gopal eventually edited the paper), and the Bethune Society.[3] Gopal Datta criticized in a speech in 1869 the lack of critical spirit among Bengalis and the system of child marriage but asserted the equality of traditional scholars with those educated in the English system. Kailas Bose, a first cousin of Vivekananda's mother, was another minor luminary of the Bengali enlightenment.[4] The Swami's grandfather, Durgaprasad, like his father before him, was probably connected with a firm of attorneys.[5] He, too, had a sound knowledge of Sanskrit and Persian. In short, the Datta family, in its professional and cultural concerns, was very much a product of early British rule. The educational and cultural ambience of that era subsumed the older inheritance of Perso-Arabic and Sanskritic learning, the former for its continued relevance to the work of administration. But the Dattas of Simla in Calcutta were unmistakably members of the new colonial élite—associates of European professional men whose lifestyle they imitated in bits and pieces.

---

* The Kayasthas' hereditary occupation was clerical and related services. Third in the hierarchy of Bengali caste Hindus, they are included among the 'clean Sudras' in the most important Smriti text recognized in Bengal. Their twice-born status was, however, firmly established in the nineteenth century.

The induction into the colonial culture went much further in the case of Vivekananda's father, Biswanath. The grandfather, Durgaprasad, renounced the world to become a *sanyasi*, probably owing to a quarrel in the family.[6] Young Biswanath's formal education was not, however, entirely neglected. He was sent to Gaurmohan Auddy's school, later known as the Oriental Seminary, read up to the pre-college level and, after matriculation, joined successively the firms of two English attorneys as an articled clerk. Higher levels of western education were not unknown in the family. Biswanath's cousin, Taraknath, was a professor of mathematics in the newly established engineering college.[7] In 1866, the then Chief Justice granted Biswanath's petition to work as attorney and proctor and he soon established his own firm. His professional career afterwards proved to be a great success. His high income allowed him to indulge his taste for luxury on a lavish scale. He was very much the successful Bengali professional of his generation who lived and worked in many 'up-country' cities, Delhi, Lucknow, Lahore, Indore, Raipur, etc., in the distant parts of Britain's Indian empire. He was a happy wanderer and all his sons appear to have inherited his love of travel. With his sound knowledge of Urdu, he proved extremely useful to the retired military officers who acted as judges in the early decades of the post-annexation Punjab. The reward for such services went beyond substantial material gains and status. His Marxist youngest son, Bhupendranath, refers with a touch of approval to his father's European friends and the elder, Mahendranath, notes that the Punjab judges held his father in high esteem.[8] In short, Biswanath was an eminently successful professional under the colonial regime, very proud of his success and not an embittered official working for alien rulers. The home in which Vivekananda grew up had prospered under the British and welcomed them as friends.

Biswanath's cultural interests straddled two worlds. Like quite a few educated persons of his generation he was a polyglot. While he knew English, Urdu, Hindi, Arabic, Persian and, almost certainly, Sanskrit, besides his mother tongue, Persian and Urdu, we are told, were the two languages he favoured. The *Diwan-i-Hafiz* was his favourite reading. At Lucknow, the citadel of Indo-Islamic culture in its later phase, he further developed his skill in classical Indian music and acquired quite a reputation as a virtuoso. One son refers to his regard for Muslim *pirs* and at least one of his close friends in Calcutta was a Muslim. He was evidently at home in the cosmopolitan and eclectic civilization of the later Mughal empire which a large section of urban Indians, both Muslim and Hindu, accepted as their shared inheritance well into the nineteenth century. He was also a practising Hindu; he introduced the public worship of the Mother Goddess in distant Lahore and was known for one traditional Hindu act of piety—charity to Brahmins.[9] While one authority 'accuses' him of ignorance of the Hindu tradition, his youngest son tells us that he learnt Sanskrit and astrology at a traditional *tol* and was an avid reader of the Srimadbhagavata. Another son writes of his eclectic spirit, the fact that he read the Bible and the Koran as well as the Bhagavat every day.[10]

The statement that Biswanath was really a product of the new western education, concerned with material welfare, his own as well as that of others, rather than Hindu spirituality appears to have been correct. With his love of Indo-Muslim cuisine, he was certainly lax in his attitude towards the maintenance of ritual purity. His travels in India made him aware of widespread superstitions in the life of the people and, true to the spirit of his times, he wrote a book denouncing such practices. He approved of Vidyasagar's agitation for the legalization of widow remarriage. The statement that, in his opinion, all worthwhile religions were to be found in the Bible may or may not be apocryphal, but he did read a few chapters from the life of Jesus every day. Mahendranath does tell us that 'people', i.e. the average middle-class Bengali, knew little of the Upanishads or Advaita in the days of Vivekananda's boyhood.[11] Evidently, such things were not a familiar part of religion or culture as understood in the Datta home. The cultural ambience in Biswanath's family was a mixture of Indo-Muslim and the new Indo-Anglian mores. But in no way was it alienated from the traditional practices and beliefs of Puranic Hinduism and the simple piety that went with it.

Expectedly, the tradition of Hindu piety was particularly strong among the women of the family. A great-grandmother had read deeply into the Puranic lore and her daughter remained an avid reader of similar literature well into her eighties. Vivekananda's first introduction to the world of Hindu devotionalism and ethical norms was through the stories he heard from his mother in his childhood. He repeatedly drew upon this storehouse of simple wisdom in his lectures abroad. Nivedita's *Cradle Tales of Hinduism*, based on stories she heard from her master, is generally traced to the same source.[12]

The new liberal spirit had, however, touched the lives of the Datta ladies as well. Biswanath's mother was educated enough to compose a sizeable work in verse, *Gangabhakti tarangini* (The River of Devotion to the Ganges).[13] His wife, Bhubaneswari, learnt English from an English missionary lady and gave young Naren his first lessons in the language.[14] She sent one of her daughters to the Bethune College (school section) and another to the Mission school at Rambagan. When neighbours objected to a widow remarriage in the locality, she with her husband protested against the persecution. The Datta ladies also responded to the new spirit of nationalism and participated in 'National' Nabagopal's Hindu Mela.[15] To repeat, the dominant influence in Vivekananda's childhood home was that of the new liberalism. However, it coexisted with the pietistic and ritual traditions of Puranic Hinduism as practised in Bengali families.

The young Narendranath, before his encounter with Ramakrishna, was very much a typical product of western education. His early intellectual development, we are told, was deeply influenced by his father. Biswanath was no believer in any simple transmission of received notions and Naren was encouraged to question every idea. Father and son had vigorous disputes and the boy participated in the learned discussions with the literati who regularly visited the Datta home.[16] An attitude of reverence towards things human, however awe-inspiring, remained for ever alien to his personality. The dreaded toughness of the youngsters in his locality, Simla,[17] appears to have assumed an intellectual dimension in his case. It saw him through all his encounters—abroad and at home. His father's advice on good manners* also appears to have struck home. If the West did in fact surprise him, the written record bears no evidence of the fact.[18]

Narendranath later faced his western audiences and eminent scholars with impressive self-assurance. It was based partly on his formidable learning and a very powerful intellect. The Reverend William Hastie (Bankim's opponent in the epistolary debate on Hindu idolatry) considered Naren a real genius. In his long pedagogic career, he said, he had never come across 'a lad of his talents, even in German universities, amongst philosophical students'.[19] Even as a rather turbulent school boy Naren had developed a love of reading. His favourite subjects at that stage were Sanskrit, English, history—especially the history of India—and later mathematics. When he was only fourteen,[20] a very learned colleague of his father was amazed by the extent of his reading. He had developed a technique which has affinities with the modern methods of fast reading. It enabled him to take in very quickly and retain vast quantities of information and ideas.[21]

---

* 'Never show surprise!'

At 16, he matriculated from Vidyasagar's Metropolitan School and was then admitted first to the Presidency College and later to the General Assembly's Institution, founded by the Scottish General Missionary Board. His intellectual interests were now marked by a degree of intensity and he began to read deeply into a very wide range of subjects.[22] As an undergraduate he specialized in philosophy and the history of Europe, both ancient and modern, but his studies were in no way confined to the curriculum. The prescribed syllabus included a fairly heavy course on English literature, with an emphasis on Shakespeare, Milton, Wordsworth, and Byron. These poets, especially Milton and Wordsworth, remained his favourite reading throughout his life. Other favourites included the *Pickwick Papers*, Carlyle's *Sartor Resartas* and *Heroes and Hero-Worship*, Emerson's *Representative Man* and, interestingly, Jules Verne's science fiction. He could recall word for word large chunks from some of the books he had read months or even years ago. His writings indicate an easy familiarity with the major works in Sanskrit literature. He too had a taste for a favourite literary pastime of his days, namely exploring the affinities and contrasts between Sanskrit and European literature. By the time of his youth, a generation of eminent writers and the growing spirit of cultural nationalism had given Bengali literature a large measure of respectability. The literary efflorescence was very much a part of his childhood environment. The poet Iswar Gupta and the playwright Dinabandhu Mitra were family friends. Naren read deeply into both contemporary and pre-modern Bengali writers. His taste in literature had, however, an element of oddity not to be dismissed as simple idiosyncrasy. His friend Girish Ghosh's *Bilwamangal*, he once commented, gave him greater pleasure than Shakespeare's plays. This statement has to be read with his words of warning to Sister Nivedita about the Tagores: 'Remember that that family has poured a flood of erotic venom over Bengal.'[23] Ghosh's play, a melodrama built around an old morality tale of a sinner's emergence into sainthood, had an obvious appeal for a man of God. On the other hand, his great contemporary's romantic poetry left him cold and the aesthete in Tagore was to him a symbol of effeminacy. It was a dangerous example for a nation already deficient in manly qualities. His eclectic tastes and wide range of interests notwithstanding, Vivekananda was an ascetic, a man in quest of God, and a spiritual leader with a particular vision of a rejuvenated India. His evident pleasure in much that the West had to offer was often overshadowed by these primary concerns.

But the wide range of his intellectual interests, a reflection of his appetite for life, should not be underestimated. After philosophy, history was his favourite subject of study, an interest he appears to have inherited from his father. He had a masterly knowledge of Indo-Mughal history and took a romantic pride in the great architectural achievements of that imperial epoch. He knew by heart large parts of that sizeable chronicle, Tod's *Annals and Antiquities of Rajasthan*, the source of many patriotic writings in the nineteenth century. The study of ancient Indian history was still in its infancy. But Vivekananda's writings and speeches are replete with insightful comments on such diverse themes as the ethnic origin of the migrants into India, the changing courses of the rivers, the nature and trends of Indian society and polity based on his extensive knowledge of literary and scriptural sources. His statements on historical processes drew upon a fantastic range of evidence from the known record of many civilizations—classical Europe, early Islam, modern Europe, and the USA.

Vivekananda's study of European history was evidently inspired by something more than mere intellectual curiosity. The themes which attracted him were concerned with the decline of great civilizations, social revolution, and the lives of heroic men. Very probably he sought in Gibbon, the historian he read with the greatest interest, some explanation of what had gone wrong with his own people. He also studied with care Maspero's history of Egypt, another record of an ancient civilization, but one which had disappeared entirely. He read extensively into the history of the French Revolution and the Napoleonic era. Napoleon and his General, Marshal Ney, were his ideal heroes, embodiments of the manly virtues which he wanted his countrymen to acquire. He was impatient with the dead wood in Indian life and one wonders if he sought in the French experience some solution for his country's predicament. Beyond doubt, he, like many others of his generation, explored the European record seeking answers to India's problems. His admiration for the West, as we shall see, might be strictly qualified, but he too was looking for lessons to be learnt from that source. Hence his persistent curiosity about the history of the western peoples, a subject he studied from a variety of angles. The curriculum itself had provided an overview of the European past, through Green's *History of the English People* and Alison's *History of Europe*. He built on that basic knowledge with extensive reading throughout his life.

Love of God and the motherland or the quest for the ultimate spiritual experience does not, however, explain all his intellectual and aesthetic pursuits. His restless energy drove him in many directions. His avid reading into a great variety of subjects was but one expression of that energy. The subjects he studied included political economy and sociology and, at one time, pathology, zoology, and physiology. He got over his early aversion to mathematics and, while at college, acquired a fair knowledge of advanced mathematics and astronomy. The *Evening News* of Detroit describes an after-dinner question-and-answer session where, for reasons unknown, the Hindu monk was asked for reading lists on chemistry and astronomy. Vivekananda readily provided two long lists in reply to these unusual queries.[24] We have direct evidence of his knowledge of contemporary physics—in his anonymous article on the now-discarded theory of ether, published in the *New York Medical Times* in 1895.[25] What he read was not always so demanding. He loved good food and, like his father, was an excellent cook. His brother, Mahendra, mentions the books he once bought from a hawker in Calcutta. These included the *Soldier's Pocket Drill Book* and a book on French cookery, the latter duly used for culinary experiments.[26] Haripada Mitra met him at Belgaum when the Swami was wandering as an ascetic with only a blanket, a pot, and a satchel—the habitual impedimenta of the sadhu's lifestyle. Mitra found that the satchel contained a single book which was on French music.[27] His interest in France acquired a new dimension during his second sojourn in England. He learnt French from his hostess, Miss Muller, and, according to his brother, Mahendra, could speak the language fluently.[28]

Naren's interest in the Indian heritage was also not confined to the religio-spiritual tradition. Kalidasa's highly sensuous poetry fascinated him, despite his ascetic ideal. He knew by heart three of the poet's major works—*Kumarasambhavam, Meghadutam,* and *Abhijnanasakuntalam.*[29] His skill as a vocalist of Indian devotional music is well known, but his introduction to the art was secular in inspiration. He was trained in several styles of classical Indian music—vocal and instrumental—by some of the great maestros of the period, both Hindu and Muslim. He learned from the latter Hindi, Urdu, and Persian songs usually sung on the occasion of Muslim festivals. He wrote at least one book on Indian music jointly with another author, which ran into several editions. He was also a skilled dancer, we are told, though one does not know in which particular style. His interest and expertise in one of India's richest and most eclectic cultural traditions had a twofold implication for his perceptions of Europe. The aesthetic appreciation of the European heritage in India was usually confined to western, especially English, literature. The relatively narrow focus of modern Indian education and Bengali urban middle-class concerns often produced a philistine outlook. Even the most sophisticated Bengalis of the period were generally preoccupied with moral judgements, historical parallels, and lessons to be learnt in their exploration of western culture—the enjoyment of European literature being the one general exception to this pattern. Vivekananda's western venture did acquire a missionary purpose, but his joy and expertise in the many facets of man's heritage rendered possible patterns of response which were neither didactic nor patriotically purposive. Classical Indian music had seams of a multi-ethnic inheritance and its protagonists at their best were free from any distressing need to feel equal or superior to other traditions. Vivekananda's trained ears discovered in western music a new source of heightened consciousness.[30] His vivid and vital personality similarly responded to much that he encountered in the West with profound delight. It was not diminished by the fact of subjection and the consequent psychological need to find faults.

Throughout the early years of his youth, there was a tension between Naren's other-worldly yearnings and the more mundane aspirations one would expect in a person of his background. After graduation, he joined the firm of his father's friend, Nimaichandra Basu, attorney-at-law, as an articled clerk. He was also studying for his Bachelor of Law degree at the time. His father encouraged his ambition to go to England and become a barrister. The court case involving family property after his father's death, in which he appeared as a witness, showed to advantage his considerable potentialities as a lawyer. In February 1884, his father made him a Freemason to help him in his future career. Then it was a common practice among aspiring Indians to become Freemasons as a likely aid to their prospects. But Naren's membership of the Anchor and Hope Lodge as well as his plans to study in England had to be given up because the family was almost pauperized by his father's death.[31]

Beyond doubt, until his final decision to renounce worldly ambitions, Naren was more than inclined to adopt the lifestyle of his forebears. In fact, he hoped to excel them by becoming a barrister-at-law. Yet even his secular intellectual concerns were overshadowed by an anxious quest which was not that of a would-be legal luminary. At college, he was primarily interested in philosophy, but his approach to the subject, then and later, was not that of an ambitious examinee. He evidently hoped to find answers to the basic problems of existence as he saw them in the writings of his favourite philosophers, Indian and western.

Naren's philosophical studies were based on a sound knowledge of logic, both Indian and European.[32] His writings provide enough evidence of his deep reading into every major area of the Indian religious and philosophical traditions—Hindu, Buddhist, and Jain. As a student in college, however, it was in western philosophy that he first sought the solution of life's conundrums. His biographers provide long lists of the philosophers he referred to or read over and over again. They include Plato, Kant, Hegel, Schopenhauer, Locke, Mill, Hume, and Spencer. Uberweg's *History of Philosophy* and Hamilton's *Metaphysics* were also in his reading list and Darwin's evolutionary theories featured in some of his philosophical discourses.[33] 'More learned than all our professors put together', wrote Professor Wright, Professor of Classics at Harvard, in introducing Vivekananda.[34] His colleagues were surely willing to treat the Swami as an equal, for he was offered a chair at Harvard.

The unfolding of Vivekananda's spiritual awareness was closely interwoven with his philosophical studies. His contemporary, Brajendranath Seal, philosopher and encyclopaedic scholar, has written very perceptively of Naren's intellectual development, as being a period of painful tension between reason and faith.[35] In his religious life, Vivekananda passed from the prayerful piety of his home environment to the austere Brahmo nonconformism in his early youth. But the 'boyish theism and easy optimism ... imbibed from the outer circles of the Brahmo Samaj' were shattered by his first serious exposure to nineteenth-century rationalism. Mill's *Three Essays on Religion* exposed for him the weakness of arguments from causality and design and the irreconcilability of evil in nature and man with an omniscient, omnipotent and benign Deity. Hume, and a little later, Spencer's *The Science of the First Principles* with its doctrine of the Unknowable confirmed him in his loss of faith 'and his unbelief gradually assumed the form of a settled philosophical scepticism'. His deep distrust of priesthood and impatience with the priestly traditions of India can also be due to Spencer's influence. While he was also influenced by Hegel and Schopenhauer besides Mill at this stage of his intellectual development, it was Spencer he accepted as his true mentor. He translated the philosopher's treatise, *Education*, and received from him an enthusiastic letter accepting, we are told, some points raised by Naren.[36] His faith in an Ultimate Reality rudely shaken, he fell back on the idea of customary morality as something to live by. Comte's Positivism provided a temporary respite from his uncertainties, but agnosticism was too anaemic a doctrine to satisfy a youth of his passionate temperament and theistic background.[37] He asked his learned contemporary, Seal, for a reading list on theistic philosophy. Seal recommended the Intuitionists and the Scottish 'common sense school'. Their stock arguments were of little help to Naren. Besides, as Seal points out, Naren, his intellectual abilities notwithstanding, had a certain impatience with bookish knowledge. He sought a validation of faith in 'living communion and personal experience', in a convincing intensity of feeling rather than sustained argument. Seal next suggested a course of readings in Shelley. The poet's pantheism and 'vision of a ... millennial humanity' contained for Naren a spiritual principle of unity. 'Hymn to the Spirit of Intellectual Beauty' moved him in a way no philosophical writing had done. His youthful mentor temporarily converted him to his own philosophical belief, the sovereignty of Universal Reason and the negation of the individual as the principle of morals. Here was an acceptable escape from scepticism and materialism, but the triumph of reason did not resolve his basic conflicts.

To repeat an obvious yet inadequately emphasized fact about Swami Vivekananda, discussed in the introductory paragraphs of this chapter, the man was more than anything else a mystic in quest of the Ultimate Reality within a specific Indian tradition. This dominant concern was the centre-point of his life and virtually nothing he sought to do was unrelated to this fundamental purpose. The fact poses a serious problem for the secular historian. Fisher's famous dictum that we do not encounter God in history ceases to apply where the chief protagonist claims with total assurance that his Master did encounter God and that similar experiences are potentially accessible to lesser mortals. The mystical states described by the Swami in his lectures on Raja-yoga, among others, are also stated to be based on personal experience. In his attempt to cope with the supranatural in the received tradition on such matters, Max Mueller spoke of the 'dialogic process', the transformation of objective reality in the process of transmission of evidence into something other than real—'that we do not and cannot know of any historical event that has not passed through' this process.[38] But Vivekananda's own half-muted testimony about his own or his guru's experiences is not covered by the dialogic process. In wishing to reject it as illusion, one recalls perforce Goethe's *obiter* that a man like Schlegel should be on his knees when he writes of Homer. For the purposes of the present chapter one can only note what Vivekananda believed beyond doubt about his Master's and his own religious life in so far as it helps us understand his personality and perceptions of the West. The social circumstances and personal development which offer insights into his religious quest are also discussed below as far as our sources permit.

Young Narendranath's emergence as a *sanyasi*—whatever anticipation of such a development one can trace to his childhood and early growth—is ultimately explained by the influence of one man, Ramakrishna Paramahamsa. The impact of this barely literate man of God on the Bengali intelligentsia has been variously explained—generally within the framework of Hindu revivalism. The most recent historical study of his ideas and role[39] has drawn attention to a hiatus in the cultural history of Bengal, between an early phase of optimism based on a faith in a glorious future under Britain's leadership and the emergence of militant nationalism. In their wilderness of uncertainties, the Bengali middle-class found some solace in the mystical teachings of the saint and their implied message restoring confidence in the inherited system of religious belief. The standard biography by his disciple, Saradananda, states explicitly that the Deity was incarnate as his guru for one specific purpose—to bring the western-educated Indians who had strayed into the blind alley of rationalist scepticism and materialist aspirations back into the Hindu spiritual and religious fold.[40] If, indeed, this ascetic's conscious or unconscious role was to rescue his misguided countrymen from western intellectual ideas and this-worldly ideology, then his influence on Vivekananda is, of course, crucial to any understanding of the Swami's interaction with the alien culture.

The facts of Paramahamsa's life are well known to every student of nineteenth-century Bengali society. Professor Max Mueller first wrote a sketch of his life for western readers in *The Nineteenth Century* and followed it up with a brief biography;[41] based on a sketch written by Saradananda under Vivekananda's instruction.[42] Besides numerous statements quoted by his friends and disciples, Max Mueller's biography of the saint may be treated as a toned-down version of Vivekananda's perception of his Master's life. The following sketch combines the incontrovertible facts of Paramahamsa's life with an account of his spiritual development as recorded in the above-mentioned biography.[43]

Gadadhar Chattopadhyay, later known as Ramakrishna Paramahamsa, was born in 1836 of poor Brahmin parents in a village near Calcutta. He moved to Calcutta in 1852 with his brother, Ram Kumar, a Sanskrit scholar, who ran a traditional seminary. Gadadhar resisted all attempts to teach him 'worldly learning' and his education stopped at bare literacy. When Ram Kumar accepted appointment as a priest on his behalf at Rani Rasmani's temple at Dakshineswar, Gadadhar's orthodox sensibilities were shocked because the patroness was of low caste and earning one's livelihood in work for such a person was ritually degrading. But he eventually compromised and in 1855–56 became the priest at the temple of Kali, the Mother, with whom he was soon in constant communication. His dark night of the soul was interpreted as insanity and, after a course of treatment, the family got him married to a five-year-old girl, Sarada, with whom he later established a partnership free of all sexuality. After a second bout of 'insanity' in 1861, he was discovered by a mysterious lady ascetic, a *bhairavi*, who introduced him to the Tantric way—later described by Ramakrishna as one of the unclean paths to ultimate realization. In 1864–65, he met the ascetic Totapuri and became an ordained *sanyasi*. His mystical discipline now entered a new phase and he began to seek God according to the beliefs and precepts of every major religion, Indian and foreign, including Islam and Christianity. He frequently entered into a state of trance and had beatific visions. The visions he had of the prophets, saints, and deities during this phase followed a standard pattern. He would see an effulgent image—of Christ or Muhammad or Chaitanya—and the image would merge into his own body. The vision expressed *inter alia* his Vedantic faith in the underlying unity of the universe, permeated by Brahman, the ultimate and the only reality. He had acquired the knowledge of Vedanta, not from Sanskrit texts, but from the oral testimony of sadhus and scholars he had met over the years. He also had a profound knowledge of the northern Indian *bhakti* traditions as professed by the mediaeval saints. His devotees believe that he attained ultimate realization through mystical disciplines prescribed by every major faith. His reaffirmation of the ancient syncretic belief—that every faith is a way to God and hence all religions ultimately contain the same truth in different forms—was based on his own spiritual experiences.

For nearly two decades, 1855–74, Ramakrishna's fame as a man of God was confined to his own locality. The metropolitan intelligentsia, in the throes of mutually contending socioreligious movements, hardly took any notice of the saint of Dakshineswar. He was a controversial figure even to the locals; many thought that he was insane or at least highly eccentric. Even later, his devotees repeatedly encountered his many detractors.

In March 1875, Ramakrishna paid a visit to the Brahmo leader, Keshab Sen, the idol of Calcutta's western-educated youth, especially those inclined towards religiosity. After a brief movement of imperfect sympathy, Keshab recognized in Ramakrishna a man of transcendent spirituality and a very close relationship developed between the two. Keshab's writings on the saint in Brahmo periodicals aroused great interest in Calcutta and, before long, a steady flow of visitors began to reach Dakshineswar. Many came out of mere curiosity, some scoffed, but many also stayed to pray. The latter included a band of idealistic young men who, led by Narendra, became his disciples. After Ramakrishna's death, as ordained *sanyasis* they went in search of God and, later, as monks of the Ramakrishna order, propagated his gospel. The belief that he was an incarnation began in his lifetime and an episode shortly before his death in August 1886 suggests that Vivekananda fully accepted this belief.[44] *Inter alia*, in an essay on Hinduism and Ramakrishna[45] he stated quite explicitly that the saint was the most perfect incarnation of the Deity born to demonstrate in his own life that it would be possible for mankind to rediscover and realize India's spiritual heritage which had been eroded over the centuries.

The fact that Naren, a follower of Keshab Sen and a young Brahmo, was one of several western-educated young men who became devotees of Ramakrishna underlines a social situation which helps explain his conversion. At one level, no special explanation of Ramakrishna's influence is necessary for anyone familiar with the practice and traditions of Hindu religiosity. The *siddha*, an adept in the mystical ways who had achieved direct knowledge of the ultimate reality, is very much an accepted part of the received tradition. Such holy men sometimes laid claims to—or were popularly believed to have acquired—*siddhis*, i.e., powers which could contravene the laws of nature. Such powers were, however, no essential attribute of a *siddha* even in popular perception and the *siddhis* are generally relegated to the lower rungs of spiritual development. In the Indian 'middle ages', unlettered men of God like Kabir, Nanak and Ruhidas, who came from the poorer and low-caste stratum of society, added a new dimension to the tradition of *siddhas*. Speaking in the language of the people, they preached devotion to a personal Deity and declared the fundamental unity of all faiths, especially of Islam and Hinduism; Ram of the Hindus and Rahim, the merciful God of the Muslims, were the one and the same in their eyes. The ascetic in quest of God commanding reverence remained very much a part of the nineteenth-century Indian tradition. Vivekananda travelling all over the subcontinent as an unknown, in fact often anonymous *sanyasi*, frequently received adoration from people in all walks of life—princes, men of learning, including many educated in the western system, as well as unlettered humble folk. There were at least three famous contemporaries of Ramakrishna in northern India—Trailanga Swami, Paohari Baba, and Raghunath Das—revered as holy men by the people, the élite very much included. The educated Bengali living outside his home province was no exception.[46] Ramakrishna's own initiation into the mystic path was helped, if not induced, by two ascetics, the *bhairavi* and Totapuri, who belonged to the same tradition of *sanyasa*, understood and held in high regard by believers in all parts of the country. For nearly twenty years before his first encounter with the Calcutta intelligentsia, Ramakrishna lived at Dakshineswar as a *sadhak* (a seeker after God) within that familiar tradition. While some considered him insane, local people accepted him as a man of God and his name was not unknown in the city. Miraculous powers, *bibhuti* or *siddhis*, were attributed to him and, as is usual in such cases, many came to him seeking cures or solution of material problems.[47]

Reverence for a man with a reputation for holiness thus requires no special explanation in the Indian context. It is Ramakrishna's impact on the Bengali intelligentsia—influenced by rationalist thought and involved in a self-conscious search for elements in the tradition of which they could be proud—that contains an element of the unexpected. But one could easily exaggerate this element. The discontinuity between Hinduism in its popular form and the lives of the western-educated Bengalis was hardly ever total. As the life stories of the saint's disciples conclusively prove, exposure to the new enlightenment was only one and, in some instances, a very small, component of their experience.[48] The cycle of rituals, worship of and reverence for the deities, belief in reincarnation and the miraculous, etc. remained an important part of domestic and religious life. It seems unlikely that the great majority of the western-educated Hindus was ever totally dissociated from this established pattern of belief and practice. High regard for a famous *sanyasi* would have been their natural response. At least curiosity about a man of Ramakrishna's reputation would have been almost universal. It is worth noting in this context that of all his numerous visitors only a certain proportion accepted him without reservation.[49] Several of his disciples, including Vivekananda, felt puzzled when they first met him. Such facts suggest that the Calcutta intelligentsia's initial excitement over Ramakrishna's saintly life, as presented by Keshab Sen, was no more than the response expected of a Hindu public in all similar circumstances.

Hindu revivalism in the late nineteenth-century Bengal was a very different kettle of fish. Western, especially missionary, criticism of Hinduism had evoked a range of responses, reasoned or angry, ever since the days of Rammohan. Generally speaking, the responses had one characteristic in common—an implicit acceptance of the criteria by which the western critics assessed Hindu beliefs and practices. Hence the anxiety to affirm the truly monotheistic character of Hinduism and the symbolic nature of image worship. The Brahmo and the neo-Hindu ideology absorbed in the process much of western liberal and even Christian values. Keshab actually preached an oriental Christ, seeking to find a common ground between the tradition of *bhakti* and unitarian principles. This pattern of response subsumed a rejection or, at least, a sense of shame about rituals and social institutions to which the vast majority of Hindus evidently had a sense of loyalty. In any case, with a burgeoning sense of national identity and resentment against colonial rule, many found the criticism of these rituals and institutions entirely unacceptable. Bhudev provided a reasoned defence of established practice in terms of national need and ethical norms. Bankim's highly erudite *tour de force* in *Dharmatattva* and *Krishnacharitra* were *inter alia* attempts to extol Hinduism à la Bankim as superior to all that the West had to offer. These intellectual defences had limited 'mass' appeal and said little to flatter the ego of an intelligentsia frustrated and humiliated by the colonial presence and with an evident sense of inferiority in relation to the master race. Bankim, in fact, harped continually on this theme of inferiority. A declaration of superiority in relation to the West was at the heart of the Hindu revival as preached by men like Sasadhar Tarkachudamani, Krishnaprasanna Sen and their followers. It claimed for Indian civilization all the scientific discoveries of the West, declared the immeasurable superiority of Hinduism over all other faiths and discovered profound scientific or spiritual meaning in current superstitions. The Theosophists with their exaltation of Hindu spirituality offered another sop to the mangled ego of the colonial élite.

Those followers of Ramakrishna who read in his life a conscious purpose to beat back the tide of western influence certainly have affinities with the revivalist ideology. Vivekananda interpreted his master's message very differently. Ramakrishna's unqualified reverence for all faiths, including Keshab's Christianized devotionalism, Christianity itself and Islam, links him

with the syncretic tradition of the Indian middle ages rather than the
nineteenth-century Hindu revivalism. If anything, this very gentle person
who once rebuked Vivekananda for criticizing certain Tantric sects[50] because
these too were paths to God in his eyes, was mildly critical of Sasadhar[51] and
the Theosophists. We have hints of a conscious purpose in his relationship
with the intelligentsia—to redress the suffering induced by excessive
worldliness and to teach people basic humility probably as the first step
towards devotionalism.[52] He also went about building up very purposefully a
group of dedicated young ascetics, under Narendra's leadership. He never
explained what their task was to be.[53] If that task was the programme
eventually chalked out by Vivekananda, it had little to do with Hindu revivalism
at home. The propagation of Vedanta in the West might have satisfied the
wounded ego of a colonial élite, but it was not the result which the Swami
had in view.

Perhaps Ramakrishna met a felt need of the urban intelligentsia not
traceable to the insecurity of their cultural self-esteem or a hiatus in their
sociopolitical aspirations. Issues of faith were quite central to the movements
and debates which agitated nineteenth-century Bengal. The controversies
among Christians, traditionalist Hindus, different groups of Brahmo and
neo-Hindus were not exclusively concerned with questions of social reform
or ritual. The nature of the Deity and man's relation to God were interpreted
very differently by Rammohan, Debendranath, Keshab, his dissident
followers, Bankim and others. If the debate on social change centred even
ostensibly round the theme of religious faith, the quintessential concerns of
religion necessarily became a major preoccupation with many. In the 1870s
and 1880s, we are told, even school students used to debate whether God
was with or without form. An anguished spiritual yearning, evident in the
life of men like Keshab, Sibnath Sastri, and Bankim in his later years was
shared by many idealistic young men.[54] Some found the nonconformist piety
of the Sadharan Brahmo Samaj or Keshab's growing devotionalism adequate
answers to their query. But the appeal of Brahmo ideals declined owing to
factional dissension among the Samajists. Neo-Hinduism à la Tarkachudamani
had little spiritual content. Vivekananda's younger brother, Mahendra, has
described popular Hinduism among the urban middle-class in Bengal around
this time.[55] According to him, the average educated Bengali had not even
heard of the Gita and the Upanishads. The Bible, distributed by the
missionaries, and some Brahmo tracts were often the only scripture they
had ever read. While the orthodox Saktas and Vaishnavas rejoiced in sectarian

rivalry, the non-sectarian Hindu knew little of Chaitanya or Vaishnavism. *Bhairavi-chakras*, esoteric circles, practising Tantric rituals which involved a great deal of sexuality, flourished in Calcutta and its suburbs. Ramakrishna's nephew, Hriday, used to participate in his youth in as many as six *chakras* a night in the Alambazar area. College students with their new Victorian sensibilities detested such practices. They lost faith in the rituals and traditional worship unsupported by any intellectually acceptable doctrine. Even the practice of obeisance, *pranam*, to one's elders fell into disuse. Young people, cynical about their own religion, found little to attract them in Christianity as preached by the Hindu-hating missionaries whose education was often very limited. The new sociocultural movements had focused attention on religion and thus produced both an uncertainty and a concern about faith and spirituality. But they had failed to provide solutions acceptable to large numbers. Keshab's inspired preaching in the *mohullas* of the city was a conscious assault on this anomy in religious life. It had considerable appeal. Many of the young people who became devotees of Ramakrishna were at first Keshab's followers. The fiery orator was a seeker after God. By his own testimony, Ramakrishna was a person in communion with the Deity. Sections of the intelligentsia, concerned about essential religiosity and tortured by doubts, accepted the soothing news as true. The news was all the more satisfying because the saint personified the tradition of syncretism.[56] One opted out of all painful controversies by becoming his devotee. And by all accounts, the man had phenomenal charisma enhanced by a rustic simplicity.

To conclude, the veneration of Ramakrishna by a section of the urban intelligentsia was based on the psychological need for a satisfying spiritual ideal, generated by decades of religious controversy. The religious idiom and overtones of the burgeoning nationalism probably enhanced that need as well as the veneration.[57] Hindu revivalism may have found some comfort in the reflected glory of a great saint, especially after he was accepted as such by eminent westerners. Ramakrishna for them might be a positive proof of Hindu superiority, but his infinite tolerance and unsectarian spirituality was hardly their cup of tea. To the majority of his urban devotees, their links with the tradition of reverence for holy men never broken, the advent of a great *siddha* in their neighbourhood must have been simply a matter of good fortune, a gift of Providence to be accepted in humility and with joy. The enthusiasm for the cult which developed around Ramakrishna did decline over time. Political fervour replaced religious concerns as the dominant preoccupation of the Bengali intelligentsia. But Ramakrishna's famous disciple and his interpretation of the Master's message were significant factors in the transition.

As noted earlier, Narendranath first sought a resolution of his spiritual crisis in western philosophy. His recourse to Ramakrishna, considered rationally, was an unlikely and almost accidental event. His passage from scepticism to unquestioning faith is partly explained by the general circumstances affecting the lives of the western-educated Bengalis discussed in the preceding paragraphs. But there is another side to the story. The Dattas of Simla, despite their involvement with the new enlightenment for at least three generations and their liberal-latitudinarian outlook, were in no way dissociated from the Bengali version of popular Hinduism. Vivekananda eventually acquired a masterly knowledge of Indian philosophy, but his basic beliefs and religious outlook were shaped by his childhood environment. Philosophical scepticism created a temporary disquiet. It never displaced entirely the faith he had accepted without question early in life. In a manner very different from Bhudev's, Vivekananda later assessed the moral and spiritual life of the western peoples using yardsticks familiar since childhood. His discipleship of the saint and scholarly studies confirmed and elaborated the values implicit in a religiosity he had absorbed almost with his mother's milk.

Narendra's grandfather, Durgaprasad, renounced the world and became a *sanyasi*. Anecdotes of his life as an ascetic were a part of the family lore. Durgaprasad's sister discovered an uncanny similarity between the new-born Narendra and his grandfather. The belief that the child was a reincarnation of the *sanyasi*, first announced by the old lady, was firmly held by many members of the family. No wonder that the child played at being an ascetic and hoped to grow instantly the *sanyasi*'s matted hair. Narendra's birth was also an answer to a prayer—to Siva. Some believed that Narendra was none other than an incarnation of Siva himself. The deity's name was frequently invoked to calm the turbulent child. His favourite game was prayer and meditation before the clay images of the deities. Rama was taken up and then discarded as an object of worship because the child, already fascinated by the ideal of celibacy, felt disgusted by his god's unworthy act—his marriage to Sita. Vishnu's incarnation was hence replaced by Siva and throughout his life Vivekananda frequently invoked the name of the deity he had learnt to adore in childhood. He often expressed his faith in Advaita, non-duality as follows: 'Siva, my lord, my real self.' His childhood ambition contained an element of prophecy; he, too, would become a *sanyasi* like the grandfather in good time.[58]

His other concerns, especially philanthropic-cum patriotic ones, notwithstanding, a personal spiritual quest was central to his aspiration. 'Every moment I think of anything else is so much loss to me', Vivekananda affirmed in a lecture delivered in New York.[59] An anguished impatience with his role as a preacher and organizer was a recurrent feature of his life.[60] His loss of faith in theism, as reported by his contemporary, Brajendranath Seal, was no more than a brief hiatus. It derived from his quest for unquestionable proof rather than any genuine disbelief. Even as a young adult, he persisted with his childhood practice of meditation. Only now it was a part of a severe spiritual regime which included celibacy and other mortifications of the flesh. His commitment to renunciation was not yet total. Dreams of worldly success and the happy life of a householder still had their appeal. But a more compelling desire—for the lifestyle of an ascetic as the way to the knowledge of the Deity—dominated his thoughts.[61] The coveted deliverance from worldly pursuits came only through his discipleship of Ramakrishna.

Naren first met the mystic in a neighbour's house. Principal Hastie had described his trances, already publicized by Keshab, in a respectful reference to the saint's spirituality. Ramchandra Datta, Naren's relation and a lay disciple of Ramakrishna, had to work hard to induce the young man to visit his guru. Naren's initial response to the suggestion was not exactly respectful: 'But he is an illiterate fool!'[62] His scepticism was not easily dispelled until one day the holy man induced in him through a mere touch the state of *samadhi*, an experience he later described more than once to his fellow ascetics and disciples: '... I saw everything melting away into the sky— homesteads, buildings, trees, the sun, the moon, everything. Then the sky itself was dissolved into nothing. I do not recall what I experienced next, but only that I was mightily scared.'[63] The guru later repeated the spiritual experiment and the disciple was no longer scared. The latter ceased to doubt Ramakrishna's statement that it was possible to 'see God' and talk with Him just as one could see and talk with a human being.[64]

The story of Vivekananda's discipleship is recorded in his numerous biographies and the accounts of his Master's life. We are told of Ramakrishna's foreknowledge that a group of pure-hearted youths would come to seek his guidance and carry on his work. Of the young acolytes who did come to him, he declared Naren to be the purest soul, an incarnation of some ancient seer born to redress the suffering of mankind, a liberated being who would leave his body as soon as he became aware of his true self.[65] The guru reinforced his disciple's longing for the life of renunciation. Strict observance of celibacy was an essential part of the regime into which Naren was initiated. The emphasis was in tune with his own culturally-determined faith in the need for total sexual abstinence as a prerequisite for spiritual realization. Prolonged abstinence, the guru affirmed, enabled the intellect to penetrate the subtler levels of consciousness. The deity could be experienced only through such refinement of consciousness.[66]

The ancient doctrine prescribing renunciation of the world and all its pleasures in quest of God was acceptable to Naren without any resistance, even though Ramakrishna offered to his lay disciples an alternative—the way of King Janaka, performing one's worldly duties with one's mind firmly fixed on God. The choice was however not offered to the select—such as Naren—who were to carry on the saint's work. The confirmed young sceptic accepted asceticism but did not easily give up his many doubts concerning his Master's life and teachings. The latter's constant communion with the Deity, he suggested, might be no more than a projection of the devotee's own thoughts. Advaita, non-duality,—the notion that everything in the universe, animate and inanimate, was but a manifestation of the one ultimate reality—seemed unacceptable to logic and common sense. He denied that he had anything to learn by way of philosophy from his nearly illiterate teacher. Total surrender to the guru's will came after searching tests and repeated experiences of *samadhi* through his grace. In the last year of his life, Ramakrishna formally initiated his small band of young disciples into monastic life and entrusted them to Naren's leadership. On his death, they banded together to practise a regime of severe spiritual discipline in conditions of extreme poverty. The quest later assumed the form of the Indian ascetic's traditional lifestyle—the way of a wandering *sanyasi* with voluntary gifts or begging as the only means of livelihood.[67]

Since Vivekananda's responses to the West had causal links with his role as a teacher—and what he taught derived much from what he had learnt from Ramakrishna—his understanding of the saint's personality and role has a central relevance to this study. To him, his guru was an incarnation, in fact the most perfect of all incarnations. Incarnations or great men—he used the two terms as synonymous—were born to restore virtue in this world. Rama, Krishna, the Buddha, Jesus and other great figures in the history of the world's religions all belonged to this category. An incarnation was a person with an inborn knowledge of the Self, indistinguishable from Brahman, for 'there is nothing to distinguish Brahman from one who had realized Brahman'. Such beings could remove the veil of ignorance from other souls as well.[68] Vivekananda described how a few days before his death Ramakrishna sat facing him in a state of *samadhi* and he felt an energy, like currents of electricity, passing into his own body. 'I have given you all I have and become a beggar', the Master told him, adding that he would render great services to mankind by virtue of the power thus given. His mission in the West and all that he achieved later in life he attributed to his guru's behest and guidance in a very literal sense.[69] The message he later set forth to broadcast as his guru's gospel had two basic themes: renunciation as the essential precondition of spiritual realization and the fundamental yearning of all souls and the existence of only 'one eternal religion' manifest in many forms, in other words, 'the wonderful truth that the religions of the world are not contradictory or antagonistic.'[70] By the same token, Ramakrishna's teaching was not to be the basis of any sect formation.[71] And in projecting his Master's life and personality in the West, he carefully avoided all references to suprarational beliefs to avoid provoking any gratuitous scepticism concerning the doctrine of Vedanta itself.

Vivekananda was very reticent about his own spiritual life. 'A hot flush and an accession of delicate *hauteur* were his immediate response, even to such merely theoretical questions as appeared to him to demand too intimate a revelation of the personal experience.'[72] A man not renowned for his modesty, he was remarkably humble in all his references to his mystical quest. He hesitated to discuss his guru's life for he confessed that he had understood very little about him.[73] Yet, he did describe to his fellow disciples the spot of bright light he used to see every night before falling asleep and how it used to burst into an all-encompassing effulgence.[74] His brother, Mahendra, has recorded in detail the intense spiritual regime of the young monks who had banded together in quest of the ultimate realization after their guru's death and their total indifference to worldly pleasure and pain.

He has also described Vivekananda's states of absorption in the realms of experience where it was impossible to reach through to him.[75] On another occasion, in London, Mahendra saw his brother dancing with joy, ecstatic with *anandam* (bliss) that filled the universe and an awareness of non-duality.[76] Vivekananda believed he remembered his past incarnations and in the last months of his life he said that he did at last know who was his real self as prophesied by Ramakrishna.[77] Yet, he laughed at the suggestion that he—'a big fat man' like him—might have 'seen God'[78] Shortly before his first voyage to the West and at the end of his long travels across the length and breadth of India, he told his fellow-disciple Turiyananda that he had not found God.[79] For our present purpose, his mystical quest is relevant for one reason. He believed in the received traditions of Indian mysticism. Its promise of spiritual realization was, in the last analysis, to him man's only worthwhile goal. He continually assessed western men in terms of their potentialities for that realization and the perceived chasm between the current reality of their life and what they could achieve.

In Vivekananda's perception, India's noblest gift to mankind was her spirituality. One of his chosen tasks was to bring this spirituality to the West and thus inform her vital civilization with a new purpose. This cherished inheritance from the Indian past was also the ultimate yardstick by which all human achievement was to be measured.

The Indian spiritual tradition was in his view encapsulated in its entirety in Vedanta, i.e., the Upanishads and the systems of philosophy which claimed to interpret these.[80] Even Buddhism and Jainism cited their authority and Vyasa sought to harmonize the doctrines of Samkhya and Nyaya with those of Vedanta. He traced the origins of all Indian sects to Vedanta because they were based on one or the other of the three systems of philosophy— Dvaita (dualism), Visishtadvaita (qualified monism or non-dualism) and Advaita (monism or non-dualism), all of which he regarded as interpretations of Vedanta.[81] The three philosophies were but three levels of interpretation suited to three possible stages in man's spiritual progress. The deepest urge of the human soul was towards a realization of non-duality, a sense of identity with the One Being manifest in infinite forms which are but appearances created by *maya*, i.e., ignorance or illusion.[82] Man's ego, 'this little personalized self', derived from a perception of duality, the sense of separateness from the Divinity manifest as the universe, and was the source of all misery. Escape from this limiting identity and thus from the snares of *maya* equalled the realization of Brahman, man's true self and the only reality underlying the universe—absolute, eternal, and changeless. This philosophical notion, Vivekananda affirmed, was also the basis of morality: 'Love everyone as your own self, because the whole universe is one. In injuring another, I am injuring myself ...'[83] Further, since the ego was the source of all misery, self-abnegation, i.e. renunciation, was the obvious path to liberation, the tearing of the veil.

The Advaitin, the believer in non-duality in Vivekananda, could have had little rapport with any element in the western religious tradition. But his own spiritual preference and the example of his Master's life emphasized a very different approach to the Deity as well—the path of *bhakti* or love-devotion. The simple piety of his childhood environment, his prayers to and meditations on the formless personal God as a young Brahmo and his profound emotions centred on the Deity as the Mother were all embedded in the tradition of *bhakti* central to popular Hinduism. Ramakrishna, despite his frequent experiences of *samadhi* which transcended perceptions of duality, was in a perpetual state of high emotion inspired by his love of the Mother. His experience of non-duality was continuous with his love for the Deity. His famous disciple adopted a very similar attitude to spirituality. Again and again, he spoke of Divine guidance in connection with his work abroad. Evidently, the referent was a personal Deity, not the Brahman beyond the reach of words or the human mind. His sense of rapport with theistic faiths like Christianity was based on the devotional trait in his religious persona.[84] His inclusion of dualism in Vedanta allowed a perception of affinity between the Indian tradition and religions centred on a personal God, the eventual basis of his claim that Vedanta comprehended every religious faith.

In his opinion—and in that of many of his contemporaries—his Master's life was the ultimate realization of religious syncretism; Ramakrishna's mystical quest provided the clinching evidence for the age-old Indian belief in the fundamental unity of all faiths which were but different paths to a common goal, namely, direct knowledge of the Deity. Naren had learnt the lesson of eclectic tolerance from the cultural ambience of his own home. His discipleship of the ultimate adept transformed that lesson into a profound spiritual conviction. His attitude to other faiths went way beyond respectful tolerance and an essential yardstick in all his assessments of other cultures was the degree of their freedom from bigotry.

His deep regard for Islam was in a way the most striking expression of his faith in the validity of all religions. This is so because he too shared up to a point the nineteenth-century Bengali Hindu intelligentsia's ambivalence in relation to the Indo-Islamic past.[85] But with him it *was* ambivalence rather than the total rejection of an earlier generation, for by his time self-conscious Indian nationalism was concerned to encompass all communities and dispel communal disharmony. His youngest brother underlines the Islamic component of his family's cultural heritage. His standard biography, compiled by his disciples, refers to his numerous friendly contacts with Muslims. His

Muslim friends and admirers included a humble school teacher of Alwar, as
well as the high ministers of the Nizam and an Amir of Kabul.[86] He flouted
without hesitation the taboo on commensality and made a point of buying
sweets from a Muslim vendor in Kashmir.[87] Sister Nivedita records his joyous
pride in the Indo-Mughal heritage, 'the great national genius that decreed
the birth of Indian sovereigns to be of a Moslem father and a Hindu mother.'[88]
He vehemently denied that such rulers were foreigners. He considered the
difference between the Hindu and Muslim worlds more apparent than real
and found the Muslims 'a generous race, at heart as Indian as the Hindus'.[89]
His highest prayer for the good of the motherland was that she might make
manifest the twofold ideal of 'an Islamic body and a Vedantic heart'.[90]

His attachment to Islam was not simply patriotic in its inspiration. The
faith revealed to the Arab Prophet was in tune with his spiritual and human
values. The affinity between Sufism and Advaita Vedanta had been
demonstrated in his Master's life. But what appealed most was the directness
and simplicity of the great message which 'deluged the world in the name of
the Lord': '... no music, no paintings, ... no priest, ... no bishop.' And, of
course, the practice of equality: if an American Indian became a Muslim,
'the Sultan of Turkey would have no objection to dining with him'. He saw
this 'practical brotherhood' as Islam's 'particular excellence'.[91] The Prophet's
greatness was proof enough that he had 'come from God'. In an explicit
reference to Muhammad's many marriages he stated that individuals of
such transcendent greatness could not be judged by common mortals or by
their standards of right conduct.[92]

The values which informed Vivekananda's world-view are perhaps most
explicit in his attitude to the Buddha and his teachings. As young acolytes,
Naren and his brother monks had taken up the study of Buddhism in both
its forms as a serious pursuit.[93] Sister Nivedita described his reverence for
the Buddha as his chief intellectual passion. The Buddha to him was the one
and only 'absolutely sane man' in human history, 'perfect ... in reason' and
'wondrous in compassion'. He alone 'freed religion entirely from the argument
of the supernatural'.[94] What appealed most was the sage's immense moral
strength, the total independence of spirit which had no need to invoke a
Godhead. The other theme continually emphasized in his discourses on the
Buddha was the grandeur of his renunciation and the totally selfless effort
to alleviate human suffering.[95] He took a patriotic pride in the fact that
Buddhism was the only religion which had proselytized without bloodshed.[96]
His respect for Buddhism was one more reason for his empathy with

Christianity, because he was convinced that 'the very teachings of Christ [could] be traced back to those of Buddha'.[97] And, of course, Vedanta was the foundation of Buddhism as of 'everything else in India' But he also believed that the doctrine of Advaita owed much to Buddhism, especially of the Mahayana school.[98] His perception of Buddhism's role in Indian history had links with his vision of the country's future glory. His ideas in this regard were necessarily influenced by the contemporary Indological concept of a 'Buddhist Age', which he considered to be the most glorious phase in the country's past. The flowering of Indian genius he traced to two interlinked factors, the decline of priestly power over petty kings through Buddhist monasticism and the emergence of pan-Indian empires under mighty rulers who unified the petty kingdoms of an earlier age. The 'revolution' reconciled royal and priestly powers.[99] But Buddhism also sowed the seeds of decline through its 'un-Hindu' error, the false belief that the same rules apply to all men, irrespective of their social roles and temperament. Renunciation, projected as the ideal for all and sundry, meant the decay of Indian civilization.[100] To repeat, Vivekananda's perceptions of Buddhism subsumed his basic moral and social concerns which were compassion and self-denial for the good of mankind and a high regard for renunciation as a way of life for the strong. Negatively, these perceptions reject priestly domination. They also project the image of a united and powerful nation, preaching its faith without bloodshed. These were the ideals he wanted his countrymen to live by. Curiously, he seems to have been least concerned with the spiritual goal of *nirvana* in projecting the Buddha's greatness, perhaps because he found it irrelevant to the needs of the weak and impoverished Indians. The spirituality he preached for the benefit of the worldly and powerful West was rooted in Vedanta.

As discussed below, he was less than sympathetic to a great deal in Christianity as practised in the West in his days. This negative appraisal was in sharp contrast to his veneration of Christ and the Christian ideal of life. The spiritual discipline he imposed on himself and his fellow disciples after Ramakrishna's death had a strong Christian component. In fact, it has been said that the banding together of the saint's disciples under Naren's leadership was an act in emulation of the example set by the apostles after the death of Christ. Probably the first book written by Vivekananda was a Bengali translation of Thomas à Kempis. The first monastery he set up was decorated with oleographs of Jesus and St Paul. The young monks celebrated Christmas and the Bible was a part of their daily reading, a source of consolation to

Naren in his days of extreme poverty.[101] He frequently alluded to the affinities between Hindu and Christian religiosity. The adoration of the child Christ reminded him of Krishna's childhood, so central to the Vaishnava devotional myths. The milkmaids' love for their Lord, he thought, had its counterpart in St Catherine's devotion to Jesus. He cited examples from the Christian tradition to explain the principle of total surrender to the Lord's will inculcated in the Gita.[102] Christianity, of course, was recognized as a dualistic faith and hence not alien to Vedanta as interpreted by him. However, even at the level of beliefs and principles, Vivekananda had more reservations about Christianity than about other non-Hindu faiths. His criticisms of Christianity as practised in the West had a sharp anti-colonial edge. Besides, it was to him historically the religion of western man. Despite his anxiety to 'condemn nothing' in other nations, states, and religions,[103] the 'us'–'they' dichotomy was very much a part of his awareness of Europe. Cultural self-assertion was one powerful element in much of what he said and did. Since religion was at the heart of his western mission, this invariably implied some claim of superiority for Hinduism *vis-à-vis* Christianity. At one level, the emphasis was simply on the fact of difference; the Hindu faith in the soul's eternity was contrasted with the Biblical belief in its finite beginning.[104] Hinduism was described as an 'ethnic' religion, not concerned with proselytization unlike the 'spreading' religions, including Christianity.[105] Something more than just difference is implied in both these statements. Sharp criticism of Christian doctrine itself is not absent from his pronouncements on the subject. On one occasion he described the prayer for personal salvation as a form of selfishness and the egocentricity implicit in the commandment—'do unto others as you would be done by'—as 'horrible, barbarous, savage'.[106] His reservations regarding Christianity were however genuine, and not merely derived from the psychological need for cultural self-assertion. His brother, Mahendra, reports his dissatisfaction with the belief in man's state of bondage and the terrifying wrath of God projected in the Bible, a text he considered suitable for 'ordinary devotees'. For the spiritually advanced, Vedanta was to be preferred.[107]

Such preference derived partly from his cultural conditioning, but it was also the end result of his intellectual and spiritual quest, though of course the two factors overlap. The very nature of the Vedantic doctrine, especially as interpreted by.Vivekananda, rejected exclusiveness in matters of belief and all claims to monopoly of truth. His perception of his Master's syncretism generated the ideal of a universal religion. It was to be attained not through any new dispensation but simply 'by recognizing the natural necessity of variation', [108] through conscious acceptance of all faiths as true, something very different from any patronizing tolerance of another man's beliefs. Each religion had its particular excellence, meeting particular needs in human beings. Quintessentially, they did not contradict, but complemented one another, for mankind had proceeded from truth to truth and not from error to truth. This universalist faith was the ultimate criterion by which every civilization was to be judged. Hence the overtones of contempt for bigotry in all its forms in the written and spoken words of the Swami.[109] In truth, however he was not uniformly indulgent to all expressions of religiosity. He described Tantric rituals as forms of diabolism, in a conversation with Nivedita.[110] He was highly critical of many elements in the Hindu tradition, especially the ritual taboos on inter-caste commensality.and the apotheosis of popular superstitions.[111] He made fun of the neo-Hindus who, in his opinion, had total knowledge of 'the movements of electricity and magnetic energy from the pigtail to the nine orifices' in the human body and hence could provide scientific justification for all ancient practices such as child marriage and pregnancy of ten-year-old girls. This, he quipped, was profoundly reassuring to all good Hindus.[112] He was not overawed even by the high Hindu tradition. He was relieved to learn, he wrote to a friend, that Rama held the *Asvamedha* sacrifice after he had banished Sita. The point of the joke was the ritual prescription that the queen had to simulate copulation with the strangulated sacrificial horse.[113] Despite his Vedantic faith, he considered the great Sankaracharya heartless and narrow-minded for he sent his defeated Buddhist opponents to death by slow fire. The Buddhist scholars who agreed to enter into debates on such conditions were also rather stupid in his opinion.[114] He was also full of contempt for modern occultism and told off Colonel Olcott for the hoaxes he perpetrated.[115] An iconoclastic rationalism was an essential component of Vivekananda's personality. He accepted the suprarational only if he felt it was validated by experience. He did not reject occult phenomena as illusory for he had encountered things he could not explain but the supernatural was irrelevant to his religious quest for it did not lead to realization.[116]

There are two basic referents in Vivekananda's thought and action. Spirituality and its cultural expression, religion, were the primary concerns of his personal life and his mission abroad. Patriotic fervour rooted in strong nationalist sentiments was the second source of his inspiration. The two are often too closely intertwined to be identified as separate elements in his awareness. He travelled West in the hope of raising funds for service to the poor in India. He stayed on for years to preach the gospel of Vedanta as the basis of a universal religion. The spiritual liberation of the West, he hoped, would lead to a new dawn for mankind. But the liberation was also to be a spiritual conquest—of the West by India. It would earn for his country the homage and material assistance of western nations, the latter leading to an escape from poverty. His efforts at home were aimed at the betterment of the poor—through education and social service. The chosen instrument for this highly secular purpose was however an order of dedicated monks and nuns, named after Ramakrishna, and non-dualist in its ideological belief. Like the protagonists of Bankim's *Anandamath*, Vivekananda considered renunciation essential for true service to the motherland. Spirituality and patriotism were evidently continuous in his awareness. Only rarely was he impatient with the duties imposed by his concern for his countrymen and longed to break away into an uninterrupted mystical quest.

Nationalism—including elements of xenophobia—was very much a part of the milieu during Naren's boyhood. The child, it appears, absorbed the new spirit very early in life. He objected to learning English, the language of the alien ruler, at the age of eight and only his mother could eventually overcome his stubborn resistance.[117] His faith in physical prowess as a necessary prerequisite for national regeneration can be traced back to his school days. He was an enthusiastic member of 'National' Nabagopal's gymnasium where young Bengalis were encouraged to shed their physical weakness through vigorous physical exercise. Naren excelled in gymnastics, wrestling, fencing, and 'lathi' play.[118] His contempt for all forms of effeminacy and the ways of the aesthete derived partly from the innate masculinity of his temperament. But he also saw in these a threat to national regeneration.[119]

The element of self-assertion and aggression in his nationalist persona was expressed in a variety of ways throughout his life. The Christian missionary with his ill-informed criticism of Hinduism in street corner speeches was a favourite object of attack in his youth.[120] The aversion developed for this type of missionary propaganda did colour his view of Christianity. He resented deeply 'the abuses incessantly hurled' at a conquered people.[121] His lectures in the USA on unwholesome Indian practices like *sati* and child marriage either denied their existence or sought to explain them away. He took pride in the fact that he had 'dared to defend his country' against the foreigners' calumny.[122] Nivedita mentions his 'splendid scorn of apology for anything Indian' and describes his 'national defence' as unreasonable and unpleasant yet superbly manly.[123] He admitted the need for social reform in India and declared that, after Ramakrishna, he followed the reformer Vidyasagar. 'But,' he commented, 'why should one advertise these [social ills] in the press for the benefit of the English? Who is a greater ass than the person who washes his own dirty linen in public?'[124] His monk's apparel, donned in Europe despite the unfriendly attention it often attracted, was in a sense a statement—a token of defiance and self-assertion. He rejected totally any westernization of Indian social mores.[125] When a fellow disciple described his guru as 'Lord Ramakrishna', he made savage fun of this Christianized style of description.[126] One is reminded of Bankim's angry snub: 'Nobody called Mr Bankimchandra lives in this house'.

Vivekananda's pride in the Indian past, especially the supreme excellence of the Hindu tradition of spiritual quest, and his spirited defence of everything Indian are in tune with the dominant ideological preoccupations of the western-educated Bengalis of his time. But his love for his country contained a unique feature—a genuine sense of identity with the poverty-stricken and oppressed masses, and indignation at the injustice heaped down the centuries on the real builders of human civilization.[127] Sympathy for the poor and championship of the oppressed were of course not absent from contemporary sociopolitical consciousness. The middle-class involvement with the indigo ryots' cause and Bankim's impassioned accounts of the peasants' miserable existence are evidence enough of such sympathy.[128] But there was little effort to translate it into any programme of effective action. Besides, the masses were unmistakably 'they' to the high-caste educated *bhadralok* Vivekananda, by contrast, wanted the new India to emerge from the peasant's shanty and the factory floor.[129] Significantly, latter generations of militant Indian nationalists were inspired by the aggressive patriotism of *Anandamath* and Vivekananda's call for renunciation in the cause of the motherland. But Bankim's discourse on the misery of the masses and Vivekananda's appeal for dedicated service to the poor had very limited impact on nationalist consciousness. The self-sacrificing revolutionaries of the early twentieth century had little understanding of the *sanyasi*'s anguished empathy with starving people. Evidently even sacrifice of life itself came easier than the effort to transcend the limits of middle-class consciousness.

Vivekananda's life experience led him beyond those limits. He gave up his worldly aspirations when he finally decided to become a *sanyasi*. Yet, until he went on his solitary journeys across India as a penniless sadhu, which were an essential part of the ordained monk's spiritual discipline, his patriotism was not notably informed by any awareness of mass poverty. In fact, young Narendra sought Ramakrishna's guidance for an entirely asocial purpose—his personal spiritual quest. The discipleship and the spiritual regime followed after the master's death also had no secular objective.[130] The illusion—*maya*—from which he sought escape surely did not exclude nationalism, with its roots in the individual ego. Ramakrishna admonished Naren to give up his selfish longing for total and uninterrupted *samadhi*, for he had duties to mankind. There is nothing to indicate that by 'duties' the guru meant any amelioration of material misery.[131] Vivekananda's awareness of the misery that was the life of the poor in India came from his experience of total destitution over a period of years.[132] Other *sanyasis* living off voluntary gifts or begging surely had similar experiences. Only, in his case the seed fell on very fertile ground—an intensely emotional temperament.[133] Besides, his great pride in India's civilization was rudely shaken by the sight of horrendous poverty throughout the land. His mission to the West was inspired directly by a desire to do something about it.[134] There is an apparent contradiction in his attitude to material misery. He had known poverty and actually experienced near starvation when his father's death ended his life of luxury and reduced his family to abject poverty.[135] His final decision to renounce worldly life came *after* this. The young monks' regime of extreme rigour at Baranagore also implied a life of great deprivation which was joyously borne, for the renunciation of lust and gold (*kamkanchan*) was one of the objects of the exercise. The hunger thus endured did not lead to any empathy with the poor. Only as a *parivrajaka*, a travelling mendicant, did he discover the reality of Indian life. Repeatedly in his later life he referred to the horrors of hunger.[136] And at the end of his solitary travels on the eve of his departure to the USA he confided to a friend that while he had not encountered the Deity of his quest, he had learnt to love human beings.[137] The lesson so learnt implied a rejection of material misery as an acceptable state of affairs. And if he looked to the affluent West for aid, inevitably he would come to admire the energy and social talent which produced the affluence. But his sense of identity with the disinherited of this earth also created a keen sensitiveness to discrimination and inequality. As an ascetic and as a nationalist from a subject race and as a believer in equality, he could never overlook the clay feet of western materialism.

The unusual character of his programme for national regeneration in the context of nineteenth-century India needs to be emphasized. Its focus was almost entirely on the poor and the illiterate. The plan was to open their eyes—through education. He went to the USA in the hope of raising funds. A band of dedicated *sanyasis*, recruited from his own social class, would use these funds to serve his 'God, the poor' of all races.[138] With maps, globes, and magic lanterns they were to go out among the lowliest, the pariahs and the *chandals*, and remove their ignorance. Evidently he expected the dispossessed to stand on their own feet and claim their own once their eyes were opened. 'The only service to be done for our lower classes is to give them education, to develop their lost individuality', he wrote to the Maharaja of Mysore. 'Give them ideas,' he added, 'that is the only help they require, and then the rest must follow as the effect'.[139] Social service, especially amelioration of suffering at times of disasters like famines or epidemics, was undertaken by fellow monks of the order he established. They had his full sympathy and support. But such efforts appear to have been peripheral to his central concern, which was restoring to the masses downtrodden for centuries by priests and conquerors alike a sense of their human worth and dignity.[140] This objective was virtually absent from Indian social thought until the advent of Gandhi.

Vivekananda's programme for national regeneration included a different prescription for the more privileged elements of the Indian society. It seems unlikely that he had given much thought to the subject before his travels in the West. He did plan to recruit a band of dedicated *sanyasis* from among young educated Indians. The object, however, was to educate the poor, though the education would include the message of Vedanta. On his return from the West, he preached a gospel of manly virtues, an ideal of western-style worldly achievements as the first step towards national regeneration.[141] Spirituality and Vedanta were not for the weak in his opinion. He did not clarify exactly how the ideal of manliness was to be achieved. For the' dedicated worker in the cause, renunciation was emphasized. Indifference to the pleasures of the world was essential in his view for all impersonal achievement. Even the hard work and concentration involved in scientific research or technological invention, he pointed out, implied a measure of renunciation.[142] But renunciation was the way of the strong. A weak and degenerate subject race first needed the quality of *rajas*, vigorous pursuit of worldly ends. Spirituality was a diet better suited to the mighty nations of this world whose material achievements had impoverished their souls. He had evident concern for the discovery of some means by which the nation could escape from poverty. He advised a disciple to try and sell Indian handicrafts abroad.[143] He suggested to Tata, a fellow-passenger on the boat during his first journey to the USA, that he should set up a factory to manufacture safety matches rather than act as the agent for a Japanese product.[144] He felt greatly inspired by the Japanese industrialization.[145] But his call for strength, self-reliance, and escape from poverty was never spelt out in any concrete programme.[146]

His emphasis on national regeneration excluded any explicit reference to politics even though many of his statements abroad contained violent criticisms of the British rule in India. 'I am no politician or political agitator', he wrote to a friend from the USA, 'I care only for the spirit ... warn the Calcutta people that no political significance be ever attached falsely to any of my writings.'[147] There is some evidence to suggest that the above statement contains an element of excessive protest. A variety of sources report his sympathy for revolutionary activities. He told his brother Mahendra that the Indian National Congress should declare independence, following the American example of the previous century, if it really meant business.[148] One of the young revolutionaries he met in Dacca reports that he advised them to take the Rani of Jhansi as their ideal, emulate the *santans* in *Anandamath*, and liberate the country.[149] In a well-known passage he cited several examples from history to indicate that many nations had progressed in the past through their enmity with other peoples.[150] He is reported to have said that statues of gold should be erected in honour of the Chapekar brothers hanged for the murder of Captain Rand. A recent article claims that the Swami was actually 'looking for young men with nerves of steel and lucid brains for an insurrection'. Apparently, he told Jatin Mukherji, the brain behind the German conspiracy plot, 'that India's political freedom was essential for the spiritual fulfilment of mankind'.[151] These statements, however, lack corroboration. On the other hand, a passage in the *Swami-sishya samvad*, universally accepted as authentic, records Vivekananda's opinion that it would be insane to plan any armed rebellion against the British.[152] The Swami, intensely human, was not always consistent in his statements. Reports of his admiration for revolutionary ardour may after all be correct. It would be the extreme expression of his impatience with political bondage. His anger at the fact of conquest significantly coloured his assessments of western societies.

Of the three thinkers discussed in this book, Vivekananda alone visited the West. He did so as a highly successful purveyor of India's spiritual inheritance and a defender of Indian life and thought against often ill-informed calumny. His encounters with western men and women, both in India and abroad, were friendly most of the time. There were, of course, the inevitable collisions with Hindu-baiting missionaries on Calcutta's streets and with racist white passengers on board trains. Racism was also a fact of life on board ships on the journeys to the West; when epidemics raged in an Indian city, only its native inhabitants were precluded from visiting ships at the harbour lest they spread infection.[153] The behaviour of the white passengers, Vivekananda noted with some amusement, did however improve once the ship had left Ceylon behind. But even in India, when he was an unknown young man and later a wandering *sanyasi*, a few Europeans he met were benign and appreciative of his great talents. Principal Hastie, as noted above, had a very high opinion of his intellect and was partly responsible for rousing his interest in Ramakrishna. As a wandering monk, he met a number of English officials at Ghazipur—including Mr Ross, Colonel Rivett-Carnac and the district judge, Mr Pennington. His exposition of Hinduism impressed them. The judge advised the young ascetic to go to UK and actually offered to pay his expenses.[154] These were happy auguries for the close personal bonds which were later to develop between the Swami and his many followers, patrons, and friends in the West.

Vivekananda's mission in the West has been covered in great detail in his several biographies, the account of his sojourn in England written by his younger brother, the reminiscences of his disciples, and finally, in magnificent detail, in Marie Louise Burke's monumental compendium of all available data on the subject. A potted summary of this massive evidence would not be very useful for our purpose. I shall merely pick out a few themes which have a direct bearing on his understanding and impressions of western civilization.

He left for his first voyage to the USA via Japan on 31 May 1893 and reached Vancouver on 14 July. His famous début at the Parliament of Religions in Chicago, noted extensively and admiringly in the American press, was followed by a hectic lecture tour in the Midwest and the East Coast. He attracted very large audiences wherever he went. In January 1894 he started a regular class on Vedanta and Yoga in New York. The effort culminated in the founding of a Vedanta Society. After a very fruitful retreat at Thousand Island Park in the summer of 1895 he left for England at the invitation of two British enthusiasts, Sturdy and Miss Muller. His sojourn in Britain, where he gave lectures and held classes till December 1896, was interrupted by a brief visit to the USA (December 1895—April 1896) and a tour of the continent. He left UK for India via Italy in December

1896. He again sailed for the USA via UK in June 1899 reaching New York in August after a fortnight in England. The highlight of the second voyage was his Californian mission. A series of lectures and classes at Los Angeles, Pasadena, and San Francisco, led to the founding of the second Vedanta Society in America, at San Francisco. In July 1900 he left USA, sailing from New York to participate in a Congress on the History of Religions at Paris. After a sojourn of some three months in Paris, he left by the Orient Express for a holiday in Egypt, via Vienna, Greece, and Constantinople, as the guest of the French prima donna, Emma Calvé. He left for India from Egypt on 26 November 1900. His plans for a third visit to the West—to the US and UK via Japan—did not materialize. He died in 1902 at the age of thirty-nine. He had spent nearly five years of his brief adult life in the West. It was in the US that he achieved world fame. The tasks he set himself were aimed almost equally at India and the West.

Only, in the West he worked out for himself a role that was very different from his role in India. The Swami sought the regeneration of his motherland and the Ramakrishna Mission was to be the instrument to achieve that end. The emphasis was on service, renunciation for the sake of one's country, and the ideal of manly qualities. The doctrine of Vedanta was almost secondary in this context. Whenever he projected it in India, the message of freedom from all fear and selflessness implicit in the ancient philosophy was underlined. For India, the ethical rather than the spiritual message of Vedanta was of supreme importance. In the West, he preached Vedanta in its resplendent spirituality as the basis of a universal religion.

The purpose of Vivekananda's visit to America was transformed in course of the first twelve months of his stay in that country. The Chicago 'Parliament' which made him famous overnight was the first turning point. Originally, the US to him was 'the only place where there was a chance of success for everything,'[155] and initially he went there to 'cull ... ideas and material aid' in order to establish an institution which would help educate the Indian masses but soon decided to work 'like any other lecturer', keeping the project in the background.[156] His lectures in this phase focused on Indian society and religion, seeking to establish that Indians were not the savages of Christian missionary propaganda and poked gentle fun at American social mores. The object was decidedly oriented to India.[157] As he had explained to his Madras disciples: 'It is for the people of India that I am going to the West, for the people and the poor!'[158] Other concerns emerged out of his American experiences. The response to his address at the Parliament of Religions was startlingly enthusiastic. The vast crowds at his lectures in the Midwest in the autumn of 1893 and his increasing familiarity with the upper strata of American society created an awareness of new possibilities. A letter written in December 1894 speaks of the Americans' social superiority and spiritual inferiority. 'We will teach them our spirituality and assimilate what is best in their society', he added.[159] 'I give them spirituality and they give me money', he wrote to another friend the following month in an evident reference to his original purpose, but an equally clear recognition of the spiritual hunger among the people who came to him.[160] His earlier vague aspiration to spread the message of Sri Ramakrishna 'from pole to pole' begins to take a definite shape around this time.[161] Already in his post-Chicago lectures there was a new emphasis on the fundamental unity of all religions. The possibility of a universal religion based simply on the positive acceptance of all faiths was also stated quite explicitly.[162] The attempt to define the fundamentals of religion went hand in hand with the aspirations towards a unified civilization of all Aryans.[163] In July–August 1894 he held a series of classes at Greenacre, Maine sponsored by the Greenacre Religious Conferences. This experience of religiophilosophical instruction, where he taught Advaita Vedanta as well as Rajayoga, is known to have been a factor in his decision to offer spiritual training to Americans.[164]

The Vedanta Society of New York expressed his conviction that the New World was in need of India's religious inheritance.[165] Gradually, his preaching came to centre exclusively on Vedanta and he wrote home asking his fellow monks to send people to assist him in his new mission of spiritual conquest.[166] His purpose at one level transcended the narrow limits of national interest. Vedanta was India's gift to the world and he purveyed it to the vigorous western nations to help them reach out towards a new fulfilment, for they alone had the strength and vitality needed for a spiritual quest.[167] The brave new world of the Swami's dream would achieve an equilibrium on the highest plane that man's material and spiritual aspirations could hope to attain. National interest was however not forgotten. Only, the plan now was not simply to raise funds, but also earn for India the status of the revered teacher and thus restructure the relationship of dominance and subjection. The western nations as India's disciples would also be her friends and offer spontaneous assistance.[168] It almost appears as if Vivekananda projected his personal experience in the USA—the enthusiastic reception, the gathering of disciples, the many friendships, and eager hospitality—into a global possibility. By a singular act of transference he conceived for India— his country, his people as he described her—the role of a spiritual guide to the West which he had acquired himself in relation to a large following of western men and women. If a citizen of a despised nation could come to be treated like a god, the cultural inheritance which had produced this transformation could lead to similar results for the country as a whole. Independence, it was implied, could follow from the redefined relationship. At noted above, the Swami had no faith in any alternative path to political freedom.

If a man's responses to an alien culture are conditioned by the way it receives him, there was every reason why Vivekananda's assessment of western society should have been overwhelmingly positive. Arguably, no other man or woman from the non-western world was treated with such honour in nineteenth-century America or Europe. The extent of his access to the social and intellectual élite in the West also probably had no parallel in the experiences of any other non-European person at the time. The implication of his great success has to be seen in the context of the fact that he arrived in the USA as a totally unknown young man. Before his speech at the Parliament of Religions at Chicago very few people had even heard of him. He achieved world stature through his exposition of Hindu spirituality first in the USA and then in England and France. The accolade in India was also inspired by reports of the honour given him in the western world. His brother, Mahendra, mentions that his personality flowered in the West and that he was not quite the same man back home. Declining health may partly explain the change so noted, but perhaps the challenge of a very difficult task and the appreciation of men and women he came to value did lead to a flowering of his personality. He spoke of divine guidance behind everything he did or said in the West.

Marie Louise Burke explains the response to Vivekananda in the USA in terms of a particular conjuncture in the country's social and intellectual life.[169] The tension between Christian fundamentalism—rejecting theories of evolution and any need for a fresh orientation in the Church's outlook—and liberal Christianity, which accepted the new knowledge and sought to socialize religion, induced an interest in other ways of thinking, even a quest for alternatives to received dogma. Transcendentalism, on the wane by the 1870s, was one expression of this quest. Other movements, like Christian Science and New Thought, though directed more towards material than spiritual welfare, also felt the need for a regeneration of the spirit.

East Coast liberal Christians, especially members of the Unitarian or Congregational churches, and the seekers after a rationally acceptable spiritual thought were among the most enthusiastic recipients of the Swami's teaching. Socially active ladies, many with university education, whose intellectual curiosity and social concern were expressed in hundreds of clubs, associations, lectures, conferences, and the like functioned within and also independently of the trends mentioned above. They accounted for a very large proportion of Vivekananda's devotees and admirers. His appeal however was not confined to people in quest of religion and spirituality. There was much to interest the secular intellectuals, especially philosophers and psychologists, in what he said. His formidable learning and the hard core of systematic argument in his exposition of Vedanta were attractive even to high-powered scholars like Professor Wright of Harvard and, later, Max Muller and Deussen. His words and personality aroused genuine interest among serious-minded men and women. This is why the more sober section of the American press covered his activities in great detail.[170] The interest which was already there was deepened and further extended. The appeal of the exotic was of course a factor in that interest. Vivekananda looked impressively handsome in his *sanyasi*'s attire. The robe and the good looks are invariably commented upon in nearly all reports of his lectures. The Minneapolis *Tribune* also commented on the attraction of his Bengali accent which 'strangely perverts the vowels sounds, and misplaces the inflection', lending thereby 'a novelty to his delivery'.[171] There was more excitement than comprehension in the popular press which misspelt his name with considerable imagination and described him as a raja, a high Brahmin, an emissary of Buddhist ecclesiastics, and 'the Great High Priest of India'.[172] The themes of his lectures were also described with similar abandon:[173] 'Karmax' (Karma?) was the mystifying title of one such lecture. Perhaps his personal charisma more than anything else explains his impact. Those who got to know him intimately or came to hear him with serious interest all commented on the one thing which they found irresistible—the genuineness and evident depth of his spirituality and total selflessness which informed his many-sided charisma. One press report expressed the hope that through his accounts of the West, India might learn to admire westerners.[174] Evidently, insecurity of the national ego was no monopoly of colonial dependencies.

The great excitement in America over this Indian man of God is now fully documented. This was a unique phenomenon specially given the time and the context. We know of the avalanche of ladies who rushed to shake his hand after the lecture at the Chicago Parliament. The Chicago *Times* described him as the person who attracted most notice at the Parliament. Harriett Monroe, the founder of *Poetry: A Magazine of Verse*, remembered her response to the famous speech as 'a rare and perfect moment of supreme emotion'. 'There has seldom been such a sensation in cultural circles in Detroit', the *Tribune* commented on the Swami's visit. He was treated as the social lion of the day in that city and the largest hall would not hold the crowds at his lectures.[175]

He received and gave affection in a simple-hearted way which may well have puzzled his American friends. Ascription of kinship in the context of close interpersonal relations is structured into Bengali social mores. Vivekananda transplanted this idiom of socially approved emotionalism in the unlikely environment of his intimacy with Americans. Significantly, he was never rebuffed. The unalloyed sincerity of his words and actions and a childlike simplicity enhanced by deep spiritual experiences probably explain the acceptance of gestures which almost certainly would have been treated as bizarre in any other person. He addressed Mrs George Hale, a lady in her mid to late forties, as mother and her daughters and nieces as sisters. The latter reciprocated by addressing him as brother. Mrs Hale had literally opened her door one morning and seen him, a delegate to the Parliament of Religions without any place to stay, seated on the pavement opposite her house. Her extraordinary generosity in inviting him in to stay with her family for an indefinite period tells us much both about her gracious kindness and the instant impact which Vivekananda often had on people.[176] The near reverential tone of his estimate of American womanhood was no doubt inspired by encounters such as this.

He was a welcome guest in affluent American homes both before and after the Parliament. Kate Sanborn, an author and lecturer, was probably the first American to offer him hospitality, in her elegant home in a New England village.[177] It was through her that he met Professor Wright whose letter of introduction gave him his entrée to the Chicago conference. After the conference he became 'one of the most popular of guests in Chicago drawing-rooms'.[178] At Detroit, he was the guest of Mrs John Bagley, the widow of an ex-governor of Michigan. The cream of Detroit society came to the first reception in honour of the Swami at her palatial home.[179] His other hosts and hostesses included the Lyons of Chicago, owners of a sugar plantation in Louisiana and a house complete with a kennel and a stable in the heart of the city, Charles L. Freer, a partner in the Michigan-Peninsular

Car Company and a great collector of Oriental art, Senator T.W. Palmer, one of Detroit's wealthiest businessmen, Representative Flagg, an uncle of Mrs Vanderbilt, Helen Gould, heiress to a robber baron, etc.[180] A full list of his acquaintances, friends, and admirers would read like several pages out of the Social Register. He met John D. Rockefeller while staying as a guest with an associate of the tycoon. His devotees suggest that Rockefeller's philanthropy was first triggered off by a harsh gibe from Vivekananda. He also met Mme Clave for the first time in the same house and this proved to be the beginning of a great friendship.[181] At least one beautiful heiress proposed marriage and she was probably not the only one to do so. His affluent hosts offered him an experience of American high life, which he came to admire as a token of high material achievement and a commendable concern for quality. It appealed to one side of his personality—his contempt for spiritless low living, repeatedly mentioned by his brother, Mahendra. The *sanyasi*'s renunciation, an act of strength, or the destitute's hunger were to him very different from the spineless acceptance of miserable living standards. American materialism might have no answer for man's spiritual needs, but the great vigour which was its source could be the basis of spirituality as well.[182] Besides, a weak, impoverished, and demoralized India would do well to attain such vigour in the first place and only then attempt the sterner task of liberating the spirit. Realization of *atman* was not for the weak.[183]

His long sojourn in the States gave Vivekananda an intimate knowledge of many facets of American life. His close friends and acquaintances included a number of leading intellectuals, some of whom were serious students of religion and philosophy. He went to Boston with letters introducing him to 'leaders of thought, action and fashion'.[184] He addressed the prestigious American Social Science Association, lectured at Smith College, and held classes for Harvard students of philosophy. Professor John Wright, the Harvard classicist, and his family were among his closest friends. William James, America's leading psychologist, was deeply interested in his ideas.[185] Walter Hines Page, editor of *Forum* and *Atlantic Monthly* and later ambassador to the Court of St James, requested him to contribute articles to his journals.[186] The very long list of his ardent admirers included the poets Ella Wheeler Wilcox and Harriett Monroe, Ernest Fennollosa, a great connoisseur of Oriental art, the famous agnostic Robert Green Ingersoll and the singer, Emma Thursby. At the Lyons home, he spent an evening with 'young intellectuals' from the university and the press who had gathered to 'show him up'. They later 'admitted that Swamiji had held his own on every point'. After the Chicago conference, he got to know a number of famous scientists who came for the International Electrical Congress. Among them were Lord Kelvin and Professor von Helmholtz.[187] The most sustained interest he roused was, of course, among liberal-spirited men and women with a deep concern for religion. The Reverend John H. Barrows, the chief organizer of the Chicago conference, who later became very hostile to the Swami, was an ardent admirer for many years. Merwin-Marie Snell, president of the scientific section of the conference, remembered him as 'beyond question the most popular and influential man in the Parliament'. He could also develop a serious dialogue with the Unitarians and the Transcendentalists, especially the Free Religious Association which was an offshoot of the Transcendental Movement and which believed in syncretism. Dr Grossman, Rabbi of the Temple Beth El, Detroit lectured on Vivekananda's teaching, contrasting it with 'the morbid ecstasy of the Chapman revival'. The philosopher, William Ernest Hocking, in his youth listened to a lecture by Vivekananda on Advaita and felt that the Swami's ideas sprang, not from books, but from his experience. His own religious conversion shaken by Spencer's dismissive treatment of spiritual enlightenment as a spiritual flurry was affirmed by Vivekananda's certitude.[188] In 1896, Vivekananda met a flamboyant celebrity, the physicist and inventor, Nikola Tesla, but only a tantalizing note from the scientist survives to tell us that this was no casual encounter.[189] His social contacts in the States were, however, not confined to the élite of wealth and intellect. One of his pre-Chicago talks was for the inmates of a prison; another was addressed to a group of children.[190] He spoke to labourers and farmers as well during his Midwestern tour.[191] The men and women who became his disciples mostly came from a relatively humble stratum of society. The students at his New York classes in 1893–5, with some exceptions, could afford only small contributions 'barely enough to maintain the classes'.[192] The disciples, however, came from a wide social spectrum. Mrs Ole Bull, the widow of a famous Norwegian violinist, Mme Marie Louise, a French emigré, well-known in New York as a 'progressive, advanced woman' who was ordained as a *sanyasin* by Vivekananda, Leon Landsberg, a Russian Jew, on the staff of a leading New York paper, who too was ordained and given the name, Kripananda; Dr Street, alias Swami Yogananda, the third disciple to be given *sanysasa* and Miss Sarah Ellen Waldo of Brooklyn were among the first to accept him as guru. Then there were the two 'Sisters', Devamata (Laura Glenn) and Christine Greenstidel.

The students who gathered round him at a retreat in the Thousand Islands Park cottage of one Miss Dutcher were all initiated by him. They were serious students of religion and philosophy and in no sense either social dropouts or 'pebbly-eyed Theosophists' in quest of a new sensation.[193]

The Swami thus encountered and was received with honour by a wide cross-section of American society. His second visit widened and deepened his familiarity with the multiple facets of life in the USA. His fame attracted people like the Mead Sisters of South Pasadena who were interested in non-denominational religion and spirituality.[194] Among them were people of 'New Thought' persuasion, especially a group centred on the Los Angeles Home of Truth, and Californian cognoscenti of metaphysics. The encounters were by no means always cordial. Though he counted Bernhard Baumgardt, Secretary of the Southern Californian Academy of Sciences and a number of "advanced" women among his new acquaintances, the intellectual challenge of his East Coast encounter appears to have been missing in the West. In January, 1900 he wrote to Sister Christine that the first boom was over.[195] His references to the effervescent quality of American enthusiasms may have been inspired partly by his Californian experience.

The high excitement which the Swami had generated in America did not have an English or European counterpart. He did have his entree to the world of social and intellectual élite when he crossed the Atlantic. He also lectured to full halls in London and elsewhere. Serious-minded men and women in quest of higher thought, old India hands, Orientalists and the truly religious, including some genuine eccentrics, were the types of people he got to know in England and Europe. Nivedita's descriptions catch the mood of intelligent earnestness in his English audiences, an earnestness which did not exclude some doubts. His remarks indicate that he rather appreciated the relative calmness of his reception in Europe. He understood it to betoken a certain seriousness of concern and a depth of feeling about his mission. He wondered if the American response was not ephemeral by comparison.

The two persons who first invited him to England were Miss Henrietta Muller who met and spoke to Vivekananda at the Chicago conference and E.T. Sturdy, an erstwhile Theosophist who heard of the Swami from his fellow-disciple, Shivananda at Almora.[196] Later developments suggest that as human beings both were somewhat unstable.[197] The same cannot be said of J.J. Goodwin, a high-earning ace stenographer who gave up his lucrative profession to follow the Swami despite his patriotic pride in Britain and her empire and profound dislike of most things Indian.[198] On his premature death in India, the Swami said he had lost his son. He received unquestioning loyalty from three other persons in Britain—Miss Margaret Noble, alias Sister Nivedita, an Irish nationalist and Captain and Mrs Sevier. Like Goodwin, they too followed him to India and unlike him accepted their Master's country as their own. Nivedita was his daughter just as Goodwin was a son. As to the Seviers, his letters refer repeatedly to the great kindness he received from them. His friends in Europe included more high-powered persons as well both socially and intellectually. While in London, he was invited out to dinner most evenings by people who belonged to the highest echelons of English society. His hosts included at least one Duke. The Duchess of Albany came to his lectures. Other visitors included a canon of the Church and a general's wife.[199] He developed an intellectual rapport and a personal friendship with two luminaries, Max Mueller and Karl Deussen. Sarah Bernhardt was another celebrity who befriended him. One of his travelling companions on the journey to Turkey and Egypt was the Carmelite monk, Père Hyacinthe who had defied the Pope and was eventually excommunicated. His host in Paris was Jules Bois, a young man interested in Vedanta as well as satanism and magic. The person whose letters of introduction smoothed his way in his Near Eastern travels was Sir Hiram Maxim, of 'Maxim gun' fame, an admirer of China and India who also wrote on religion and philosophy.[200] In short, even though Vivekananda's sojourn in Europe was shorter than in the New World, it was not just a casual visit. His encounters covered a wide enough social spectrum to afford a rounded view of European life and mores.

Neither in the USA nor in Europe were his experiences uniformly positive. He had his fair share of racially motivated insults in the USA. At Baltimore, white hoteliers refused to admit him; in New York, the hair-dressers' saloons showed him the door; in Boston, urchins gave chase to the strangely clad sadhu; in London, an obdurate retired official from India hurled insults at a meeting; on board ship, two English missionaries indulged in vile abuse of Hindus and Hinduism until the formidable Swami threatened to throw one of them overboard.[201]

But these were pinpricks compared to the campaign of slander in America describing him as a fake and a debauch.[202] Fundamentalist Christians, especially missionaries who projected an image of India as a benighted heathendom and Midwestern 'church women', found both his defence of Hindu ways and criticism of current Christian practice unacceptable. The Ramabai Circles, who supported the efforts of the Maharastrian 'feminist' to raise funds for improving the condition of Indian women, were alarmed by his statements challenging their view of Indian womanhood. The Brahmo preacher, Protap Mazoomdar, who had achieved some fame in the US and participated in the Chicago conference was plainly jealous. The sum total of their propaganda was that Vivekananda was neither a Brahmin nor a genuine *sanyasi* and that he represented nobody. And, of course, there were dark hints about his relationship with his female admirers. The campaign eventually failed, because in response to the Swami's appeal his friends and admirers organized mammoth meetings in Calcutta and Madras congratulating him on his achievements in America. Reports of these meetings, published in the American press, helped counter the slanderous propaganda. He was, however, helped above all by his friends in the US, especially the ladies who had an unquestioning faith in him and hence fought back the evil rumours with great energy. At the end of the day, the Swami had more friends than enemies. There is very little trace of bitterness in his memories of the West.

Since these personal experiences, pleasant and unpleasant, did leave their mark on his assessment of the West, certain relevant facts should be noted in this context. Vivekananda had nothing but contempt for compromise, diplomacy or tact in any form and his public utterances were often abrasive in the extreme—especially on such matters as Christian missions, western colonialism and the image of India in the West. All religions might be based on the same fundamental truth, but his uncompro-mising rejection of the notion of sins and sinners as acceptable concepts and equally emphatic projection of non-duality were off-putting even for many who genuinely admired him. Profoundly respectful to what he considered the essence of Christianity and Christ's divine mission, he berated much of what to him was false or pernicious in Christian belief and practice. His utterances could therefore be deeply offensive to many Christians. He did not care, for he was aware of no malice in himself. Some of the hostilities he faced were no doubt due to bigotry, but some were traceable to wounded sensibilities. The tensions in his relationship with some of his followers, like Leon Landsberg, Sturdy, Miss Muller, Nivedita and at times even Goodwin, derived at least partly from his impatience with any infringement of his personal freedom as a *sanyasi*, though such an explanation has little relevance to the defection of Sturdy and Muller. Mahendra mentions how in London Saradananda lived in fear of Vivekananda's anger, a trait he seems to have acquired abroad. Always a fighter, he had fought hard and successfully to survive in the West. Some at least of the conflicts he faced were of his own choosing. They gave him a fresh perspective for assessment of western life balancing his experience of sympathy and friendliness. Interestingly, he took a very detached view of the hostility he encountered. He repeatedly stressed the absence of jealousy as a characteristic virtue of western public life.[203] Perhaps his judgement was influenced by his experience of hydra-headed enmity on his return home.[204] The youth of India might have rejoiced in replacing the horses of his carriage with their own selves, but he offended the orthodox and reformists alike by his open criticism of priestcraft, theosophy and Brahmo insincerity. The Theosophists, as noted earlier, had won the gratitude of many Indians through their homage to the Hindu tradition. Some of Vivekananda's most ardent admirers were members of the society, but the Swami brushed aside their request that he should not speak of their hostility to him in America. He made many powerful enemies through this refusal. Among them were the neo-Vaishnavas led by Sisir Kumar Ghosh and his very influential daily, *Amrita Bazar Patrika.* The virulence of the campaign against him in India, especially Bengal, probably penetrated his shield of equanimity. He told Tilak that a man's leadership was accepted relatively easily away from his home base. These words, no doubt spoken in sorrow, help one understand why he could look back on his conflicts in the West without bitterness. Compared to what he had to endure at home, the campaign of calumny he had faced in the USA probably seemed mild.

In concluding this discussion on aspects of the Swami's life-experience which have a bearing on his responses to the West, I should like to emphasize certain features of his personality. As a nineteenth-century Indian patriot, he shared the growing sense of helpless rage against the fact of alien rule. The rage was helpless because he too saw no light at the end of the tunnel in the foreseeable future.[205] His plans of campaign in the West were among the several contemporary prescriptions for national regeneration and self-respect accepting the fact of British rule. Despite his evident anger and the fact that his admiration for the British was arguably more reluctant than that of many of his contemporaries, his indifference to things of this world— his very genuine spirituality—and a powerful intellect gave him a capacity for objective assessment. He also gave and returned affection with a simple-hearted innocence. Not mere gratitude, but a very warm appreciation of friendship informs his statements on the western, especially English,

personality. Finally, Vivekananda's written and spoken words on western
life have a unique quality hardly ever to be found in any other Indian
writing on the subject at the time—an almost frivolous sense of fun. The
dour seekers after wisdom from the East were at times baffled by what must
have seemed like levity in his conduct. To him, the Creator was no sombre
Deity and His creation was a source not only of joy but amusement.[206] His
racy style in Bengali made not infrequent use of slang to very good purpose.
Besides, his appetite for life, untarnished by any desire for possession, fostered
a lively interest in virtually everything he saw. This believer in non-duality
could shift from the sublime to the mundane with unnerving ease. After one
of his lectures on Vedanta, there was a pensive pause and a cryptic comment
followed. The Swami said, 'Now I know how they do it'. The 'it' under
reference, he disclosed, was not *nirvikalpa samadhi* but mulligatawny soup.[207]
He responded to Europe as an intellectual and a man of God. But another
side of his personality—a fun-loving and somewhat mischievous child—keeps
peeping through his high purpose all the time.

II

Swami Vivekananda's well-known essay, *Prachya o Paschatya* (*The East
and the West*) begins with a classic statement on mutual perceptions:[208]

'Horrendous onslaughts of cholera, decimation caused by epidemics,
malaria chewing into the bones and marrow, recurrent bouts of devastating
famines, a battleground of disease and misery, a vast cremation ground
strewn with skeletons where all hope, enterprise, joy and enthusiasm have
perished and therein the yogi deep in meditation in quest of *moksha*—this is
what the European traveller sees [in India].

'Three hundred million subhuman creatures, their souls crushed for
centuries under the feet of everyone, compatriots and aliens, coreligionists
and people of other faiths alike, capable of slave-like industry, listless like
slaves, without hope, without any past or any future, concerned only with
bare survival in the present by any means available, with the slave's proneness
to jealousy, intolerant of their compatriot's success, cynical and without
faith like men who have lost all hope, stooping to low cunning and trickery
like the jackal, the ultimate in selfishness, bootlickers to the powerful, verily

the god of death to the powerless, weak, devoid of any moral stamina, spread all over India like maggots feeding on stinking rotten flesh—this is our image in the eyes of the English official.

'Intoxicated by the heady wine of newly acquired power, fearsome like wild animals who see no difference between good and evil, slaves to women, insane in their lust, drenched in alcohol from head to foot, without any norms of ritual conduct, unclean, materialistic, dependent on things material, grabbing other people's territory and wealth by hook or crook, without faith in the life to come, the body their self, its appetites the only concern of their lives—such is the image of the western demon in Indian eyes.'

Such negative perceptions, he pointed out, derived mainly from the superficial observation of the unenlightened. The Europeans, living in the elegant parts of the metropolis, compared the dirty native quarters with the clean cities of Europe. The only Indians they met were those serving under Europeans. They naturally could not believe that any worthwhile qualities might survive beneath the dirt and servility all around. The Indians were similarly repelled by the Europeans' sanitary habits, the fact that they ate anything and everything and the unseemliness of their ballroom dance. Indian society was closed to the *mlechcha*, the unclean alien, and the Europeans looked down on the slave-like dark-skinned native.[209]

Such perceptions were not without any basis in facts. They were false because they were superficial and took no note of the fundamental human reality under the surface of external conduct.

The concept of cultural relativism projected in Bhudev's writings appeared under a different rubric in Vivekananda. He spoke of each race or culture having a distinctive outlook or attitude (*jatiya bhav*), a moral purpose and implied by that term something approaching national character.[210] In his view, each individual had an outlook on life of which his external conduct was only an expression. Since a nation was but a collection of individuals, it had correspondingly a collective outlook. The collective outlook was linked to qualities dominant in the culture. So long as a people or a culture survived, its outlook met some need of human society. Europe's dominance was to be explained with reference to the historic necessity fulfilled by its cultural attitudes. A nation could be judged only in terms of their ethical goals. 'We must look at them through their eyes. To look at them through our eyes or at us through theirs are both mistakes.'[211]

He summed up in a single phrase the essential difference between Indian and western concerns. The West was dominated by their pursuit of *dharma*, while the central concern of Indian culture was *moksha*,[212] the liberation of the soul. *Dharma*, as explained by the Swami, was the ideal of the good life, a morally acceptable pursuit of legitimate material ends. The *dharmic* way recognized that it was for the strong man of courage to enjoy the world. It encompassed the manifestation of manly prowess, the use of diplomacy and armed strength in the pursuit of political goals, strenuous effort to gain wealth which allowed an affluent lifestyle as well as philanthropy. *Dharma* was action-oriented and a laudable ideal, for only a person whose soul had been purified through right action, the 'virtuous one', was entitled to seek *moksha*.[213] European culture embodied this high ideal. The Christian ideal of peace with all, non-injury to one's enemy and renunciation of this ephemeral world had little practical bearing on European life. On the contrary, Krishna's teaching in the Gita appeared to have borne fruit in the West. The call to action—to destroy one's enemies and enjoy this life on earth—was at the heart of western culture. *Rajas*, the element of manly and this-worldly virtues, was the dominant trait in the European personality driving western man to the ends of the earth in pursuit of material ends. By contrast, it was in India that one encountered a feeble-minded acceptance of the call to renunciation. The myth of gods and *asuras* (demons) offered, in the Swami's opinion, a paradigm of the contrast between the West and India. This statement, he was careful to explain, contained no value judgement for the ways of the Puranic deities were not quite exemplary. By comparison the *asuras* had a relatively clean record. The relevance of the myth consisted in the fact that the gods put their trust in God and the life hereafter, while the *asuras* were concerned to enjoy this life on earth. Hence 'you (Indians) are the offsprings of the gods and the westerners are descended from the *asuras*.'[214]

His considered judgement at the end of his exercise in comparison was that 'they are all right, so are we, but goodness manifests itself in a variety of ways'.[215] His specific statements on various occasions, especially in the West, at times depart from this broadminded appraisal. His criticisms of western ways and ideals are seldom as severe as his castigations of Indian society, but one is often left with the impression that his ascription of superior spirituality to India was really a claim to overall superiority. In his statements in India, especially his Bengali writings, such claims are markedly absent; the emphasis, if anything, is on poverty, weakness and social degeneration.

In one speech in Detroit, he asserted that India was the 'most moral nation' ascribing thereby a relative inferiority to the West in matters ethical.[216] In another lecture at Minneapolis[217] he stated: 'You of the West are practical in business, practical in great inventions, but we of the East are practical in religion.' He developed his argument pointing out that American labourers and farmers were well-informed about politics, and supported one or the other of the two major political parties. They were also well-posted on the gold standard controversy. But their ignorance of religion was abysmal whereas the Indian peasant, ignorant of politics, knew of monotheism, deism and the like. In a grand assertion of superiority derived from spiritual excellence he told his brother, Mahendra, in London that there was no reason to stand in any awe of the westerners. They understood the business of this world and little else. Their spirit was that of a trader and it would be very long before they sorted out the puzzle that was India. 'You can walk over them as if they were so many insects', he advised Mahendra, an evident reference to his guru's words that men lusting after women and gold were no different from worms.[218] Another statement made to Mahendra also suggests a claim to superiority on grounds which were human rather than ethical. Action in Europe, he said, was inspired by a sense of duty; in India, love was the source of all inspiration.[219] In a slightly different mood, he once told Nivedita, 'You western folk want action! You cannot perceive the poetry of every common action of life.'[220] He illustrated his statement with stories from the Buddha's life—the bereaved mother consoled through the knowledge of death's universality, the Enlightened One offering his body to save the goats meant for sacrifice and so on. By contrast, the crucifixion appealed to the action-oriented ancient Romans because they saw it as high drama. The implied claim was to a refinement of spiritual sensibility in India not to be found in the West.

This perceived dichotomy in basic attitudes was seen to be manifest in the history of the two cultures as well., Vivekananda interpreted the evolution of European society partly with reference to the *devata-asura* paradigm discussed above and partly by reading into the historical overview based on contemporary scholarship what he considered the dominant traits of western civilization. The paradigm and the analytical insights were, of course, closely interlinked. His gods, the *devatas*, were the settled agrarian societies of the ancient world, the civilizations of Asia's river valleys which created the early urban cultures. The *asuras* were the nomadic people, the hunters, food-gatherers and pastoralists who entered into relationships of both conflict and exchange with the gods. The lifestyle of the gods produced weak bodies, with low levels of endurance and agile intellects generating *inter alia* technological progress. The *asuras* excelled in physical prowess, a capacity for hard labour and great endurance.[221] Their habitat was either hilly areas or along the sea coasts. The hunting and pastoral occupations gradually gave place to or were supplemented by other more aggressive means of livelihood—plunder, acts of brigandage across land or sea. While all human societies were the products of racial admixture, the *asura* element played a dominant role in the origin of the European peoples. Vivekananda refers to the waves of migration from Asia to Europe in prehistoric times but, expectedly, traced the beginning of western civilization to Greece. Here too he emphasized the migration of civilization and people from Asia Minor to the Mediterranean islands and the influence of Egypt on the early island cultures.[222]

But his sensitive mind was attracted so profoundly by the civilization of ancient Greece that the element of cultural self-assertion, the need to feel equal if not superior to manifestations of excellence in the West, is almost absent in his statements on the subject. His admiration for Greece reflected his great delight in things French, especially Paris, his 'Heaven on earth' for he too believed that the spirit of Greek culture had been reborn in France. He described the ancient Hellenes in a lyrical passage:

> There is a small country in the eastern Mediterranean wreathed by chains of beautiful islands. There once flourished a not very numerous race of great genius—handsome with perfect features and yet with iron muscles and nerves of steel, light of limb yet formidable in their industry and supreme in their skill to create this-worldly beauty.[223] Their achievements were without precedent ... . This tiny nation of superb prowess has no parallel in the history of mankind. Wherever men have progressed or are progressing in this worldly knowledge or skills—study of society, military science, the art of government or the fine arts such as sculpture—there you find the impact of ancient Greece.

Bengalis over the last half century had drawn inspiration from the Greek masters as reflected in European literature. Nineteenth century Europe was the heir and pupil of ancient Greece. Vivekananda quoted with approval a contemporary opinion that the Greek mind had created whatever nature had not. Greek religion, a thing of great beauty, might be dead because it was not embodied in scriptures, but its influence was writ large on the religious belief and practice in Europe.[224]

This recognition of unparalleled excellence and mankind's debt to Hellenic civilization was, however, informed by his perception of Europe's basic concerns. The Greek mind, like its modern European heirs, sought the solution of life's problems as 'of all the sacred problems of Being by searching into the external world'. It looked outwards because the Greek civilization flowered in an invigorating climate and a natural setting 'which was more beautiful than sublime, generous yet simple.'[225] Its concern, inevitably, was to analyse the external world. Hence it produced 'all the sciences of generalization', an expression used by the Swami to mean ideas and theories which offered general explanations of nature and human conduct. Looking outwards, the excellence of their thought was manifest in a high capacity for 'expression',[226] i.e. articulation. Modern Europeans had inherited this great gift.

But the Greeks, unlike the ancient Indians who came of the same stock, did not look inwards or make any serious effort to pry into the secrets of existence beyond the life of the body. Their ideas on life after death were childish and puerile, their heaven 'very much like this world minus all its sorrows'.[227] Their ideas of religion went no further. By contrast, the Hindus, living in a world surrounded by the sublime Himalayas and great forests and watered by mighty rivers, lived in humble awe of their environment. Even the climate discouraged physical effort and their thoughts turned inwards, into an enquiry into the nature of self and existence, unconcerned with whatever was not sublime. India hence missed out on the great qualities developed in ancient Greece and inherited by her nineteenth-century heirs— enterprise, love of freedom, self-reliance, an unshakeable capacity for endurance, practical skills, social solidarity and a hunger for progress.[228]

Vivekananda was convinced that a mingling of the two cultures was at the root of much that had happened in the world since that historic encounter. 'Once in remote antiquity the encounter between Indian philosophy and Greek energy triggered off the emergence of great nations like the Romans, the Iranians et al. After Alexander's conquests, the clash of these two mighty waterfalls flooded half the world with spiritual waves which bore the names of Jesus and others.' The civilization of modern Europe was similarly founded on a fresh mingling of cultures traceable to the rise of Islam. The time had come for a revitalization of human society through the mutual assimilation of the two cultures—the East and the West.

The Swami's vision of the future—in which India's spiritual heritage would play a crucial role and his people, poor and without self-respect, living in a state unworthy of their inheritance, would learn from the West the latter's concern with life on this earth—was never very far from his mind. His encomium on Greece occurs in an essay entitled *Vartaman samasya* (Today's Problem). And while his historical perceptions underlined the fruitful encounter between Europe and India, his 'East' did frequently encompass other regions of Asia—an expression of a new awareness of the 'they' and 'us' dichotomy. His cultural self-assertion included especially the world of Islam. The new mood in Indian nationalism which he shared and fostered was anxious to claim the Indo-Islamic heritage as its own, a basis of pan-Indian unity. Hence his emphasis on the Arab role in creating modern Europe. The new-found pride in an Asian identity was also expressed in his admiration for Japan and the future he saw for China. In short, there is almost always an ideological context to his observations on the West—even when he responded with spontaneous admiration to facets of western life, past or present.

Unqualified admiration was, of course, not the dominant note in his sweeping surveys of the European past. Vivekananda was concerned on the one hand with explaining the present in relation to Europe's victories in her quest for power over nature and other nations and on the other with trying to visualize a cultural synthesis between the East and the West. In all this his statements repeatedly emphasize certain value-oriented notions. The *asura* inheritance of Europe, i.e., aggressive energy and a proneness to violence generated by the life-experience of non-agricultural societies, is a major theme in his understanding of western history. That inheritance was seen to be modified by the intermingling of many elements, ethnic and cultural. The word 'barbarian' occurs repeatedly in this context. This preoccupation with the barbarian ancestry of modern Europe was very much a part of nineteenth-century Bengali perceptions. Bhudev and Bankim, as noted above, return to this theme repeatedly. But even in his emphasis on the barbarian element in Europe's ethnic composition, Vivekananda underlines his perception of synthesis, especially that fact that the wild medieval ancestors of the highly civilized nineteenth-century westerners were but the *asuras* from Asia's steppes and wild terrain. But Asia, to his understanding, had made other more direct contributions to the evolution of western culture, sometimes as a giver of gifts, at others as a powerful catalyst. His hopes of a future world civilization with a universal religion based on a Vedantic synthesis found support in this analysis.

In his travelogue of a journey to Europe, he described the Mediterranean as an area almost uniquely redolent with memories of the past where the civilizations of three continents had met and intermingled.[229] This was where modern civilization was born, the end result of a 'grand synthesis' spread over many centuries. 'Different races, people with different colours of the skin, many cultures, traditions of learning and ways of life' contributed to that synthesis. Egypt, Babylon, the Phoenicians, the Jews, Iran, Greece and Rome among others contributed to it, bringing together the genius of the Aryans and the Semites. The likelihood of a direct Indian contribution to the early origins of the Mediterranean and, through that channel, modern western culture was not overlooked. Vivekananda referred to the theory that 'Punt', the land beyond the seas wherefrom the Egyptians first came according to their legends, was Malabar. Their first King, Menes, had a name remarkably similar to that of Manu, the father of the human species in Hindu myths.

The waves of migration from Asia was a second source of the synthesis.[230] These migrants, he pointed out, were barbarians, who remained for the most part in a state of utter barbarism. They developed only a few isolated islands of civilized life. The founders of Roman civilization were also described as barbarians who defeated the culturally advanced Etruscans and adopted their knowledge, skills and various arts to become civilized themselves. Their empire was based first on the conquest of European peoples, mostly in a state of barbarism. Beyond the frontiers to the north were other barbarians, pushed by fresh waves of Asian *asuras* to descend on the Roman Empire, effete through an excess of wealth and luxury. Asia contributed a positive element of civilization through the Jews, conquered by Rome and scattered all over their empire. They brought with them their new faith, Christianity. Europe was born out of this continuous conflict, the advent of many *asura* races and the clash of differing systems of belief. The ethnic products of the new synthesis included many racial types—ranging from dark to very fair, blondes and brunettes and with a variety of eye colours. Some were very similar to the Hindus in their features, others were flat-faced like the Chinese. But they had one characteristic in common. They were 'barbarians, utter barbarians', continually at war with one another. The northern barbarians were but brigands and pirates who seized every chance to cause havoc among their more civilized counterparts in the south. These hordes of brutish barbarians—their kings and queens included—came under the authority of the two heads of the Christian churches, the Pope in Rome and the Patriarch at Constantinople. Bhudev conceded an element of civilizing influence to the formal acceptance of Christianity by Europe (though he did not think that Christ's message went very deep into the European soul). It is not clear that Vivekananda had a similarly positive assessment of the Christian impact on Europe's middle ages. He referred somewhat disrespectfully to the authority exercized by Popes and Patriarchs. His exact words are: '*sakaler upar kartali chalate laglo*' ([they] started bossing over everyone).

The truly civilizing influence on medieval Europe was again traced to Asian sources, specifically to a new manifestation of the region's spiritual inheritance. Vivekananda built on the scholarly opinion of the time that the pre-Islamic Arabs were uncivilized, 'nearly brutish' as he put it. These brutish hordes were transformed through the advent of a man of God, Muhammad, and they burst upon the world with irresistible energy. The tidal wave hit Europe from both east and west, and the Arabs brought to Europe's barbarians two distinct inheritances, the Greek and the Indian. The Moorish conquerors generated a high civilization in Spain. They established the first universities in the West, drawing pupils from Italy, France and even far off Britain. Princes and nobles now came to Spain to learn from the Arabs their arts of war and civilization. The Swami traced the origins of European feudalism itself to Arab models. He described the 'Muslim' system of fiefs in conquered territories, the king parcelling out the land among his generals, keeping a chunk for himself and the generals retaining armed men for the king's service in lieu of paying revenue for their land. But he noted a difference between the 'Muslim' system and its European imitation. Evidently, the former was more equitable in his eyes because it encompassed countervailing powers—the king, feudatories, armed men and the rest of the king's subjects. In Europe, the kings and nobles reduced the rest to near slavery. He was under the impression that every person in Europe was under the firm control of one noble or another, obliged to fight whenever called upon to do so.

Asia contributed powerfully to the growth of Europe's medieval civilization through one more climacteric episode—the Crusades. He traced the origins of that story to the emergence of another group of *asuras* from Asia, the Turks or Tartars as he called them. He did not have for these barbarians the same respectful regard as he had for the Arabs, despite the former's achievement as conquerors and conversion to Islam. To his knowledge, this particular branch of *asuras*, with one exception, the Mughals in India,[231] had little concern with the arts of civilization. War was their sole preoccupation. 'One seldom encounters warlike prowess where this ethnic strain is absent.' The Russians owed their fighting qualities to the Tartar component of their ancestry, because they were three-quarters Tartar. The Tartar conquests once covered more than half the civilized world. A vast territory stretching from Egypt and Southeastern Europe to India and China was once under their sway.

Vivekananda, quite pragmatically, traced the origins of the Crusades to Turkish expansion which was responsible for the destruction of the Caliphate, the occupation of the Christian holy places, the embargo on pilgrimage and attacks on Christians. This view of the Crusades, a popular version of scholarly consensus on the subject at that time, was supplemented by an explanation which expressed the Swami's highly individual perception. He thus described Europe's response to the Turkish attacks on Christians. 'The leaders of the Christian faith were infuriated; Europe was full of their barbarian followers. The kings incited their subjects. Hordes of Europe's barbarians marched to Asia Minor to liberate Jerusalem. Some perished fighting among themselves, some died of diseases, the rest were decimated by the Muslims. But the wild barbarians were in a fury—more the Muslims slaughtered, more they kept coming. It was the unflinching wrath of primitives. Sometimes they plundered their own side; if food was in short supply, they made a meal of Muslims. The English King, Richard, it is said, had an especial liking for Muslim flesh.'[232] The conflict, in his view, ended as all conflicts between civilization and barbarism would do; here he contradicted his own view that an infusion of *asura* blood was essential for martial ardour. However, he concludes, that though Jerusalem was not liberated, Europe began to learn from Asia her arts of civilization. The 'skin-clad eaters of raw flesh'—the English, the French, the Germans, etc—started their journey towards a better way of life, emulating the example of their Muslim enemies. Some Crusaders, like the Knights Templars, even acquired a taste for Asia's philosophical thought. Their ideas approximated the doctrines of Vedanta and they mocked the crudity of medieval Christian thought.

By the end of the middle ages, the basic traits and pronenesses of European civilization were fully articulated. A temperate climate and hilly sea-coasts provided the environmental background. The human component consisted in the end product of endless intermingling among many racial groups, the *devatas* and the *asuras* both contributing their fair shares. The people of Europe, strong and war-like, were always at war; to fight, in self-defence and in defence of the faith, was their dominant concern. 'He who could yield the sword was supreme; he who could not, surrendered his liberty to live under the shadow of some hero's sword.' The other concern was trade. 'For this civilization, the sword was the means [for the attainment of given ends], heroism the aid, and enjoyment [of life] in this world and the next the only end.' As he once told his disciple, Sarat Chakravarti, the Europeans were the children of Virochana, the great demon of Indian mythology, who concluded that *atman*, the Self, was nothing but the human body.[233]

This end product was contrasted with the Indian ideal—a settled agrarian society's love of peace and the quiet life which allowed the necessary respite for thought and the civilizing arts. Pleasure acquired a mental and intellectual rather than a physical connotation in this context. The ephemeral, hence illusory, character of this life on earth was noted and peace sought in intellection and the renunciation of worldly things. 'The sword was placed at the feet of learning and virtue, its only task was to defend virtue and afford protection.' *Dharma*, the norms of righteous conduct, reigned supreme and everyone was free under its ever vigilant eyes. It should be noted that Vivekananda himself repeatedly questioned this idealized picture, especially in his emphasis on India's record of utter disregard for the rights of her downtrodden masses. But he invoked the image of a luminous serenity and a just society as a positive counterpoise to his dark picture of Europe's violent past.

The emphasis on violence in his interpretation of European history of course had a contemporary referent—the aggression which led to colonial expansion. This theme crops up invariably in almost every major statement on the West in nineteenth-century Bengali writings. Marie Louise Burke has culled from the American press reports of Vivekananda's several angry outbursts on the unchristian aggression of the Christian nations, especially the English and brother Mahendra tells us how the Swami once lambasted an uncivil heckler in London with an account of Britain's violent misdeeds in India. In his summing up of European history he returns to this favourite theme of nineteenth-century Bengali writings on Europe. 'Whenever any country falls into their clutches, the Europeans destroy the aboriginals and live in comfort (in their land) ... . Having no home of their own, they wander around in a desperate quest of livelihood and look around for people to plunder and massacre ...'. 'When have the Europeans done any good to any non-European people,' he asked. They had never shown any capacity to civilize relatively backward people, he added, in an obvious reference to vaunted western claims and what, to his understanding, was a very different story—the evidence of India's history. He referred to the destruction of native populations in Australia, New Zealand, the Pacific islands, and Africa which were slaughtered like wild animals. 'Progress of civilization', western-style, simply meant gaining one's ends by justifying what was evidently unjust. Europe lauded Stanley's sense of justice in flogging his Muslim guards for stealing 'a mouthful of food'. To Europeans in the throes of their famous progress, suicide, adultery and abandoning one's wife and children were but 'minor misdemeanours'.

Europe, he concluded, sought triumphant survival at the cost of other people's lives. India's Aryans had instead attempted to elevate all elements in human society through the caste system. The purpose of that institution was to provide a niche for everybody according to their level of development as a basis for steady growth into high civilization. 'In Europe, the powerful triumph, the weak perish; every social code in India is meant to protect the weak.'[234] To repeat, Vivekananda presented a very different picture of Indian social reality, past and present, while admonishing his countrymen to set their house in order.

His statements on the origins and character of modern Europe, however, express sophisticated perceptions of a very complex reality, though here too his low opinion of the Christian influence and deep regard for the Greek heritage are quite evident.[235] He referred to Rome's discipleship at the feet of the defeated Greeks and translated the nineteenth-century notions of the Dark Ages in terms of a historical phase when learning and civilization disappeared, its chronological beginning identified with Europe's conversion to Christianity. There is an implicit hint of causal connection made explicit in his assessment of Christianity as a historical force, discussed below. He believed with his contemporaries that the fall of Constantinople, the westward flight of Greek scholars, and the revival of Greek learning explained the Renaissance and the beginning of civilization in England, Germany, and France. Italy was reborn. For the rest of Europe, revival of Greek learning included the first birth of civilization.[236] He emphasized in this context the role of critical scholarship. Textual criticism and later the material sciences expressed, in his opinion, the growing refinement of the European intellect.

He placed a startling construction on one product of this refinement—
the Reformation. He considered the message of renunciation for all and
sundry, received from the Buddha in India and from Jesus in Europe, as a
prescription for disaster so far as human societies were concerned. The
pragmatic good sense of the Indian tradition had provided for four-fold
objectives of human life which included material ends and bodily pleasures.
Besides, the caste system acknowledged the need for different codes suited
to differences in aptitudes and inclinations. The ideal of renunciation had
led to a precipitous decline in civilization—in ancient India as well as medieval
Europe. 'Afterwards, fortunately for them, the Europeans became
Protestant' and shook off the religion of Jesus; they breathed a sigh of
relief.'[237]

A straightforward preference for France and her civilization also coloured
his understanding of modern European history. His direct experience of
that country was limited to a few months of sojourn, but evidently this brief
encounter had made a profound impression. In explaining the historical
evolution of Europe since the Renaissance, he introduced an unorthodox
concept—the relative age of societies as a determining influence. By the
time of the Renaissance, the Italians were an ageing people as were the
Indians around the same time. The efflorescence of Indian civilization under
the Mughals was a flash in the pan for the decrepit ancient society lacked
the energy to sustain it. Similarly, the Italians of the Renaissance showed
signs of life only briefly and then went to sleep again. The youthful and
vigorous French people became the true inheritors of this new civilization,
which later vivified the culture of other European nations. He attributed
the spread of western influence in Asia also to the French. The waves
traceable to the Renaissance thus reached even India's shores. The cultural
influences at work in Japan were also traced to the same source.[238]

His empathy with the poor and the downtrodden inspired a measure of
enthusiasm for the French Revolution. His brief account of revolutionary
France contains no criticism of the violence. All his implied criticism is
directed at the 'oppressors of the people'—the kings and the aristocrats. His
concluding statements on the revolutionary wars are adequate evidence of
his sympathies: 'Liberty, Equality, Fraternity—the barrel of guns and the
sharp edge of swords drove this message deep into the bones and marrow of
Europe. Thereafter, Napoleon became emperor: his object was to make the
great Kingdom of France strongly united and fully equipped.' He described

Napoleon's downfall and France's defeat in the Franco-German War in a tone of deep regret.[239]

His enquiry into the origins of modern European societies directed his attention to the theory of evolution. He noted that the theory was widely accepted as a satisfactory explanation for the emergence of natural species as also for the development of human cultures from rudimentary beginnings to the level of high civilization. The theory had, however, other implications for him linked to his ideological concerns. In all systems of belief other than the Indian—he pointed out—the different species of plant and animal life were considered distinct creations of the Deity, unrelated to one another. The Indian seers who, looked inward rather than outward, unlike the western thinkers, realized early that the apparently unrelated species were in fact closely interlinked—that indeed all created things and the Deity too were so related in an all-encompassing unity. European scholarship had reached the same understanding through the material sciences. The theory of evolution was one expression of this emerging perception of unity, though neither India nor the West had yet discovered how the One became many. If evolution was seen to be one expression of Advaita, non-duality, one of its end results was a movement towards the grand synthesis, the millennial destiny of mankind; plant and animal species moved to new habitats through human intervention, leading to cross-breeding with the indigenous varieties and the emergence of new species. Thus both nature and her product, man, were on the high road to the close intermingling of apparently discrete elements.[240]

Unity in the Infinite might be the only metaphysical truth and harmonious synthesis man's ultimate destiny, yet in the interim ceaseless conflict, born of nationalism and the aggression inherent in western culture, were identified as the dominant facts of nineteenth-century European politics. Franco-German rivalry was at the heart of this conflict—with France longing to avenge her defeat and her rival's strength, based on newly centralized authority, rushing towards new heights of power. All German-speaking territories excepting Austria were under her control. Germany was the first country to introduce compulsory education on pain of punishment. By the nineties of the century, she was reaping the benefits of the seed thus sown. Her infantry was the best in Europe, her navy tried hard to excel all rivals, and her manufactures, the Swami believed, had already proved superior to England's. German products and entrepreneurs were on the ascendant in England's own colonies. Other nations had accepted the leadership of Germany in China.[241]

The decline of Austria was noted as another potent fact likely to influence the course of European history. Her aspiration to status and glory was still there, but the power to realize it was gone. Her defeat by Prussia precipitated her decline. If Turkey was the sick old man of Europe, the Swami commented, Austria was her sick old woman. As the only surviving Catholic emperor in Europe—Spain and Portugal did not count—the Austrian Habsburgs enjoyed Papal support. But the Pope's political power, though not his authority in religion, was confined to the Vatican and Italy, having shaken off the Austrian yoke, was now her enemy. But newly independent Italy was herself in deep trouble as her military and imperial ambitions, prompted by Britain, had only led to heavy debts and defeat at the hands of the Abyssinian emperor.[242]

If struggle for supremacy was one source of conflict, the upsurge of nationalism—the urge to political unification of people belonging to the same race and religion and speaking the same language—was another. The Swami felt sure that Germany would try to swallow the German-speaking part of the Austrian empire after the old emperor's death. This would be resisted by Russia and since Turkey was Russia's traditional enemy, the German emperor had of late become especially cordial to Europe's sick man. Vivekananda's venture into political analysis reveals a shrewd insight into the state of international relations in the late 1890s. Written in 1899, his comments anticipate correctly the alignment of forces in the War which would break out in another fifteen years.[243]

Nationalist aspirations, he explained, were one major factor in the decline of both Austria and Turkey. Neither had the strength to weld together the many ethnic groups under their control into any effective unity. The Hungarian and Greek elements in the Austrian empire were never fully integrated with the German-speaking subjects. The Hungarians were ethnically close to the Turks and after repeated struggles remained only nominally subject to Austria. Serbia and Bulgaria had similarly achieved virtual autonomy though still formally under Turkey. The freedom attained at the cost of much bloodshed still demanded a heavy price. Since the whole of Europe had become mutually hostile armed camps, in order to survive the small nations on their way to independence also had to arm—a luxury they could ill afford. Vivekananda traced the new concern for military preparedness to France's defeat in the Franco-Prussian War. She introduced conscription out of an angry desire for revenge and from a sense of insecurity. Germany who had 'provoked a lion' felt constrained to reinforce her armed strength in reply. Other nations followed suit, inspired by mutual apprehension. Every country with the

exception of England had introduced conscription. Vivekananda wondered
if England would not follow suit after her experience of the Boer War.
Meanwhile, she was concentrating on her navy and colonization. The Balkan
states, emerging out of the Turkish empire, were as poor as India, and yet
they were forced to build up European-style armies, complete with highly
expensive modern weapons. Their peasant populations dressed in rags so
that the nation could pay for this white elephant and their cities teemed
with soldiers in gaudy uniforms. Wherever one went in Europe, one saw
'soldiers, soldiers and more soldiers'.

Commenting on the same phenomenon a few years earlier, Bhudev had
sought to draw a moral lesson regarding what India should learn to avoid
from the example of the West. But the *sanyasi*, inspired by the manifestation
of *rajas* in the West and her ideals of liberty, underlined a very different
message. 'Independence is preferable to slavery in golden chains a million
times even if the former meant semi-starvation and tattered rags for one's
apparel. The slave's fate is hell, in this life and in the next. The Serbs,
Bulgars *et al* are the butts of the Europeans' ridicule. The latter poke fun at
their mistakes and inefficiency. But can anyone learn to work in a day after
such long servitude? Of course they will make mistakes—do so a hundred
times; they will learn from their errors and once they have learnt, they will
do things right. Even the very weak becomes strong and the ignorant wise if
they are given responsibility.'[244] Acquisition of strength rather than moral
rectitude was at the core of Vivekananda's message to his countrymen. He
looked to Europe for object lessons which could rejuvenate India. At times
he found it in unexpected places like the Balkan states emerging from
centuries of alien rule.

His ardent patriotism notwithstanding, Vivekananda had an amused
awareness of the absurdities it could lead to. He made ribald fun of Hindu
revivalist claims to scientific reasons for popular superstitions. The European
patriot, he noted, could be as stupid at times. He described, tongue in
cheek, the new concern in France for old glory after her humiliating defeat
by Germany. One manifestation of this concern was the cult of Napoleon,
which produced *inter alia* a spate of books and plays on the Emperor. The
Swami's friend, Sarah Bernhardt, had made a hit in a new play on the
tragic fate of Napoleon's son—his virtual incarceration at Schonbrunn, the
attempted escape and premature death. *L'Aiglon* had become a craze with
patriotic French men and women. Vivekananda was witness to a bizarre
episode on a visit to the Schonbrunn. A group of French tourists eagerly

wished to see the rooms where the Baby Eagle had slept and played and an Austrian janitor—to whom Napoleon was no doubt a *bête noir*—showed them round, his face glum but his reluctance repressed for worldly considerations.[245]

The less amusing aspects of aggressive nationalism were of course not overlooked. The warships of Europe's powerful nations were seen to be always on the move, to fish wherever the water was troubled and secure the self-interest, trade and dominance of the countries concerned. Fuel, especially coal, had acquired a new importance for war would stop access to the sources of supply. Every country sought sources of coal under its own control. The most lucrative sources were under English occupation. Next came France, and the rest did their best to secure their own sources by hook or by crook. Since the Suez Canal was under French control, the English maintained a firm hold on Aden, while the others had got their footholds along the Red Sea. Italy, free after centuries of servitude, also felt the urge to conquer. Since imperial aspirations were not on in Europe, and Asia was being swallowed by the lords of the jungle, only a few bits of Africa were left for the latecomers. Italian hopes in that direction first shrank before France's menacing posture. Their next venture from their toe-hold on the Red Sea—a British gift—the war with Abyssinia, fared worse.[246] Russia, whose Christian affiliations had affinities with that of Abyssinia, was said to have had a hand in the matter.

The above account of nineteenth century power games and mutual aggression paraphrases Vivekananda's description, written in very racy Bengali which is difficult to translate. He considered the clay feet of the gods with his characteristic lack of reverence for the mighty. At least in this particular passage, however, he passed no moral judgement. There is only a faint hint of a chuckle. The Swami had seen through the pretences of high civilization.

He interpreted the long-term trends in human societies, especially those of Europe, in terms of another paradigm, the division of mankind into four varnas. As a tool of analysis, he found it relevant to all societies and all times.[247] I have noted above his admiration for the caste system as a civilizing institution. Elsewhere, he described the origins of the division of labour enshrined in the caste system as follows:[248] 'One group of people began to produce consumer goods using their hands or skills. One group guarded the goods so produced. Everyone began to exchange these commodities and

some smart alecs appeared from nowhere to appropriate the lion's share as
their pay for carrying these things from one place to another [Thus] one
person cultivated, another guarded, a third carried the product and a fourth
bought it. He who tended the plough received peanuts [for his troubles];[249]
he who acted as the guard, seized a part of the produce by force at the very
outset. The bulk went to the trader, the one who transported the stuff. He
who purchased, had to pay for all these people! The guard came to be
known as the king, the porter as the merchant. These two did no work, but
lived off the fat of the land by trickery.[250] He who produced the goods
clutched an empty stomach and prayed to God for his mercy.'

In *Vartaman Bharat* (India Today), he described a scheme of social
evolution in which the four varnas succeed one another as repositories of
power and authority. Though the direct referent of this analysis, at times
abstract, was the Indian past, its universal context and specific relevance to
the western experience were made quite explicit.

The rule of each varna we are told had its plus and minus points. The
priests or Brahmins ruled by virtue of their intellect and sanctity of character
based on self-restraint and spirituality. They alone had access to the
transcendental reality, a yearning for which was built into the human psyche.
Their power was thus not based on physical prowess. Worshipped like the
gods, they had no need to earn their living by the sweat of their brow. Kings
intoxicated with power and wealth bowed before the priests' sanctity. As
the first source of enlightenment and the harbinger of a consciousness that
transcended crudely material concerns, the priests were the first men to be
worshipped in every society. But the very nature of their profession contained
the seeds of deception and deviant conduct. Power as expressed through
things material was obvious and comprehensible to everyone. It allowed no
scope for any obscurity. But where its container and field of expression was
the intangible world of the human mind and its source such elusive things as
a mere word enunciated in a particular way, an incantation or some mental
exercise, when even material ends like success or revenge were sought
through occult non-material means, the practitioners tended to live in an
obscure world where nothing had the clarity and directness of daylight. The
end product of such preoccupations was disingenuous narrowness of outlook
and extreme intolerance born of envy. The person who claims sole access to
deities, the givers of all desired gifts, or the power to fight back unseen evil
and all these in ways not obvious to others, develops a vested interest in
secrecy. Selfishness and hypocrisy are natural results of such secrecy.

Knowledge itself declines through lack of open cultivation and free exchange. What survives of it stagnates, because the priests trace it to divine origin. A degenerate priesthood, devoid of learning and all manly virtues, desperately tries to hold on to inherited privileges. Hence the conflict with other peoples.[251] To repeat, the immediate referent of this powerful castigation was no doubt India's Brahmins. His many comments on Christian priests and missionaries suggest that he saw them in a very similar light.

The second caste, the Kshatriya warrior, was described in terms which leave one in no doubt as to their meaning: '... one finds in kings, lions among men, all the good and evil qualities of the king of animals. On the one hand, the lion's sharp nails tear apart without hesitation the heart of animals who feed on leaves and grass so that the king may eat his fill. On the other hand, the poet tells us, a lion, even if famished, would not kill for food the baby fox that had sought his protection'.[252] The Kshatriya virtues and vices may be the obvious referents of the metaphor, but the British, or the western, lion destroying peace-loving races could not have been far from the Swami's mind.

The warriors' advent was seen to have other implications as well for social evolution. The divinity attributed to the king implied a willing concession of godly pleasures. Hence the grand palaces, royal gardens, great works of art, and costly silk which replaced the simpler and more natural habitat and articles of consumption. Intellectuals and artists abandoned physical labour for more refined pursuits and created the arts to entertain the kings. Urban life developed around the courts, while the villages were in eclipse. And just as the priests seek a monopoly of all knowledge, kings try to monopolize power leading to inevitable conflicts between the ruler and the ruled. Their outcome determines the course of social evolution. Vivekananda stretched a point to claim that such cleansing conflicts were not unknown in Indian history, but his 'model' was clearly derived from the western experience.

The western referent becomes most explicit in his discussion of the third phase in the evolution of society—when the Vaisya, the trader, assumes supreme power.[253] If the Brahmin's authority derived from the power bestowed by his learning and the Kshatriya warrior had ruled by the might of his sword, the Vaisya supremacy was based on the infinite power of money thus described in a dramatic statement: 'Oh Brahmin', says the Vaisya, 'by its grace I shall buy forthwith all your spiritual wealth and religious merit, all your knowledge and learning. Oh King, through its benign favour, all your weaponry and valour will now be employed to serve my ends. Those factories, very high and extensive, are my beehives. Look, how the Sudras in the guise of numberless worker bees are storing honey there ceaselessly. But who will drink that honey? I. When the time is ripe, I squeeze out all the honey from their bottom.' Under the Brahmins and the Kshatriyas, society had accumulated learning and culture. Under Vaisya rule, all energy was focused on accumulating wealth. It had the power to beguile all the four castes. The Vaisya is forever careful lest the Brahmin seizes his wealth by fraud or the Kshatriya by force. The traders are forever united to protect their self-interest. They terrorize the world with the power of credit. They are forever vigilant so that royal power may not create any obstacle to their accumulation of wealth. Hence their anxiety to curtail royal authority. But they have no desire to see that power descend to the Sudras.

The Vaisyas were the great conveyers of civilization. They went everywhere carrying the art and learning of one country to another. The arteries of trade acted as so many veins carrying the accumulated lifeblood of culture to all parts of the human society. Civilization benefited thereby. The world Vivekananda knew was firmly under the control of western Vaisyas.

Vivekananda admired the immense power of western capitalism and appreciated its contribution to world culture. He however refused to concede all its claims to have helped mankind's progress towards a higher destiny. He was far from impressed by the way democracy functioned in the West. Senates, parliaments, vote by ballot etcetera merely camouflaged one universal phenomenon—all societies were controlled by the powerful, driving the rest like so many sheep in any direction they liked. But, he asserted in a patriotic mood, power in Indian society belonged to the virtuous and one did without the rigmarole of majority vote and the like. Indians lost out thereby on their chances of political education, but they were also free from 'the band of thieves who sucked people's blood in every European country and thrived on it'. He described European politics as a 'feast of bribery, robbery in broad daylight', which destroyed all one's faith in human nature. The reins of government were firmly in the hands of the rich who robbed the people and then sent them off to distant lands as soldiers. Victory means more wealth for them bought at the cost of poor people's lives.[254]

Vivekananda looked forward to the time when the Sudras, the toiling masses, would inherit the earth.[255] The power and wealth of Brahmins, Kshatriyas, and Vaisyas alike were based on their toil, but they had no share in the wealth they created. They constituted the vast majority of mankind, but they were still incapable of solidarity and hence naturally subservient to others, but there was hope. A two-way vertical mobility had become a feature of modern societies. Sudras in high places and the high castes in lowly occupations were no longer a rarity. History had many examples of such mobility. Rome's 'Sudra' slaves had emerged as Europe's valiant Kshatriya warriors. Once mighty China was well on her way to Sudra status, while Japan had emerged from that lowly niche and was climbing fast towards the rank of the high varnas in the hierarchy of nations. Thus, if Sudra nations could aspire to Kshatriya or Brahminhood, indeed there was hope for the downtrodden masses. A time would come, Vivekananda prophesied, when the Sudras would dominate mankind. They would do so, not through their transformation into any higher caste, i.e., as priests, warriors or merchants, but in their very role as the toiling masses. The transformation would begin, he said with uncanny foresight, in Russia and China.[256] The first light of the new dawn was already there on Europe's horizon. Socialism, anarchism, nihilism *et al*, were the harbingers of the revolution to come and the haves were worried beyond measure by these portents. Both Bankim and Bhudev commented on the egalitarian ideologies of Europe. The former declared his early enthusiasm for the egalitarian cause as misconceived after mature consideration. Bhudev always regarded it as unnatural, a perversion of generous sentiments. Vivekananda felt no need to qualify his hopes for the time when the poor would inherit the earth in a strictly material sense. The empathy developed during his years of wandering in India was not confined to the Indian masses. The Swami had two lines of exit from the limiting boundaries of his patriotism—the transcendental doctrines of Vedanta and a passionate sense of identity with starving people all over the world. Neither was a basis for objective assessment, but if they caused distorted vision, the distortion expressed systems of value very different from the xenophobic resentment against the ruling race's advantages in civilization.

His hopes for the world's Sudras were however qualified by a realistic appraisal of trends in western society. The fact that caste in Europe depended not on birth but on one's work and achievement was identified as a barrier to the rise of Sudra power. The masses everywhere had very limited scope for upward mobility. The few exceptional persons who succeeded in acquiring wealth or high education were absorbed into the upper strata of society. The masses derived no benefit from their achievements. Moreover, the worst failures from the upper strata increased the number of the underprivileged.

The Swami's prognosis was based on a belief central to his entire way of thinking. Whatever the source of power in society—be it learning, force of arms or wealth—it derived ultimately from the masses of the population. Alienation from this fundamental source of strength meant weakness for the leadership. This is how priestly power, weakened by their alienation, had fallen before the warriors' onslaught and the Kshatriyas in their turn had to surrender their authority to the traders who had secured the people's support. Now that the Vaisyas had gained their ends, they were busy creating a chasm between themselves and the masses 'and this is where the seed of ... [their] destruction is being sown.' He traced Europe's emergence as a high civilization to the education and emancipation, however limited, of the masses. To his understanding, the flotsam and jetsam of other countries, discarded as so much rubbish, were the true backbone of American society. This perception was obviously linked to his understanding of the Indian problem which inspired his social ideology. The relevant passage concludes: 'It does not matter if the aristocrat, the learned, the wealthy listen to you or not ... their function is merely decorative ...'[257]

If caste in its western incarnation was a major trait of European civilization, a more obvious feature of western life embodying its characteristic strength and limitations was Christianity. There are apparent contradictions in Vivekananda's assessment of Europe's religion. His remarks on the subject range from adoration and high praise to almost xenophobic expressions of resentment. In fact, they reflect different levels of perception rather than actual contradiction. The mystical-syncretist content of his religious faith induced an attitude of adoration towards Christ and Christianity. The doctrine and dogma were compared inevitably to Vedantic subtleties and found lacking. The new discipline of higher criticism had raised basic questions disturbing to the believer. Here he found reasons to doubt the Christian claim to superiority which had offended Hindu sensibilities at least since the early decades of the nineteenth century. His criticisms of Christian dogma contain more than a hint of cultural self-assertion—a distinct projection of Hinduism's superior wisdom, refinement and spirituality. Alleged affinities and historic links are stressed in this context. The critical note becomes razor sharp in assessments of Christianity's role in history—the record of fanatical intolerance and un-Christian aggression by Christian nations. The missionaries and their work are attacked in vehement language, which almost suggests a measure of intolerance he otherwise rejected as an unacceptable component of religious ideology.·

I have discussed in the first part of this chapter young Narendra's deep admiration for the life of Christ, the fact that he translated *The Imitation of Christ* into Bengali, and found solace in the Bible in his days of extreme poverty. Celebrating Christmas Eve became a part of the Mission's ritual calendar.[258] The rationale of his criticisms is traceable in the first place to a distinction which was of great importance to him—between religion and creeds. 'Religion', he explained, 'is the acceptance of all existing creeds seeing in them the same striving toward the same destination. Creed is something antagonistic and combative. There are different creeds because there are different people, and the creed is adapted to the commonwealth where it furnishes what people want. As the world is made up of infinite variety of persons of different natures ... so these people take to themselves that form of belief in the existence of a great and good moral law which is best fitted for them. Religion recognizes and is glad of the existence of all these forms, because of the beautiful underlying principle.'[259] The principle enunciated in this passage, and the Swami's comments on the Christian creed, do not indicate a total acceptance of other ways of religious life. Like the two other thinkers discussed in this volume, he too was unhappy with the Christian doctrine of renunciation as the highest goal for all men irrespective of their personalities and conditions in life. He made a distinction between 'true Christianity' and dogma. The former, it appears, he identified with the essential teaching of Jesus—both moral and spiritual. 'Dogma' was the elaborate system of beliefs developed by the Church over the centuries. He had little patience with the latter. The notion that souls were immortal but had a finite beginning was to him a crude and erroneous idea.[260] The sacrament—the transmutation of bread and wine into Christ's flesh and blood—was described as a ritual traceable to primitive practice with cannibalistic nuances and hence repellent.[261] He detested the continuous reference to blood in Christian preaching.[262] In one speech, he described the Christian creed as 'horrible, barbarous, savage', not because of its symbolic preoccupation with blood, but in view of a perceived crudity in the admonition, 'do unto others as you would be done by'. He saw in this adage not altruism but an egocentric concern with self-interest. The Christian conception of a personal Deity and a heaven from where the good Christian could gaze down from time to time 'into the other place and see the difference' was also ridiculed. He contrasted this with the Hindu doctrine 'that all non-self is good and all self is bad'.[263]

Such visceral responses occur more often in his lectures and casual statements than in his systematic written comments on Christianity. His impatience with Christian claims to superior rationality is however recorded as part of his considered opinion. 'Now there is a craze in every country to find scientific evidence for the absurd religious myths', he wrote apropos of an American missionary's claim that science had proved the legend of Moses and his followers crossing the Red Sea on foot to be true.[264] In a more serious review, he summed up the results of nineteenth century Biblical studies and higher criticism, questioning many popular beliefs regarding Christianity. He referred to the basic affinities of all Semitic faiths which could be traced back to the ancient Mesopotamian cultures. He noted the barbaric practice of child sacrifice to please the gods and the erotic cults which had developed around the worship of Baal or Moloch. The relatively recent origin of the Old Testament, probably not earlier than 500 BC, the Babylonian sources of its myths and ideas, the absence of any belief in the hereafter or soul are all mentioned in the same work. An unfavourable comparison with the Indian tradition, the latter's antiquity, originality and superior insight into matters spiritual, is implied, though not explicitly made as in his Detroit lecture mentioned above. The belief in a life hereafter, resurrection, and the Devil is traced to Iranian influences and the period when the Jews were ruled by the Medes. The theory that the Judaic Yaveh himself was of Egyptian origin is cited, underscoring the relatively late, derivative and synthetic origins of the Judaeo-Christian faith. The idolatrous traditions of Judaism—the phallic symbol in the temple at Jerusalem and the ball of Ephraim—the sacrifice of the first born, and the institution of temple prostitutes are all described in the same context as if in reply to western criticisms of Hindu idolatry, sexual immorality, and barbaric practices. The results of higher criticism are next cited, questioning the historicity of Christ himself. Vivekananda referred to the silence of the contemporary historians—Josephus, Philo, and Greek writers generally—on Christ, Christians and the crucifixion though they referred even to the minor Jewish   ts of the period. Only three of the four New Testament gospels had stood the test of scientific analysis and even that only as later works copied from some early text. The New Testament doctrines, he added, were already parts of the Jewish religious idiom before the advent of Christ, especially as articulated by preachers like Hillel. He concluded this discussion in a tone of mild ridicule; scholars were gradually unravelling the truth about Christianity, but of course it was easier to make drastic statements about other people's faiths than about one's own.[265]

The element of cultural self-assertion is most explicit in the claim of the Hindu origin for Christianity. The language used, even more than the thesis itself, provides the clinching evidence: 'Our religion is older than most religions and the Christian creed—I do not call it a religion, because of its antagonistic features—came directly from the Hindu religion. It is one of the great offshoots.' He traced specific elements in Catholicism—the confessional, the belief in saints etc.—to Hindu antecedents adding how a Catholic priest, probably Bishop Bigandet, was punished by the church for recognizing the obvious Hindu origins of Christianity.[266] The Christian Mother of God and the Hindu mother goddess were identical in his view—a point made by Bhudev as well. He saw in European life and their treatment of women an element of Sakti worship.[267] In his travelogue, he developed this theme with reference to historical evidence—the influence of Asoka's missionaries to Ptolemaic Egypt on the growth of mystical sects like the Therapeuts, Manichaes etc. and their impact on the development of Christianity.[268]

Despite his perception of affinities between Christianity and the Hindu tradition, he was severely critical of the historical role played by institutionalized Christianity in the West. He refused to concede it any civilizing influence and drew a sharp contrast with Islam in this context. In the first three centuries of its existence, Christianity unlike Islam had hardly made any mark in the world. Even after 'Constantine's sword' established it firmly in the Roman empire, it did little to advance human civilization materially or spiritually. 'How did the Christian religion reward the scholar who proved that the earth was not stationary? When was any scientist approved by Christianity?' Their theological writings had nothing to offer by way of scientific or practical knowledge. The Church remained hostile to 'profane' literature and the modern man who accepted science could not at the same time be a sincere Christian. The New Testament had no words of praise, direct or indirect, for the sciences or the arts. By contrast, there was not a single branch of science or the arts not approved or encouraged in the Quran and the Hadith. Europe's leading thinkers—Voltaire, Darwin, Buchner *et al*—were cursed by Christians. Islam, on the other hand, considered them theists who merely lacked faith in prophethood. If it was a question of tolerance of other cultures, Islam's record was infinitely superior. It had protected aborigines, their languages and their culture and had no record of genocide. But where were the Arabs in Spain and the aborigines in Australia? How had Christians treated the Jews in Europe? The only humane feature of European culture approved by the Gospel was charity. Otherwise, all its progress was through revolt against Christianity. 'If the Christian faith still had its power in Europe, it would have burnt alive scientists like Pasteur and Koch and impaled men like Darwin.' Christianity and civilization had parted ways in modern Europe and civilization was determined to deprive its old enemy, the clergy of their control over educational and other charitable institutions. The creed survived through the adherence of ignorant peasants, for the urban poor were openly hostile to it. In Muslim countries by contrast all institutions were based on Islam and the theologians highly respected as were the teachers of other faiths.[269]

He saw bigotry, intolerance and aggression as the chief traits of historical Christianity. These had nothing to do with Christ's teachings, he was careful to point out.[270] The light of Graeco-Roman culture was extinguished, thanks to Christian bigotry and the Goths' barbarism. Ignorant and bigoted Christians destroyed pagan Alexandria and burnt down her famous library.[271] Their fanaticism sought victims in their own society, to wit, the institution of witch-hunting. Compared to its record of sadism, the custom of *sati* had many redeeming features. The *sati* was an honoured person, not an outcaste.[272] The tradition of intolerance was still fully alive. He found its extreme expression in missionary propaganda, specially in America, against the Hindus, which portrayed them as inhuman savages with mothers throwing their children into the mouths of crocodiles and husbands burning their wives alive.[273] He condemned the methods of conversion which presented a fake picture of Hinduism and took advantage of the poverty of the masses. To him such converts were no better than perverts.[274] The intolerance was not confined to the ignorant missionaries. In explaining the reasons why a Parliament of Religions could not be held in Paris, Vivekananda wrote of the Christians' sectarian bigotry. The Catholics, he pointed out, had come to the Chicago Parliament with hopes of influencing Protestants. Other Christians had seen in that conference a chance to blow their trumpets for the benefit of sundry heathens. But as things had turned out differently, their enthusiasm for a universalist synthesis had suffered a serious setback. The Catholics, dominant in France, had developed a special disinclination.[275]

The Swami's sharpest barbs were aimed as expected at the Christian nations' record of aggression. In a speech at the Chicago Parliament he ridiculed the notion that non-Christians should accept Christianity because the Christian nations were the most prosperous. He remarked that Christian England, in her prosperity, had 'her foot on the neck of 250,000,000 Asiatics'. Prosperity of Christian Europe began with Spain's invasion of Mexico. 'Christianity wins its prosperity by cutting the throats of its fellow men. At such a price the Hindu will not have prosperity'.[276] Evidently, beyond a point, the line of demarcation between religion and politics looked very thin to this Asiatic subject of a Christian nation.

His assessment of Europe's other cultural artifacts is generally marked by admiration and at times an acceptance of values alien to the Indian tradition. This is particularly true of his approach to the fine arts, even though his views on the subject are not free from contradictions. He appreciated the aesthetic sensibility expressed in western lifestyle and regretted its disappearance from the Indian art of living. He admired the western art collectors, but of course the poverty-stricken Indians could not emulate them. He conceded unquestioned superiority to the traditions of painting and sculpture in Europe and added, 'we have always been incompetent in these two fields', citing the examples of the images of the deities as well as Ravi Varma's paintings. Interestingly, he saw some merit in the art of the Bengali *patua* and the gilded paintings of Rajasthan.[277] His sensibilities rejected soulless decoration—the flowery exaggeration of later Sanskrit literature as well as the baroque exuberance of Indian temple sculpture.[278]

His scattered remarks on the subject suggest that he found two very different traditions of art most appealing—classical Greek sculpture and Indian Buddhist art—for two very different reasons. In his brief yet perceptive account of the Greek sculptures at the Louvre, he commented on the 'Asian' element in both Mycenaean and early Hellenic art traced to contact and conflict with Egypt and Babylon. He saw the distinctive feature of Greek art in its effort to imitate nature absent in the Asian traditions. He however found archaic Greek sculptures rather lifeless, with fixed expressions, rigid stances and the drapery lacking in plasticity. He next quoted with evident approval a French art historian who traced the vitality of classical Greek sculpture to its rejection of all formal cannons of art. In recording the critical consensus on the decline of Greek art after Alexander, he expressed his personal distaste for decorativeness and the preoccupation with mere size. He concluded this discussion with a disparaging reference to the later Greek art's proneness to copy old models or, at best, reproduce in exact detail an individual's face.[279]

His dislike for the exact imitation of nature in art is also expressed in his comments on the Dutch paintings at the Kunsthistorisches in Vienna. He saw in these nothing but attempts to copy nature exactly—especially in the still lives, and too little effort to 'unravel beauty'.[280] The implication of this rather cryptic statement is best understood if read with his observations on the nature of art.[281] Art, to deserve the name, must express an idea. One should do this even in making the articles of daily use. Art removed nature's veil to reveal the beauty underneath. Modern art, in India as well as in Europe, had lost all originality in his view for it followed in the footsteps of the photographer. Every culture had its distinctive 'character' expressed in its social mores as much as in the creative arts. He observed a quality of pointed sharpness in Europe's artistic expression. They threw their hands and legs about when they danced, their instrumental and vocal music reminded him of the bayonet's thrusts. Dance and music in India had by contrast a rounded quality, rising and melting like waves.

At this point, he introduced his favourite theme of the contrasted preoccupations of European and Indian culture—with materialism and transcendence respectively. Materialistic Europe accepted nature as the 'primary basis of art'. Cultures which aimed at a transcendent ideal used nature to express the 'identity'. But great excellence was achieved in pursuit of both ends. The best in European art conveyed the feeling of a true segment from nature. The best products of Indian sculpture carried one beyond nature to an ideal world. In the last analysis, he found nothing anywhere else in the world which could be compared with the best in Buddhist sculpture. The statement may express an actual preference natural in a sensitive mystic. But perhaps cultural self-assertion is not entirely absent from it.[282]

His respect for many areas of western scholarship was, however, total. He described in his travelogue the techniques and methods of the new 'scientific history'—specially the use of archaeological and epigraphic evidence and the evaluation of raw data. Research on Egyptology and the ancient Near East and Old Testament studies are mentioned respectfully in this connection. He noted the special contribution of different European nations to particular branches of study. The Germans, the French and the Dutch contributed a great deal to Indology. The English apparently pioneered research in many areas such as Assyriology, Egyptology, Hebraic and Biblical research and then withdrew. He remarked on the persistent inhibitions regarding the critical study of Christianity and cited the bowdlerization of

Maspero's *Histoire ancienne orientale* in its English translation meant to soft pedal conclusions unacceptable to orthodox Christians. But he hoped that the courage of conviction with which western scholars stated brutal truths about other religions would be evident in Biblical studies as well before long.[283] Now that the violent persecution of earlier times was no longer in vogue, scholars had become more outspoken than before. But the threat of social opprobrium had not disappeared. He also discussed the findings of nineteenth-century ethnology which questioned the ancient belief in man's common ancestry. While accepting implicitly the theory of physically distinct racial types, he underlined the conclusion that all races in the modern world were of mixed origin.[284]

He focused more on the achievement of western Indology than on other areas of western scholarship. The lengthy discussions on European social thought found in the writings of Bhudev and Bankim are almost entirely missing here. Vivekananda had a specialist's knowledge of ancient Indian civilization, central to all his intellectual and religious concerns and he commented on western scholarship in the field with assurance and a measure of detachment. At most, he shows a streak of impatience with some European pronouncements on the Indian tradition. There is no trace of the angry rejection one comes across in Bhudev or Bankim.

He recognized a spectrum as well as some evolution over time in the attitudes of European Indologists.[285] He referred to the early and not very well-informed excitement over Sanskritic learning which inspired one scholar to identify Kalidasa's Sakuntala as 'the high watermark of Indian philosophy'. They were followed by a reactionary and mostly ignorant band of critics who 'ridiculed everything from the East'. Their special delight was in attributing everything Indian to the genius of other races. 'Suddenly, on one fine morning, the poor Hindu woke up to find that everything that was his was gone; one strange race had snatched away from him his arts, another his architecture, and a third, whatever there was of his ancient sciences; why, even his religion was not his own!'[286] Then came 'a new type of Sanskrit scholars, reverential, sympathetic and learned'. He considered Max Mueller, whom he described to his disciple as the incarnation of Sayanacharya,[287] the great commentator on the Vedas, as the link between the older type of scholarship and the new. He did not agree with all that the Professor said, e.g., the latter's refusal to acknowledge Hindu influence on ancient Greek thought until he had unquestionable evidence that at least one pre-Alexandrian Greek had learnt Sanskrit. By the same logic, Vivekananda argued, one could not speak of Greek influence on India until one had unquestionable evidence that at least one Indian had learnt Greek.[288] Yet, he acknowledged the great debt Hindus owed him 'for the preservation, spreading, and appreciation of the literature of our forefathers'. If Max Mueller was 'the old pioneer', Paul Deussen was one of the younger avant-garde who moved away from the primarily philogical interest, which 'had hidden long from view the gems of thought and spirituality' to be found in the Sanskrit scriptures. Deussen's interest in the Upanishads was especially welcome because of his training in Greek and modern German philosophy and his courage in declaring openly his high opinion of Vedanta. Such genuine friends of India would help check the petty chauvinism extolling every superstition as well as the demoniac zeal denouncing the received tradition.

His regard for the European Indologists notwithstanding, Vivekananda had serious misgivings about many of their pronouncements. At the Paris Congress of the History of Religions, 1900 he had intended to question the consensus view that Vedic religion centred round the worship of personified material objects—the sun, fire etc. He quoted the Atharvaveda to challenge the identification of the *sivalingam* with the phallus and prove that it was recognized to be one with the Brahman. The theory propounded by a German scholar identifying the *salagrama* as a *yoni* symbol struck him as even more preposterous.[289] He also rejected the view that the Indo-Aryan migrants into India seized by force the land belonging to the aboriginals or that the Ramayana was a mythical account of the Aryan conquest of the barbarous south. The Rakshasas, he argued, were if anything more civilized than the people of Ayodhya and the Vanaras were allies, not a conquered race. Such interpretations merely reflected a projection of Europe's own record of aggression into a context where it was totally inappropriate.[290] The claim to India's morally superior traditions, the effort to elevate rather than uproot or exploit less fortunate people was the basis of these statements.

Perhaps the most attractive parts of Vivekananda's writings on the West are the passages where the ideological concerns are least obvious and his love of life comes through. The vigorous fun-loving child of an affluent home who delighted in culinary experiments, had an expert's knowledge of music and once excelled in manly sports remained very much alive under the ochre robes. The 'refined enjoyment' of life in Europe reminded him of Kalidasa's word pictures in *Meghadutam* depicting the civilized pleasures of another people in another age.[291] Always the concerned intellectual and patriotic man of religion, one of his best known passages[297] on Europe begins with the expected query: why was the rest of the world subject of Europe? What explained her total triumph in this age? His answer is a shade less expected. To understand Europe one had to understand France and her great city Paris, the epitome of modern European life. Western civilization with its lights and shades had reached its final apogee in that great city. His description of France reads like an apostrophe: 'The climate is temperate and the soil very fertile. There is no drought, nor any excess of rain. Ah, that cloudless sky, mild sunshine, the greenness of her grass, the low hills, clusters of bamboo, small rivulets and waterfalls! There is beauty in that water, enchantment in the land, intoxication in the air and sheer joy in her sky. There is a touch of beauty, a fulfilled longing for the delicate in those mansions fit for the king of gods, heavenly gardens, bowers and even the peasant's fields.' Paris to him was 'the heaven on earth, the ever joyous city.' Nowhere else did one encounter this continuous celebration of life. 'London and New York had wealth; Berlin had her fair share of scholarship and intellect; but they lacked the soil of France, and lacked above all the French people ... . This wonderful French personality is like a reincarnation of the bygone Greeks—ever full of joy, ever enthusiastic, utterly frivolous yet capable of great profundity, given to excitement in all their activities, but easily discouraged if there is any obstruction. But that despair does not darken the French face for long, for their spirit revives very soon.'

The rest of Europe accepted the University of Paris as their model. The scientific associations of the world copied the French Academy. Paris was the mentor in the art of colonial expansion. The terminology of military science remained French for the most part, whatever the language. Paris was the source of all western philosophy, science and arts. Others merely copied them. The French were truly urbane; beside them all others were country yokels. What the French did, the Germans, the English and others imitated decades later. Her revolutionary slogans, no longer potent in the country of their origin, had transformed Europe, still busy working these out in their lives. He almost agreed with the view that a nation's progress depended on the closeness of her contact with Paris. If anyone had any new idea to offer to the world, he should broadcast it in Paris. Artists, musicians, dancers all sought their first laurels in this city, for fame was theirs if she accepted them.

The Swami defended his beloved city against the familiar calumny of debauchery. The English, he said, were the worst detractors. The wealthy foreigners, whose idea of pleasure was the satisfaction of crude appetites, did see in Paris only the means for the indulgence of their vulgar tastes. Other western cities were not short of prostitutes, 'only the difference was that in other countries sensual pleasures had a brutish quality, in Paris, civilized Paris, even the dirt was wrapped in gold leaf; a peacock dancing with its feathers spread out is not the same as a pig wallowing in the mud'. Anyone who made some money rushed to Paris; kings and emperors came there for a purifying bath under false names. Most of the obscene entertainment was for the foreigners, the stupid rich from other countries. The French, careful with their purse, milked them with elegant courtesy and smiled to themselves.

This encomium on the French and their city led to a discussion of social mores—especially family life and the man-woman relationship—in different western countries. Vivekananda approached the topic without any moral preconceptions. He wrote with verve and considerable amusement about cultural differences, comparing different countries and, of course, Europe and India. He appears to have been constantly tickled by the fact that what is considered extremely proper in one country was the height of rudeness in another, especially in matters concerning 'the primeval joke of the human body'. The high eclecticism he had learnt from his guru, the Hindu tradition, and a natural sense of humour rendered cultural relativism an evident and amusing fact. His Bengali style—vivacious, racy and rich in Calcutta slangs, communicates to the reader his sense of fun at the absurdity of all social codes.

He found American, German and even English society relatively open as compared to the French.[293] The Americans invited even a casual acquaintance to be a guest at their home and so did the Germans. The English did the same only a little later. The French opened their doors only to intimate friends. Unmarried girls lived a secluded existence and marriages were more or less arranged. But the fun-loving French had ballerinas performing on all social occasions, a practice which could convey wrong impressions about their social mores. Their dance, especially in the nude, might appear obscene to an Indian, but evidently the French took it rather casually. It is a remarkable fact that the *sanyasi* too was not excessively bothered by their insouciance. The English with their long faces and joyless lives objected to the obscenity which they found quite acceptable on the stage. '... The English and the Americans make a point of seeing these things and then go home to denigrate [the French]'.

He noted one universal characteristic in social attitudes towards man-woman relationship: an indulgent view of male polygamy, and a very different attitude towards feminine sexuality. Only, the Frenchmen were a shade more tolerant—the way the rich were in all countries. Besides, he noted, Europeans generally took an indulgent view of male sexual excesses, though there was a very different set of rules for women. He added that in fact parents felt a little worried if a young man remained entirely indifferent to women, lest he turned out to be a sissy. The westerner insisted on one quality in men—manliness. 'Their 'virtue' and our '*viratva*'* are really the same word.'

The purpose of this discourse is explained in a succinct statement of Vivekananda's faith in cultural relativism. 'The reason why I say all this is that every nation has a distinctive moral purpose in life. Their ways should be judged in terms of that purpose. To see them through our eyes would be as mistaken as seeing us through theirs.'[294] The spiritual motivation of Indian culture as contrasted with western materialism is introduced into this discussion, but the emphasis here is clearly on the fact of a difference in outlook and not on any claim to superiority or self-assertion. Salvation, he wrote, was the ultimate object of Indian life. Celibacy was essential to attain that end. The Europeans wanted, above all, to enjoy life and hence celibacy was not an important prerequisite for their purpose. The reason for Europe's persistent concern with feminine chastity was traced to a curious physiological theory—that women became infertile if they were promiscuous.

He was, however, profoundly, and very favourably, impressed by the treatment and status of women in the West, especially the USA. He noted one basic difference between women's role in India and its western counterpart. In India, she was the mother; in the West, her main function was as the wife.[295] The contrast with the condition of women in upper-caste Bengali society and the fact that he counted among his friends some high-powered artists and very privileged society ladies probably explain his somewhat exaggerated estimate of women's role in western society. 'In the West, women own the kingdom, have all the power: 'they have the supreme authority', he wrote to Swarnakumari Devi, Tagore's eldest sister.[296] He

---

* The word literally means heroism. Here it is evidently used in the wider sense of manly qualities.

saw in the western treatment of women an element of veneration which he equated with the Hindu worship of Sakti, the Divine power manifest in nature as a feminine principle and embodied in the Mother Goddess. The veneration of Mary, as noted above, was to him just another way of worshipping Her. And while the worship of Sakti was confined to a few places of pilgrimage in India, it was an uninterrupted ritual in the West. Its social expression was the privilege accorded to women in every sphere of life. The origins of the code of chivalry, which he interpreted as the worship of Sakti, were traced to the Moors 'with whom began the flowering of (modern} civilization in Europe'. As they lost this fine tradition, they went into decline surviving in a state of semi-barbarity in one corner of Africa. The power, Sakti, they lost was transmitted to Europe. 'The 'Mother' abandoned the Muslims and took her abode in the Christians' home.'[297] Western nations were worthy of praise for the reverence in which women were held and the gentle consideration with which they were treated.[298] The Americans excelled in this respect. He recorded his highest praise in a letter to Swami Ramkrishnananda—in a language full of racy idioms for which there are no equivalents in English: 'Oh boy! am I dumbfounded by my encounter with their girls!* ... . They are [like] the Goddess Lakshmi herself in their beauty and [like] Saraswati, the goddess of Learning in their qualities [of the head]. I am their adopted brat, and they, my boy, are indeed the Mother Goddess incarnate ... . Your men are not worth their toe-nails and I better say nothing about your women!' He referred to the horrendous Hindu practice of marrying off girls at the age of ten by way of contrast. If only one could produce a thousand such women in India, there was some hope for the country.[299] Vivekananda was particularly impressed by the large proportion of girls in the American universities and the fact that many women earned their living. He found their practical abilities quite overwhelming. As his own talents in that direction were not very pronounced, he admitted that he could not have got done 'a quarter of a quarter' of what they achieved.[300]

In the same letter, he commented on the American family system, marriage and courtship, so different from their Indian counterparts. It is the language rather than the substance of his description which conveys his sense of amusement: 'In this country, the most important relationship in

* The original sentence is worth quoting for those who understand Bengali, 'eder meye dekhe amar akkel gudum baba!'

marriage is through the daughter not the son. The son becomes a stranger after marriage and it is the daughter's husband who frequently visits her parents' home ... . Marriage is quite a problem in this country. First, a girl must find an acceptable bridegroom. Secondly, she must have enough money. The gay Lotharios are expert in flirtation—but they perform a vanishing trick before they are caught. The girls dance and romp about until they catch a husband, but the boys are anxious to avoid the trap. It goes on like this until there is an incidence of 'love' [sic]—then alone does marriage take place.'*[301] Elsewhere he described the European nuclear family but unlike many of his compatriots he saw in it no element of egocentric selfishness.[302] The Swami, despite his admiration for the 'reverence' with which women were treated in the West, did not always share that reverence. Watching from the window of his London house the crowds of women on the busy street below, he once improvised a far from reverential doggerel in Bengali:

> Here come the hussies with parasols
> Their heads in pretty bon-nets
> Tonnes of flour on each face
> Who knows from how many baskets.[303]

He added an explanatory note, as his brother records: 'One could scrape [that powder] with a shovel.'[304] The man who could joke about the Mother Goddess was of course even less inhibited about her earthly incarnations. Besides, he made one important exception to his adoration of American womanhood—the 'church women' as he described them. The term was used with reference to the extremely bigoted harridans who had unleashed a campaign of calumny against him. He saw these patronesses of the church, especially in the Midwest and the South, as narrow-minded and often very frustrated human beings. His understanding of what really bothered them did not however induce any hypocritical words of kindness.[305] An impulsive person, Vivekananda could be quite abrasive and never bothered to offer high-minded rationalization for his vigorous criticism of things and people he disliked.[306]

His amused tolerance rooted in his awareness of cultural relativism did not usually desert him. The well-known passages in his *The East and the*

---

* The last four sentences read as follows in the original: 'Chhonra betara iyarki dite badai majbut—dhara debar bela pagar par. Chhundira neche kunde ekta swami jogad kare, chonda betara phande pa dite bada naraj. Ei rakam karte karte ekta love haye pade, takhan sadi hay.'

West on the contrasted notions of propriety and cleanliness in the two cultures offer a fine example of his response to other ways of life.[307] He explained the contrasts as being the results of environmental, especially climatic factors— but only partly so. Even the differences in such apparently trivial matters expressed a fundamental difference in outlook and objectives.

He wrote at some length on the attitudes to nudity, partial or total. Anything beyond the loin-cloth 'to cover one's shame' was a superfluity in hot countries and served no purpose other than decoration. People in cold climes dressed heavily perforce. The love of self-decoration was hence expressed in clothing and its changing fashions, for ornaments worn on a bare body would spell death in such climates. In India, by contrast, there was a craze for changing fashions in ornaments. Besides, western ideas on matters of propriety in dress were also partly climatic in origin. One went forth fully covered out of necessity as much as for reasons of etiquette. But this was not the whole story. Women in the West were permitted a low neck-line, but had to cover their legs. In India, propriety demanded that women should cover their faces, no matter if the sari pulled up to produce a long enough veil thereby failed to cover the bottom (a slight exaggeration, this!). The dancers and the tarts in Europe bared their bodies to attract men. Their Indian sisters were fully covered, only ladies went about half bare-bodied. Since women in Europe were fully dressed all the time, bare flesh appeared especially attractive. Covered limbs were more enticing where bare ones were commonly visible. A remarkably shrewd observation for a *sanyasi*! He further noted that European men had no sense of shame about nudity among themselves. Father and son could go bathing together in the nude—something unthinkable in India.

The excretory processes were unmentionable and, of course, totally unactable in public in Europe and America. Such delicacy of feeling, in Vivekananda's opinion, was impossible in a country where people ate oodles of cereals and vegetables and drank gallons of water. One had to get rid of the vast quantities the body failed to absorb. By contrast, the meat-based western diet, washed down with wine or beer, was insignificant in volume and so was its end product. 'Compare a cowshed or a horse stable with the cage of a lion or a tiger', was his clinching comment on this fundamental issue. But he did dilate at some length on the social consequences of western dietary-cum-excretory habits. Excretion in any form and stomach trouble were totally tabooed themes in one's conversation with women in England and America. One went to the toilet stealthily. Girls would rather die, refusing to answer nature's calls, than mention the unmentionable in front of men. The French, however, were a shade less inhibited about such things and the Germans even less so. Anglo-Saxon prudery, it was noted, imposed further taboos on conversation. 'Leg' was not a word to be uttered in the presence of ladies. The French had no such inhibitions, while the Germans and Russians indulged happily in smut.

But romance and love—subjects tabooed in India—were perfectly admissible topics of conversation between parents and children. A father teasing his daughter about her lover, an unthinkable violence to rules of distance and deference in the Indian context, was common enough in the West and people saw nothing improper in kissing or embracing publicly. Vivekananda's clinical detachment in observing other ways of life was evidently disturbed by such exhibition of affection if carried beyond a point. He wrote with distinct disapproval of two hapless fellow passengers on board ship, an American clergyman and his wife who spent four hours each day on the deck, cuddling each other. The couple had produced six children in seven years. Vivekananda commented, 'It is difficult to figure out this European civilization. If we rinse our mouths or brush our teeth in public—they comment 'How barbarous!' But wouldn't it be better if these cuddlings were done in private?' As the offending male was a clergyman, a cryptic comment followed on the benefits conferred by Protestantism on Northern Europe through its rule permitting the clergy to marry: Even if the rest of the English people perished and only their clergy survived, the latter would bring back the population level to the *status quo ante* in two decades.[308]

By and large, Vivekananda's comments on European social mores stop short of ethnocentric value judgements. Curiously enough, his conscious effort to judge 'them' by 'their' standards did not quite succeed when it came to questions of personal cleanliness, especially sanitary habits. The Hindus, he claimed, of all peoples had the highest standard of bodily cleanliness. They alone used water to clean themselves after answering nature's call. The West had been rescued from nauseating barbarism in these matters only because the Chinese had taught them the use of paper. The practice of taking a bath was also virtually unknown in Europe, though the English had introduced it at home after their contact with India. Only the rich bathed regularly, especially in America. 'The Germans rarely [took a bath], the French never.' The Russians and others, who were really *mlechchas*, unclean barbarians, were of course strangers to the habit. The Italians and Spaniards, devoted to garlic, never touched water despite the heat and the resulting sweat. 'The stink of their bodies is enough to scatter fourteen generations of unholy spirits, never mind the mere ghost who is but a suckling babe [in the face of such menace]'.[309] In 'Paris, the capital of [world] civilization, Paris, the heaven on earth', his hosts looked for a hotel which had bathrooms. The 'peculiar' facility was not available in twelve of the city's top hotels.

The attitude to cleanliness was also traced to the basic pronenesses of western civilization. Their emphasis was on externals—on looking rather than being clean, an end easily achieved by washing only one's hands and face. Hence the secrecy about all uncouth bodily action—the taboo on rinsing one's mouth or spitting in public. This meant unwashed mouths after meals and, inevitably, bad teeth, but no matter. Indians by contrast carried on their ablutions in public to the accompaniment of violent noises. The Europeans blew their noses into their handkerchiefs and the mucous, beautifully wrapped, went into their pockets. The very idea of such a practice would be nauseating to Indians. The latter, however, had such an aversion to dirt that they allowed garbage to gather and rot at their doors rather than remove it. They were happy so long as they did not have to touch it. The western chef, clad in spotless white, had never heard of the practice called bathing. He returned from the toilet or blew his nose and then kneaded the dough without bothering to wash his hands. The milkwhite bread served on china plates by waiters with gloved hands was made out of dough kneaded under the feet of half-naked men whose flowing sweat enriched the flour. The Brahmin cook never forgot to bathe and cooked with meticulous cleanliness but his dhoti carried a thick layer of dirt. 'The Hindu is forever looking for inner cleanliness. Outer cleanliness is the westerner's aim.' 'The Hindu wraps the Kohinoor in a piece of rag; the Europeans keep a clod of earth in a box of gold.' The difference went deeper. 'Why do we bathe?— lest we violate the rules of right conduct; the westerner washed his hands and face—only to be clean.' The moral purpose of a culture was evidently manifest in everything one did—great or small. But perhaps not quite so. The amoral environment also helped create differences in social mores. The taboo on belching would be cruel in a country where nature and diet ensured indigestion. And Europe had to tolerate the blowing of one's nose in public because there the common cold was an integral part of the human condition.

The moral criteria also got somewhat confused when it came to the question of diet, though the Swami was on surer grounds as to its physiological implications. Indian vegetarianism led to diseases of the stomach. The

Europeans' meat diet led to heart and lung diseases. But he believed in a causal connection between the nature of one's illness and mental attitudes. Apparently, diseases of the chest—especially pthisis—sustained optimism, while stomach ailments engendered pessimistic thoughts and other worldliness.[310] As to the debate on the morality of meat eating, he was content to present a resumé of the debate. The new debate in Europe on the possible ill effects of the habit was mentioned without comment. A normative statement linked the issue of diet to the question of higher purpose. The Hindus unlike the rest had recognized correctly the need for different rules for different people according to their profession and conditions of life. Meat eating was certainly barbarous and vegetarianism a morally worthy practice. However, the latter was all right for a life of holiness, but if one wanted to survive the struggle for existence—so long as the world was ruled by the strong, meat eating was essential for ordinary mortals. 'Or else the weak would forever be trodden under the strong man's feet,' for history showed that the meat-eating nations had always excelled not only in war but also in the quality of their intellect.[311] His admiration for Europe's dietary habits was however not unqualified. He described with a touch of disgust the practice of hanging venison and game birds for days. The taste for strong meat and cheese was to him no different from a liking for rotten food.[312] Its origins were traced to the hunting stage of European civilization. What was once a necessity became a fashion later on. Besides, Christianity, uniquely among all religions, imposed no taboo on food. The Jewish taboos were, however, noted. Their content might be different, but these restrictions had an obvious affinity with their Hindu counterpart.[313]

Vivekananda identified better food as one cause of the westerners' generally better health. Climate and better living conditions were other contributory factors. But the most important reason was, to his understanding, the practice of late marriage. It explained why in Europe a man was still considered young at forty and a fifty-year-old woman not described as old. By contrast, a Bengali was past his youth at thirty.[314]

Despite their inferior health, he considered the Hindus the most handsome people on earth. The Europeans' superior health did not preclude infirmities which affected their looks. Baldness and bad teeth were very common in the West. Stupid social habits which disfigured the human body were no monopoly of India. Europeans might not pierce their ears and noses to enhance their beauty, but their tight belts and corsets and mountains of clothing had the effect of bending the backbone and displacing internal organs. Such indeed were the results of their concern for a fine figure.[315]

Besides, better health did not automatically result in superior courage or character. His assessment in this regard referred, not to India's élite, but the lower orders, 'oppressed over many millennia', for whom he had not only sympathy but genuine respect. He was deeply impressed by the dignity, courage and quiet efficiency of the Bengali crew on the *s.s. Golconda* which took him to Europe in 1899. He referred to the growing prejudice in England against them because they took away jobs which could have gone to white workers. The prejudice was rationalized into a racist stereotype—that the Indian crew lost their nerves if there was any trouble. It was the white sailors, not the black ones, Vivekananda commented, who got drunk and were paralysed with fear in the face of danger. The Indian crew never touched alcohol and not one among them ever acted in a cowardly fashion. In India, it was the leadership, not the rank and file who were lacking in courage.[316]

There are glimpses of a sympathetic concern for the predicament of Europe's proletariat in the Swami's writings. An excess of machinery had reduced human beings to the level of mindless automatons. Extreme specialization in factory production meant endless repetition of boring, minute actions. People spent their whole lives producing pinheads or feeding yarn into a machine. If they lost the one specialized job they had learned to do, they perished.[317] Soul-destroying uniformity reducing people to the slavery of mindless habit was creeping into all areas of modern industrialized society. The growing uniformity of food and dress all over Europe was seen as a sign of decay. Like the Hindus who mindlessly followed the ancestral ways, modern Europeans were also falling into a groove. When men became machines, civilization did not survive very long.[318]

Moral judgements and comparisons with Indian ways were, however, not the only referents in Vivekananda's comments on western life. As noted earlier, he responded with childlike pleasure and an intelligent curiosity to much that he saw and experienced. Contemporary stereotypes did not dominate his assessments and often one comes across statements reflecting a freshness of response. He also focused on the distinctive features of the different western cultures. Despite his delight in Paris, it was Rome that he enjoyed most. He admired greatly the modernity of ancient Pompeii, a city which in his opinion had everything except steam power and electricity. He rated her art as much superior to that of modern Europe.[319] Constantinople with her narrow alleys, dirt and wooden houses he found charming, with a 'beauty born of strangeness'.[320] He appreciated in the Hungarians their warlike skills and generosity traceable to their 'Turkish (i.e., Mongol) forefathers as well as their excellence in music and the fine arts.[321] But Vienna, 'an imitation' of Paris, bored him. He invoked a simile from the Indian culinary experience to describe his experience of travels in Europe: 'To see [the rest of] Europe after Paris—is like tasting [the sour] tamarind sauce after a sumptuous meal.'[322] He considered only three European nations civilized—the French, the Germans and the English. The rest were no better off than the Indians. The majority was on a level of culture so low that Asia offered no parallels. Countries like Serbia and Bulgaria, with their earthen huts, poverty and dirt were worse off than even the poorer parts of India. Their love of pigs guaranteed filthiness. 'A single pig produced more filth than two hundred barbarians could have done.'[323]

France and her capital were to him the ultimate in western civilization. All civilized westerners emulated the French in food, dress and etiquette. French was the language of culture in Europe. Local costumes still survived in Europe. But the skirt-clad Greeks and Russians in Tibetan garments adopted the French style of dress as soon as a person become a member of 'polite society'. The Swami did not, however, fail to notice that London had overtaken Paris as the pace-setter in men's styles.[324]

He was struck by the contrast between the French and the Germans, fast emerging as a great nation—the former a dark-haired, slightly built race, dedicated to the arts, pleasure-loving and the last word in sophistication and the latter, their rivals, blonde, large and elephantine in their crudity. 'There is not city in the western world except Paris; the rest are imitations of Paris—or rather, attempts at imitation.' But the refinement of Parisian art was not to be found in its crude German, English or American imitations. 'Even the display of military power had an aesthetic quality in France; there was something frightening even in Germany's artistic efforts. The face of French genius was charming even when enraged; even the smiling face of German genius had an awesome quality. French civilization was nervous, it melts in the air like musk or camphor and fills the space with fragrance; German civilization was muscular, heavy like lead or mercury and lies immovable wherever it is placed. German muscles can keep hitting endlessly without any sense of fatigue; the French had soft, almost feminine bodies, but when they concentrated and hit hard, the stroke had the power of a blacksmith's blow [on the anvil]. The enormous German palaces built in imitation of the French could well be stables for elephants or camels. Even a multistoried French building had an airy quality as if it was meant for the habitation of fairies.'[325]

The German influence was strong in America teeming with German migrants.[326] But Vivekananda did not consider America a distinct civilization. It was only an offshoot of Europe, especially an imitation of English ways.[327] Yet, he was full of admiration for the great country where he went to seek help for India's poor. Her genius for organization, the virtual abolition of poverty and her effort 'to break down the barriers of this little world' were worthy of emulation by every country.[328] He appreciated the American spirit of independence and their love of work. Their ways might be lacking in restraint, but these were preferable to the inertness of Indian life. He was especially impressed by the way America treated her migrants. The Irish poor who arrived on her shores without a trace of self-confidence, abject and fearful, were transformed in a few months. Back home, they were objects of contempt, born and bred in a culture of hopelessness and denied political freedom by the ruling English. Americans gave them hope and courage by treating them as human beings. Such spectacular results of changes in the psychological environment contained obvious lessons for India.[329] Even their own poor were full of hope in this land of opportunity.[330] The US to him was a young country, full of fresh energy and ever ready to welcome anything new. Vivekananda even preferred modern American furniture to heavy European antique. The electricity they had harnessed for man's use seemed to be present in all their actions. The young in India had much more to learn in New York, than in London.[331] Despite his experiences of racism, to which he referred with amusement, he found the Americans less prejudiced than the English, at least in relation to India.[332] They were far superior to Indians in their social virtues, specially their ability for cooperative action and absence of jealousy in public life. Such jealousy in Vivekananda's opinion was a characteristic failing of subject peoples. He found it powerfully present among the American blacks who, like the Swami's contemporary Indians, reacted with malice towards the few of their own people who achieved a modicum of success.[333]

The Americans were a people with many positive qualities. They were truthful and kind by nature. But all their effort was centred on the body and all their energy spent on satisfying its needs, keeping it in shape and embellishing it in thousand ways, '[They have] a thousand variety of implements to pare their nails, ten thousand for cutting their hair and, as to perfumes and cosmetics, the number is truly infinite.' 'They are a fine people in every way', Vivekananda concluded, 'but this satisfaction of appetites is their true God. Hence the rivers of wealth, floods of beauty, waves of learning and surfeit of luxury.'[334] They were the richest people on earth and ate better and spent more than other nation. They were given to excess in all their habits of consumption. At the height of winter, they would not drink a glass of water without a chunk of ice in their well-heated rooms.[335] Beyond a point, he found 'this busy, meaningless, moneymaking life', the American love of razzmatazz hollow and tiresome.[336] They had very little concern with true spirituality. Their religious enthusiasms were little more than a craze. What they looked for was not spirituality, but the occult. Their scoundrels sought easy ways out of the feared consequences of their sins and the unscrupulous clergy took full advantage of their anxieties. While he appreciated the welcome extended to him in the USA, he had serious doubts about the depth of spiritual concern which apparently inspired it.[337]

Vivekananda saw a strong contrast between the English and the American personality. He found in the former a quality of seriousness and commitment to what they considered worthwhile. The American was effervescent by comparison.[338] He had strong, almost xenophobic, prejudices against the English before he visited their country. As a child, he had resisted learning the language of the hated foreigner.[339] Mrs Wright described one ferocious outburst against the English during the Swami's sojourn at Annisquam, Massachusetts: '... just a little while ago they were savages ... the vermin crawled on the ladies' bodices ... and they scented themselves to disguise the abominable odour of their persons.' He went on to describe the English as 'quite savage'; the alleged savagery was the result of the harsh northern climate. Their lip service to Christianity and, their civilizing mission were mere hypocrisy for 'in their hearts there is nothing but evil and every violence.' He added a prophecy: that there would be 'another invasion of the Huns' for the Chinese would sweep over Europe and the dark ages would come again. 'The vengeance of God' would come as a punishment for oppressing other people just as it had come upon India. This was his first public speech in the USA, albeit to a small audience, and he gave full vent to his strong feelings against British rule. He compared its contribution to Indian life with the legacy of the Hindu and Muslim past and came up with a familiar cliché: 'nothing but mounds of broken brandy bottles' was Britain's gift to India.[340]

He never lost his deep resentment against the fact of British rule and some of the negative assessments of the English which inevitably followed from it. The conversations recorded by his brother during the sojourn in England contain a number of highly critical comments. The English were tyrannical and ungrateful. Cruelty and selfishness were integral parts of the English personality. Hindus fought Britain's wars for her, because the British were a cowardly people. The Indian sepoys' valour won the Victoria Cross for British soldiers. And so on. Some day the Indians would 'squeeze you like lemon', he once told his hapless English devotee, the patriotic Mr Goodwin.[341]

'My ideas about the English have been revolutionised', he wrote to the Hale sisters after a few months spent in England. 'I now understand why the Lord has blessed them above all other races.' They were steady, sincere and capable of great depths of feeling. He described the famous English reserve as 'a crust of stoicism on the surface'. Once that crust was broken, one discovered great human qualities. These qualities, he implied, included a capacity for genuine friendship.[342] He found them generous and read into this quality an unexpected dimension: 'they understand a bit of renunciation, here—the deep English character'.[343] His optimism about the potentialities of Vedantic teaching in England—the conviction that his work would 'have more hold on England than America'—was based on his faith in the mature judgement of the educated Englishman and 'the tremendous tenacity of the English character'.[344] He admired their patriotism which counterbalanced the trait of selfishness. Besides, the one deficiency in the Indian character which vitiated their public life was totally absent in England. The English were 'the least jealous of each other ... and that is why they dominate the world. They have solved the secret of obedience without slavish cringing.' Hence they were law-abiding and yet enjoyed great freedom.[345]

Vivekananda's insights into the English social culture are not all that different from the familiar stereotypes. There is, however, one important difference. He arrived at his conclusions from personal experience—almost as a reluctant convert. One referent of his assessments was a comparison with Americans who had lionized him. His reception in England was not half as enthusiastic as the excited American response to the handsome *sanyasi*. He was also fully aware of English attitudes to the 'natives' of India. Of all his English friends, he considered only two, Captain and Mrs Sevier, totally free from prejudice, 'the only English people who do not hate the natives, Sturdy not excepted'. They were also the only ones who, in his estimate, did not go to India 'to patronise us'.[346] His English experience—which included the eventual break with Sturdy and Miss Muller who had first invited him—was not uniformly pleasant. His positive assessments in the context of his strong feelings against British rule in India suggests a capacity for objective judgement. Much of the intellectual effort by India's nationalists to analyse their historical predicament was concerned with such objectivity in assessing the West, especially England. The effort was not always successful. But to see its results simply as expressions of ambivalence is to underestimate their complexity. Colonial rule was beyond doubt an enemy to Vivekananda and his contemporaries who shared such sentiments. But they found it necessary to assess the enemy's true strength—its source in the history and culture of England. The relevant preconceptions included an element of admiration. Given the complexity of the Indians' relations with the ruling race—especially the possibility of friendly encounters—the admiration could subsume some affection, especially at the level of contact between individuals. Hence mutually opposed elements coexisted in all such assessments. To repeat, the fact indicates complexity rather than inconsistency or ambivalence.

The same complexity marks the Swami's view of the British rule in India and, as has been noted, he was not alone in this. Many of his statements on the subject—especially the ones expressing his strong gut reactions—are very similar to other nationalist critiques of the colonial presence. His lectures in the USA were full of the familiar diatribes. Britain's civilizing mission in India as elsewhere depended on the sword. Its symbols were the 'Bible, bayonet and brandy'. They had sucked India's blood 'for their own pleasure' and carried away vast stores of wealth. They added insult to injury by a constant denigration of the unhappy victims of their conquest. Their chief gifts to India were poverty, degeneration and an intolerant faith.[347] On the positive side, never before had India known a machinery of government so powerful and all-pervasive.[348] 'The householder had no problems under British rule.[349]

His seriously considered judgements—especially in his Bengali writings—however offer a somewhat original and far more sophisticated analysis of Britain's role in India. His paradigm derived from the caste system—the thesis that over time the world had witnessed the succession of different varnas to the position of supreme power—was central to his analysis. The most striking fact about the British rule was its basis in the merchant's power. The English character itself had developed around their commercial skills and concerns. Exchange and fair sharing were at the heart of their social culture, just as the French were concerned above all with political liberty. The English readily conceded social superiority to the King and the aristocracy, but would insist on careful accounting if they had to part with money. The King's attempts at arbitrary exaction led to the Civil War.[350] Hence British rule in India meant the Vaisya's supremacy. The Vaisya ruler facilitated the movement of goods from one end of the country to the other. 'The same effort was forcing the penetration of ideas from distant lands into the very bones and marrow of India.' The end results were mixed and uneven, but the clash of ideas, indigenous and alien, had produced at least one fortunate consequence. There were signs of a very slow awakening.[351]

The worst evil, as he saw it, was not exploitation but the slow death of the intellect and spirit under the tyranny of alien regulation which allowed no freedom of thought or action. He regretted that the leaders of Indian society were also anxious for fresh laws and rules, as if the country did not have enough of these.[352]

His explanation of the exploitative nature of colonial rule and racial discrimination was certainly original. Conquest by an autocratic ruler did not, in his view, usually lead to racial discrimination, for under such a regime everyone regardless of race or colour was denied all access to power. Racial pride or privilege has little scope in such a situation. But when the conquering nation was under democratic rule, the effort which could have gone into the welfare of the vanquished was usually expended on keeping the subject people under permanent subjection. He was not unduly worried by the fact of racial discrimination, the Englishman's contempt for the dark-skinned native. The Indians practised far worse discrimination within their own society.[353] Besides, the Anglo-Indians' hauteur had forced a measure of egalitarianism on Indians. They were all on the same plane in their degraded status as 'natives'.[354] The levelling process was not entirely negative. British policy had had some impact on the hereditary privileges in Indian society. An aborigine could now compete with the Bengali children at school, thanks to British policy.[355]

Vivekananda noted with some amusement England's desperate anxiety to retain her Indian empire traceable to the belief that they would be ruined if they lost India. Hence the concern to remind the Indians continually of England's power and glory. England, he commented, had no reason to worry so long as she retained her heroic qualities, perseverance and patriotism which won for them their empire, and their commercial skill, assisted by science and technology, which had reduced once self-sufficient India to the status of her market. But if they lost the qualities of character on which their greatness was founded, self-glorifying propaganda—wasteful of resources and energy which could have better uses—would not serve any purpose.[356]

Denationalization of certain elements in Indian society was to him—at least as much as to Bhudev and Bankim—possibly the worst consequence of alien rule. He ridiculed the pathetic anxiety to imitate the English and claim a relationship with the rulers via the new theories on race. 'Nowadays one hears from all castes that they are pucca Aryans .... And also that they are the same race as the English, in fact, first cousins .... They have come to this land from sheer kindness of heart—just like the English .... And their religion is just like that of the English. Their forebears were indistinguishable from Englishmen; only the [tropical] sun has darkened their skin .... [But] the government says, everyone [in India] is a native [sic]. What is the point in dressing up? How will your hats and all help you? If you do your best to blame the Hindu and stand apart, close to the English, your share of kicks and blows will be more, not less .... All the European ways we had learnt were alas lost under the white man's boots.' 'Glory unto the British government! Long live your throne, your crown; let your seat of power remain immovable'.[357] In a very different vein he stated his sense of grief at the sight of Indians in western attire. He wondered if people so dressed were ashamed to acknowledge their poor, illiterate countrymen as their own people. The Parsees nurtured on Indian soil for fourteen centuries had ceased to be 'natives'. 'And the Europeans have taught us that those ignorant, illiterate people of the low castes, clad only in loin cloth are non-Aryans. They are no longer our own!'[358]

Vivekananda's mission itself was his answer to the question which bothered the Bengali intelligentsia of his time: what should one learn from the West and what should one reject? He proposed a fair exchange of ideas, a synthesis based on national dignity. One had to learn from the West, but not accept without discrimination their criticisms of Indian society or even their patronizing appreciation of things Indian. He referred in this context to one of Ramakrishna's gibes—a question he put to an educated Bengali who expressed his admiration for the Gita: 'From which sahib did you hear that?' He acknowledged that the Hindu society lacked the strength to resist the flood of ideas from the West. He was not sure that this was undesirable. Centuries-old institutions would be swept away by the tide of new influences.[359]

But he himself rejected many of these institutions as inhuman. Especially, if India's hopes for the future lay with her Sudras, the oppressed masses, the damned heritage which denied them human dignity had to go.

Unlike Bhudev and Bankim, Vivekananda was not initially concerned with exploring what to learn and what to reject from western civilization. He went out with total confidence in India's spiritual inheritance to seek help for India's poor, and with somewhat vague hopes of assistance for the introduction of new technology. He was also sure that the poor in India had to be rescued from their ignorance with the aid of the new knowledge—with maps, globes and magic lanterns. No detailed investigation of western culture was necessary to arrive at this conclusion. His interest in western civilization was roused by the experience of direct encounter. It is not traceable primarily to his concern with the Indian predicament or to his academic knowledge of European thought and culture. Even the question insistently present in the awareness of the colonial intelligentsia—what to accept from the West— occurs almost as a postscript to his delight and amusement in what he saw in Europe and America. He found little to condemn except the oppression inherent in imperialism. His perceptions were informed by a simple dichotomy—'us' and 'they'—equated with spirituality and this worldliness respectively. But he saw the latter as an admirable manifestation of *rajas*, manly vigour, a necessary step to higher things. Indians sunk in *tamas*, pure inertia, and all that is brutish in man, had to emulate that quality first.

Notes and References

1. Bhupendranath Datta, *Swami Vivekananda* (in Bengali), Calcutta, BY 1383 (AD 1976), 91.
2. Mahendranath Datta, *Swami Vivekanander balyajibani*, Calcutta, BY 1366 (AD 1959), 3–4.
3. BD., SV, 93–4.
4. Ibid., 94f, 119f.
5. Ibid., 98.
6. Ibid.
7. BJ, 51–2.
8. BD., SV, 101; BJ, 49–50.
9. See footnote 8.

10. Ibid; BJ, 51; Swami Saradananda, *Sri Sri Ramakrishnalila-prasanga*, Calcutta, BY 1390 (AD 1983), vol. 2, part 5, 199–200. The publishers, Udbodhan Karyalaya, have not numbered this edition of the famous biography of Ramakrishna by one of his disciples. Also see Swami Gambhirananda, *Yuganayak Vivekananda*, part I, Calcutta, BY 1384, 19–20.

11. Mahendranath Datta, *Sri Ramakrishner anudhyan*, 2nd edn., Calcutta, BY 1361 (AD 1954), 12,14; also his *Srimad Vivekananda Swamir jibaner ghatanabali*; 4th edn., I, 63–4; also Sailendra Nath Dhar, *A Comprehensive Biography of Swami Vivekananda*, part I, Ist edn., Madras, 1975, 4–5.

12. BJ, 6–8; Dhar, I, 6, 11.

13. BD., SV, 97, 125.

14. BJ, 58.

15. Dhar, I, 11.

16. Gambhirananda, *op. cit.*, I, 55; Mahendranath Datta, Ghat., I, 4th edn., BY 1884 (AD 1977), 10.

17. Mahendra Datta mentions that the Simla boys were notorious for their 'dare-devilry'. 'They feared nobody, were no respecters of persons and told off people as they pleased.' This description does in a way fit the young Naren as well as the great Swami in his maturity. See RKA, 20–1.

18. *The Life of Swami Vivekananda* by His Eastern and Western Disciples, 5th edn., I, Calcutta, 1979, 44.

19. Ibid., 48.

20. Ghat., I, 10; Dhar, I, 44.

21. Life, I, 45.

22. Also see S.P. Basu, *Vivekananda o samakalin Bharatvarsha*, IV, first reprint, Calcutta, BY 1388 (AD 1981), 203. His intellectual interests and wide range of reading are discussed in all his biographies. Some of the relevant information comes from the reminiscences of people who knew him at different stages of his life. See Life, I, 41, 45f, 106f, 107f; Ghat., II, 131–4. 142; Haripada Mitra's reminiscences in *Viswavivek*, edited by A. Bandyopadhyay, S. Basu and Samkar, 2nd edn., Calcutta, 1966, 45–8; B. Majumdar, '*Swami Vivekanandar itihas chetana o rashtriya adarsha*' (Swami Vivekananda's Consciousness of History and Political Ideals), ibid., 262f; RLP, V, 72; Swami Gambhirananda, *op. cit.*, I, 65; Pramathanath Basu, *Swami Vivekananda* (in Bengali), I, 2nd edn., Calcutta, BY 1356 (AD 1949), 60–80. Each of these works and articles contains some significant

information not found in the others. Their statements are confirmed by the internal evidence of his own writings and the detailed narration of his numerous encounters in the West, supported by documents in Marie Louise Burke's *Swami Vivekananda in the West—New Discoveries*, (hereafter Burke), 3rd edn., Calcutta, 1983, a six-volume work of which the first four have been published so far.

23. Ghat., I, 101; S.P. Basu, VSB, IV, 203. Also see. S.P. Basu, ed., *Letters of Sister Nivedita*, I, Calcutta, 1982, 82.

24. Burke, I, 364–5.

25. Ibid., III, 54–9.

26. Ghat., II, 164.

27. H. Mitra, *Parivrajak* (The Wandering Monk) in *Viswavivek*, 45.

28. M. Datta, *Londone Swami Vivekananda*, II, 3rd edn., Calcutta, 158–9, 176; Ghat., II, 166.

29. Ghat., II, 166.

30. For Vivekananda's musical skills, see Basu, I, 72–6; B.N. Datta, *Swami Vivekananda—Patriot-Prophet*, Calcutta, 1954, 86, 115; Priyanath Sinha, *Chhatrajivan* (In His Student Days), *Viswavivek*, 29, 33; Swami Prajnananda, *Samgitsadhak Swami Vivekananda* (Swami Vivekananda as a musician), ibid., 237–49; *Bharatiya o europiya sangit sambandhe swamijir mat* (Swamiji's Views on Indian and Western Music), ibid., 249–51.

31. Life, I, 116–18; BD., SV, 141; Basu, I, 117–18.

32. Ghat., II, 166.

33. For Vivekananda's philosophical studies, see Ghat., I, 98–101, II, 163–4; Basu, I, 94f; Life, I, 107–11.

34. Burke, I, 27.

35. Seal's article, published in *Prabuddha Bharata*, April, 1907 and again in the *Brahmavadin* next month, is reproduced *in extenso* in Life, I, 107–11. Also see Basu, I, 94–6.

36. Ghat., II, 163–4; Basu, I, 92.

37. Basu, I, 95.

38. Max Mueller, *Ramakrishna—His Life and Sayings*, 2nd edn., Calcutta, 1984, 25–9.

39. Sumit Sarkar, 'The Kathamrita as a Text; Towards an Understanding of Ramakrishna Paramahamsa' (Mimeographed, Nehru Memorial Museum and Library, Occasional Papers on History and Society, No xxii), New Delhi, 1985.

40. RLP, ɪ, chap. 1. The chapter is entitled 'Yug-prayojan', i.e., 'The Need of the Age'—Saradananda writes elsewhere (V, 3): '... India had been saved in her great crisis by virtue of the Master's effort to establish dharma in this age by living his exemplary life over twelve long years before the eyes of westernized people whereby the deluge of western ideas was beaten back.' The theory of reincarnation is firmly stated in Life, ɪ, 62, 183.

41. *Ramakrishna—His Life and Sayings*, first published in 1898.

42. Londone, ɪ, 41.

43. I have used the 2nd Indian edn. (Calcutta, 1984). For a brief chronology, see RPL, ɪ, 145–6, ɪɪ, 410–14.

44. Life, ɪ, 183.

45. Reproduced in RLP, *Gurubhav*, 8.

46. See Sister Nivedita, 'Glimpses of the Saints', *The Master as I Saw Him*, 11th edn., Calcutta, 1972, 154–61.

47. RLP, *Gurubhav, uttarardha*, 278f.

48. See *The Apostles of Sri Ramakrishna*, compiled and edited by Swami Gambhirananda, Calcutta, 1967; *The Disciples of Sri Ramakrishna*, Mayavati, 1943. Swami Brahmananda's (né Rakhalchandra Ghosh) mother was a devotee of Krishna and his own favourite 'game' in childhood was the worship of Kali. He 'had great devotion to gods and goddesses'. Saradananda's (Saratchandra Chakravarti) father and grandfather were also profoundly religious and Sarat in his boyhood preferred images of deities to other toys. Yogananda, after he was given the sacred thread, spent a lot of time in meditation and worship. Almost all the devotees, *sanyasi* or householder, whose life stories are known, had a similar background of Hindu religiosity. Any reference to Hindu revivalism to explain their attachment to a famous mystic is entirely superfluous. Hindu thought and practice were a living reality in their lives. The conscious and often distorted self-assertion implicit in revivalism was irrelevant to their conversion to *sanyas*.

49. See BD., SV, 185–6.

50. Sister Nivedita, *The Master as I Saw Him*, 168.

51. He advised Sasadhar to acquire some more spiritual power before preaching. Sri Ma (Mahendranath Gupta); *Sri Sri Ramakrishna Kathamrita*, Ist complete edn., published by Ananda Publishers, Calcutta, 1983, ɪ, 110. He also wondered if the access to supernatural powers claimed by the Theosophists was of any use in one's quest for God. Contemporaries like Protap Mazoomdar saw him as the 'apostle of union and reconciliation'. See Brajendranath Bandyopadhyay and

Sajanikanta Das, *Samasamayik drishtite Sri Ramakrishna Paramahamsa* (Sri Ramakrishna Paramahamsa in the Eyes of His Contemporaries), 2nd edn., Calcutta, BY 1359, 19.

52. RLP, *Gurubhav uttarardha*, 201, 206.

53. *Dharmatattva*, a contemporary periodical sympathetic to his ideas, affirmed in 1882, 'His Deity continuously presses him to preach the gospel. He is very reluctant. He prays that this purpose be achieved by the few pure-hearted individuals who were around.' See Brajendranath Bandyopadhyay and Sajanikanta Das, *op. cit.*, 27.

54. For a discussion of evolving religious sensibility in nineteenth century Bengal, see Bipin Chandra Pal, *Character Sketches*, Calcutta, 1957, especially the chapters on Rammohan, Keshab, Aswini Kumar and Aurobindo.

55. See his RKA, 13–28. Mahendra mentions elsewhere that the Gita was not easily available in Bengali before 1887. Ghat., I, 134.

56. The underlying unity of all faiths was preached as his message in *Tatvamanjari*, a journal edited by his devotee, Ramchandra Datta. ibid., 72f.

57. See chaps, 1 and 3 above.

58. Ghat., I, 2–7, 15; Bj. 9, 10–11; Dhar, I, 14–17, 39; Basu, I, 318, Nivedita, *The Master as I Saw Him* (13th edn., Calcutta, 1983), 164.

59. 'My Master', *The Complete Works of Swami Vivekananda* (in English) 11th edn., IV, Calcutta, 1978.

60. For example, Sister Nivedita (*op. cit.*, 113) reports the following statements: 'Who was he that he should feel responsible for teaching the world? ... Even work ... was nothing but illusion.' 'There was nothing to be desired, but the life of the wanderer, in silence and nudity, on the banks of the Ganges.' See also ibid., 109 and Burke, II, 107.

61. RLP, V ('Thakurer divyabhav o Narendranath'), 66–9; for his occasional worldly aspirations and yearning for a householder's life, see CW(E), II, 98.

62. RKA, 21, 23–5; VSB, I, 307.

63. Saratchandra Chakrabarti, *Swami-sishya-samvad*, 5th edn., Calcutta, BY 1389 (1982), 138; see also Nivedita, *op. cit.*, 115–16; RLP, v, 92.

64. RLP, V, 59, 65, 96. Naren's disbelief concerning the doctrine of non duality was finally dispelled by a similarly induced experience of *samadhi* (ibid., 149).

65. Ibid., 97f, 100.

66. Ibid., 208. Also see RKK, 37, 58f.

67. RLP, v, chaps. 3–12; Life, I, chaps. VII, X–XVIII; RKA, 85, RKK, 998.

68. SSS 146, 185. The same work (p.60) records a statement by Vivekananda that two days before his death the guru told him that He who was Rama and Krishna was now incarnate in his body as Ramakrishna, and not merely in the Vedantic sense, i.e. the notion that Brahman is manifest in all beings. Vivekananda added, 'We heard this repeatedly from our Master, but still cannot believe in its truth entirely ...'.

69. Ibid., 58, 193; Burke, II, 380, 381, 390.

70. See 'My Master', CW(E), IV, 180.

71. Ibid., 62.

72. Nivedita, *op. cit.*, 83.

73. SSS, 146.

74. RLP, v, 103–4.

75. Ghat., I, 78, 79, 84–5.

76. Londone, III, 7, 41.

77. Londone, II, 89–90, 94–5, 96; Nivedita, *op. cit.*, 164; Life, II, 517.

78. Life, II, 520.

79. Ghat., III, 124.

80. Vivekananda lectured and wrote on Vedanta extensively. A summary statement of his ideas is given in his lecture entitled, 'The Vedanta Philosophy', CW(E), vol. 7, 357–65; also see 'The Vedanta Philosophy and Christianity', ibid., VI, 46–8, 85. For an illuminating assessment of his interpretation of Vedanta, see Rabindrakumar Dasgupta, 'Vivekanandar Vedanta', *Visvavivek*, 306–21.

81. See his lecture on 'The Vedanta in all its phases', CW(E), III, 322–49.

82. Nivedita explains (*op. cit.*, 17) Vivekananda's interpretation of *maya* as follows: '... that shimmering, elusive, half-real half-unreal complexity, in which there is no rest, no satisfaction, no ultimate certainty, of which we become aware through the senses and through the mind as dependent on the senses. At the same time—And That by which all this is persuaded, Know that to be the Lord Himself!'

83. 'The Vedanta Philosophy', *op. cit.*, 364.

84. For a discussion of Vivekananda's views on the affinity between Christianity and Hinduism, see the second part of this chapter.

85. He referred, for instance, in a letter to Sir Subrahmanya Iyer to India's 'Centuries of Servitude'. The next sentence refers to the stagnation of Hindu civilization 'during the Mohammedan tyranny, for then it was not a question of progress but of life and death'. See 'A plan of work for India', CW(E), IV, 373.

86. See Life, I, 265–8, 279–80, 374f; Ghat., II, 136.

87. Life, I, 268; Nivedita, *op. cit.*, 76.

88. *Op. cit.*, 42.

89. Life, I, 357.

90. Nivedita, *op. cit.*, 204.

91. 'The way to the realization of a universal religion', CW(E), II, 371.

92. Lecture on 'Mohammed' delivered on 25 March 1900 in the San Francisco Bay Area, CW(E), I, 481–4.

93. Ghat., I, 27, 36, 42, 151.

94. Nivedita, *op. cit.*, chap. XVIII.

95. Sister Nivedita to Sister Christine, 27 January 1900 quoted in Burke, II, 271, I, 269; Life, I, 172, 335, 388, 527.

96. Burke, I, 316–17.

97. Lecture on 'India's gift to the World', reported in *Brooklyn Standard Union*, 27 February 1895, CW(E), II, 510.

98. 'Buddhism and Vedanta', CW(E), V, 279; Life, II, 614.

99. 'Vartaman Bharat' (India Today) (hereafter VB), CW(B), VI, 225. Also see the report of his lecture on Buddhism in the *Chronicle*, San Francisco, 19 March 1900 reproduced in Burke, II, 351f.

100. *Prachya o Paschatya*, 153, CW(B), VI.

101. Ghat., I, 28–9, 36, 94, 111, 171–2.

102. Londone, II, 107–9.

103. Burke, II, 155.

104. CW(E), VI, 85.

105. CW(E), II, 379.

106. The statement occurs in a report of Vivekananda's lecture on 'The Divinity of Man' at Detroit dated 17 February 1894 in the *Free Press* of 18 February 1894 reproduced in Burke, I, 337. The relevant passage is somewhat obscure and may be a garbled version of what Vivekananda actually said.

107. Ghat., I, 82–3.

108. CW(E), II, 382.

109. 'The way to the realization of a universal religion', CW(E), II, 358–74; 'The ideal of a universal religion', CW(E), II 375–96. Vivekananda referred to Ramakrishna's homely analogy in explaining the *raison d'être* for many religions: a mother cooked highly spiced dishes for some of her children and very bland food for the less sturdy stomachs. SSS, 25.

110. Nivedita, *op. cit.*, 168.

111. SSS, 78; *Bhavbar katha*, CW(B), II, 45.

112. *Bhavbar katha*, CW(B), II, 45–6.

113. Letter to Swami Brahmananda, 1895, CW(B), 107.

114. SSS, 114.

115. Ghat., II, 171; VSB, III, 82–5; for his open conflict with the Theosophists after his return from the USA, see VSB, 3, III, 36, 70–1.

116. SSS, 85f.

117. Life, I, 28–9.

118. Ghat., I, 7, 11, II, 168; Bose, I, 76f. '*Lathi*', a stick made of bamboo, was used as a weapon in Bengal and '*lathikhela*'—stick play—was a highly developed form of martial art.

119. VSB, IV, 201.

120. RKA, 12–13.

121. Burke, II, 182.

122. Ibid., II, 346, 416; I, 47–8, 191, 197, 202, 205, 334–5, 339; CW(E), II, 515–17; IV, 198–202.

123. Nivedita, *op. cit.*, 44; S.P. Basu and S.N. Ghosh, *Vivekananda in Indian Newspapers, 1893–1902*, Calcutta, 1969 (hereafter VIN, 180, 273).

124. *Viswavivek*, 49; VIN, 274.

125. He considered dark-skinned Indians in western attire a revolting sight, CW(B), VII, 217.

126. VIN, 107, Ghat., III, 98.

127. He said on one occasion that he wished that he was a pariah, VSB, III, 200; also *Parivrajak*, 106.

128. See chaps. I and II above.

129. *Parivrajak*, 82, in CW(B), VI.

130. His brother, Mahendra, describes this phase of his life (see Ghat., I) in great detail and offers a picture of exclusive devotion to a mystical quest.

131. The likelihood that Ramakrishna's concerns were entirely asocial has been discussed above.

132. See Ghat., I, 17, 23, 63, 157; II, 155, 170; III, 125; Londone, I, 161–3; II, 167.

133. See Nivedita's account of his reminiscences of poverty and hunger, *op. cit.*, 60f; also Life, I, 354 for an account of his days as the guest of a family of sweepers.

134. Life, I, 343f. See *inter alia* his letter to Sivananda from the US, CW(B), VII, 74–5.

135. Ibid., I, 120f.

136. See footnotes 127 and 128 above.

137. Ghat., III, 124.

138. Ibid., II, 20; Burke, I, 367; VIN, 700–2.

139. CW(E), IV, 362.

140. Nivedita points out that while 'the nursing of the sick and the feeding of the poor, had indeed from the first been natural activities of the Children of Ramakrishna' these things 'were considered from a national point of view' after Vivekananda's return from the West. *op. cit.*, 35. He explained the object of the Ramakrishna Mission as 'first the gift of food, then the gift of learning and then the gift of knowledge', SSS, 126f.

141. 'You who cannot feed the [starving] people, are incapable of mutual co-operation for the common good', he wrote in *Prachya o paschatya*. 'You [have the impertinence to] run after salvation!' (153, CW(B), VI). The passage which follows is an impassioned call to manly action: 'The earth is for the enjoyment of heroes—reveal to the world the heroism in your nature ...'. His oft-quoted advice to India's youth recommended football in preference to the Gita as a way to heaven. CW(E), III, 242.

142. Nivedita, *op. cit.*, 18–19.

143. 'Throw all [your] concern with religion into the Ganges for the present and march into the struggle for existence', he advised Sarat Chakravarti and told him to go and hawk the products of Indian handicrafts in the streets of Europe and America. SSS, 105–6.

144. Ghat., III, 2; VSB, 243–6, 252–60.

145. He actually wanted that Indian young men should visit Japan in large numbers. Life, 398–9.

146. Hemchandra Ghosh, a revolutionary, however refers to a fourfold programme chalked out by Vivekananda: service to the people,

abolition of untouchability, starting gymnasiums and a library movement. BD., SV, 305–8.

147. Burke, II, 167f.

148. Londone, I, 191.

149. Jadugopal Mukhopadhyaya, 'Deser muktiprayasi swamiji' (Swamiji in Search of the Country's Liberation), *Viswavivek*, 260, 261.

150. VB, 243. The relevant passage reads as follows: 'Unqualified patriotism and unqualified hatred of the Persians in the case of the Greek people, hatred of idolaters in the case of the Arabs, hatred of the Moors in the case of Spain, hatred of Spain in the case of France, hatred of France in the case of England and Germany and hatred of England in the case of America were certainly a major factor ... in the progress of the [said] nations.' (Translation mine).

151. Prithwindra Mukherji, 'Bagha Jatin: Only Man M.N. Roy Blindly Obeyed', *The Statesmen* (Delhi and Calcutta), 25 March 1987, 6.

152. SSS, 7.

153. *Parivrajak*, 75, 85, CW(B), VI.

154. Ghat., I, 194; Life, I, 231.

155. Letter to Professor Wright, 26 October 1893, Burke, I, 164.

156. Ibid., 162, 163, 164, 468, 470.

157. Ibid., 52.

158. Life, 1st, edn., II, 278.

159. Letter to Haripada Mitra, 28 December 1893, CW(E), V, 327.

160. Letter to Ramakrishnanda, January, 1894, ibid., VI, 255.

161. Ibid., VI, 267.

162. Burke, II, 346, 352–3.

163. Life, I, 510f.

164. Burke, II, 369.

165. Ibid., 229.

166. Ibid., 176.

167. Ibid., I, 465–8.

168. SSS, 7f; VIN, 105f.

169. Burke, I, 219f.

170. Ibid., 110.

171. Ibid., 218.

172. Ibid., II, 203, 209.

173. Ibid., 219.

174. Ibid., 273.

175. Ibid., I, 86–7, 366, 373, 381.

176. Ibid., 60, 278–84.

177. Ibid., 21f.

178. Ibid., 99.

179. Ibid., 290f.

180. Ibid., 150f, 363, 427; II, 24.

181. Ibid., I, 483f, 487f.

182. SSS, 16.

183. POP, 155f, CW(B), VI; Letters to Brahmananda, 1895, CW(B), VII, 109.

184. Burke, II, 25.

185. Ibid., I, 35f, 52.

186. Ibid., II, 130–1.

187. Ibid., I, 43, 157–8, 159f, II, 138.

188. Ibid., I, 85, 95, 161, 197f, 343f, 346.

189. Ibid., III, 503f; VSB, II, 51.

190. Burke, I, 58.

191. Ibid., II, 368.

192. Life, II, 14.

193. Ibid., chap. 26.

194. Ibid., II, 482f.

195. *Op. cit.*, chaps. I and II.

196. Ibid., 41.

197. VSB, I, 93f, 105f.

198. Ibid., 86.

199. Londone, I, 122; II, 81, 89, 106.

200. Life, II, 547–8, 555; *Parivrajak*, 122–3, CW(B), VI.

201. Life, I, 456, II, 161; VIN, 700; Burke, II, 195.

202. Burke, I, chaps. 7 and 8; Life, I, 518f.

203. Letter to Ramakrishnanda, 25 September 1894, CW(B), 5: 'Whatever one does, some people will give cheers and some act as enemies.' In another letter to Ramakrishnanda in 1894, he implied that cowardly jealousy was a characteristic trait of subject people. Ibid., 58.

204. For detailed accounts of the hostility to Vivekananda, see Ghat., III, 11–12, 76f; VSB, I, 45f, 275f; II, 151f, etc; VIN, 154, 157–8, 182f; Burke, II, 40, 79, 82f, 300f; I, 400f.

205. He told Narendranath Sen, the editor of *Indian Mirror*, quite explicitly that it was entirely illusory to expect that India would achieve freedom by defeating the British because the latter's supremacy in things material was unshakeable. SSS, 7. He also told Aswini Kumar Datta quite categorically that he had no faith in the Congress. Life, ɪɪ, 354.

206. SSS, 21.

207. Life, ɪɪ, 497.

208. POP, CW(B), vɪ, 149–50. All translations from Vivekananda's Bengali writings quoted in this chapter are mine. Accurate rendering of his meaning and style into English is almost impossible. I have tried to convey the same without departing very far from a literal translation.

209. Ibid., 150.

210. Ibid., 196.

211. Ibid.

212. Ibid., 152f.

213. Ibid., 154.

214. Ibid., 168.

215. Ibid., 163.

216. Lecture delivered at the Unitarian Church, Detroit, 14 February 1894 reported in the *Free Press*. See Burke, ɪ, 307F.

217. Reported in *Minneapolis Journal*, 27 November 1893. ibid., 194f, 197.

218. Londone, ɪɪɪ, 47.

219. Ibid., ɪɪ, 5–6.

220. Nivedita, *op. cit.*, 219.

221. POP, 203f.

222. Ibid., 205.

223. '*Vartaman samasya*' (Today's Problem), Introduction to the magazine *Udbodhan*, CW(B), VI, 29–30.

224. 'My Plan of Campaign', CW(E), ɪɪɪ, 217, 'The Religion we are born in', ibid., 455.

225. 'The Vedanta in all its Phases', ibid., 330; 'The Work Before Us', ibid., 270; 'Vedantism', 434; 'Hindu and Greek', in *Notes of Class Talks and Lectures*, ibid., vɪ, 85f.

226. 'The influence of Indian spiritual thought in England', CW(E), ɪɪɪ, 440.

227. 'Vedantism', ibid., 437–38.

228. *Vartaman samasya, op. cit.*, 32.

229. *Parivrajak*, CW(B), VI, 107, 113ff.

230. Ibid., 250f.

231. *Parivrajak*, 137.

232. Ibid., 207.

233. SSS, 7.

234. POP, 210–12.

235. *Parivrajak*, 108ff.

236. POP, 192.

237. Ibid., 157.

238. Ibid., 192–3.

239. Ibid., 198–9.

240. Ibid., 199–201.

241. *Parivrajak*, 125–7, 128–9.

242. Ibid., 129–30.

243. Ibid., 132–3.

244. Ibid., 134–5.

245. Ibid., 130–2.

246. Ibid., 95.

247. 'The four castes headed by the Brahmins are to be found in all societies since ancient times', VB, 229.

248. POP, 203–4.

249. Vivekananda use the pregnant Bengali phrase 'ghodar dim', i.e. horse's egg, to describe the producers' reward.

250. The literal translation of the relevant passage '*phanki diye mudo marte laglo*' would be: 'began to eat the fish-heads by tricking everyone'.

251. VB, CW(B), VI, 233–5.

252. Ibid., 235.

253. Ibid., 239–40.

254. POP, 161–2.

255. VB, 240ff.

256. Sister Christine, *Reminiscences of Swami Vivekananda*, quoted in Burke, I, 35; VSB, III, 450–68.

257. *Parivrajak*, 117–18.

258. Ghat., I, 111.

259. Report of an interview in *Free Press*, Detroit, 14 February 1894, quoted in Burke, I, 299–300.

260. CW(E), vi, 85.

261. Ibid., ii, 379.

262. Burke, ii, 30.

263. *Parivrajak*, 94–6.

264. Ibid., 115–17.

265. See fn. 251 above.

266. POP, 151, 190–1.

267. *Parivrajak*, 97.

268. POP, 212–13.

269. 'Plea for Tolerance', a report on Vivekananda's lecture published in the *Commercial*, 17 January 1894, Burke, i, 249.

270. *Parivrajak*, 97.

271. 'Women of India', report on a lecture published in the *Tribune*, Detroit, 1 April 1894. Burke, i, 447–8.

272. Ibid., 128, 222–3.

273. Ibid., 201.

274. 'Pari pradarsani' (The Paris Exhibition), CW(B), vi, 47.

275. Dubque (Iowa) *Times*, 29 September 1893, Burke, i, 112.

276. POP, 214–15.

277. 'Bangla bhasha' (The Bengali Language), CW(B), vi, 36–7.

278. *Parivrajak*, 142–4.

279. Ibid., 132.

280. These were made in course of a discussion with the Bengali painter, Ranadaprasad Dasgupta, SSS, 186–9.

281. The report on a lecture delivered at San Francisco, 'On Art in India', records a somewhat blunt statement: 'India led in music, also in drama and sculpture'—too bare to be quite accurate. It surely does not convey the complexity of Vivekananda's ideas on the subject. See CW(E), iv, 196–7.

282. *Parivrajak*, 108–11.

283. Ibid., 111–12.

284. 'On Dr Paul Deussen', CW(E), iv, 272–7.

285. Ibid., 275.

286. SSS, 34–5. Also see 'On Professor Max Muller', CE(E), iv, 278–92.

287. 'Pari pradarsani', CW(B), vi, 49–50.

288. 'Pari pradarsani', CW(B), vi, 48–9.

289. POP, 209–11.

290. SSS, 16.

291. POP, 191ff.

292. Ibid., 195f.

293. Ibid., 196.

294. 'The Women of India', CW(E), vii, 505.

295. Letter dated 6 April 1897, CW(B), vii, 377.

296. POP, 190-1.

297. Interview with Swami Vivekananda, *Free Press*, Detroit, 14 January 1894, Burke, i, 302.

298. Letter dated 25 September 1894, CW(B), vii, 8.

299. Ibid., 6, 8.

300. Ibid., 6.

301. 'Siver bhut' (Siva's Demon), CW(B), vi, 53.

302. '*Chhati hate, tupi mathay aschhe jata chhunri Mukhe mekhechhe tara mayda jhudi jhudi*'—Londone, i, 91.

303. Ibid., 92.

304. VIN., 699.

305. There is a fine example of this refusal to rationalize his outbursts of temper in his conversation with Aswini Kumar Datta. When Aswinibabu asked if it was becoming of him to describe the Madras Brahmins as 'the Pariahs of the Pariahs', he replied: 'I never said I was right. The impudence of these people made me lose my temper, and the words came out. What could I do? But I do not justify them.' See Life, ii, 355.

306. POP, 168-72, 187-90.

307. *Parivrajak*, 93.

308. It is quite impossible to convey the power of Vivekananda's language in translation: 'Se gayer gandhe bhuter chauddapurush palay, bhut to chhelemanush!', POP, 169.

309. POP, 165-6.

310. Ibid., 173-5.

311. He commented, 'More rotten the cheese, more it was full of worms, more was it to the taste of the English', ibid., 182.

312. Ibid., 183.

313. Ibid., 165.

314. Ibid., 165-6.

315. *Parivrajak*, 80-1.

316. Ibid., 74.

317. Ibid., 133.

318. CW(B), VII, 363.

319. *Parivrajak*, 139.

320. Ibid.

321. Ibid., 133.

322. Ibid., 134.

323. POP., 185.

324. *Parivrajak*, 126.

325. Ibid.

326. *Tribune*, Detroit, 18 February 1894, quoted in Burke, I, 367–68.

327. Burke, I, 147, 156, 164, 241, 303; letter to Haripada Mitra, 28 December 1893, CW(B), VI, 389.

328. Ghat., III, 21–2, 25; Letter to Swarnakumari Devi, 6 April 1897, CW(B), VII, 375.

329. CW(B), VI, 389.

330. Londone, I, 198–9; II, 58; III, 21; letter to Ramkrishnananda, 19 March 1894, CW(B), VII, 412.

331. VIN, 106. He thus described one of his experiences of racism: 'And whatever aspirations I had of becoming an European was fulfilled totally by the American God. Oh the pangs of an unshaven face! But as soon as I entered a barber's saloon, I was told: "Those looks will not do here!"' He first thought that his *sanyasi*'s attire was the source of trouble and was about to put on western clothes, when a kindly American explained that the robe was preferable to European attire. The latter would mean the risk of lynching. And when he experienced similar treatment in shops, 'the land of the Americans appeared as pleasant as one's own country'. *Parivrajak*, 76.

332. Burke, II, 370; letter to Ramkrishnananda, 19 March 1894, CW(B), VI, 413, 414; letter dated 1895, ibid., VI, 166; letter to Haripada Mitra, 28 December 1893, ibid., 389; letter to Ramkrishnananda, 1894, CW(B) VII, 58.

333. Letter to Ramkrishnananda, 25 September 1894, CW(B), VII, 8.

334. Letter to Ramkrishnananda, 19 March 1894, CW(B), VI, 409; also letter dated 1894, ibid., 453; Londone, I, 95.

335. Burke, II, 215, 346, 379.

336. See fn. 322 above, 7.

337. Burke, II, 370.

338. Letter dated 5 December 1895, CW(E), VI, 351.

339. BJ, 57–8.

340. These statements occur in a sketch written by Professor Wright's wife which was based on notes taken at the time of Vivekananda's first visit to the Wright family. The relevant passages are not included in his biography complied by his disciples where the sketch is reproduced (Life, I, 406–9). For the excluded passages, see Burke, I, 31–3.

341. Londone, I, 176–7, 181, 182, 185–7.

342. Letter to the Hale sisters, 28 November 1896, CW(E), VI, 384.

343. Letter to Mrs Bull, ibid., 367.

344. Letter dated 5 December 1895, ibid., 351.

345. Letter to Miss Waldo, 8 October 1896, ibid., 376.

346. Letter to Miss Noble (Sister Nivedita), 29 July 1897, ibid., VII, 512.

347. Burke, I, 33; II, 108, 290, 312, 313.

348. VB, 243–4.

349. Letter to Pramadadas Mitra, 3 March 1890, CW(B), 320.

350. POP, 159.

351. VB, 243–4.

352. Ibid.

353. Ibid.

354. *Parivrajak*, 75.

355. '*Jnanarjan*,' (Acquisition of knowledge), CW(B), VI, 39.

356. VB, 245.

357. *Parivrajak*, 76.

358. VB, 248–9.

359. Ibid., 247–9; *Vartaman samasya*, 33–4.

Select Bibliography

Bandyopadhyay, A., S. Basu and Sankar (eds.), Viswavivek, 2nd ed., Calcutta, 1966.

Bandyopadhyay, Brajendranath and Sajanikanta Das, *Samasamayik drishtite Sri Ramakrishna Paramahamsa*, 2nd edn., Calcutta, 1952.

Basu, Pramathanath, *Swami Vivekananda*, 2 vols., 2nd edn., Calcutta, 1949.

Basu, S.P., *Vivekananda o samakalin Bharatvarsha*, 5 vols., 1st reprint, Calcutta, 1981.

Basu, S.P. (ed.), *Letters of Sister Nivedita*, 2 vols., Calcutta, 1982.

Basu, S.P. and Ghosh, B.K. (eds.), *Vivekananda in Indian Newspapers, 1893–1902*, Calcutta, 1969.

Basu, S.P. and Ghosh, S.N. (eds.), *Thakur Sri Ramakrishna o Swami Vivekananda—Girishchandra Ghosh*, 2nd reprint, Calcutta, 1981.

Basu, Swapan, *Banglay nabachetanar itihas* (1826–1856), 2nd edn., Calcutta, 1985.

Burke, Marie Louise, *Swami Vivekananda in the West: New Discoveries*, 4 vols., 3rd edn., Calcutta, 1983.

Chatterjee, C., *Sri Sri Latu Maharajer smritikatha*, Calcutta, 1940.

Datta, Bhupendranath, *Swami Vivekananda—Patriot-prophet*, Calcutta, 1954.

_____ *Swami Vivekananda*, Calcutta, 1976.

Datta, Mahendranath, *Sri Ramakrishner anudhyan*, 2nd edn., Calcutta, 1954.

_____ *Swami Vivekanander balyajibani*, Calcutta, 1959.

_____ *Srimad Vivekananda Swamir jibaner ghatanabali*, 3 vols., 4th edn., Calcutta, 1977.

_____ *Londone Swami Vivekananda*, 3rd edn., 4th reprint, Calcutta, 1977.

Dhar, S.N., *A Comprehensive Biography of Swami Vivekananda*, 1st edn., Madras, 1975.

Forbes, G.H., *Positivism in Bengal*, Calcutta, 1975.

Gray, J.N., 'Bengal and Britain: Culture Contact and the Reinterpretation of Hinduism in the 'Nineteenth Century', in R. van M. Baumer, *Aspects of Bengali History and Society*, Honolulu, 1976.

King, U., 'Indian Spirituality, Western Materialism: An Image and its Function in the Reinterpretation of Modern Hinduism', in *Social Action*, vol. 28, 1978.

_____ *Sri Sri Ramakrishna kathamrita* (*Sri Ma kathita*), 1st edn., Calcutta, 1983.

Mueller, Max, *Ramakrishna—His Life and Sayings*, 2nd edn., Calcutta, 1984.

Mukherjee, H., *Vivekananda and Indian Freedom*, Calcutta, 1986.

Pal, Bipin Chandra, *Character Sketches*, Calcutta, 1957.

Rolland, Romain, *The Life of Vivekananda and the Universal Gospel*, translated by Malcolm-Smith, E.F., 10th reprint, Calcutta, 1984.

Sarkar, Sumit, 'The Kathamrita as a Text: Towards an Understanding of Ramakrishna Paramahamsa' (Mimeographed, Nehru Memorial Museum and Library, Occasional Papers on History and Society, no. xxxii), New Delhi, 1985.

Sister Nivedita, *The Master as I Saw Him*, 11th edn., Calcutta, 1972.

Swami Ananyananda, ed., *Reminiscences of Swami Vivekananda—by His Eastern and Western Admirers*, 3rd edn., Calcutta, 1983.

Swami Gambhirananda, ed., *The Apostles of Sri Ramakrishna*, Calcutta, 1967.

_____, *Yuganayak Vivekananda*, 3 vols., Calcutta, 1977.

Swami Nikhilananda, *Vivekananda—A Biography*, Calcutta, 1975.

Swami Pavitrananda, ed., *The Disciples of Sri Ramakrishna*, Mayavati, 1943.

Swami Saradananda, *Sri Sri Ramakrishnalila-prasanga*, 2 vols., Calcutta, 1983.

Swami Vivekananda, *Inspired Talks*, 15th edn., Madras, 1986.

Swami Vividishananda, *A Man of God*, Madras, 1957.

Tagore, Rabindranath, *Reminiscences*, 6th reprint, London, 1942.

The Life of Swami Vivekananda, by His Eastern and Western Disciples, 2 vols., 5th edn., Calcutta, 1979.

Tripathi, Amales, *The Extremist Challenge*, Calcutta, 1967.

chapter **5**

Afterword

The Bengali intelligentsia in the latter half of the nineteenth century developed an almost obsessive preoccupation with the West. This concern offers a contrast with the inward-looking ideology of Indian nationalism in the Gandhian era. In the latter phase, the European models of political and social life had become either marginal to the conscious projections of current programmes and future goals or so much a part of accepted values that continual reassessments were no longer found necessary. Bhudev, writing in the 1880s, speculated on the probable personality of the future national leader who would—i.e., should, combine the inherited Indian values with a knowledge of the external world derived from western learning. By the 1920s, the anxious enquiry into Euro-American mores as a basis for such projections had become irrelevant. Some four decades of organized nationalist politics had produced alternative models of leadership. Whether these were western in origin or not was not a question worth any serious attention any longer. The political processes had also generated firm expectations of a parliamentary form of government in the future, so that enquiries into its suitability for India would have seemed strange. Such speculations were in fact virtually overlooked when anyone made them. Similarly, the new militancy of nationalism ascribed a measure of odiousness to the westernized lifestyle. Exaltation of the *swadeshi* rendered discussions on the denationalizing effects of imitating Englishmen superfluous, even though such imitation did not of course disappear from Indian life overnight.

I have drawn upon examples from the arena of political ideology and related fields because here the changes in intellectual concerns can be seen most clearly. Furthermore, nationalism was at the heart of the preoccupations and enquiries focused on Europe in the late nineteenth century Bengal. A widened social base, some measure of self-confidence and experience of and preparation for political activism had at least partly rescued the Bengali intelligentsia from their earlier sense of inadequacy by the 1920s. The new preoccupations built around current activity and future hopes also de-emphasized the Hindu past and its glorification. The process of politicization had become increasingly secular in outlook, even though the emerging communal problem inhibited its healthy potentialities. Admittedly, precise investigation would modify this very general assessment of changes in attitudes.

However, my purpose in commenting on the changed concerns of the twentieth century is to underline the factors which help explain the earlier preoccupations of the Bengali intelligentsia, namely, the anxiety to understand the West, compare her civilization with that of India, discover at least some points where India was equal if not superior to Europe and decide what to adopt and what to reject from the culture of the politically dominant nations. The questions which our protagonists sought to answer were nearly all within the limits of such concerns. So long as nationalism was to a large extent an anguished awareness in the mental world of the intelligentsia, it generated anxieties about the image of one's culture in the eyes of the world. These were aggravated through the apprehension that the negative assessment by the dominant race, whose judgement one often accepted implicitly, might after all be valid. Political activism which would act as a palliative before long seemed a very distant possibility even in the 1890s. That activism was also an effective outlet for the resentment which induced enquiries into Europe's many failings.

If group anxiety about the relative status and worth of one's own culture was one factor which explains the preoccupation of the nineteenth century Bengali intelligentsia with the West, natural curiosity, intellectual excitement and the facts of attraction and repulsion *vis-à-vis* a civilization totally different from one's own have causal links with specific features of the perceptions discussed in this book. The anxieties were rooted in the structure of the relationship between the ruler and the ruled. The monopoly of ultimate power and the highest status by the ruling race and the consequent exclusion from the same of the entire indigenous population were built into the colonial experience. The white man was the boss. The colour of his skin was the symbol of authority. However high one's status in indigenous society the chances of offensive behaviour from a white fellow passenger on trains could never be precluded. The Indian official could never hope to reach the highest rungs in the bureaucracy. The perceived arrogance of one's official superiors was a fact of daily experience to men highly regarded in Indian society. Laws and rules which regulated even the minutiae of the lives of the indigenes were decided by the alien bureaucracy. The new academic myth that effective authority was vested in locally powerful men had no relevance to the life of the Bengali intelligentsia. Anxiety and a sense of inadequacy were inevitable products of a relationship so structured. But it coexisted with a very different and in many ways amorphous feature of the colonial situation: the contact between two distinct cultures which permitted a wide range of possibilities in terms of life experience. A more limited range of alternative possibilities was not absent even within the framework of the structured relationship itself. But the milieu of culture contact was rich in the possibilities it offered. The storehouse of western civilization had very different things on offer and experience determined one's choice of interest as well as the pattern and depth of response. High office and the authority to make decisions might be closed to the Bengali intelligentsia. Books and western ideas were not. Besides, ever since the days of Rammohun Roy the Bengali intellectual had had experiences of happy encounters with educated Europeans. Travel and study in Europe increased the scope of such encounters even though few Indians travelling in the West escaped entirely the experience of racial humiliation. But, to repeat, the contact between two different cultures, even under colonial rule, was necessarily unstructured. Our three protagonists, like many of their contemporaries, posed essentially similar questions in their exploration of western life. But their answers covered a range of approaches. They focused on different things. The end results of their enquiry were also very different in essential substance and, even more, in differing shades of meaning. And this is so, despite the fact that all three can be located within a narrow span of the nineteenth century ideological spectrum. They were all very Hindu, with an avowed pride in their Hindu identity.

But were all three Hindus in the same sense of the word?

Bhudev's Hinduness was firmly rooted in the punctilious observance of ritual conduct as prescribed in the Smritis, the ultimate criterion by which the orthodox Hindu would judge a person's claim to twice-born status. One wonders if he would have approved of Vivekananda's deviations from orthodoxy, especially the fact that the Swami went through no ritual purification on his return from across the black waters. He rejoiced in the system of values on which the high-caste extended family was based. Child marriage was more than acceptable to him. He abhorred the degradation of the untouchable but saw great merit in the caste system. His future hopes

were built around plans for resuscitating the Brahmins' glory. He donated
his life's savings for this cherished end. But he also held Islam in high
regard.

Bankim's *vita religiosa* began with a sceptical outlook. He was according
to his own statement an atheist in his youth, though peculiarly ambivalent
about the high emotions of the *bhakti* cult. In his total admiration for rational
enquiry and the experimental sciences, he had an open contempt for much
in the Hindu past. He rejected totally the prescriptions of ritually correct
conduct. He saw the caste system as a device for inhuman exploitation, the
reason for India's decline. His faith therefore in the excellence of Hinduism
should not be taken at its face value. What he admired was a synthesized
world-view of his own creation which drew as freely on Comte, Spencer and
Mill as on the Gita and the Mahabharata. Incidentally, he rejected *sanyasa*
and referred disparagingly to the new craze for asceticism, even though
Vivekananda's ideal of renunciation for service to the nation has affinities
with the world-view projected in *Anandamath*. His encounter with the
Paramahamsa was not a success.

By any criterion, the Hindu heritage meant very different things to
Vivekananda and Bankim. Vedanta and non-duality, the promised realization
of the ultimate reality, were at the heart of India's religious tradition, so far
as the Swami was concerned. That message, as the basis for a universal
religion, would take mankind to a new fulfilment. India, in her degradation,
could not of course expect to skip a vital stage and hope for Vedantic self-
knowledge with weak bodies and famished stomachs. Hence the emphasis
on *rajas*. And, of course, *rajas* was essential for national liberation. His
dreams of national regeneration come close to those of Bankim. The latter's
evocation of two symbols of power, Vishnu the Protector, fully armed, and
the Mother Goddess, with weapons in her ten hands, has more to do with
the manipulation of an ancient cultural idiom in the unlikely context of
nationalism than with *bhakti* as understood by the traditional Hindu.
Vivekananda's emphasis on *rajas* similarly invokes a paradigm from the
Sanskritic culture. There is nothing especially Hindu about it. In fact he
discovered a superabundance of *rajas* only in the West. His description of
Brahmins as 'wicked priests' and the emphasis on ritual minutiae as a religion
of 'don't touchism' [sic] would not have amused Bhudev. And, unlike Bankim,
he never retracted his denouncement of the inhuman oppression built into
the Hindu social system. The two had one thing in common in their attitude
to the Hindu past: they were far from being uniformly laudatory. Bankim

could describe the great embodiment of virtue in the Indian tradition, Yudhishthira, as an ass for gambling away his wife and his kingdom even though he was only following the Kshatriya's time-honoured code. Vivekananda referred gleefully to the little business between the queen and the dead horse, a part of the Asvamedha ritual. Such levity would have been unthinkable to Bhudev.

I have argued that despite their emphasis on the Hindu identity, it is a mistake to identify these three and many others who partly shared their outlook (like the Brahmo champion of Hinduism, Rajnarayan Basu) as protagonists of Hindu revivalism, a term which justifiably has a connotation of social and political reaction. Such reactions in the context of modern Indian history have several referents. Of these, three are most relevant in the present context—attitudes to social reform, the Muslims and the Indo-Islamic past and, finally, the masses of the population and necessary changes for the betterment of their condition.

It is certainly true that Bhudev was opposed to any change in established social practices, not as a 'revivalist' but as a defender of a system into which he was born and which he found, as social institutions go, not worse than any other. He compared the fate of the Indian widow with that of the English spinster and concluded that the former was not worse off. Further, reforms in such matters were for him peripheral to the all-important task of national regeneration. Widow remarriage had not helped significantly either the Muslims or the lower castes. If attitude to Muslims is one criterion for assessing a nineteenth century Bengali intellectual's involvement in Hindu revivalism, Bhudev should perhaps be described as an opponent of the movement. He did not approve of the early nationalists' delight in the alleged resistance of Hindu patriots against Muslim tyranny. His assessment of the Muslim contribution to the Indian heritage was overwhelmingly positive. His visions of India's future emphasized a shared destiny for the two communities. His concern for the masses was expressed in the policies he advocated and, where possible, implemented as an educationist *inter alia* free primary education for all, the aborigines included. He saw India's bondage as a divine punishment for her social inequities. He explicitly rejected the egalitarian doctrines as fake and condemned as anti-national* the objection to the existence of a handful of rich people in Indian society. The few

* He pointed out that only 3 per cent of India's population had an income of Rs 500 or more per annum and less than 600 families an annual income of one lakh or more.

wealthy persons had, in his view, a role to play in protecting India's economic interest against the alien onslaught. The implied policy of class collaboration in the national interest anticipated the outlook of Indian nationalism in a later phase. 'Conservative' rather than 'revivalist' or 'reactionary' is perhaps the appropriate label for Bhudev's ideological position. But his conservatism contained a strong element of radical thought.

It is more difficult to locate Bankim at any precise point in the ideological spectrum of the day. His own uncertainties and shifts in attitudes over time are the chief reasons for this difficulty. He was surely not enthusiastic about social reforms like the legalization of widow remarriage, but he acknowledged that such remarriages should be allowed. He had also accepted *in toto* the British historians' projection of the Indo-Islamic era as an age of Muslim tyranny. I have cited evidence to show that this academic perception was translated in his case into gut reactions which we now describe as communalism.

At a slightly later date, the Hindu communalist was seen justifiably as a political reactionary. It is, however, well to recognize that in Bankim's days, unfortunately, the nationalist perception of Indo-Islamic history saw the Muslim dynasts as tyrants. By association, the Muslim fellow subjects of the empire were also painted black, just as the crime of conquest was attributed to the entire English people, and not to any particular section of English society. Only a few intellectuals saw quite early the fallacy and dangers of communalism. In contemporary eyes Bankim's image should perhaps be redeemed by his impassioned critique of exploitation in Indian society. He rejected his treatise on equality as erroneous, but never retracted his description of the Bengali peasant's horrendous fate. Of course, the highly talented deputy magistrate was not a revolutionary. He prescribed reform, not abolition, of the zamindari system, partly because he, as an avowed friend of the British, did not want them to go back on their promises. It may not be irrelevant to point out that socialistic India has not bettered significantly that fate of the marginal peasant described by Bankim. This creative artist, torn by conflicts, is perhaps the most interesting of our three protagonists as an individual. It is difficult to subsume the complexity of his concerns and attitudes under any label.

Vivekananda, like Bankim, considered the nineteenth-century programmes of social reform peripheral, if not irrelevant, to the task of national reconstruction. He was particularly irritated by the recourse to an alien administration for achieving improvements in Indian society. The continuous harping on the evil customs of the Hindus, to the delight of foreigners, hurt his national pride. He rejected much in the Hindu tradition which he rationalized in his statements abroad. The changes he sought in Indian society were far more radical than any programme conceived by his contemporaries or forebears. He wrote off India's élite as the living dead, mummies who should make way for the rightful heirs, the oppressed masses who had always been denied their inheritance. He assigned to the intelligentsia a very limited task—to make the masses aware of their power and provide them with the physical and mental nourishment they would need to achieve their destiny. This was not exactly the goal one would associate with Hindu revivalism or even with colonial middle-class ideology. His radical outlook was also manifest in his attitude to Islam, especially its role in India. There are hints of pan-Asianism in his proud claim asserting the Islamic origins of modern European civilization. He contrasted Islam's civilizing role in history with Christianity's record of bigotry and persecution. His pride in the Mughal heritage was marked by highly charged emotions. To see the youthful *sanyasi* as a protagonist of Hindu revivalism with its connotation of social-political reaction is to misread his message. He projected abroad the least denominational features of Hindu thought. His purpose in doing so was rooted in the hopes of a mystical millennium—all mankind led by the mighty westerners under Indian guidance, reaching fulfilment and brotherhood in the realization of *atman*. In the process, the dominant West would bow before India as their teacher. These were the hopes of a radical nationalist who was also a mystic. He deployed what to him were the most potent tools in the Indian inheritance for human welfare and national glory. To repeat a point already made, all the three protagonists discussed in this book distanced themselves from the revivalist claims to Hindu foreknowledge of western scientific discoveries. Vivekananda made ribald fun of electromagnetic theories explaining Indian superstitions.

The attitudes of the three very individual thinkers to the question of Hindu identity and the dominant politicocultural issues of the time indicate the differences in their life experiences and personalities. The latter in turn, I have argued, have an important bearing on what they looked for and discovered in European civilization, which informed the finer nuances of their perceptions of the West. Bhudev and Bankim both belonged to a high subcaste of Brahmins and worked in the colonial bureaucracy but were almost poles apart as individual human beings despite the similarities in their background and education. The severe discipline of a Brahminical upbringing left its mark on Bhudev. He looked like a Hebrew prophet in his advanced years. His contemporaries suggest that even as a schoolboy he was formidable in his puritanism and strict adherence to ritual codes. His style of writing, clear, precise, direct and entirely free from the flowery exuberance one associates with much of nineteenth century Bengali prose, reflects a completely disciplined personality. Except for a brief and unsatisfactory venture into writing a novel he stuck to his forte—didactic and sociological treatises based on great erudition and Brahminical certitudes. Except for a very short-lived flutter in early adolescence, he never suffered from culture conflict. Values, derived from nineteenth century western thought and world-views, did inform his outlook. This is most clearly noticeable in his enthusiasm for Positivist ideals though one reason for his enthusiasm was the exaltation of the priestly caste in Comte's philosophy. But he appears to have been genuinely unaware of the western influences he had unconsciously absorbed into his value system. So far as his self-image was concerned, he was nothing but a learned Brahmin following in the footsteps of his forebears. At the level of values, anything the West had to offer was incomparably inferior in his eyes to the received wisdom. This conviction was generated by the conditions of his life, especially his deep attachment to the emotional ambience of the Bengali 'joint family'. Individualism was destructive of that ambience and hence to be rejected. Arguably, his declaration of faith in the moral superiority of Hinduism was not an attempt at cultural self-assertion or at least not consciously so. It expressed a genuine belief which he wanted his countrymen to share. As a patriot, he sought national regeneration built around this faith. Defence of the received system of values was at least as important to a people as the defence of territorial sovereignty.

He aimed at objectively exploring western history and civilization and was fully aware of how one's hopes and preferences could influence one's judgement. At the same time, his very impressive *Essay on Society* was avowedly an exercise in proving conclusions at which he had already arrived. Western history to him was an object lesson in what mankind should avoid. Hindus need learn from the West only their practical skills and social solidarity. The latter and its highest expression, patriotism, were necessary for survival but in Bhudev's scale of values these were allotted a rather low rung. Patriotism, if unchecked, led to self-aggrandisement and hence aggression. Its end product was the criminally violent act of conquest.

Ultimately, it would lead to wars which would destroy western civilization. He explored western history to unravel the root of that violence and discovered it in individualism—to him an apotheosis of selfishness, exaltation of property rights, an amoral loyalty to national interests, and the heritage of the barbarian hordes who destroyed the Roman empire. Christianity, with its limited message for man's worldly life and accepted more in name than in fact, acted as a mild corrective of the immoral selfishness at the root of all western endeavour.

The entire exercise develops around the theme of morality, or rather the all-encompassing concept of *dharma*, right conduct. This anchor sheet of the good life as conceived in Brahminical doctrine was the ideal by which Bhudev and his forebears lived. He used his knowledge of western thought to judge the west in terms of an ill-defined yet perfectly understood code on which his own culture was based. Patriotism to him was a defence of that culture as well as its further growth.

There is something very Gandhian in his rejection of western values. The future India of his dreams as described in his imaginary history of the country stops short of encouraging industry and trade beyond a point, for unrestrained greed, whether individual or national, led to selfish aggression and conflict. England's wealth was the source of her moral decline. Like Gandhi, too, he is not particularly excited by the varied spectacle of western civilization. His biographers tell us of his interest in European literature, especially Goethe. He also had plans to write a treatise on western art. But his voluminous published works bear little evidence of his pleasure in western literature. One wonders if the projected volume on western art would not have focused on the themes which most concerned him—moral purpose, religious ideology, and historical circumstances which in their mutual interaction determined social evolution and all its expressions. His statements on western life have a richness of texture and reflect a powerful intellect as well as profound erudition. Every argument is supported by evidence and the West to him is not an undifferentiated mass reducible to set clichés. The cultural variations over space and time are carefully noted. But all this intellectual effort was geared to a single purpose—an argument to establish conclusions derived from culturally determined moral premises. He advised his countrymen not to learn from Europe anything but her skills in practical matters. He used his profound readings into western thought and culture to justify this advice. In short, despite the wide scope of his statement and the extensive data on which it was based, his enquiry had a limited objective and was rooted in a preconception.

Bankim, unlike Bhudev, was above all an artist, who as a novelist learnt his craft from western models. Europe's literature and social thought fascinated him. He had an untutored admiration for western painting and sculpture which he considered superior to the Indian inheritance. In fact, he was convinced of modern Europe's incomparable superiority in the arts of civilization over all human achievements in earlier ages and in other parts of the globe. He was equally convinced of degradation and inferiority of contemporary Indians, especially Bengalis of his own class. His was an avowedly self-conscious quest for the limitations of western civilization and for areas of cultural achievement where India could claim to be superior. He considered national pride an essential precondition for national regeneration. An unrelieved sense of inferiority could not be a source of pride.

If Bhudev was a model of Brahminical self-discipline, a man in command of his emotions, Bankim was the archetypal Bengali creative artist-cum-intellectual—passionate, conflict-ridden and inspired by a love of reason which was not always very consistent with his strong emotional drives. His patriotism had an impassioned quality and there was something almost personal in his sense of humiliation at the fact of political dependence. The colonial context, rich in possibilities of unpleasant encounters with the master race, provided the basis for a series of humiliating experiences which mortified this very proud and sensitive man. His admiration for the West was counterbalanced from time to time by almost xenophobic outbursts. Yet the dominant concern in his explorations of western life was a quest for things to learn. A convert to liberal-humanist ideology, he, like his contemporary, Akshay Datta, identified rational enquiry and experimentation as the source of Europe's excellence. His emotional faith in social justice as a high value probably derived as much from his exposure to the Bengali peasant's misery as from his study of western social philosophy. But his faith was articulated in terms of categories derived from the latter source. He eventually discovered a world-view and philosophy of life, traced to Hindu sources, and hence projected as an adequate basis for national self-respect as well as regeneration. His later novels underline this ideology; the fictional struggle for political liberation in *Anandamath* is inspired by it. Here was an escape route from a sense of inferiority. But the ideology, as his contemporaries recognized, drew heavily on Bentham, Mill, Comte and Matthew Arnold. Bankim explained away his western sources either as affinities, not borrowings (the philosophers he borrowed from were but 'European Hindus') or as dim and belated gropings of Europe towards truths discovered by the ancient Hindus. The element of cultural self-assertion in these statements expressed one tendency in contemporary public life. But it also embodied a more constructive quest— for a satisfactory philosophy as the basis of individual and national life. This quest was a crucial feature of early nationalist thought. Indian nationalism, arguably, was never entirely divorced from this search for a wide-ranging philosophy of life in any of its manifestations.

Bankim's liberal humanism explains the absorption of western values into the moral and cultural discipline he prescribed for his countrymen. The denial of his debt reflects the colonial élite's sense of inadequacy in relation to the politically dominant race and its civilization. But the *Dharmatattva* and the ideal of *nishkama karma* express concerns which are not exclusively public. Bankim included in one of his didactic dialogues a thinly veiled account of his agonized quest for a satisfactory philosophy, for some meaning in life almost since his childhood. This is a pattern of anxiety to which his pre-colonial forebears were almost certainly strangers. The tradition provided the answers, even if the questions did arise in the individual soul. Bhudev is a prime example of such certainty and there is no reason to consider him an atavistic survival. His brief uncertainty caused by exposure to western-style rational thought was quickly corrected under parental guidance. Bankim, it appears, began to wonder what it was all about as a precocious boy. He had little experience of Brahminical discipline and not much of parental guidance. His youthful exuberance generated feelings of guilt. Faith in rational thought, acquired in early youth, undermined loyalties to traditional belief. The much admired western culture was represented by a system and people he came to dislike, and probably hate. Hence the arduous investigation of the Mahabharata and the Gita to discover a satisfying philosophy which would deliver him from his *angst* and be at the same time acceptable to his nationalist ego. But western values had entered his very soul. No way could he exorcise the ghost from his synthesized philosophy of life.

As a sensitive artist and a man very much in love with life, he savoured western literature with undisguised pleasure. The comparisons with Sanskrit poetry were attempts to widen and deepen the literary experience, not compensate for any sense of inadequacy. He had plans for travel in Europe. Very probably, he would not have discovered in the West data for a moral argument if his plans had materialized. His intellectual and artistic involvement with western humanism, like that of his senior contemporary, Michael Madhusudan Datta, was part of a developing concern going back to the early decades of the century. It transcended and survived the sense of inadequacy and resentments inseparable from the colonial nexus. The intellectual excitement over western humanism was the one product of the encounter between two dissimilar civilizations least tarnished by conflict. It created and sustained an interest in the many facets of western culture—its intellectual and artistic achievements as well as the excellence and oddities of lifestyle.

Our third protagonist, Vivekananda, was a western-educated Hindu *sanyasi* who accepted a nearly illiterate holy man as his guru. His travels in India as a wandering ascetic in search of God led to his discovery of Indian poverty. His early middle-class patriotism, submerged under his mystical yearnings, resurfaced with a new edge—a determination to awaken India's masses to a sense of their dignity and power. He went to the West to secure the wherewithal for his new objective. There he developed other aspirations— salvation of mankind, no less, and, in the process, the elevation of India to the status of world's guru. He did not travel to America to learn from the West. What he had learnt of western thought as a student had become largely irrelevant after his initiation into the discipline of Indian mysticism. The band of youthful ascetics led by him studied *inter alia* Christianity and European history, even chanting 'Vive la republique' like some holy *mantra*. The secular studies were however traceable to the intellectual concerns of the Bengali intelligentsia and were not central to the ascetics' spiritual goal. Only, Vivekananda's later plans to awaken the masses were built round an educational programme which would introduce the unlettered to a knowledge of the world around them. His was truly an unintended discovery of the West, and also an unexpected success story. He responded with characteristic ebullience, delighted and amused by much that he saw or experienced. An extraordinary literary talent flowered under this impact, producing some of the most marvellous prose in the Bengali language. They record the vivid impressions of a person of immense vitality, responsive to but not hungry for life. His commitment to the mystical goal was qualified only by patriotic concerns. He does appear to have been totally free from any personal aspirations and transcended the longings of the flesh. Yet cultural self-assertion is not absent from his statements. His strong feelings against colonial rule were expressed in almost racist terms. He repeatedly laid claims to India's moral superiority in his lectures in the US and tried to explain away

India's unwholesome social customs. His criticisms of Christianity in history and his uninhibited resentment against Christian missionaries echoed his anti-colonial sentiments. These were also the basis of his claims to Asian, especially Indian, superiority in matters religious.

His western experience made him aware of something he had not set out to discover—the vitality of Euro-American civilization which he translated as *rajas* in terms of a Sanskritic cultural idiom. He prescribed an attitude of renunciation as the way to liberation to his western devotees. He preached *rajas*, western-style, to his countrymen with no holds barred. This was very different from the counsel of selective approach—either gingerly emulation of western technological and social skills or a synthesis of eastern and western values offered as authentic Hindu doctrine. He too explored the fundamental pronenesses of eastern and western civilizations, accepting the simplistic dichotomy which still survives as a respectable paradigm. That dichotomy was equated with another: preoccupations with the body and the spirit, materialism and spirituality. Two very different notions are intermingled in this thesis. Projection of eastern or Indian spirituality as opposed to western materialism has obvious resonances of cultural self-assertion. But it is well to remember that the paradigm did not refer to contemporary Indian reality. Vivekananda had discovered Indian spirituality in the life and teachings of his guru after a hard and highly sceptical search. To him it did represent the acme of human aspiration. He had found nothing comparable in the living traditions of the West. He saw in the West, on the other hand, a manifestation of power geared to material ends which too had no parallel in the Indian experience. He not only acknowledged the excellence of Europe's high civilization, but saw in western vigour a moral quality essential for the transition to *sattva*, spirituality, the ultimate stage in man's evolution. The dichotomy he projected was thus at one level a theoretical statement of observed facts, not a claim to cultural superiority. One has to read it with his almost ecstatic account of Paris—the readiness to recognize merit even in her immoral pleasures; he saw in these the beauty of a dancing peacock.

This book deals with the perceptions of three influential thinkers who both reflected and shaped powerful trends in the life of nineteenth century Bengal. I have argued that their perceptions were determined partly by those features of the colonial nexus which impinged uniformly, more or less, on everyone's life. The stereotypes of Europe's superior power and inferior morality derive from the colonial élite's emotional responses to that nexus. Our protagonists did not reject the stereotypes. But they did discuss these in very different terms and emphasize very different facets. Besides, they talked of many things which were not parts of any simple pattern. The differences in their approach and substantive statements reflect the diversity in life experiences and personalities, an important dimension of the concrete historical experience which has not been adequately emphasized in the literature on colonial or pre-colonial India. I am not arguing here in favour of a disaggregated approach as the high and exclusive road to historical truth or the negation of analytical frameworks which have a general relevance. Only, if the discipline has a humanistic dimension, the specificities of experience and individual variations can illuminate past reality in a way not open to analysis of trends and social categories. Besides, I have tried to show that the specificities have an explanatory value. They also reveal the complex nature of interactions, the alternative possibilities of response and perception created by the encounter between different cultures and even by the conditions of colonial rule. To take the most obvious and least noted example, the culture of the dominant race did not uniformly dominate colonial élite consciousness. Bhudev rejected spontaneously nearly all its values and advised others to follow suit. Vivekananda advised emulation as an *ad hoc* step towards higher things and even that in terms of an idiom and value system alien to western culture. The three *gunas* have little meaning in the Euro-American context.

The perceptions discussed here are archetypal rather than typical. These embody at a high level of articulation a range of ideas which were either in the air at the time or which were introduced into the cultural vocabulary of the élite by our protagonists and other publicists. Nationalist consciousness was informed by these perceptions. These were also parts of an ongoing enquiry which was not exclusively ideological in purpose. Many of the statements discussed here are addressed to intellectual or cultural queries inspired only by intelligent curiosity. Ideology itself had a scope which transcended politics. It subsumed values, world-views and, at a more mundane level, standards of behaviour and social conduct embodying values which remained unstated. The western model was seldom found irrelevant to any area of life. It could, of course, be emulated or rejected *in toto* or in part. As often, it was simply assessed as something very different which one might admire or criticise but in no case adopt as the basis on which to build one's life.

The Bengal Renaissance:
Reconsidering Revisions

This memorial lecture was delivered at Jadavpur University, Calcutta, to mark the centenary of the birth of Professor Susobhan Chandra Sarkar.

I

First, I should like to thank the organizers of these lectures for inviting me to speak to you today. Professor Susobhan Sarkar profoundly influenced the thinking and outlook of generations of students. I feel highly privileged that I happened to be one of his many pupils whose intellectual development was thus shaped. I also remember with gratitude the fact that I got to know him personally and received his undemonstrative affection. I chose as the subject of my talk today a theme to which he returned again and again, a subject which to him was of more than academic interest and, to my understanding, should be so to all of us for it concerns the definition of our own identity. What I shall say involves controversy. I offer my comments in the spirit which Professor Sarkar sought to instill in us—a belief in the necessity to differ without disrespect for those with whom one disagrees. His Marxist convictions did not eliminate his essentially liberal outlook.

The earlier historiography on the subject, and indeed the continuing popular perception of the historical phenomenon in question, were, in their naïveté, something of sitting ducks. It was inevitable that at some point in time people would shoot these down. That the Marxists took the lead in the matter and the postmodernists followed in their footsteps are facts of our intellectual history in recent times. But non-Marxist historians such as the late Professor Amales Tripathi also objected to perceptions which saw nineteenth century Calcutta as a reincarnation of quattrocento Florence. Only, he was more respectful than his radical colleagues towards our intellectual forebears.

The easiest duck to shoot in this particular scene was Sir Jadunath Sarkar's embarrassing conclusion that Plassey was the harbinger of a new dawn which put to shame even the splendours of Renaissance Florence. The great historian was an uncompromising believer in the redeeming qualities of British rule. Be it said to his credit that he was consistent in his belief and action: he never compromised with or accepted the patronage of the post-Independence regime which he loathed. There is a lesson in such consistency for the contemporary critics of western dominance and our much maligned nation state.

The Marxist critique of the older perceptions had its first systematic expression in 1972, the bicentenary year of Rammohan's birth. Its major conclusions are contained in a volume of essays edited by V.C. Joshi entitled *Rammohan Roy and the Modernisation of India.* Two of the most influential contributions in this volume, by Barun De and Sumit Sarkar respectively, questioned the validity of the perceptions which project the Raja as the pioneer of modernization and westernization in India and the assumption that unqualified benefits flowed from these two processes. The essays raised doubts regarding Rammohan's commitment to modernity and identified elements of ambivalence in his attitude to the less savoury features of Hindu belief and practice, to wit caste hierarchy, rules of ritual purity, enforced celibacy of widows, and so on. Sarkar found in Rammohan's life a pattern of retreat from the bold rationality of the *Tuhfat* which questioned the supernatural beliefs to be found in all religions; contemporary authorities who spoke of the Raja's anxiety to please all and sundry were quoted in the essay. A more serious flaw in the eyes of the Raja's radical critics was his faith in the regenerative possibilities of British rule, especially the absurdity of his expectation that collaboration with European colonizers might transform India's society and economy. The many deficiencies in his role as a thinker and reformer derived from this one central flaw: his glaring failure to perceive the reality of colonial subjection.

The argument progressed through Ashok Sen's well-known essay on Vidyasagar's elusive milestones and Ranajit Guha's essay on *Nildarpan,* written before he stood forth as the leader of the intellectual movement centred on the Subaltern Studies. The basic idea in these essays is simple enough: the worthies of the so-called Bengal Renaissance were petty collaborators of the colonial regime, alienated from the masses, with no aspiration towards class hegemony, and totally incapable of advancing social production. Their influence limited to a tiny minority, they were unlikely initiators of industrialization and did not even try to forge a broader social consensus. Their English education, far from being a blessing, was a disaster for it raised insuperable barriers between them and the underprivileged. Knowledge of Persian, which had acted as a channel of cultural communication between educated Hindus and their Muslim counterparts, also disappeared under colonial rule. The intellectual advantages derived from that now lost source, such as access to the rationalist traditions of the Mutazilla school, ceased to be a part of the intellectual equipment of the bhadralok. A social class burdened with such handicaps and frailties, and faced with the historic situation in which they thrived, was both incapable of generating any revival and, of course, any transformation of the society and economy. Their puerile and half-hearted initiatives at reform inevitably produced the backlash of Hindu reaction. Sasadhar Tarkachudamani's dazzling idiocies, anticipating those of Dr Oak, and the monstrous agitation against the Age of Consent Bill were the ultimate end products of the famous Renaissance. The attempts at reform were now well and safely buried. One central concern of nineteenth century reform, altering the status and condition of women, also ended in failure, thanks to the Hindu reaction. Such in short is the story of the Bengal Renaissance. The word 'renaissance', like the word 'nationalism' in the Indian context in more recent writings, is encased in inverted commas to signify the authors' distance from the perceptions implied by those words. Incidentally, these exercises in debunking, despite their radical origins, are highly popular with overtly or covertly imperialist historians. They are immensely pleased that the originators of protonationalist ideas have at last been shown up by their own countrymen. Such delight, of course, has no relevance to any assessment of the theses in question. I start with the assumption that the radical critics as well as the imperialist historians may well be right.

The other sitting ducks, besides Sir Jadunath Sarkar's embarrassing assessment, were the hagiographical writings on the nineteenth century worthies which often passed as sober history and shaped the popular perception of our social and intellectual past in recent times. There were obvious elements of misleading hero-worship in this literature, exaggerations which deserved to be cut down to size. But the very fact of these exaggerations underlines a psychological necessity which is not irrelevant to our discussion, a topic to which I shall return at the conclusion of my lecture.

Sumit Sarkar's later studies, especially his essays written in the 1990s, have certainly deepened our understanding of the social processes at work in nineteenth century Bengal. Three of his conclusions, and the research on which these are based, are especially important. First, he drew attention to the diversity of the colonial middle class, particularly the role of the traditional pandits and their social background. This emphasis is of value in explaining the persistence of strongly conservative elements in the middle-class outlook. Second, he unravelled the complexity of individual roles which could range from totally reactionary to almost radical positions depending on the particular issues, so that any simple classification of the intelligentsia as conservative, radical or liberal would be misleading. Third, he worked out a chronology of sociocultural history in which the changing material conditions are seen to engender a loss of faith in the regenerative potential of colonial rule and in the last three decades of the century the frustrated middle class finds solace in the consolations of religion, especially such as were offered by the semi-literate holy man, Ramakrishna. These developments facilitated the Hindu revival or reaction. The argument is developed in Amiya P. Sen's very impressive monograph on Hindu revivalism in Bengal, which has unfortunately not received the attention it deserves.

The scholars associated with the Subaltern Studies collective, especially Partha Chatterjee, based their critique on distinctly non-Marxist premises. In their analysis, the material base and the dialectics of historical change lose their importance. Instead it is centred on relationships of power, of dominance and subjection, imperialist projects of cultural hegemony in which western education is projected as the main instrument for what in plain English can be described as brainwashing. Following Edward Said's *Orientalism* and using techniques of deconstructing texts, they emphasize the construction by the imperialist West of an essentialized Orient different from and inferior to Europe's high civilization. Cultural propaganda, using western education as a conduit, successfully implanted this belief in western superiority into the consciousness of the colonial middle class. Orientalist paradigms thus proved to be a powerful tool of cultural and political domination. Indian nationalism, strictly within inverted commas, was a by-product of Orientalist projections of the Indian past, which tickled the vanity of the complex-ridden Bengali intelligentsia. Their agenda, strongly pro-imperialist in outlook, had no place for the masses. Their programmes of reform, so-called, accepted the premise that post-Enlightenment social rationality was a feature of western society and gave it its characteristic superiority. That rationality itself was part of dominant Europe's multifaceted self-projection as a superior civilization. The middle class, by accepting western education, had slavishly surrendered to western domination. This implied a total alienation from the autonomous pre-colonial consciousness of the people embedded in the culture of the distinct communities, the real base of South Asian societies. Nationalism, so-called, an alien ideology slavishly adopted by the middle class for their own ends, had no roots in this pristine consciousness of the subaltern classes or communities. The Subaltern Studies scholars totally reject the notion that an élite leadership mobilized the masses for the anti-colonial struggle for freedom—'the freedom struggle'—which to some British historians is a ludicrous figment of the Indian imagination besides being a prime example of Babu English. Brilliantly documented essays and one remarkable monograph, by Shahid Amin, have established that the masses responded to the call of the nationalist leadership only when it corresponded to their own perceived needs as autonomous agents. But echoing for once the Marxist analysis of R.P. Dutt, the Subaltern Studies scholars conclude that their participation in the nationalist struggle did the masses no good. The western-educated élite eventually created a nation state which was an unnatural imposition on the communities and only a source of oppressive domination. The denial of its legitimacy and the empowerment of the communities were the only acceptable paths to an equitable future.

One dimension of this analysis took on the so-called reforms aimed at ameliorating the condition of women. In one of his essays Sumit Sarkar discusses the relative failure of these reforms, eventually stifled by the rising tide of social reaction. Partha Chatterjee questions this thesis and argues instead that in this one area, that of gender politics, the bhadralok did achieve what they had set out to do, namely a reconstitution of patriarchy in terms of their new needs and aspirations. This particular thesis has gained wide acceptance among feminists, especially in the United States.

II

I have presented to you a thumbnail sketch of complex, highly sophisticated, and very serious historical research, which has achieved a well-deserved centrality in the historiography of India over the last three decades. Such sketches invariably water down and somewhat distort both the results of the research in question and the methods adopted to arrive at them. I trust, however, that I have not seriously misrepresented the positions taken by my colleagues whose theses I am going to question. I also owe an apology for going overground familiar to many in critiquing the positions I have discussed briefly.

Let me begin with some initial concessions to the critics of the Renaissance concept. I too do not feel that Renaissance is the appropriate description for the literary-intellectual efforts of the nineteenth-century Bengali bhadralok or their undoubtedly limited initiatives in the arena of social reform which was confined strictly to their own social class. They themselves ascribed no such grandeur to their modest efforts. Bankim, as Sumit Sarkar notes, placed the Bengali Renaissance in the sixteenth century. The term used to describe the new consciousness, creativity, and social initiatives was *naba-jagaran*, new awakening, and I am not sure when the term was first invented. The Bengali bhadralok had a fairly low opinion of his own station in life and the achievements of his class. From the beginning of print culture—from the writings of Bhabanicharan Bandyopadhyay and others, through Bankim's caustic essays on the babu, to Rabindranath's famous description of the children of Bengal with their plump well-oiled sleepy bodies, and later Nirad C. Chaudhuri's vitriolic portraits of Bengalis— the Bengali intellectual has rarely had a good word to say about his own class. The radical critique, it seems to me, is in a direct line of descent from the nineteenth century self-deprecation of the Bengali intelligentsia. The 'unhappy consciousness' of which Sudipta Kaviraj writes was no occasional product of melancholy introspection, but entrenched at the very heart of the bhadralok's colonial experience. In his private letters Bankim repeatedly refers to the Bengalis as mere servants of the British, without any power or status. This sentiment was by no means confined to him alone.

Much has been written about the role of the bhadralok as enthusiastic collaborators of colonial rule. Perhaps there is some overstatement here. Let us start with Rammohan, who certainly believed in the beneficial impact of continued British rule. He also had a low opinion of his ritual-ridden society which, he thought, killed all initiative. He felt, perhaps somewhat naïvely, that contact with educated Europeans might help cure these frailties. The allegation that he had no appreciation of the true nature of colonialism is, of course, true, but no one did at that point in time, not even the noble subaltern gifted with an autonomous pre-colonial understanding of social reality. What is singular about Rammohan is that he was the first person to speak of India as a politiocultural entity, to envisage a future 'in hundred years' time' when the country would be free, but who hoped that the day would not come too soon for his countrymen to learn from contact with Europe. As the Vishwa Hindu Parishad (VHP) programme for the revival of Hindutva, centred on a pristine pre-colonial consciousness, unfolds itself, one wonders if Rammohan was entirely mistaken. A pioneer is not a person who works out a complete agenda for the future; he/she only initiates ideas and actions which acquire a life of their own over time. In this sense there is nothing false about Rammohan's role as a pioneer. Our contemporary critics, arguably, are his intellectual progeny. I do think he would have approved of them.

The successive generations which followed expressed their anti-colonial attitudes and their burgeoning national consciousness in a wide variety of ways. One must remember that we are talking of a tiny group of people, with little economic and no political power, drawn from a range of social groups which were mostly created directly or indirectly by the functioning of colonial rule. Commerce, the mainstay of the urban economy in Bengal, was firmly in British hands, as was banking, insurance, and transport. There was only a handful of wealthy Bengalis, enriched by dealings with the Company and/or the Permanent Settlement. But the class which could aspire to high office both under the nawabs and in the early days of Company rule was now reduced to seeking employment in the lower levels of the bureaucracy or was confined to the profession of the petty vakil. The post of a deputy collector was the height of their aspiration. In 1867 only 13,431 persons earned Rs 75 or more per month in Bengal. Of these, less than 50 per cent were Bengalis. Actually the proportions changed somewhat for the better by the late 1880s and there were also a few successful professionals by then. But this was hardly an adequate social foundation for launching or even for perceiving the possibility of an anti-colonial agenda.

The Bengali intellectual might not be able to understand the true nature of colonial rule, although in the last decades of the century Bholanath Chandra and R.C. Dutt were analysing the devastating impact of colonialism. Earlier

Lal Behari De and Bankim had described the condition of the peasantry and passionately denounced the causes of peasant misery. To quote Bankim's words, he refused to sing the praises of British rule so long as such misery persisted. True, he accepted the theories of the classical economists which had been implicitly rejected by R.C. Dutt, but it is well to remember that rival theories explaining economic processes persist till today. Agendas for economic reconstruction with an emphasis on the eradication of poverty have a long history in Bengal. They date back to Bhudev's imaginary history of India and the *Samajik Prabandha* (incidentally, the measures he recommended might please the contemporary critics of foreign investment). Accepting the fact of colonial rule as something which was beyond their power to remove, they instead suggested plans for capturing the vantage grounds of the economy and society. Rabindranath, following the same logic, worked out detailed schemes for rural reconstruction which anticipated many of Gandhi's ideas. The beginnings of contact with the working class also go back to this period. The initiatives of Keshabchandra and Sasipada Banerji were not in the tradition of Victorian slumming, but were genuinely intended to alter the conditions of the workers. The concern recurs in one of Sibnath Sastri's novels. To repeat, they were, of course, not revolutionaries any more than the current day Indian leftists are. But they did mark the beginning of middle-class initiatives and an awareness which laid the basis of more systematic efforts to empower the workers, or at least to secure for them acceptable living conditions at a later date. These efforts too were middle class in their origin.

One of the many criticisms of the social class in question was its inherent incapacity to induce irreversible changes in the economy or, industrialization in other words. The story in this respect is more complex than the critique suggests. Amiya Bagchi has drawn attention to the causal links between the differing records of colonialism in various parts of India and the regional differences in the history of industrial development. N.K. Sinha describes the retreat of Bengali capital from modern enterprise after the failure of the Bengal Bank and the way in which the Bengali partners of European investors were cheated and ruined owing to the absence of laws limiting liability. Incidentally, a fair measure of industrial growth under colonial rule was by no means impossible, as the experience of western India proves. In his monograph on the inter-war years Basudev Chatterji has shown the two faces of Indian enterprise: one benefiting from Pax Britannica and even the twisted development of the infrastructure which hence cooperated with the colonial ruler; the other opposing and pressing for a more positive framework of state policy until the entrepreneurial class came to perceive nationalism as the ideology which reflected their interests. Despite all the negative factors at work, Bengali enterprise did not die out entirely; the details of that story are narrated in the Bengali monograph *Lakshmir Kripalabh—Bangalir Sadhana* by Viswakarma.

One of the major points in the critique of the Renaissance paradigm relates to the impact of western education. Sumit Sarkar refers to one disastrous consequence: a total alienation from the masses. The Subaltern Studies scholars see it as an instrument of subordination, its willing recipients surrendering slavishly to an alien ideology contrived to perpetuate western domination. More than one nineteenth century worthy, Bankim in particular, was aware of the divisive implications of western education, particularly of the language barrier it was creating between the privileged and the masses. The intellectuals and creative writers sought to counter this tendency through a new concern with developing the Bengali language. Hence the *Bangadarshan* at least intended to reach out to people who did not understand English, Keshab's *Sulabh Samachar*, and Rajnarayan Basu's somewhat quixotic club where one paid a fine for using English words in one's conversation. Moreover, the bulk of the nineteenth century writings on matters of social concern were produced in the mother tongue. I note with regret that we who try to sell our academic products on the world market, including the most radical among us, have not emulated our unworthy forebears.

The critique of western education includes an element of populist nativism. English learning is supposed, among other things, to have severed our links not only with mass culture but also with the enriching tradition of Persian-based education. Especially regretted is the loss of Mutazilla rationality. I gather from the *Encyclopaedia of Islam* that the Mutazilla was a doctrine rooted in mediaeval Islam and centred on the question of free will versus predestination. Rammohan may have derived the style of argument in the *Tuhfat* from the academic tradition of the *madrassas*, but not the substance. Other traditions of rationality were also at work. As Sibnath Sastri informs us, the rejection of idol worship and in fact any belief in God in the case of his father was a product of his training in *nyaya*, but it did not affect his very active acquiescence in orthodox practice. Neither Mutazilla nor *nyaya* dislodged Hindu orthodoxy from its throne of privilege. Like the establishment today, Hindu orthodoxy in the past had nothing against radicalism so long as its postures did not go beyond hot words. I do believe that our loss of Persian education, like the present generation's total unfamiliarity with Sanskritic learning, implies a cultural impoverishment. If our poet had access to Persian like his father, the inspiration he derived from Kalidasa would have been supplemented by one from Hafiz and we would have been enriched by one more element of grandeur in his poetry. But to suggest that Mutazilla rationality was somehow superior to the rationality of western derivation, especially what is now described as 'colonial rationality', is really the height of nativist absurdity. And the view that this loss by itself severed the cultural link with the Muslim intelligentsia is also invalid, simply because the shared knowledge of English, accessible to many as opposed to the handful of people who knew Persian, created channels of communication among all educated people. The new print-culture further facilitated such communication. If the two communities drifted apart, western education was hardly a major contributory factor in that process.

The concept of post-Enlightenment rationality in its social context, especially its colonial variant, has been a butt of much derision in recent years, particularly among radical postmodernists on American campuses. This has helped install the incomprehensible on the throne of privilege, displacing logical argumentation, a product of vile rationality. We are perhaps witnessing the advent of a dark age in the literal sense of the term when mystic communion between the dispensers of the unintelligible and their clueless acolytes will be the centre-point of all intellectual enterprise. In fact in some areas of academe that age is already with us.

Jokes apart, the western claims to superior social rationality treated as an analogue of scientific reason is indeed unacceptable. But to proceed to the other extreme of relativism and treat all beliefs and practices as equally worthy of respect is certainly absurd from the perspective of human welfare. The acceptance of the pre-colonial autonomous consciousness of unlettered communities as something sacrosanct and superior to the rationality of western derivation is also ludicrous, to say the least. There is one simple logic behind such rejection—that of the minimum requirements of human welfare in purely physical terms, if nothing else, which all members of the species share. To wit, beliefs and practices which severely limit longevity, help spread diseases, and ensure a high rate of child mortality are equally painful in their consequences for the subaltern and the privileged alike in all societies. If pre-colonial consciousness were treated with unqualified respect, our average life expectancy in India would still be 29 years, child mortality would remain pegged at above 20 per cent, and the Kumbha *melas* would regularly be followed by cholera epidemics as was the case in the past. One can go further. Unqualified respect for indigenous beliefs and practices would imply the continued celebration of widow burning and child marriage. We owe nearly all that has made our life, including that of the oppressed, a shade more tolerable than in the past to the application of humane rationality to human affairs. That this instrument of understanding and social engineering, like theoretical science itself, has been actually used to reinforce colonial domination is no argument for throwing the baby out with the bath water.

It has been suggested, as we have seen, that the imperialist project of cultural domination was a total success. Not so. I have argued this point at length elsewhere and shall not repeat what I have already said. Briefly, it is my contention that different elements of our intelligentsia responded very differently to the contact with western ideas. Even the most ardent westernizer accepted from that vast storehouse only what appealed to them in the light of their historical experience and cultural preferences. Few ideas likely to bolster the faith in British rule in perpetuity were among these. The ideology of the French Revolution was unlikely to enhance loyalty to the British throne. During their spiritual apprenticeship Vivekananda and his fellow disciples used to chant '*Vive la republique*', not 'God Save the Queen'. In fact, at one point, the educational policy makers who introduced 'the tyranny of English poetry', including that of the iconoclastic Shelley, considered removing English history from the syllabus lest the babus get ideas unsuitable to their station in life. Of course, one could cite against such evidence the babus' repeated declarations of loyalty to the colonial ruler. But such loyalty was always hedged in with qualifications and its appeal declined sharply by the end of the nineteenth century.

Over time, the Bengali intelligentsia developed a highly sophisticated critique of western civilization which had many dimensions. Unqualified acceptance of western superiority was no part of that corpus. Even the immature Derozians saw in the British exclusiveness and monopoly of privileges a reflection of Brahminical hierarchy. I argue that the western contact was a catalyst which engendered processes of thought and action that acquired an autonomous life of their own. They hardly ever replicated any western model. The allegation of slavish and denationalizing surrender implies a misreading of what actually happened.

Here I want to introduce a more general issue: the subject of cultural influence in different historical settings. It is simply not true that the acceptance of the ideas of non-indigenous origin is invariably linked to relationships of power. If we accept for the moment Toynbee's notion of the contemporaneity of all history, the Roman adoption of Greek culture, the civilization of a weak and defeated people often dispensed by slaves, offers a case in point. So does the spread of Indian influences all over East and Southeast Asia, totally unconnected to political power. One has to locate the whys and hows of cultural influence in the specificities of historical situations. A simple equation with domination and power is simplistic and contrary to known facts.

Even the cultural supremacy of the West in modern times is not invariably related to political and economic domination. From Peter the Great's Russia to post-Meiji Japan and Ataturk's Turkey we note an eagerness to adopt western models. Interestingly, even in Japan this concern was by no means confined to science and technology. One post-Meiji doggerel, popular with the young intellectuals, pointedly expresses the new preoccupation:

Dekansho Dekansho Dekansho
Half the year we live with them
And the other half we sleep

The first three words are not Japanese but an abbreviation of Descartes, Kant, and Schopenhauer, homogenized into a philosophical Trinity. Even the Derozians, allegedly slavish imitators of the West, could not have improved on this.

One particular allegation against the impact of western education relates to the false perceptions of our history, especially the Indo-Islamic era. It is certainly true that we owe the unholy belief in oppression by Muslim rulers to British historians and the paradigm of a Hindu struggle for freedom against their misrule also to the same source. I should like to make two points in this connection. First, this view was challenged early and then repeatedly. Bhudev, the believer in Hindu orthodoxy, rejected it without qualification and ascribed it to the British historians, as well as to the educated youth who had come under their influence. His position, in short, was close to that of our contemporary critics. Then, in the pages of *Bangadarshan* itself we come across an anxious statement advising against the continuous struggle against *jabans* on the Calcutta stage because such heroism, painful to Muslim brothers, was unlikely to help in building a nation. Vivekananda, notwithstanding his one statement which reflects the British perception, was enthusiastic in his admiration for the achievements of the Mughals and their policy of dynastic marriage alliances with the Rajputs. If the Hindutvabadis were aware of the fact, their enthusiasm for the prophet might have been somewhat less.

Unfortunately, the negative perception of 'Muslim rule' (I have argued elsewhere why the term is inappropriate: briefly, the fact that the ruler was Muslim, and often even she/he was not, does not mean that the Muslims were rulers) cannot be attributed to British historiography alone. Bharatchandra writing in the mid-eighteenth century, speaks on the one hand of the fundamental unity of all religions, but on the other, of the *jaban* Alivardi's iconoclastic activities, eventually punished by Shiva. Abdul Odud, one of the most ardent advocates of communal amity, argued that communalism has a history going back to pre-British times. So did Muhammad Habib and Mushirul Hasan. One needs to explore the implications of such statements. I for one reject Bayly's view that "communalism then was what communalism is now", because the former was not rooted in any struggle for political power, but was a social phenomenon which never engendered horrendous violence on a mass scale. But projecting images of perfect mutual understanding interrupted by the colonial intervention perhaps misrepresents the historical truth. And if secularist historians do not analyse the facts of our past misfortunes and find ways of integrating the results into our agendas for the future, we end up yielding ground to the likes of Arun Shourie and Sitaram Goel whose central concern, it seems, is to generate malice towards one community. The emerging common sense regarding past relations between Hindus and Muslims is already dangerously close to their jaundiced views.

The nineteenth century reformers have been accused either of failing to implement their programmes of reform or, worse, in matters concerning gender, being only interested in the reconstitution of patriarchy. It helps to underline in this context what they were up against: the sheer power of Hindu orthodoxy. During his agitation against *sati*, there were three attempts on Rammohan's life. He did not give up. Was this person likely to suck up to people and compromise with orthodoxy out of sheer timidity? Our expectation that any individual should be totally consistent in his life and outlook is highly unrealistic. In our own lives, we do without such consistency quite happily. Rammohan, despite his rejection of idolatry, was of orthodox

Brahmin origin. Often life habits have a stronger hold on us than intellectual beliefs. It is quite possible that he did share with fellow Brahmins their sensibilities regarding ritual pollution and never lost entirely his regard for the scriptures. Bipin Pal tells us that many in his father's generation had no faith in idol worship, thanks to Islamic influence, but continued to stick to orthodox practice. Perhaps acknowledging the genuine ambivalences in Rammohan's outlook is a more realistic reading of his life than the accusation of timid compromise. Again, the failure of Vidyasagar's initiative in introducing widow remarriage was surely no part of reconstituting patriarchy. He took up arms against one of the most deep-rooted prejudices of Bengali Hindu society and suffered financial ruin in the process. He could get a law passed, but the prejudice remains unshaken even today. The majority of the reformers did have strong conservative leanings, an acceptance of patriarchy with qualifications. Within those limits, they tried to introduce minimum improvements in the lives of middle-class women. Theirs was no revolutionary agenda, but nor were they in the business of reconstituting patriarchy. Even conservative thinkers such as Bankim and, of course, Rammohan compared unfavourably the condition of women in bhadralok society with that of animals. Their actions did not match their words, yet their words reflect a new sensibility, not a cynical agenda for perpetuating male domination. And there were a few who were willing to risk much in support of bolder actions. The young leaders of the Sadharan Brahmo Samaj were among them. Sibnath Sastri tried to persuade his second wife to accept divorce and remarry. Durgamohan Das arranged the remarriage of his widowed stepmother. Men like these were not inclined to put any restrictions on women's rights. And when R.C. Dutt described the condition of women in Victorian England as one of veiled bondage, concluding that the only way to their emancipation was through economic independence, he too was holding no candle for patriarchy. Social change in such matters has been slow in realization everywhere. Laurence Stone has traced how in England change began within a limited social space and over a long period became part of accepted practice. In the highly conservative bhadralok society the resistance to change was much stronger. The fact that yet substantial changes did take place within a relatively short time surely owes something to the ideas and initiatives of the nineteenth century reformers.

The alleged failure of reforms, a questionable proposition, has been attributed partly to the Hindu reaction described as a revival. I have questioned that particular paradigm, because the forces of conservatism remained very strong from the days of Radhakanta and Bhabani Bandyopadhyay onwards. The new spate of reactionary efforts in the last quarter of the century owed much to the several decades of experience in organized activity and an awareness of unacceptable criticism familiarized by the print culture. The cultural self-assertion challenged the reformers' perception of Indian society, but they did not stem the course of reform. Many of the ideas projected by the Brahmos and liberal Hindus gradually became a part of the accepted norms over time and were implemented inevitably over a long period. There was high drama in the Hindu reaction, but there is nothing to show that it produced any renewed commitment to orthodoxy among the majority who had never deviated from it.

I find one received wisdom reiterated in the contemporary critique particularly unacceptable. Ramakrishna's life and preaching and Vivekananda's agenda, I submit, had little to do with the Hindu reaction. The mystic was not in the business of preaching Hinduism. He represented in his life two older traditions—one of mediaeval *bhakti* with strong syncretistic leanings and the other of the mother cult as manifested in the life of Ramprasad. But his *bhakti*, like Ramprasad's, and his mystic experiences were informed by a Vedantic awareness of non-duality. He preached, if that is the right word for his recorded dialogues, not a synthesis but equal respect and acceptance of all religions as true, a point emphasized by his famous disciple. And as to Vivekananda, I do not see how anyone who has read his Chicago speech and his fiery denunciations of Puranic Hinduism can project him as a protagonist of Hindu revival. Ramakrishna has been accused of accepting the status quo and of criticizing the reform initiatives. These issues were very marginal to his concerns but his anguished longing to distance himself from worldly men has to be built into any total picture of the man. Vivekananda's avowed agenda was a regeneration of the masses through education so that they could realize their power. The much abused contemporary expression 'empowerment' is perhaps relevant in this context. He distrusted the babu as much as the contemporary critics of babudom do. How exactly he stemmed the tide of Brahmo influence, which never had more than a few thousand converts, or saved Bengalis from conversion to Christianity, which never cut much ice with the bhadralok, is not clear to me. The agitation against the Age of Consent Bill was no product of Ramakrishna's influence. The law against *sati* had prohibited a custom which affected relatively small numbers, yet it had generated massive protest. Seven decades later we have this attack on the core of patriarchy which would affect every bhadralok home. Even without any Hindu reaction, resistance was inevitable. To somehow trace its source to the influence, among others, of Vivekananda, who saw child marriage as one of the worst blots on Indian civilization, is rather absurd.

III

Is there anything worthy of admiration or emulation in nineteenth century Bengal for Bengalis today, even in the light of our very different concerns? Are there achievements there which have enriched our lives or given us any legitimate basis for a positive self-image?

If an answer to that query is formulated in the light of current radical yardsticks, the answer, of course, will be disappointing. If we are to judge our forebears in terms of their commitment to the anti-colonial struggle, the liberation of the masses or the undermining of patriarchy, their record will not appear earth-shaking. But I submit that these are unrealistic criteria by which to judge a colonial middle class with strong roots in a conservative society and dependent for its survival on the colonial regime. Yet many of these yardsticks, which we take for granted now though we do mighty little to live by them, can be traced back to these people who spoke and acted in ways which could induce change against tremendous odds. The phenomenon in question was not a Renaissance of the Florentine variety, but it was a seed time rich in possibilities. Among its major contributions was the gradual imagining of a nation which would be based on the willing union of diverse cultures. They also took the first steps towards realizing this possibility. Here we have the beginning of a unique experiment in world history, the creation of a nation state based on the consent of some hundred or more ethnic groups. True, little was done for the dispossessed then and not much has been done for them since. But our nineteenth century forebears focused on their problem for the first time in the history of our culture. The sensibilities which inform egalitarian ideologies today were first born in that time. An awareness of the horrors of patriarchy was a part of that new sensibility.

Then we have a rare outburst of literary and intellectual creativity which has few parallels outside Europe. Its climax was the life and work of a genius who has enriched our lives. We have also the beginning of a great curiosity about the world at large, an agenda of scholarship which in 1917 the Sadler Commission considered something unique. The ambition towards encyclopaedic scholarship and an openness to new ideas remain a part of Bengali culture. The post-modernists among us are a striking example of such openness. It would be unfair to describe their initiatives as derivative, though derivation from an alien culture is not necessarily an intellectual or moral sin.

Perhaps the most striking feature of the nineteenth century experience was the advent of very remarkable men—remarkable in their humane concern for society, in their courage and commitment to unpopular causes, in their willingness to suffer for such causes, and for the excellence of their creative endeavours. Few societies produce such a galaxy of human beings in the course of a relatively short time. The hagiography exaggerates their achievements and slurs over their deficiencies. But one has to place such exaggerations and omissions in the context of the colonial experience, the continuous reminders of one's low status in the world and the worthless lives. The great men, even when one rejected their counsel, were there to demonstrate that at least some among the subject population could rise above the limitations of their constricted lives, achieve creative excellence, and exemplify a superior morality. Hence the hagiography. And hence the need for us to appreciate their worth and their achievements. Their initiatives induced significant processes of positive change in the society and created a tradition of scholarship and intellectual creativity. They did not produce the results one had expected. The responsibility for the failure lies less with them than with the later generations and very adverse historical developments. Many societies have periods of high creativity which are not repeated in later epochs. I think we would be justified in concluding that, renaissance or no renaissance, the nineteenth and early twentieth centuries constitute such a period in the lives of the Bengali middle class. Our failure to recognize the fact diminishes us.

IV

To conclude, the critiques of the 'renaissance' paradigm, whatever their validity, do us some harm. I have tried to show that their validity is questionable and at best has to be qualified. Any culture needs a positive self-image to thrive. This does not mean that one has to concoct a heroic past where none such exists. But given the shallowness of our contemporary lives, the pervasive hypocrisy, and the preoccupation with narrow self-interest, be it of the individual or one's factious group, it helps to remember that it was not always so. That our society produced men and women who lived high moral lives and who were willing to risk a great deal for the things they believed in may not be an unworthwhile message to convey to our youth. The contrary message couched in the often incomprehensible language of high élitism does not fortunately enter popular consciousness: the school textbooks continue to speak of the renaissance and that is what most educated Bengalis still believe in. But they do so at a level of no longer acceptable naïveté. The intellectual skills and scholarship which go into debunking our past achievements could be better used to underline some worth in that past, partly to help us understand our own origins. If the young intellectuals are trained only to look for the alleged inadequacies in terms of inapplicable and hence unacceptable criteria, then eventually they will look for mentors among the least worthy members of our society. And if we preach rejection of our nation state, arguably the greatest achievement of our people, great despite the evident inadequacies of our successive governments and the many failures of our democracy, then it is incumbent on the critics to suggest a viable alternative. They have failed to do so even at a theoretical level. Again, such intellectual rejection does not affect popular perceptions in India; they gain currency mainly on American campuses and are highly popular with the reactionary elements in western societies who share the radicals' distaste for the nation states of the Third World, though for very different reasons. The imperialists, old or new, have never been reconciled to the fact of decolonization. We hence have this strange convergence of opinion between extreme radicals and extreme reactionaries. This should not bother us unduly. Only, if the gifted young in our own society are preoccupied with rejections and negative paradigms, worthless and often vicious people take the place which should be theirs as the formers of opinion and the initiators of social action. It is needless to emphasize that this is already happening to a dangerous extent. That is one major reason why we need to take a fresh look at nineteenth century Bengal.

Bibliography

Amrita Bazar Patrika, 1871–1970.

Abhedananda, Swami, *Amar jibankatha*, Calcutta, 1964.

Akhandananda, Swami, *Smritikatha*, Calcutta, BY 1357 (1952).

Ananyananda, Swami (ed.), *Reminiscences of Swami Vivekananda—by his Eastern and Western Admirers*, 3rd edition, Calcutta, 1983.

Bagal, Jogeschandra, *Hindu melar itivritta*, Calcutta, BY 1357 (1968).

Bandyopadhyay, A., S. Basu and Samkar (eds.), *Viswavivek*, 2nd edition, Calcutta, 1966.

Bandyopadhyay, Brajendranath, *Bangiya natyasalar itihas*, Calcutta, BY 1340 (1933).

Bandyopadhyay, Brajendranath and Sajanikanta Das, *Sahitya-sadhak charitmala*, vols. 1–9, 5th edition, Calcutta, BY 1364 (1957).

―――――, 1376 (BY 1369). [N.B. The number of editions into which the different volumes ran is not the same.]

Samasamayik drishtite Sri Ramakrishna Paramahamsa, 2nd edition, Calcutta, 1952.

Bandyopadhyay, Srikumar, *Bangasahitye upanyaser dhara*, Calcutta, 1954.

Banerjea, Surendranath, *A Nation in Making Being the Reminiscences of Fifty Years of Public Life*, London, New York, etc., 1925.

Bangadarsan, 1872–6.

Basu, Jogindrachandra, *Model bhagini*, 4 parts, Calcutta, BY 1293–5 (1886–8).

Basu, Jogindranath, *Michael Madhusudan Datter jivancharit*, BY 1300 (1893).

Basu, Pramathanath, *Swami Vivekananda*, 2 vols., 2nd edition, Calcutta, 1949.

Basu, Rajnarayan, *Atmajivani*, Calcutta, BY 1315 (1908).

_____, *Sekal ar ekal*, Calcutta, Sakabda 1800 (1878).

_____, *Briddha Hindur asa*, Calcutta, 1886.

_____, *Rajnarayan Basur baktrita*, 2 parts, 3rd revised edition, Calcutta, Sakabda 1793(1871).

Basu, S.P., *Vivekananda o samakalin Bharatvarsha*, 5 volumes, 1st reprint, Calcutta, 1981.

_____, (ed.), *Letters of Sister Nivedita*, 2 vols., Calcutta, 1982.

Basu, S.P., and B.K. Ghosh (ed.), *Vivekananda in Indian Newspapers, 1893–1902*, Calcutta, 1969.

Basu, S.P., and S.N. Ghosh (eds.), *Thakur Sri Ramakrishna o Swami Vivekananda—Girischandra Ghosh*, 2nd reprint, Calcutta, 1981.

Basu, Swapan, *Banglay nabachetanar itihas* (*1826–56*), 2nd edition, Calcutta, 1985.

Baumer, Rachel van, (ed.), *Aspects of Bengali History and Society*, Honolulu, 1976.

The Bengalee, 1895–96.

The Bengal Harkaru, 1839–43.

The Bengal Spectator, 1842–3.

Bhudev jibani, printed and published by Kasinath Bhattacharya, Chinsurah, BY 1318 (1911).

The Brahmavadin, 1895–1901.

Buckland, C.E., *Bengal under the Lieutenant-Governors*, Calcutta, 1902.

Burke, Marie Louise, *Swami Vivekananda in the West: New Discoveries*, 4 vols. (published to date), 3rd edition, Calcutta, 1983.

Chakrabarti, Ajit Kumar, *Maharshi Debendranath Thakur*, 1st edition, Calcutta, 1916, new edition, 1971.

Chandra, Bipin, *Origins of Economic Nationalism in India*, New Delhi.

Chatterjee, Partha, *Nationalist Thought and the Colonial World: A Derivative Discourse?*, Delhi, 1986.

Chattopadhyay, Bankimchandra *Bankim rachanavali*, 2 vols., edited by J.C. Bagal, Sahitya Samsad, Calcutta, 1953–69.

_____, *English Works*, edited by J.C. Bagal, Calcutta, 1983.

——, *Bankim granthabali*, edited by B.N. Bandyopadhyay and S. Das, Calcutta, 1938–42 (known as the Centenary Edition).

——, *Bankim rachanavali*, 2 vols., Patra's Publication, Calcutta, 1983.

——, English translations of Bankim's works [Only the works directly relevant to the present study are listed below].

——, *Durgeshnandini*, tr. Charu Chandra Mukherji, Calcutta, 1880.

——, *Kapalkundala*, tr. H.A.D. Philips, London, 1885; tr. D.N. Ghosh, Calcutta, 1919.

——, *Bishabriksha*, tr. Miriam S. Knight, London, 1884.

——, *Chandrasekhar*, tr. M.N. Raychaudhuri, Calcutta, 1904, tr. D.C. Mullick, Calcutta, 1905.

——, *Rajani*, tr., P. Majumdar, Calcutta, 1928.

——, *Krishnakanter uil*, tr. Miriam S. Knight, London, 1895; tr. D.C. Ray, Calcutta, 1918; tr. J.C. Ghosh, New York, 1962.

——, *Anandamath*, tr. N.C. Sengupta, Calcutta, 1914.

——, *Debi Chaudhurani*, tr. S.C. Mitra, Calcutta, 1946.

——, *Sitaram*, tr. S. Mukherji, Calcutta, 1903.

——, *Indira and Other Stories*, tr. J.D. Anderson, London, 1919.

——, *Samya*, tr. M.K. Haldar in *Renaissance and Reaction in 19th Century Bengal*, Calcutta, 1973.

——, *Essentials of Dharma*, tr. M. Ghosh, Calcutta, 1979.

——, *Sociological Essays: Utilitarianism and Positivism in Bengal*, tr. and edited by S.N. Mukherji and M. Maddern, Calcutta and Sydney, 1986.

Chattopadhyay, C, *Sri Sri Latu Maharajer smritikatha*, Calcutta, 1940.

Chattopadhyay, Sachischandra, *Bankim jibani*, Calcutta, 1901, 3rd edition, 1931.

Chaudhuri, Niradchandra, *Bangali jibane ramani*, Calcutta, 1968.

Das, Satyaranjan, *Bangadarsan o bangalir manansadhana*, Calcutta, 1974.

Das, S. K., *The Artist in Chains: The Life of Bankimchandra Chatterji*, New Delhi, 1984.

Dasgupta, Rabindrakumar, *Bankimchandra* (incomplete), *Kathasahitya*, 1963.

Datta, Akshay Kumar, *Dharmaniti*, Calcutta, 1856.

_____, *Bharatvarshiya upasak sampraday*, Part I, Calcutta, BY 1277 (1870), Part II, Sakabda 1804 (1883).

Datta, Bhabatosh, *Chintanayak Bankimchandra*, Calcutta, 1961.

Datta, Bhupendranath, *Swami Vivekananda—Patriot-Prophet*, Calcutta, 1954, *Swami Vivekananda*, Calcutta, 1976.

Datta, Hirendranath, *Darsanik Bankimchandra*, Calcutta, 1940.

Datta, Mahendranath, *Sri Sri Ramakrishner anudhyan*, 2nd edition, Calcutta, 1954, *Swami Vivekanander balyajibani*, Calcutta, 1959.

_____, *Srimad Vivekananda Swamir jibaner ghatanabali*, 3 vols., 4th edition, Calcutta, 1977.

_____, *Londone Swami Vivekananda*, 3rd edition, 4th reprint, Calcutta, 1977.

Datta, Mahendranath and Sadasivananda, Swami *Kasidhame Swami Vivekananda*, Calcutta, BY 1332 (1925).

Dhar, S.N., *A Comprehensive Biography of Swami Vivekananda*, 1st edition, Madras, 1975.

Duff, Alexander, *India and Indian Missions, including Sketches of the Gigantic System of Hinduism, Both in Theory and Practice*, Edinburgh, 1840.

Forbes, G.H., *Positivism in Bengal: A Case Study in the Transmission and Assimilation of Ideology*, Calcutta, 1975.

Gambhirananda, Swami (ed.), *The Apostles of Sri Ramakrishna*, Calcutta, 1967. *Yuganayak Vivekananda*, 3 vols., Calcutta, 1977.

Gogerly, G., *The Pioneers: A Narrative of Facts connected with the Early Christian Missions in Bengal*, London, n.d.

The Hindoo Patriot, 1857–60, 1872, 1879, 1894,1896.

India Gazette, 1830, 1833.

India Education Commission, 1882, *Report*.

Joshi, V.C. (ed.), *Rammohan Roy and the Modernisation of India*, Vikas Publishing House, Delhi, 1975.

Kakar, Sudhir, *The Inner World: A Psycho-analytic Study of Childhood and Society in India*, paperback, 2nd edition, Delhi, 1986.

Kaviraj, Sudipta. *The Unhappy Consciousness: Bankim Chandra Chattopadhyay and the Formation of Nationalist Discourse in India*, Delhi, 1998.

Kling, Blair B., *The Blue Mutiny: The Indigo Disturbances in Bengal 1859–1862*, Calcutta, 1977.

The life of Swami Vivekananda, by His Eastern and Western Disciples, 2 vols., 5th edition, Calcutta, 1979.

Ma[hendranath Gupta], *Sri Sri Ramakrishna kathamrita*, Calcutta, 1910; Ananda Publishers' edition, Calcutta, 1983.

Majumdar, Bimanbihari, *History of Political Thought from Rammohan to Dayananda (1821–84)*, Calcutta, 1934.

Majumdar, Mohitlal, *Bankim baran*, Calcutta, 1949; reprint 1964.

Mitra, Kishorichand, *Memoirs of Dwarkanath Tagore* (revised and enlarged edition), Calcutta, 1870.

Mitra, Lalit Chandra, *History of Indigo Disturbance in Bengal with a Full Report of the Nil Durpan Case*, Calcutta, 1903.

Mueller, Max, *Ramakrishna—His Life and Sayings*, 2nd edition, Calcutta, 1984.

Mukherjee, H., *Vivekananda and Indian Freedom*, Calcutta, 1986.

Mukhopadhyay, Bhudev, *Bhudev-rachanasambhar*, Calcutta, 1962.

———, *Bibidha pravandha*, 2 parts, Part I, 1895, Part II, 1905.

———, *Achar pravandha*, 1895, 3rd edition, Chinsurah, BY 1324 (1917).

———, *Sikshavishayak prastab*, 1856; Hugli, BY 1288 (1881).

———, *Banglar itihas*, Part III, 1904.

———, *Parivarik prabandha*, 1882, 11th edition, Chinsurah, 1939.

———, *Inglander itihas*, 1862, 5th edition, Hugli, BY 1295 (1887).

———, *Unavimsapuran*, 1866.

———, *Dinalipi*, quoted extensively in biography by M. Mukhopadhyay.

Mukhopadhyay, Kailas, *Sayings of Bankimchandra*, n.d.

Mukhopadhyay, Mukundadev, *Bhudev-charit*, 3 vols., Calcutta, BY 1324 (1917), 1334 (1927).

Nikhilananda, Swami, *Vivekananda—a Biography*, Calcutta, 1975.

Nivedita, Sister, *The Master as I saw Him*, 11th edition, Calcutta, 1972.

———, *Notes of Some Wanderings with the Swami Vivekananda*, 4th edition, Calcutta, 1957.

Pal, Bipin Chandra, *Memories of My Life and Times*, 2nd edition, Calcutta, 1957.

_____, *Charitra-chitra*, Calcutta, 1958.

_____, *Character Sketches*, Calcutta, 1957.

Pavitrananda, Swami (ed.), *The Disciples of Sri Ramakrishna*, Mayavati, 1943.

Philips, C.H. (ed.), *Historians of India, Pakistan and Ceylon*. London,

Poddar, Arabinda, *Bankim manas*, Calcutta, 1951, 2nd edition, 1955.

Prabuddha Bharata, 1897–1901.

Ray, Alok, *Alexander Duff o anugami kayekjan*, Calcutta, 1980.

Ray, Gopal Chandra, *Anya ek Bankimchandra*, Calcutta, 1979.

Raychaudhuri, Girijasamkar, *Bhagini Nivedita o Banglay biplabbad*, Calcutta, 1960.

Raychaudhuri, Sunitiranjan, *Unis satake nabyahindu andolaner kayekjan nayak*, Calcutta, 1983.

Reymond, Lizelle, *The Dedicated: A Biography of Nivedita*, New York, 1953.

Rezaul Karim, *Bankimchandra o Musalman Samaj*, Calcutta, 1944.

Rolland, Romain, *The Life of Vivekananda and the Universal Gospel*, tr. by Malcolm-Smith, E.F., 10th reprint, Calcutta, 1984.

Samajpati, Sureschandra, *Bankim prasanga*, Calcutta, 1922; new edition, 1982.

Saradananda, Swami, *Srisriramakrishnalila-prasanga*, 2 vols., Calcutta, 1983.

Sarkar, Sumit, 'The Kathamrita as a Text: Towards an Understanding of Ramakrishna Paramahamsa' (Mimeographed, Nehru Memorial Museum and Library, Occasional Papers on History and Society, No. xxxii), New Delhi, 1985.

Sarma, Ramdas, [alias Indranath Bandyopadhyay], *Bharat-uddhar Kavya*, Calcutta, 1877.

Sastri, Sibnath, *Ramtanu Lahiri o tatkalin bangasamaj*, Calcutta, 1903.

Sengupta, Subodhchandra, *Bankimchandra*, Calcutta, 1945.

_____, *Bankimchandra Chatterji*, Delhi, 1977.

Sinha, N.K. (ed.), *The History of Bengal* (1757–1905), Calcutta, 1967.

Sen, Amit, *Notes on the Bengal Renaissance*, Calcutta, 1946.

Sen, Priyaranjan, *Western Influences on Bengali Literature*, Calcutta, 1947.

Sherring, M.A., *The History of Protestant Missions in India*, London, 1884.

Smith, George, *The Life of Alexander Duff, D.D., LL.D.*, London, 1900.

Swami Vividishananda, A Man of God, Madras, 1957.

Tagore, Rabindranath, *Reminiscences*, London, 1917.

——, *Jivansmriti*, BY 1319 (1912).

Tarkachudamani, Sasadhar, *Dharmabyaksha*.

Thakur, Debendranath, *Atmajivani*, edited by Satischandra Chakrabarti, Calcutta, 1962.

Tripathi, Amales, *The Extremist Challenge*, Calcutta, 1967.

Vivekananda, Swami, *The Complete Works of Swami Vivekananda*, 8 vols., 1st edition, 1907–22, 15th edition, 1977. [The number of editions for the different volumes varies].

——, *Swami Vivekanander vani o rachana*, 10 vols., 6th edition, 1982.

——, *Inspired Talks*, Madras, 1908.

Weitbrecht, J.J., *Missionary Sketches in North India*, London, 1858.

Index

stereotypes of, 343
Vivekananda's comparison with
Indian, 260
European expansionism, 198–9
onslaught on non-Europeans,
275
European feudalism, Arab origins,
273
European history, Bankim's partial
admiration, 174
European literature:
Bankim's interest, 174
and patriotism, 174
European Orientalism, 177
Bankim's disquiet, 180
handicaps of, 178
no angry rejection by
Vivekananda, 293
European perception of India,
Bankim's parody of, 164
European social mores, 301–4
European tradition, 4
decline of hospitality, 89
forbearance not part of, 74
inferior to Aryan, 10
strength of, 157
evolution, theory of, 277

Family life:
in America, 298
in Europe, 296
Faust, 171
Ferguson, 179
Fourier, Charles, 169
France:
contrast with Germany, 305
Vivekananda's preference for,
277, 296, 305
Franco-German rivalry, 277–8
Franco-Prussian War, 279
Free Mason Lodge
Bhudev's membership of, 45

Free Religious Association, 260
French Revolution, 87
saved Europe, 159
Fundamental pronenesses of
civilizations, 343
future, Vivekananda's vision, 270

Gall, Benjamin *see* Benjamin Gall
Gandhi, 138, 251
Gandhian era, 331
rejection of western values, 339
Gagananda, Sanskrit scholar, 106
Garfield, 88
Garibaldi, 4, 14
General Assembly's Institution, 225
George Campbell, 191
George Hale, Mrs 258
Gibbon, 226
Girish Ghosh, 225
Gladstone, 166
Gopal Datta, 221
governmental process, Bankim's
cynicism, 199
Govinda, Bhudev's second son, 57
Grant, J.P., 118, 122
Greek civilization:
Greek sculpture and Vivekananda,
291
Vivekananda's admiration for,
271
Grossman, Dr, 260
Gupta, Ishwar *see* Ishwar Gupta
Gyananwesan, 7

Haladhar Tarkachudamani, 107
Halford, 47
Hamilton, 229
Haripada Mitra, 227
Harish Mukherjee, ed., *Hindu
patriot*, 14
Harriet Munro, 258, 259
Hastie, Reverend: 8